FLORA of JERSEY

FLORA of JERSEY

by Frances Le Sueur

*with notes on the occurrence of species
recorded for the other Channel Islands*

*Colour plates from watercolour
drawings by Pandora Sellars*

Société Jersiaise

First published in 1984 by
the Société Jersiaise, Jersey, C.I.

ISBN 0 901897 11 6

Designed by James Sellars
Typeset by Anton Graphics Ltd.
Produced by MRM (Print Consultants) Ltd.

*To the members of
the Botanical Section of the Société Jersiaise
who combed Jersey for records for
the distribution maps*

Contents

COLOUR PLATES

BLACK AND WHITE ILLUSTRATIONS

(All the photographs were taken in summer 1984.)

MAPS

Acknowledgements

This Flora could not have been produced without the help of many specialists who with courtesy and kindness have assisted with difficult groups. Their names will be found in the appropriate places in the Flora but I would particularly like to thank D. E. Allen who came and looked at our brambles, Professor J. P. M. Brennan for working through large numbers of Jersey specimens of the Chenopodiaceae and Amaranthaceae, Dr A. Melderis for his work on Jersey's grasses, Dr A. J. Richards who cheerfully accepted many parcels of dandelions for identification and Dr R. H. Richens for unravelling the mysteries of Jersey's elms.

As botanical knowledge increases it becomes progressively more difficult for amateurs to undertake investigations which require advanced laboratory techniques, so students who do such work are welcomed. As will be seen below, the sea-lavenders were investigated by Dr M. J. Ingrouille for his doctorate and the sheep's-fescue group is currently under review by M. Wilkinson, a student of Dr C. A. Stace at Leicester University, as was M. J. Ingrouille. In 1983 R. W. S. Knightbridge, an M.Sc. student, undertook a detailed survey of wet meadows. Many of his finds are incorporated in the Flora.

Over the years the main recording work was done by Miss P. Donaldson, J. C. Fluck, Mrs D. L. Le Quesne, Mrs M. L. Long, Miss D. C. Mauger, Mrs L. A. Morris, Mrs E. Melville-Towers and the writer; other helpers for shorter periods included Mrs R. Adams, Mrs J. Brooks, Mrs V. Dorey, Miss E. H. du Feu, Miss F. M. Evans, Miss P. K. France, Mrs P. Green, Mrs K. Le Sueur, Mrs J. Petre, Mrs M. Pett, Dr & Mrs D. H. Phillips, Mrs J. Powell, A. J. Robinson, Mrs B. Savage, Mrs K. M. Stone, Miss E. F. P. Thompson, Mrs M. Tessier-Yandell and Mrs E. Whiteside.

The names of recorders of the less common species are given except when the record is the writer's, and it will be seen that visitors have helped greatly. Many also worked with us on the map scheme, and the enthusiasm and encouragement of Mrs J. Russell, Dr and Mrs J. G. Dony and the late J. E. Lousley will long be remembered. David McClintock, author of *The Wild Flowers of Guernsey* and co-author with the writer of the original Checklists of Alderney, Sark and Herm, has always been ready to share his great fund of botanical knowledge and experience, and his help in many diverse ways over the last twenty-five years is much appreciated.

I should also like to thank the Island Development Committee for permission to use some of the maps from the *Island Plan* Vol. 1, R. R. Le Sueur for adapting them as necessary, drawing the physical features map and taking black and white photographs, R. P. M. Paton for drawing the original 'squared' map used to show the distribution of the different species, Jurat M. G. Lucas for help with the Jersey-Norman-French names, Joan Stevens for answering many questions about the history of Jersey, R. and M. L. Long for their support over the years and finally the trustees of the Meaker Trust for a generous donation towards the cost of production of this *Flora of Jersey*.

xii

Foreword

Jersey has been fortunate in having had for more than a century a succession of devoted and skilled botanists who have recorded the contemporary flora.

Since its publication in 1903 the Flora of Jersey by L. V. Lester-Garland has remained the standard work on the subject, highly reliable and much consulted by specialists, but of little popular appeal, because only the Latin Linnaean plant names were given. For forty-five years, from 1915 to 1960 Mr. T. W. Attenborough was secretary of the Botanical Section of La Société Jersiaise and published annual reports of newly discovered plants. He was then succeeded by Mrs. Frances Le Sueur. She had been a member of the Société, and an active local botanist, since 1950 and had absorbed much of Mr. Attenborough's life-long store of knowledge, to which she has continued to add. She certainly has a greater knowledge of Jersey's flora than anyone else now living, and probably than anyone in the past. She has now written a completely new Flora of Jersey which fully maintains the accuracy of Lester-Garland's work, and far surpasses it and all other publications in completeness, convenience and readability. In particular she has given English as well as Latin names, and where possible also Jersey-Norman-French ones. All plants reliably recorded as growing wild in Jersey are included, as well as garden escapes which are likely to be found in an apparently wild state. The book is amply illustrated with colour plates, black-and-white photographs, and maps.

To natives of and residents in Jersey this will prove an incomparable reference work, while to the visitor it will serve as an introduction to our flora which contains so many plants characteristic of more southerly areas, and which are rare or absent on the mainland of Britain.

A. E. Mourant F.R.S.

Preface

The Flora Explained

This Flora provides information on the wild plants of Jersey from the time when records began until the end of 1983. It will not be complete for the obvious reason that many plants will have flourished, withered and perished without a botanist recording their presence. Also many specimens, still awaiting discovery, must lie in old herbaria. Lester-Garland in his excellent 1903 Flora only gave records of plants which he himself had seen growing or which he himself had seen as herbarium specimens in Jersey except in species like Rubus. He ignored the vast volume of information in herbaria outside Jersey and in the many papers on the flora of Jersey published in botanical journals. His Flora is almost a time capsule showing the wild plants of the island between 1896 and 1903 with only a few additions from earlier years, mainly J. Piquet's. It was therefore felt that any new Flora must include as much information from the past as possible, even though it would have been easier to have dealt with only, say, post-1950 records. Also there was considerable criticism locally for many years of the way Lester-Garland had relegated records of species which he had not seen, to a list of errors, ambiguities etc. These are now back in the body of this Flora with as much information as possible about them. As will be seen, some have been proved correct but his rejection of a great many has been vindicated.

It may be pointed out that in doing so, I am being inconsistent, since it is stated under 'Botanists in Jersey', to which reference should be made, that two sets of records, J. Dickson's and Frère Louis-Arsène's, have been rejected and are not included in this Flora. To include literally hundreds of extra records which produce a false impression of Jersey's flora, only then to deny them, would seem a useless, costly exercise and would 'blur' the outline of Jersey's flora as known to generations of dedicated botanists.

Many herbaria in England have been searched for Jersey specimens. Dr H. J. M. Bowen began the search in the Druce herbarium, Oxford; Miss P. Ross listed the many Jersey specimens in the Tullie House Museum, Carlisle; D. McClintock has been untiring in his efforts to trace Channel Island material in herbaria wherever he has been, and I have spent much time in Oxford searching for Piquet's specimens and in Cambridge for Babington's. Lester-Garland's specimens are at Kew where Dr P. J. Cribb looked up a few queries. This is time-consuming in the extreme and when confronted with massive major herbaria like those in the British Museum, Kew and the older universities, one can only dip in here and there. One finds what one is looking for (or not as the case may be) and little more. Perhaps by the time the next *Flora of Jersey* is written, all this information will be on computers, including an essential entry as to whether or not critical specimens have been authoritatively checked, but perhaps by then the *Flora of Jersey* itself will be on computers. I would like to thank the staff of the various herbaria who have always been most helpful and have almost made the searching a pleasure.

Specimens labelled only 'Jersey' or 'Guernsey' have been treated with caution both in this *Flora of Jersey* and in McClintock's *The Wild Flowers of Guernsey* especially if the species is unknown in the island from which the specimen is claimed but well known in the other. Confusion of island names is not new, nor is it confined to botanists. In Edward II's reign (1307–27) Geoffrey de Carteret petitioned the King (Ancient Petition No. 2693) 'for remedy' because in a letter of Privy Seal which should have given his father tithes in the parish of St Ouen in Jersey, Guernsey was written instead of Jersey and until this was changed 'the attorneys . . . would do nothing'.

The order and nomenclature of *Flora Europaea* (Tutin *et al.* 1964–80) have been followed, except where recent advances in knowledge have necessitated name changes. The Botanical Society of the British Isles recommended (*B.S.B.I.News* 32, p. 24) that the names in the *Excursion Flora of the British Isles* (Clapham *et al.* ed. 3, 1981) be used if different from those in *Flora Europaea* and this has been done. Unfortunately the order in the *Excursion Flora* is sometimes different from that in *Flora Europaea*; in these cases *ad hoc* solutions have been found. In a few species like the Bamboos and the Sea Lavenders, yet more recent name changes have been used. Wherever there has been a departure from the name in *Flora Europaea*, then the *Flora Europaea* name has been given in brackets and likewise with the names in Lester-Garland's *Flora of Jersey*.

The English names used are mainly those in *English Names of Wild Flowers* (Dony, Rob & Perring 1974) a list recommended by the Botanical Society of the British Isles. Extra names have occasionally been added. Only one Jersey-Norman-French name has been given for each species but different parishes often have different names for the same species. The one name given here will give access in the *Dictionnaire Jersiais-Français* (Le Maistre 1966) to the others and to a wealth of information concerning them. At Jurat M. C. Lucas' suggestion, instead of the name being given in artificial isolation, it is given in the way it would be used by anyone speaking Jersey-Norman-French and I am much indebted to him for his help with this.

Records of rare or interesting species have been given in the Société's *Annual Bulletin* for many years. One of the first undertakings of the Botanical Section when it was revitalised in the 1950s was the collection of records for the *Atlas of the British Flora* published by the Botanical Society of the British Isles in 1962 and it was on this that the Jersey distribution map scheme was based.

Unfortunately in 1960 when the map scheme began, no maps of Jersey with the UTM Km grid existed. The official map produced for the States of Jersey by BKS Air Survey Ltd in 1958 had a grid showing only latitude and longitude in minutes so this was used with an extra latitude line drawn in to show half minutes. Each 'square' on the maps is therefore a rectangle half a minute of latitude by one of longitude, approximately 1.15 sq. Km in area. No map is given if a species was found in less than five squares; nor is one given where recorders may have found precise identification difficult, or had problems in deciding how 'wild' a garden escape was. Unless stated to the contrary, maps include all subspecies, and occasionally composite maps of two or more species are given.

A 'dot' is in a square if that particular species was seen in that particular square between 1960 and 1970. Only one plant may have been seen or the species may have been abundant every year. The maps show distribution only: the quantity, rare, occasional, frequent, common or abundant is given in the text.

In the early 1970s when the problems posed by a herbarium made by Frère Louis-Arsène were becoming apparent, and it was realised that a new *Flora of Jersey* would have to wait until they were resolved, it was decided that the maps would be of more value in years to come, if they were restricted to the years 1960–70, rather than if they were open-ended in time. Most of the distributions are still the same, but where they are known to have altered, this is made clear in the text. Occasionally, if the species is a newcomer, the map shows its distribution up to 1983 and this is also stated.

To put each species into its Channel Island context, a brief indication of its status, if present, in Guernsey, Alderney, Sark and Herm (G, A, S, H) is given. The information for Alderney, Sark and Herm is from checklists compiled by Le Sueur & McClintock in the 1960s, updated for Alderney by Dr H. C. Prentice in 1974 and for Sark by Mrs M. Marsden in 1979. Later information was supplied for Alderney by the late N. V. Mendham and for Sark by Mrs M. Marsden. Recent Herm records are from the *Transactions* of the Société Guernesiaise. Guernsey records are from *The Wild Flowers of Guernsey* (McClintock 1975) with later ones supplied by D. McClintock. It will be noticed that many records given for Jersey in the 1920s and 1930s in *The Wild Flowers of Guernsey* are missing from this Jersey Flora. These came from the herbarium of Frère Louis-Arsène before it was analysed in detail and until this was done, the records had to be accepted as genuine.

The number of species, subspecies and hybrids entered in the Flora is well over 1,500 but the number is irrelevant since the interest of an area's flora does not depend on the quantity of different species present, and also the number could have been considerably increased (or decreased) according to the ideas of the recorders about garden escapes. This is too complicated a subject to discuss here but it should be pointed out that the problem is perhaps more acute in Jersey than in most places in the British Isles because of Jersey's mild climate. On the whole if a species was recorded, then it is given here but had a thorough search been made, particularly in the 1950s and 1960s when sacks full of garden rubbish were often emptied in odd corners or in old quarries, and had every species seen growing outside a garden for a year or two been entered in the Flora, it would have read more like a book on gardens than on wild flowers. Now that there is tight control over all dumping, including garden rubbish, fewer transitory garden escapes occur.

Future workers will find that much of interest in Jersey's flora still remains to be discovered. Some difficult groups have not been thoroughly investigated. For example water-crowfoots were often seen in the late 1950s and Professor C. D. Cook identified all specimens sent to him then as hybrids. Since that time water-crowfoots have been scarce in spite of many wet areas remaining apparently unchanged, but search should be continued for the parents. Conversely, the parents of numerous hybrids mentioned in *Hybridisation and the Flora of the British Isles* (Stace 1975) grow in Jersey, and though some hybrids are given in this Flora, many others are likely to occur. Few deliberate searches, like the successful search for the hybrid between the common Thrift and Jersey Thrift, have been made.

Nevertheless it is possible that easily identifiable species, known to have been present in Jersey since records began, will prove the most interesting. During the thirty years that the records for this Flora were being compiled, there were extraordinary, short-lived resurgences or scarcities of several species. Why? The times of plenty are much more exciting than the times of scarcity and are easier to notice but both exist, even in species usually common. The most dramatic changes occurred in Clustered Clover, Slender Bird's-foot-trefoil, Ox-eye Daisy and Wild Carrot and this latter then had a 'knock-on' effect on Carrot Broomrape. Details are given under the species concerned. Long-term studies of the interaction of plants with one another and with their surroundings over restricted areas of Jersey would be of great interest. It is hoped that the *Flora of Jersey* will encourage such studies.

Frances Le Sueur,
Les Hâtivieaux,
Jersey,

1   Rugged cliffs at Le Val Rouget, St Mary, on the north coast

Introduction

Physical Features

Jersey, the largest of the Channel Islands, lies in the Bay of St Malo only about fifteen miles off the French coast. The Channel Islands, map 1, were part of the Duchy of Normandy when its ruler conquered England in 1066 to become William I of England. Jersey, like the rest of the group, has remained firmly attached to the English Crown though the continental lands of the Duchy were lost in the following centuries.

The Bailiwick of Jersey, a political entity, includes two groups of uninhabited islets, Les Écréhous and Les Minquiers, as well as the main island. Les Écréhous lie about 7 miles north-east of Jersey and Les Minquiers about 12 miles to the south, so that both are about halfway between Jersey and France but in different directions. In 1956 the International Court of Justice at The Hague upheld Jersey's sovereignty over these reefs, a claim which had been disputed by France. On a low spring tide, an ormering tide, extensive areas of rocks are exposed on both reefs but when the tide rises to its full height, little remains above the surface of the sea. At Les Minquiers only one small islet, La Maîtresse Île, has enough soil to maintain a cover of vegetation. At Les Écréhous there are two, Le Maître Île and La Marmotière, both also small.

2   Cows grazing a water-meadow at Trinity

3   Ferns self-sown on a set of granite steps in St Mary

Jersey is rectangular in shape with its south-west corner lying at 49 deg. 11 min. N., 2 deg. 15 min. W. It measures approximately 10.8 miles (17Km) east–west and 6.8 miles (11Km) north–south but its area is only about 45 square miles because of irregularities in the coastline. The land slopes roughly from north to south with the highest elevation being just over 400ft, map 2. Most of the north coast is edged with rugged cliffs and these extend some distance down the north-west. There are also cliffs at the west end of the south coast and a few rocky outcrops elsewhere but in the main, the east, south and west coasts have long sandy beaches backed by wide coastal plains. The high land in the north acts as a watershed so short streams run quickly down to the north coast while longer ones flow more slowly to the south through beautiful valleys in the interior of the island, map 3.

Geology and Archaeology
A geological survey recently completed by the Institute of Geological Sciences should be consulted for details of Jersey's geology. Briefly, sedimentary shales laid down 1,000–700 million years ago were partially covered by volcanic ash. Folding of the rocks was followed by more volcanic activity which resulted in intrusions of newer rocks like the granites through the shale. Weathering and erosion then led to the formation of conglomerate. It will be noticed that none of these rocks is basic, like limestone, yet the island does contain lime-loving plants. These are able to grow because of the constitution of the soil cover which is not derived entirely from the rocks.

The 'surface' geology is shown in map 4. By weathering and erosion over the millenia, head, a mixture of coarse rock rubble with silt and sand, was formed to a depth of about 80ft. This was then covered by loëss, the dust blown over Europe after the glaciations when the retreat of ice left enormous deposits of dry silt in northern Europe. Alluvium is a mixture of head and loëss. Gradually by further weathering and erosion, the present soil of Jersey was formed. Most soils in the interior are deep and well-drained but on high land near the coast the rock is often near the surface and the soil is then poor and acidic. Inland behind the sandy bays, deep drifts of blown sand occur, overlying the original surface.

Comparatively small changes in sea level can produce great changes within the Channel Islands, and it is thought that Jersey was isolated from the continent several times, and then rejoined, before the final break came. Deposits of pre-Flandrian peat occur and that at Fliquet Bay, St Martin, has recently been analysed in detail by G. R. Coope, R. L. Jones and D. H. Keen (*Journal of Biogeography* (1980) **7:** 187–195). Its age is not precisely known but it was laid down in a time of deteriorating climate not later than the beginning of the Devensian (Wiechselian, Würm) glacial and possibly earlier. It is therefore at least 20,000 years old. Pollen grains in the lower depths indicate that the peat was formed from a sedge swamp near the sea with a few trees and shrubs like Scots Pine, Birch and Juniper. Pollen grains in the higher levels indicate a more inland, colder flora with more herbaceous species and yet fewer trees though the flora is still predominantly that of a marshy area. All Scots Pine, Birch and Juniper now in Jersey have been planted by man comparatively recently, but some of the herbaceous species whose pollen was specifically determined in the pre-Flandrian peat are once again naturally part of Jersey's wild flora. These include Thrift *Armeria maritima*, Sea Plantain *Plantago maritima*, Common Sorrel *Rumex acetosa* and Common Nettle *Urtica dioica*. How long ago they finally returned naturally to Jersey is unknown.

4 The cliffs of the south-west where warmth-loving species like the Sand Crocus and the Spotted Rock-rose flourish

Deposits, including layers of peat of Flandrian age, i.e. post glacial, occur in several places round the coast. Pollen from this newer peat was analysed by Dr and Mrs H. Godwin in the 1930s and the results were published in the *Bulletins Annuels* of the Société Jersiaise. A more detailed investigation of the deposits is now being undertaken, one of the objects being to date as closely as possible when Jersey finally became an island. Jersey was the last of the Channel Islands to be isolated and this may in part account for the differences in vegetation between the islands. Except in special cases no mention is made in the body of the Flora of the numerous genera and species whose pollen has been found in peat, because insufficient is at present known about their subsequent history in Jersey. Members of the Archaeological Section of the Société Jersiaise now investigate the flora in any excavation they undertake and it is hoped that this will eventually lead to a knowledge of Jersey's flora in the time before written records began.

Climate

Details of wind, temperature and precipitation in Jersey, compiled by the Meteorological Office of the States of Jersey over recent years from Jersey Airport Meteorological Station 276ft above sea level, are given in the accompanying table.

Jersey, because of its position off the coast of Europe in the comparatively warm waters of the Atlantic, has a more equable climate than places at a similar latitude in continental Europe. And because plants and animals normally of south Europe or the Mediterranean can live further north up the warm Atlantic coast than they can in continental Europe, many of these species reach Jersey. Some such species are at their northern limit, like the Broad-leaved Sea-lavender *Limonium auriculae-ursifolium* for which Plémont is the most northerly locality known. Others are towards the extreme end of their northern range. For example, although Jersey Thrift *Armeria alliacea* has a few outposts further north along the European coast, it does not occur in the other Channel Islands or in mainland Britain.

This normally equable climate only rarely gives way to freak weather of exceptional rain, snow, wind, heat, cold or drought, but when it does, these can produce great changes in the flora, some permanent, others only for a year or two. Freak conditions must have occurred throughout the centuries, as for instance in 1771 when snow, frozen on top, lay 17ft deep near Town Mills. The effects of such weather, or of abnormally hot and dry weather, on natural vegetation or wild life was not considered worthy of notice in the past. Even T. W. Attenborough in lengthy Société Jersiaise botanical reports for 1916 and 1917 mentions the serious drought of 1916 only casually and makes no mention of the long, severe frost of 1917. This frost lasted at Rosel Manor from 22 January to 16 February and reached down to −7 deg. C (20 deg. F). Its effects on the exotic vegetation in the Manor grounds are described by the Seigneur in the Société's *Bulletin Annuel* (1918). This frost must surely have had an equally devastating effect on warmth-loving aliens growing in the wild but not thoroughly established.

In recent years there were freak conditions of frost in 1962/63, of wind in 1964 and of heat and drought in 1976 and 1983. The great frost of winter 1962/63 culminated in January 1963 when the edge of the sea froze and St Ouen's Pond was covered by ice in places 8–9in. thick. The lowest screen temperature was −11 deg. C (12 deg. F) at Jersey Airport on 20 January and the lowest grass temperature was −16 deg. C (3 deg. F) on 19 January at the Maison St Louis Observatory. This resulted in some of the Mediterranean elements of the flora being very scarce for a year or two. One of the established species worst affected was Great Quaking-grass *Briza maxima* which had previously been plentiful and which took several years to recover. Some garden escapes which looked like becoming part of Jersey's established flora in the wild were wiped out. Belle de Nuit or Marvel of Peru *Mirabilis jalapa*, for example, which had been flourishing on most of the old rubbish dumps for some years, has not been seen regularly since, other than in gardens.

On 9 October 1964 the tail end of a hurricane hit Jersey. The wind averaged 78mph for more than an hour with the highest gust being 108mph from the west. The greatest damage was to trees. Many were uprooted while all the young growth of others was burnt off on the windward side by the salt-laden winds. Gorse bushes on the foothills behind St Ouen's Bay were broken off at the base by the force of the wind. Perennial species like Sea Beet *Beta vulgaris* subsp. *maritima* growing by the edge of the coast have substantial roots to anchor them against strong winds, so though their leaves were shredded or blown off completely, they recovered quickly. On the other hand Beetroot *B. vulgaris* subsp. *vulgaris* in gardens was blown out of the ground as were a good many wild plants.

The summer of 1976 will long be remembered for its scorching heat, month after month, and its drought. Winter 1974/75 had been dry; summer 1975 was Jersey's normal 'good' summer with little rain; winter 1975/76 was again dry. The result was that springs were low when the drought of 1976 began. The following year Cornish Moneywort *Sibthorpia europaea*, usually a locally common species of damp shady hedgebanks, could hardly be found even in places where previously it had been dominant. Only now, some years later, is it back in fair quantity. Some trees, including several of the planted birches, died. But many species seemed to revel in the heat. For the next few years there was an even great glorious abundance of wild flowers on the cliffs and dunes than usual. Some rare species appeared in such quantity in 1977 and 1978 that there was more each year than in all the previous ten or twenty years put together. Details of this increase are given under some of the species concerned. Why this increase occurred is unknown. It may be that in the long hot summer, sun-loving plants were able to set abundant seed for the following years, or it may be that seed already present and lying dormant was activated by the heat to germinate the following year.

Temperature deg. C. (1951–80)	Jan	Feb	March	April	May	June	July	Aug	Sept	Oct	Nov	Dec	Year
Daily maximum	7.7	7.8	9.7	11.7	14.9	17.6	19.3	19.5	18.0	14.9	11.1	9.1	13.4
Daily minimum	3.7	3.4	4.4	6.1	8.6	11.3	13.2	13.7	12.7	10.4	7.0	5.1	8.3
Mean	5.7	5.6	7.1	8.9	11.7	14.5	16.3	16.6	15.3	12.7	9.1	7.1	10.9
Extreme maximum	13.3	16.2	20.1	21.8	27.3	31.9	34.6	31.2	30.7	22.9	17.3	15.7	34.6
Extreme minimum	−11.0	−7.1	−4.7	−0.9	0.0	6.0	8.4	8.1	5.6	3.4	−2.1	−8.2	−11.0
Sunshine in hours (1954–80)													
Monthly average	58.8	86.6	146.7	189.4	241.2	242.8	245.7	226.9	168.1	126.2	71.5	52.4	1856.4
Rainfall in mm. (1951–80)	94.1	74.2	63.5	48.0	52.2	41.0	42.0	57.1	70.7	75.7	111.3	104.5	834.3
No. of rain days (0.2 or more) (1951–80)	20.1	16.8	15.5	13.0	12.7	10.3	10.8	12.0	14.5	15.2	18.9	20.3	180.1
No. of days of snow or sleet (1951–80)	3.5	3.6	2.3	0.9	0.1	0.0	0.0	0.0	0.0	0.0	0.5	1.9	12.8
Snow lying at 0900	0.9	1.3	0.4	0.0	0.0	0.0	0.0	0.0	0.0	0.0	0.1	0.4	3.1
Air Frost	3.8	4.0	2.0	0.1	0.0	0.0	0.0	0.0	0.0	0.0	0.2	2.5	12.6
Wind (1958–80)													
Hourly mean speed in knots	13.9	12.9	12.6	12.4	11.5	10.8	10.7	11.2	11.7	12.2	13.9	14.6	12.4
Highest hourly wind				68 knots (78 mph) from 280° for the hour ended 1400 on 9 October 1964									
Highest gust				94 knots (108 mph) from 270° at 1325 on 9 October 1964									

Habitats

Because of the physical features, the geology, the climate and the way man has used the island (*q.v.*) Jersey in 1983 has a rich diversity of habitats. The inland valleys are deep, well-watered and sheltered. The valley bottoms are usually grazed except for parts of some of the larger valleys which contain reservoirs for the water supply of the island. Most of the valley sides are clothed in natural woodland of Oak, Elm, Sweet Chestnut and Ash, map 5, though now Elm is dying and Sycamore is increasingly invading the woodlands. The high land of the interior has a good soil cover and is intensively farmed leaving only minor patches of scrubland.

The most interesting habitats botanically are on or near the coast: the cliffs, the coastal heaths, the dunes, map 6, and the salt and fresh water marshes. Jersey has a 40ft tide at some springs, so salt spray can drench the cliffs, and if the high tide is accompanied by strong winds the spray can be blown far inland across the dunes. Species near the base of the cliffs must therefore be able to withstand large amounts of salt water pouring over them occasionally, and those which can withstand it, like Thrift *Armeria maritima*, occur all round the coast. Higher up, the cliffs vary considerably in their vegetation. Along the south and west, the cliffs and cliff-top heaths face the sun for a large part of each day so tend to be warm and dry. Their vegetation, which is low, open and contains warmth-loving annuals like the Spotted Rockrose *Tuberaria guttata*, differs from that of the north coast where the cliffs are in shade for long

5 L'Île Percée, off Noirmont, showing large patches of Hottentot-fig where the islet's natural vegetation
   used to grow

periods and are more moist. Here the vegetation cover is closed and larger species, perennials like
Pendulous Sedge *Carex pendula* and Tutsan *Hypericum androsaemum*, can be found.

   The dune systems of the coastal plains still survive on Gorey Common, Ouaisné Common and inland
behind St Ouen's Bay. The largest and deepest system is that of Les Blanches Banques on Les
Quennevais at the south end of St Ouen's Bay. It is on these dunes, calcareous because of the mollusc
shells in them, that Jersey's lime-loving flora, which includes such calcicoles as Rock Hutchinsia
Hornungia petraea, grows. In 1973 Dr D. S. Ranwell of the Institute of Terrestrial Ecology surveyed the
dunes of St Ouen's Bay on behalf of the Public Building and Works Committee of The States and
confirmed their value. Later two papers by Dr Ranwell were published by the Société Jersiaise (*Annual
Bulletin* **21**: 381–391 and 505–516). In the second of these papers he states that the St Ouen dunes are
among the ten largest single dune systems in the British Isles and are remarkably rich in species.

   The coastal plains also contain extensive fresh water marshes, map 7, towards their inland edge:
Grouville Marsh behind Gorey Common, Ouaisné Common Marsh behind St Brelade's Bay, the wet
meadows east of Les Prés Trading Estate inland from St Clement's Bay and the wetland round St Ouen's
Pond. This reed-fringed pond which has an open water area of over 30 vergées is the only large naturally
occurring fresh water pool in the island. The salt marshes of the past have gone, see below, but small
areas behind the sea walls are awash with salt water on many high tides and though not typical salt
marshes, they contain a salt marsh flora.

Wild Life

Only occasionally in this Flora is reference made to the wild life of the island, the mammals, birds, insects, etc., yet the flora lives in association with this wild life, of which a general account is given in *A Natural History of Jersey* (Le Sueur 1976).

The wild life may determine whether or not an immigrant species will survive to become part of the wild flora. Insects in Jersey can pollinate Butterfly-bush *Buddleja davidii* from China but not Fig *Ficus carica* from the south of France. Butterfly-bush has therefore become established but Figs are incapable of reproducing themselves. Narcissus bulbs are unpalatable to small mammals whereas Crocus corms are one of the favourite foods of bank voles which are abundant in Jersey. The result is that while feral Narcissi abound in the countryside in spring, discarded Crocus corms seldom survive for long and there are no masses of Crocus flowers in gardens year after year.

Any changes in the wild life may well be accompanied by changes in the flora. The most spectacular was the increase in vegetation on the cliffs and dunes when myxomatosis almost wiped out the rabbit population in the late 1950s. The vegetation grew luxuriantly in the absence of grazing. At first all species seemed to benefit but soon coarser grasses like Cock's-foot *Dactylis glomerata* began to crowd out the more delicate species. Now, with the return of rabbits, an equilibrium has been restored. A more gradual, but perhaps greater, change is being wrought by a virulent strain of the fungus *Ceratocystis ulmi* which is carried from one elm tree to another by the elm-bark beetle. This strain of the fungus was confirmed in elm trees in Jersey in 1974 and elm trees are still dying from its attacks. Elms were once the commonest trees in Jersey yet eventually none may be left.

Man probably introduced myxomatosis deliberately and he may have brought Dutch Elm disease accidentally, so causing these changes. Some account of the effect man has had on the flora of Jersey is given below.

6   L'Île Agois, St John, still with a good cover of vegetation on top including Wood Small-reed which is rare in Jersey

7   Les Quennevais dunes, one of the richest dune systems for wild flowers in the British Isles

8   A sand blow-out on Les Quennevais which may first be colonised by Marram and Sea Stock

Man and the Flora

Man has been changing Jersey's flora since he began farming in Neolithic times over 5,000 years ago. Only hunters had either lived in or visited the island until then and they made little impact on the flora. But with the development of a settled farming community, the land was gradually cleared of forest and cultivated.

When the archaeological investigations now in progress are completed much more will be known about the early history of Jersey's flora. Though written records specifically of the flora do not begin until 1690 some information is given incidentally in documents, mainly legal, in earlier centuries. It is clear that in Plantagenet and Tudor times Jersey was a corn-growing land with few trees. Many records exist indicating that up to the sixteenth century wood was scarce. J. H. Le Patourel (1937) pointed out that though the King's revenue between 1199 and 1399 was, with a few exceptions, characteristically Norman, there was no revenue from forests or anything on forest jurisdiction. This implies that there was no wooded area big enough to be worth bothering about in spite of the *Extente* of 1274 mentioning the Fief des Arbres in St Lawrence. The records contain many references to timber having to be sent from England to repair the Castles and as late as 1558 a memorandum in the *Calendar of State Papers Dom. Eliz.* (p. 485) states '. . . timber . . . cannot be had in the isle.'

The scarcity of wood is also shown by the difficulty of obtaining fuel. Old records show that vraic (seaweed) and Gorse were used extensively. G. F. B. de Gruchy, Seigneur of Noirmont, considered the Court of the Fief and Siegneurie of Noirmont, which was in full activity between 1550 and 1645, to have been more or less unchanged from the Middle Ages. He gave extracts from the *Rolls* of the Court (G. F.B. de Gruchy 1926) and commented that, 'Fuel, in the absence of coal and the scarcity of wood, was difficult to get in sufficient quantity; this explains the tenants' care to protect their rights on the commons.' In 1553 a lawsuit was brought by a tenant who had sold a Gorse côtil to another tenant on condition that the buyer delivered a load of fuel (Gorse) to the seller on St Michel de Mont Gargene's Day – but he had not done so. In 1559 a woman cut and took away fuel from Noirmont Common against the orders of the Seneschal and the tenants. As well as proceedings being taken against her it resulted in the re-statement of the orders for the care of the Common.

The Courts of the Fiefs and Seigneuries gradually fell into disuse but regulations for the care of the two Commons at Noirmont, La Commune de Haut, Portelet Common, and La Commune de Bas, Le Ouaisné Common were published as late as 1889. Gorse, Western Gorse and Heather could only be cut at Portelet in September, October and November, only with a sickle or billhook and only by tenants whose beasts had not grazed the Common; at Le Ouaisné they could only be cut after a decision of the tenants.

A changing economic climate in the seventeenth century when the production of cider apples became highly profitable and knitting became more remunerative than working in the fields, brought about great changes on the face of the island and was largely responsible for the inland landscape we know today. Jean Poingdestre (1609–91), a Lieutenant-Bailiff of Jersey, stated in 1682 in *Caesarea or a Discourse of the Island of Jersey* that the island '. . . lay heretofore, about a hundred years since, allmost open, with few Inclosures in it & very fewe Orchardes . . .' He considered that Jersey would have been in danger of becoming a continuous orchard if the States had not passed a law in 1673 forbidding the planting of new orchards on good land, though trees could still be planted on côtils where a plough could not go. The law also forbade the building of any house if it had less than twenty vergées of ploughable land round it.

Huge hedges had been built round the orchards to give shelter to the apple trees and Falle in 1694 was worried about the future of agriculture because he reckoned that the hedges, fences, roads and houses, together with the gardens round the houses and avenues leading to them, took up nearly one third of the island's land. There were so many trees, particularly inland, according to Falle, that from high ground the whole island looked like a continuous forest although there was not a wood to be seen and only a few coppices. The trees which created this impression were in the hedgerows and orchards. He went on to say, 'Nothing can be imagined more delightful than the Face of the Island, when the Trees, which are set among the High-ways, and in the Avenues of Houses are covered with verdure, and the Orchards are full of Blossoms . . . But still it must be confessed that so much shade is prejudicial to the growth of Pasture and Corn.' It was during this period that the island became unable to support itself agriculturally.

9 The marsh at Grouville, now much reduced in size

10 St Ouen's Pond and the surrounding reed bed

Though vraic, Gorse and Bracken were still used in the seventeenth century, and later, as fuel in the kitchen for cooking, wood had become the normal fuel. Poingdestre stated that 'wood', by which he meant trees, was plentiful all over the island, not only in set rows along the highways but also along fences and hedges where it was lopped every five or six years. This 'wood' was almost certainly elm trees, the ancestors of the hedgerow elms of today which are still lopped in the same way and which are suffering from Dutch Elm disease. Elms are dealt with in detail in the body of the Flora but it should be noted here that the hybrid elm, common in Jersey, so closely resembles elms in parts of Normandy that Dr R. H. Richens and Dr J. N. R. Jeffers, authorities on elms, suspect a common origin. It may well be that when supplies of young cider apple trees were required for the new orchards they were imported from Normandy and that elm suckers to plant in the hedgerows for shelter were obtained at the same time.

Poingdestre also mentioned the hedging plants used in 1682, stating that 'Besides which [i.e. the 'wood'] the hedges are planted with white and blacke thorne & with willowes . . .'

Whitethorn, now more commonly called hawthorn or May, was planted thickly on huge earth banks built up six or eight feet high round the fields and along the roads. Many of these high hedges, which were sometimes faced with stone, remain today and are similar to ones which occur in Normandy from where they were probably copied. Falle who was critical of these hedges in 1694 because they wasted land, prophetically commented that they would serve as ramparts against an enemy 'to whom we might dispute every field'. Those in Normandy were used just so in 1944 by the Germans against the advancing American army. As well as giving good shelter and making a stock-proof hedge, hawthorn was a valued part of the fuel used in bread ovens because it imparted an excellent flavour to the bread.

Blackthorn hedges, smothered in white flowers on bare dark branches in spring and bearing sloes in autumn, still survive – and more are now being planted. No work has as yet been done on the age of hedges in the island but some of the present blackthorn hedges seem very old.

This change from open land used for growing corn with temporary fences which were removed to let animals graze after the corn was harvested, to land enclosed in small areas surrounded by permanent hedges on all sides, must have produced many changes in the flora, apart from the huge increase in the number of trees and hedging plants.

The distribution of cider apple orchards in 1795 is shown in map 8. They began to disappear in the nineteenth century when arable land again became more profitable, but the hedges on the whole remain though in the last fifty years some have been removed for ease of farming. Many of the fields are small, the average size being only about four vergées because of the laws of inheritance in the past, so Jersey has considerably more hedges per square mile than most countries in western Europe, map 9.

There are strict regulations governing the cutting of roadside hedges and hedgebanks. On a given date in the first fifteen days of July and again in September each year, parish officials tour their parish to see that the *branchage* has been done. If any owner of a property has not cut back the vegetation on his hedgebanks or has allowed trees or bushes to overhang the roads, he is fined for each infraction. The clearance must be twelve feet vertically across the whole width of the road except above a footpath where the clearance need only be eight feet. No owner cuts higher than is essential to escape a fine, so after twelve feet the trees grow at will. Where there are trees on both sides of a narrow road they often meet above the middle of the road creating a tunnel of green. Alas, with the demise of many elms through Dutch Elm disease, such tree-enveloped roads are disappearing.

Potatoes became an important crop last century particularly after about 1870 and tomatoes which are grown mainly out-of-doors in fields in Jersey, were in peak production from about the 1920s to the 1950s. They are now declining because their production is so labour intensive. Neither potatoes nor tomatoes survive for long unaided in the wild but reminders of some crops look like remaining permanently in the countryside. For example bulbs of many of the older narcissi grown for the cut-flower trade flourish on hedgebanks. The Jersey Agricultural and Horticultural Society (later the Royal Jersey Agricultural & Horticultural Society) began experimenting to improve crops almost immediately on its formation in 1834. Many of the species newly introduced in its first few years were to improve pasture for cows, for example Timothy Grass which is still used, but a few species, like Rough Comfrey, survive out in the wild though they may not have been in cultivation for some considerable time.

Against this changing agricultural background, there was comparatively little change in the town and the villages or in trade and industry likely to affect the flora until the beginning of last century. Advances in technology and in wealth then began to allow projects to be undertaken which had far-reaching effects.

The most obvious changes in the flora came through the draining of low-lying land in St Clement and behind St Aubin's Bay and the building of the sea walls. A glance at some of the old records shows what a wealth of marsh-loving plants used to grow in these wet areas, particularly in the St Lawrence–St Peter Marsh which stretched roughly from Bel Royal to Beaumont. Many of the species still grow elsewhere in Jersey's remaining wetlands but Adder's-tongue Spearwort *Ranunculus ophioglossifolius*, a rare species in England, was last seen about a century ago. Earlier it had been reported as plentiful in the Marsh.

Lester-Garland complained in 1903 that the costly sea walls which were being built were obliterating the botanical features of the foreshore. The beautiful Cottonweed *Otanthus maritimus* was probably lost through this in St Ouen's Bay. Sea walls continued to be built, including many during the German Occupation (1940–45), with the result that only in one very short length of Grouville Bay is there a natural meeting place of the beach with dunes. The disappearance of the rare Purple Spurge *Euphorbia peplis*, last recorded in 1903, was almost certainly caused by the disappearance of its habitat, the region of the foreshore where high tide and vegetation used to meet. Occasionally vegetation begins to grow where sand and shingle pushed up against a sea wall by a spring tide are not washed away by the following high tides. So far Purple Spurge has not reappeared before the 'beach' has been swept away again, but it yet may.

11 Sharp Rush and Great Fen-sedge at the outer edge of the reed-bed round St Ouen's Pond. (Though July, the reed-bed is still showing the pale dead reed stems of last year because, except at the inner edge, the first growth of new reed has been attacked by the Reed Wainscot Moth.)

12 Farmland in St Clement with small fields and many hedges, a landscape typical of much of Jersey's interior

Though the building of the sea walls destroyed one valuable habitat, it has created another. The salt marshes of the Middle Ages which gave the Samarès region its name were enclosed and cultivated long before Lester-Garland's time. This century, spring tides crashing against the sea walls and pouring sea water or salt spray over the land immediately behind the sea walls, have created thin strips where salt marsh species grow in several bays. Species like Sea Purslane *Haliminione portulacoides* whose existence in Jersey Lester-Garland queried, now grow locally in quantity beside newer arrivals like the 'mesem' *Disphyma crassifolium* which comes from salt marshes in South Africa.

Advances in technology also eased transport both to and from the island and within it. This opened up Jersey to a much greater flow of people and plants from outside than in the past and allowed people to go from one side of Jersey to the other in about half an hour whereas in the past it had taken half a day. Such mobility, combined with an increasing population, meant that popular areas like Les Quennevais dunes were beginning to suffer badly from erosion in the 1960s and 1970s. Cars were excluded in the mid-1970s and since then the dunes along the west coast have been declared by The States to be a natural park, Les Mielles, whose beauty will be preserved and whose animals and plants will be conserved by The States throughout all the foreseeable future. The dunes of Les Quennevais and the equally large, highly valuable botanical area of Les Landes de l'Étacq and Grosnez were protected from development in the past by accident. Until 1956 they were owned by the War Department of the British Government which up to about the First World War (1914–18) used them for training exercises for soldiers stationed in Jersey. In 1956 they were sold to The States of Jersey which accepted a recommendation by the Public Works Committee in 1958 that they should be left in their natural state.

Individual species have occasionally become established as a result of some peculiar episode in history, as for example Cherry Laurel *Prunus laurocerasus*, a native of the Balkans. There are no political parties in Jersey now but early last century the Rose and Laurel Parties flourished in the bitterest opposition to one another. G. R. Balleine in *A History of the Island of Jersey* (1950) stated that 'Gardens with laurel hedges still show where Laurel supporters lived. No Rose-man would allow that accursed shrub on his land'. In the survey 1960–70, see p. x v i far more Laurel bushes were found in semi-wild situations than one would normally expect in similar places in England. One can only presume that they date from this Rose and Laurel period. (Did Laurel supporters deny themselves the pleasure of Roses in their gardens?)

As this Flora goes to press Volume 1, *Surveys and Issues*, of the Island Development Committee's Island Plan is being debated by The States. Jersey has a magnificent wild flora. Lester-Garland wrote in 1903 that '. . . few botanists would have expected to find so bright a gleam of the sunshine of the Mediterranean so far north.' This is still true today. Many outsiders do not realise that in spite of Jersey being a major tourist resort and an international finance centre taking full advantage of modern technology, the island remains largely unspoilt and so therefore does its flora. A glance at the body of the Flora will show that few important species have been lost over the centuries. It may be that because the island slopes from north to south, facing the sun as Poingdestre (1682) described it, open farmland, map 10, is still profitable and glasshouses, common in the sister island, are not needed. Also, because much of the north coast is inaccessible, shipping and commercial activities have been concentrated along the south coast, mainly near St Helier, so that there has not been a suburban sprawl over the countryside.

The President of the Island Development Committee, Deputy Norman Le Brocq, states in the *Foreword* to Volume 1 of the Island Plan that one of the aims of the Plan will be to show 'how we can retain, maintain and manage our beautiful countryside'. Success in this will ensure that the present richness of Jersey's flora continues.

13 A tree-lined road in St Ouen

Botanists in Jersey

The earliest known list of Jersey plants was compiled in 1689 by Dr William Sherard (1659–1728), a noted botanist after whom the Sherardian Chair of Botany at Oxford is named. The list was published in John Ray's *Synopsis Methodica Stirpium Brittanicum* in 1690. Until then, the only references to plants were incidental ones in the *Extentes*, the *Rolls* of the Courts and similar documents, except for an unsatisfactory reference to some Jersey plants which may have been Ribwort Plantain in Gerard's *Herball* in 1597. Only fifteen species were on Sherard's first list (ten flowering plants, one fern, one chara, one fungus and two seaweeds) but they were all species which he considered unusual. And still today, many British botanists see some of these species for the first time in Jersey.

Differing accounts have been given by Babington (1839), Lester-Garland (1903) and Attenborough & Guiton (1918) of the species Sherard claimed to have seen and of his comments on them. Except for the numbers at the side, which are for ease of reference later, the following is therefore an exact word copy of an Appendix in the first edition of Ray's *Synopsis* (1690, pp. 238 . . .) in the University Library, Cambridge.

'Appendix
Plants observed in Jersey *by the same Mr* Sherard.
  (i) Gnaphalium ad stoechadem citrinam accedens *F.B.* An Gnaph. Plateau fecundum *Clus. Hist. On the Walls and dry Banks very common.*
  (ii) Lycopsis *C.B.* Echii altera species *Dod.* p. 680, cujus icon hanc nostram bene repraesentat. *In the sandy Grounds near St Hilary plentifully.*
  (iii) Cistus flore pallido punicante macula insignito *C.B.* Tuberaria minor Myconi *Lugd. On the West-side of the Island near* Grosnez Castle.
  (iv) Scrophularia Scorodoniae folio *H. R. Blaef. auct. By the rivulet sides betwixt the Port and St* Hilary.
  (v) Filix elegans Adiantho nigro accedens segmentis rotundioribus. *On the Rocks on the North side.*
  (vi) Equisetum sub aqua repens, ad genicula polyspermon. *In Sir* Phil. Carterets *Fish-ponds.*
  (vii) Fungus, Crepitus lupi dictus, coronatus & inferne stellatus. *In the sandy grounds near the shore on the East-side.*
  (viii) Geranium saxatile lucidum foliis Geranii Robertiani. An Geran. Robertianum. *'Tis of the saxatile kind, having frequent joints. In several places near the shore. I have since found it near* Swannigh *in* Dorsetshire. Geranium saxatile Robertino simile Anglicum *Schol. Botan.*
  (ix) Spergula semine foliaceo nigro, circulo membranaceo albo cincto *Hort. Blaes. On the shore everywhere. I have found it near* Southampton. *I know not whether all our* Maritimae *be not* sem. foliaceo. *Yea they are so; and possibly this may be no other than the common maritime* Spergula.
  (x) Alga folio membranaceo purpureo, Lapathi sanguinei figura magnitudine. In littus rejectum. *Mr* Newton *showed it me since gathered in* Ireland *by Dr* Moulins.
  (ix) Gramen Arundinaceum acerosa gluma. *'Tis different from* Parkinson's. *On the seacoast over against* Normandy. *Mr* Bobert *will have it to be the* Gram. paniculatum folio variegato *C.B. only not striped.*
  (xii) Gramen Alopecuroides spica aspera brevi *C.B. Common on all the sandy Grounds.*
  (xiii) Euphrasia latifolia viscata serrata *H. R. Blaes. In moist places near the Port. I take it to be the* Euphrasia lutea latifolia palustris *Cat. Ang. Doubtless it is so. Observed first by me in several Places of* Cornwal.
  (xiv) Alsine spuria pusilla repens foliis Saxifragae aureae *Cat. Ang. On a moist Wall near* Greville.
  (xv) Fucus Gallo pavonis pennas referens *C.B. On the Rocks towards* Normandy *plentifully.*

   Hae tres plantae in Synopsi habentur, verum quia rariores & minus obviae sunt, loca ubi sponte proveniunt plura adnotasse convenit.'

In the second edition (1696), again consulted in the University Library, Cambridge, the species were incorporated in the main body of the work. Only the flowering plants and ferns were investigated. Entries for the species (i), (iii), (iv), (v) and (xiii) were on pages 82, 203, 161, 51 and 163 respectively and were either the same or had unimportant changes. Species (ii) was called 'Wall Bugloss', p. 119, and species (xiv) 'Small round-leaved Bastard-Chickweed', p. 211. The entry for species (xi) was slightly changed to emphasise that Sherard thought it different from Parkinson's which was called 'Great Reed-Grass with chaffy Heads', p. 255, and the entry for species (xii) had extra Latin including, 'Gramen cum cauda leporis aspera, sive spica murina *JB*' and the English name Rough-eared Foxtail-Grass, p. 251. Species (viii) and (ix) were missing but the following extra species were included, labelled (xvi) and (xvii) here for ease of reference.

After a description of a grass which in Linnean binomials would be *Briza media*, an entry, p. 254, ran:

(xvi) 2. Gramen tremulum minus, panicula ampla, locustis parvis, triangularis. *Mr* Sherard *first found in* Jersey, *afterwards in many meadows in* France. *Small quaking grass with triangular heads.*

and under the general heading of Gramina Avenacea Festucae & Bromi dicta, p. 261, there was more Latin followed by several grasses which included:

(xvii) 4. Festuca Avenacea sterilis paniculis confertis erectioribus, aristis brevioribus. *Wild Oat-grass or Drank, with a more compact Panicle, and more erected spikes with shorter awns. Found by Mr* Sherard *on the sandy grounds in* Jersey *plentifully.*

The third edition of Ray's *Synopsis* (1724), the Dillenian Edition, contained all the Jersey records of the first two editions with one exception and there was one extra species. The exception was species (ix) the *Spergula*, given in the first edition but omitted from the second. In the third, the species was mentioned, p. 351, but only as being in Ireland. The extra species, (xviii) below, was described, p. 429, as:

(xviii) 5. Juncus acutus maritimus caule triquetro, rigido, mucrone pungente. *Pluk. Alm.* 200 . . . triangularis Jersejanus D. Sherard *Buddl. H. S.* 34 In Insula Jerseia a D. Sherard inventus.

14 Hedgerow elms dying from Dutch elm disease, a common sight in recent years

James Petiver in a short paper on rare plants in the Royal Society's *Philosophical Transactions* (1712, p. 375) gave some of Sherard's Jersey records and said that the island would be well worth visiting. J. E. Smith noted several of Sherard's Jersey records in *Smith's English Botany* (1824) but there was almost a note of desperation in his comments under *Echium vulgare*, Viper's-bugloss: '. . . nor have I ever been able to detect a second species [of *Echium*] in England, whatever may be found in Jersey; on which some authentic information, by means of specimens or seeds, is very desirable. Possibly *E. plantagineum* . . . may be the plant of Ray and Dodonaeus.' He was right: *E. plantagineum*, Jersey or Purple Viper's-bugloss, is the *Echium* commonly found in Jersey whereas *E. vulgare*, the common Viper's-bugloss of England, has always been rare in Jersey and at present, 1983, cannot be found.

The problems of identification arise because Sherard had to use the voluminous Latin descriptions of pre-Linnean days and unfortunately the specimens in his herbarium at Oxford are not localised. Nevertheless nine of the fourteen flowering plants and ferns would seem easily identifiable as: (i) *Gnaphalium luteo-album* Jersey Cudweed; (ii) *Echium plantagineum* Jersey or Purple Viper's-bugloss; (iii) *Tuberaria guttata* Spotted Rockrose; (iv) *Scrophularia scorodonia* Balm-leaved Figwort; (v) *Asplenium billotii* Lanceolate Spleenwort; (xiii) *Parentucellia viscosa* Yellow Bartsia; (xiv) *Sibthorpia europaea* Cornish Moneywort; (xvi) *Briza minor* Lesser Quaking-grass; (xviii) *Scirpus pungens* Sharp Club-rush.

Of the remaining five species, the *Geranium* would seem to be *G. purpureum* Little Robin which any botanist visiting Jersey today is still likely to see. Babington, who omitted Sherard's record, did not mention it but he may not have regarded it as a species separate from *G. robertianum* Herb Robert.

Three species (xi), (xii) and (xvii) are grasses. Species (xi) was identified as *Cynosurus echinatus* Rough Dog's-tail by Smith (1824) and this has been accepted by following botanists. Druce (1916) clouded the issue by mistakenly stating that Babington had identified it as a *Bromus*. He did not: Babington's *Bromus* was species (xvii) which is probably not precisely identifiable. The nomenclature of this Bromus group is confusing and Sherard's record has variously been interpreted but most botanists consider that *B. madritensis*, which still occurs here, fits the description best. The third grass (xii) has caused much argument and unless a localised specimen can be found it is probably unidentifiable. *Phalaris arundinaria* Reed Canary-grass, *P. minor* Lesser Canary-grass and *Calamagrostis epigeos* Wood Small-reed have been suggested.

The *Spergula* (ix) was presumably given for Jersey in error in the first edition since it did not appear in the second, and in the third it was given only for Ireland. Druce (*Journal of Botany* 1916, pp. 335–336) and Attenborough & Guiton did not realise it was withdrawn and refer it to *Spergularia media*, a sea-spurrey unknown in the Channel Islands. The confusion is further compounded by Attenborough & Guiton remarking on its 'exceedingly luxuriant growth in Jersey', though both were well aware that it had never been seen here!

Babington included a Sherard record of *Juncus acutus* which he claimed was in the third edition of the *Synopsis*. This record has not been traced and it is thought that he accidentally used species (xviii) twice, once correctly as *Scirpus pungens* and then in error as *Juncus acutus*.

Between 1730 and 1740 a shadowy figure, the Rev. W. or Mr Clark(e) or Clerk(e) contributed specimens from Jersey to the Dillenian herbarium, Oxford (Clokie 1964; Druce & Vines 1907). The specimens, which are still in the herbarium, are *Potentilla anserina* Silverweed, *Gnaphalium luteo-album* Jersey Cudweed, *Polycarpon tetraphyllum* Four-leaved Allseed, *Euphorbia peplis* Purple Spurge, *Parentucellia viscosa* Yellow Bartsia, all labelled as from Jersey, and *Rumex maritimus* Golden Dock from either Jersey or Guernsey. In the Druce herbarium a specimen of Jersey Cudweed is labelled Jersey, 1720 (*sic*), the Rev. W. Clarke, ex Hb Dillenius, but Dillenius did not form his herbarium until after 1724.

The next information on Jersey's flora came from John Finlay (1760–1802) a Lieutenant in the 83rd Regiment, the Royal Glasgow Volunteers, and later a Captain in the Royal Engineers (McClintock 1972). Finlay wrote to Sir Joseph Banks on 22 February 1787 telling him of *Romulea columnae* Sand Crocus in Jersey. The Rev. J. Lightfoot entered the record in his copy of Ray's *Synopsis*, and also that in 1787 Finlay had recorded *Silene gallica* var. *quinquevulnera* a beautiful variety of Small-flowered Catchfly and *Mibora minima* Early Sand-grass. Five Companies of the 83rd Regiment, which was formed in 1778 and disbanded in 1783, were usually in Guernsey and five in Jersey from 1779 to 1782. Finlay was

15 A strip behind the sea wall in St Ouen's Bay where salt marsh conditions prevail

16 Salt marsh species including Sea-purslane and the South African 'mesem' Disphyma growing behind the sea wall north of Le Braye Slip

with one of the Guernsey Companies. He presumably visited Jersey and, as the Sand Crocus record was from sandy ground near Grouville, it is likely that when he was in Jersey he was visiting the Jersey Companies of his Regiment which were stationed at Fort Conway, now Fort Henry, Grouville.

These records are doubly interesting to a Jerseyman because the 83rd Regiment played a decisive part in the defeat of the French at the Battle of Jersey in 1781 and Finlay may well have known some of their men who lie buried in Grouville Cemetery.

Finlay's letter to Sir Joseph Banks did not give the dates of his finds but there is no record of his having visited the Channel Islands again so it is assumed that they were made between 1779 and 1782.

In 1831 Professor Mariano La Gasca y Segura (1776–1839) who had been living in England as a political refugee from Spain, came to Jersey for health reasons. Earlier he had been Professor of Botany at Madrid University, and in his exile both in London, c. 1824–31, and Jersey 1831–34, he studied the plants which he saw. He seems to have taken an active part in island life and acted as one of the judges at the first 'Floricultural Department' Show organised on 14 May 1834 by the newly formed Jersey Agricultural & Horticultural Society. In a report on the Show he was described as 'formerly Curator of the Royal Gardens at Madrid'. His list of Jersey plants, dated 8 October 1834, was published at the end of the fifth (1838) *Annual Report* of the Jersey Agricultural & Horticultural Society, pp. 65–70.

Lester-Garland (1903), who was scathing in the extreme about La Gasca's list, stated that he had ignored it. *'Requiescat in pace'* were his final words (p.x). Following botanists have been less critical. While it is true that several species on the list are highly unlikely to occur in Jersey, others were probably temporary garden escapes which La Gasca was used to seeing in the wild in Spain and which some botanists might record today. J. E. Lousley described La Gasca's London work as useful and interesting (pers. comm.), and so is his Jersey list. It should perhaps be pointed out here that Lester-Garland, so critical of La Gasca's errors, stated that the list was given in the Report of the J. A. & H. S. for 1839 whereas it was for 1838, and in spite of his stating that he was not including La Gasca's records, not even in the list of ambiguities and errors at the end of his Flora, he included several in that list.

A manuscript list of species which the French botanist J. Gay saw when he visited Jersey in summer 1832 is in the library at Kew. The list contains some species reported to him by La Gasca whom he met in Jersey. A few of these do not occur on La Gasca's own list.

Several English botanists also visited the island in the 1830s. W. C. Trevelyan (1797–1879) came in August 1833 and confirmed Sherard's *Echium* as *E. plantagineum*. Joseph Woods (1776–1864) spent a week in Jersey on his way back from France in 1836 and William Christy spent about three weeks in October 1836 in Jersey. A valuable account of the species Christy saw, mainly in the west of the island, was published in the *Magazine of Natural History, New Series* (1837) **1**: 25–28. The climax of this sudden activity came in 1839 when C. C. Babington (1808–95) who had visited the Channel Islands in 1837 and 1838, published his *Primitiae Florae Sarnicae*, or *An Outline of the Flora of the Channel Islands*. His visits to Jersey were comparatively short being only from 16 July to 11 August 1837 and from 1 (or 2) June to 22 June 1838, yet McClintock's comment in *The Wild Flowers of Guernsey* (1975) that he 'produced a neat, clear and permanently useful "outline" as a result of his two visits to Guernsey' could equally well apply to Jersey.

Few of Babington's own records have been proved wrong. The one usually quoted is *Plantago media* Hoary Plantain, a species unknown in Guernsey and an extreme rarity in Jersey but which Babington stated was common in both islands. Most of the erroneous Jersey records came through his uncritical use of Professor La Gasca's and Bernard Saunders' notes. An entry in Babington's diary for 1837 runs: 'Aug. 7. Called upon Mr. B. Saunders of the Caesarean Nursery, who showed me a list that he had formed of the native plants of the island, and allowed us to extract those names which did not come in our list.'

Bernard Saunders (1792–1859) ran the Caesarean Nurseries for many years. He took an active part in the work of the Jersey Agricultural & Horticultural Society being on its Board of Management from its foundation in 1834 until his death. That he was a brilliant nurseryman is obvious from the prizes which he won against intense competition at local Shows and from the descriptions of his Nurseries. Babington was perhaps too young to argue with anyone so well-established in the horticultural trade in Jersey or too inexperienced to doubt the records. Lester-Garland (1903) commented that Saunders '. . . was an intelligent Nursery gardener, and had a very interesting collection of cultivated plants, but he was not a sound botanist, and his records are worth no more than those of the Professor [La Gasca].'

Babington's copy of his Flora, annotated by him, is now in the Botany School Library, Cambridge University. He crossed out Saunders' name whenever he received another record of a species which he had recorded only on Saunders' authority, and gave the new record. This perhaps indicates that he was not entirely happy with Saunders' notes. Unfortunately he replaced many of them with records sent by Joseph Dickson and added new ones of Dickson's.

Joseph Dickson (1819–1874) wrote to Babington on several occasions between November 1839 and June 1848 and an article 'Notice of a few rare Plants, collected principally during the Autumn of 1839, in Jersey' by Dickson appeared in the *Magazine of Natural History* (1840, pp. 226–230). Lester-Garland (1903) did not mention Dickson so either he was unaware of the article or he ignored it. Perhaps having been so scathing about La Gasca's, he could find no words for Dickson's. Out of a list of 181 species, mostly British natives, more than twenty per cent would seem to have no connection with Jersey, species such as '*Gentiana campestris*' Field Gentian and *Parnassia palustris* Grass of Parnassus.

In a letter to Babington he claimed to have found *Campanula rotundifolia* Harebell, which was on his list together with '*C. hederacea*', in plenty in Vallée des Vaux. No one else has recorded Harebells in any Channel Island and Vallée des Vaux has been well botanised over as it is close to St Helier. Babington entered Dickson's *Aster linosyris (Chrysocoma linosyris)* Goldilocks with a query in his Flora. The record for Jersey in the *Atlas of the British Flora* (1962) is based on a specimen labelled as collected in 'Jersey' in 1840 by Dickson. The species, a perennial, grows as a great rarity on a few limestone cliffs in England. There is no such habitat in Jersey and there never has been.

No record made by Dickson, whether supported by a specimen or not, has been used in this Flora: Lester-Garland's benediction for La Gasca's list would seem more appropriate here. Dickson lived in Jersey for many years practising medicine but after this initial interest in botany in his youth, he seems to have studied it no more. This may have been because of the arrival of Jean Piquet on the scene.

Jean Piquet (1825–1912), who was apprenticed to the pharmacist John Ereaut in St Helier at the age of twelve and began his own pharmacy business when he was twenty-two, was interested in plants throughout his long life. Specimens collected by him bear dates ranging from 1847 to 1911. A few years after his death his main herbarium was sold to G. C. Druce. Unfortunately it left the island and is now in the Druce herbarium, Oxford. A second collection is in the Société Jersiaise herbarium. A manuscript list with '*Catalogue of Plants Indegenous to Jersey one of the Channel Islands by J Piquet 1851*' on the title page is in the library of the Société. A few additions and alterations were made to the list later at various undated times. In 1853 an article 'A few Notes on the Botany of Jersey; including a List of Additions to Mr. Babington's "Primitiae Florae Sarnicae," by M. Piquet' written by N. B. Ward was published in the *Phytologist* (**IV**: 1090–1094). Piquet's main work 'The Phanerogamous Plants and Ferns of Jersey' appeared in the *Bulletin Annuel* of the Société for 1896, pp. 361–382, and a supplement to it was published in the *Bulletin Annuel* for 1898, pp. 90–91.

Piquet stated in the introduction to his 1896 list that he had never seen many of La Gasca's and Saunders' species which Babington mentioned in his Flora. He therefore omitted them, with the result that Lester-Garland (1903) could write of Piquet's list: 'Most of the imaginary species have disappeared, and it represents the results of fifty years' study of Jersey plants by a keen and intelligent observer.'

Piquet introduced a few species. This, which was the custom of the time, was not frowned on as it would be today, and he made no secret of it. Marsh Marigold, Hare's-tail Grass, Sweet Flag and White Bryony are all known to have been introduced by him. Some survived; others doubtless perished. R. A. Mollet (1886–1961), Honorary Secretary of the Société Jersiaise for many years, told me that in his boyhood he often went out walking with Piquet, and that in suitable places Piquet would scatter seeds which he had gathered in other parts of Jersey. What effect this has had on the distribution of wild plants in the island is unknown but probably not a great deal. If the habitat was right the species was probably there already and if it was wrong they would not survive even if the seeds germinated.

In the year 1896 in which Piquet published his list of Jersey plants, Lester-Garland (1860–1944) arrived in Jersey to take up his appointment as headmaster of Victoria College and he remained in the island until he retired in 1911. His name was Lester Vallis Lester until 1903 when he added Garland to his surname to become Lester Vallis Lester-Garland. The records in his book *A Flora of the Island of Jersey*

(1903) are almost faultless and to have such a base from which to work has been invaluable. Critics objected to the 'List of Errors, Ambiguities, and Plants recorded for Jersey on Insufficient Authority' at the end of the Flora but this brought order out of chaos and Lester-Garland has been proved right in an overwhelming number of cases. A more valid criticism by T. W. Attenborough is that because Lester-Garland had no head for heights he did not search the cliffs properly. Also he seems to have ignored the many references to Jersey plants in the botanical magazines of last century and he searched no herbaria in England for Jersey specimens, not even Babington's at Cambridge.

Another fault has become more serious as the years have passed. The Flora is a strictly scientific work for scholars with no concessions to the non-botanist. No English name occurs anywhere; nor does a Jersey-Norman-French one. This is in sharp contrast to Marquand's Guernsey Flora which was published two years earlier. The result is that there has never been a simple way for ordinary people to find out what grows in Jersey, and consequent on that, when the conservation of wild plants on the dunes was first discussed, many people were unaware that there was anything worth conserving.

Shortly after Lester-Garland's Flora was published T. W. Attenborough (1883–1973) began visiting Jersey and eventually, in 1911, he came to live at 10, Conway Street to run his father-in-law's chemist's shop. He was to become the island's principal botanist for over fifty years. The Botanical Section of the Société was formed in 1914 and he was its secretary from 1915 until 1960. During his early visits to Jersey he met Jean Piquet often and came to know him well, thus discovering much unwritten information about Jersey's flora. His chemist's shop was a Mecca for visiting botanists as well as for local people who wanted information on plants and he would stop making up a prescription if anyone carrying a wild flower walked into his shop. Everything else had to wait while he discussed it with them.

Most of the island's botanists in the past were pharmacists like J. Piquet and T. W. Attenborough since a knowledge of plants was essential in those days in order to prepare drugs. A *Hortus Siccus*, now in the Société's possession, was made by G. Ereaut in 1847 and contains upwards of 200 pressed plants, several of them being new records for the island. John Ereaut was awarded a medal by the Society of Pharmacists of Great Britain for a collection of plants in 1857. The medal was given to the Société in 1957 but not the collection which seems to have vanished. Specimens prepared by E. Duprey in 1859, by F. Piquet in

17 The extensive heathland at Grosnez where Gorse, Western Gorse, Heather and Bell Heather grow in profusion

Professors Grubdust and Buffelskopf setting off in search of the Jersey Fern and eventually being brought a 'specimen' of it. See p. xli   (Reproduced with permission from a copy in the Library of the Société Jersiaise.)

1869–71 and later by F. G. Piquet are in the Société herbarium and Duprey wrote an article 'La Flore des Vieux Châteaux à Montorgueil' published in the Société's *Bulletin Annuel* for 1894.

Dr Martin M. Bull (1820 or 21–1879) practised medicine in St Helier from 1859 until his death but strangely his few records do not begin until 1872 when suddenly, with the tracking down of *Ranunculus paludosus* Jersey Buttercup, he emerged on the scene as a highly competent botanist. He seems to have worked with Piquet because specimens of most of his discoveries are in the Piquet herbarium now in Oxford. Druce wrote in the *Journal of Botany* (1879, pp. 119–120) that his death, '. . . had deprived the Channel Islands of its most energetic botanist.'

Adolphus J. Binet (1858–1936) who worked for the Jersey Savings Bank, kept a botanical diary from 1877 to 1929. Most entries are from 1877 to 1892 but in 1919 and 1920 there is another burst of botanical activity. The diary, which contains much valuable information and is now in the Société library, gives an insight into the problems of botanists in the past. First, transport was difficult. He walked to Plémont and Grosnez, presumably from his home in Val Plaisant, St Helier, to look for flowers on 30 March 1877, but from 1888 to at least 1892 he rode a tricycle when he went out botanising. Secondly, identification of Jersey species rare or unknown in England was troublesome and in his diary he recorded his struggles with some of them, for example *Dianthus gallicus* Jersey Pink, which he was the first to find, and *Gnaphalium undulatum* Cape Cudweed.

Another amateur botanist Stanley Guiton (1875–1935), a corn merchant, was responsible with T. W. Attenborough for the formation of the Société's Botanical Section in 1914. He contributed records from the late 1890s to his death and wrote a small book *Hints on Collecting and Preserving Plants* (1905). Some of the most beautiful specimens in the Société's herbarium are his work.

Religious men from France have contributed many records. In 1881 Père Vaniot made a herbarium of several hundred species mounted on sheets only 8in. x 6in. He was one of a group of Jesuits who came to Jersey in 1880 because of the introduction of anti-religious laws in France. He seems to have worked alone, for there is no mention of him by other Jersey botanists. His herbarium eventually came into the possession of Père Burdo who gave it to the writer, insisting that it was meant for students only and that it was not worth putting in the Société's main herbarium. On the contrary it has proved extremely valuable and several records from it are given in the Flora. Père C. Burdo (1881–1961) who botanised in Jersey in the mid-1920s with Attenborough, added a few specimens before his archaeological work at La Cotte, St Brelade, became of over-riding importance.

In 1923 Les Frères de l'Instruction Chrétienne established a school in Jersey and Frère Ariste who first came to Jersey in 1922 taught chemistry and natural science at the school until 1931. During that time he formed an excellent herbarium now in the possession of the Société Jersiaise, a herbarium which proved invaluable in assessing another made mainly over the same years, that of Frère Louis-Arsène.

Frère Louis-Arsène (1875–1959) was also a member of Les Frères de l'Instruction Chrétienne but when he was stationed in Jersey (1921–52) he was involved in the administration of the Order as a whole and he was not part of the local teaching staff. His hobby was botany, and he formed the inevitable herbarium. The publication of this Flora has been delayed because of the problems his herbarium has posed. Almost every species which Louis-Arsène knew had been recorded for Jersey in the past, he claimed to have found and collected, mainly in the 1920s. The herbarium was analysed in detail in a paper in 1982 in *Watsonia* (**14:** 167–176) and readers are referred to it. Specimens of common plants labelled as gathered from localities in the wild in Jersey, would certainly be so gathered, but one can say with almost equal certainty that many rarities, similarly labelled, were not. Between these two extremes, lies a huge 'grey' area. In this Flora no record has been accepted from Louis-Arsène's herbarium, unless there is corroborative evidence from contemporary herbaria, usually Ariste's, that the specimen supporting the record was gathered in the wild in Jersey. This is a departure from botanical tradition where normally a dated, localised specimen is taken as proof of a record. The 'Hastings' Rarities' showed that it should not be in ornithology; nor should it be in botany.

Meanwhile Babington's Flora had drawn the attention of leading English botanists once again to the wealth of interesting plants in the Channel Islands and transport was easier. Many visited Jersey and some, like G. C. Druce, returned several times. Indeed after the finding of *Anogramma leptophylla*, the Jersey Fern, by Miss Julia Marett in 1852, so many came that a botanical skit *An Excursion to Jersey* by Professors Grubdust and Buffelskopf was published in 1860. The Professors spent days searching in vain for the Jersey Fern, and many nights in lively company, until finally the Constable of St Brelade said he would get them a specimen of this most valuable Jersey plant. He did and they bore it back to their lodgings in triumph only to be told by their landlady that it was a Long Jack, a tall Jersey cabbage. In spite of this satire, visiting botanists too numerous to name individually here, have made invaluable contributions both this century and last to the knowledge of Jersey's wild plants, as will be seen in the body of the Flora.

In Jersey itself, the Société's Botanical Section which had become moribund in the 1930s after the death of Stanley Guiton, was resuscitated in the 1950s. People interested in the flora of the island have met weekly or fortnightly at the Museum for almost thirty years and visiting botanists have been welcomed. T. W. Attenborough stated at one of the early meetings that the attractions of the plants of the cliffs, the dunes and the coastal wetlands were such that there were parts of the interior which had never been searched botanically as far as he knew. From this, the distribution map scheme was born and members of the Section were responsible for collecting the records. Members continue to search the island for new species, to monitor changes in the old and to help students with research.

18 Tree-mallow on Les Minquiers

The Flora

PTERIDOPHYTA

LYCOPSIDA

SELAGINELLACEAE

Selaginella kraussiana (G. Kunze) A. Braun

Mossy Clubmoss

This small plant from South Africa and the Azores is used as a decorative edging in greenhouses and occasionally in church decoration, which may explain its occurrence in the cemetery opposite Grouville Church where Mrs D. L. Le Quesne found it growing well at the foot of a wall in 1964, and just outside the door of St Luke's Church where Mrs E. M. Towers found it in 1970. It is still at Grouville but has gone from St Luke's.

G rare.

ISOETACEAE

Isoetes histrix Bory

Land Quillwort

No satisfactory record. The entry in the third edition of Sowerby's *English Botany* (1863–1892) and the label 'Jersey, H. E. Fox' on an undated specimen in Hb Oxford almost certainly confuse Jersey with Guernsey, where the species has been known since 1860.

G local; A rare.

SPHENOPSIDA

EQUISETACEAE

Equisetum fluviatile L.

Water Horsetail

(E. limosum)

Occasional in wet places but in quantity where it does occur. The maps of this and the following species show slightly different distributions which are still roughly those given by Lester-Garland in 1903.

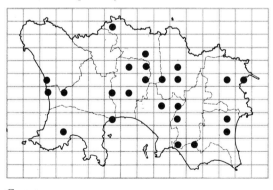

G rare.

E. palustre L.

Marsh Horsetail

Wet places but less often than the preceding species and not in such quantity.

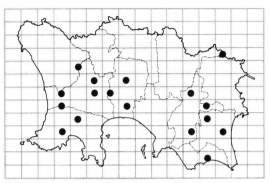

G local; A occasional; S last record 1896; H 1837 and 1962.

E. arvense L.

Field Horsetail

d'la **coue d'rat**

Frequent in fields, on roadsides and a persistent problem in many gardens.

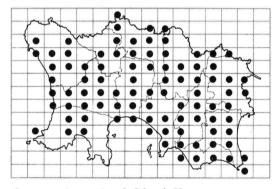

G scarce; A occasional; S local; H rare.

E. telmateia Ehrh.

Great Horsetail

G two localities, post-war; A rare.

FILICOPSIDA

OPHIOGLOSSACEAE

Ophioglossum lusitanicum L. **Early Adder's-tongue**

No satisfactory record. A specimen labelled 'Jersey 1858' is in Hb Oxford; Sir Rawson W. Rawson collected a specimen labelled 'Jersey 1862' and plants were sent to the Royal Botanic Gardens, Edinburgh, in 1880 'from Jersey' by B. H. Hossack. There is no local knowledge of this species in Jersey in spite of much searching both now and in the past. None of these records is localised so confusion between Jersey and Guernsey, where the species is well-known, is suspected.

G rare; A misreported; S ?1888.

O. vulgatum L.   **Adder's-tongue**

Found by Piquet in Samarès Marsh in 1898 and recorded as plentiful there in 1902 by Guiton. The site has now gone with the building of Le Squez high-rise flats. Its only other known locality was north-east of St Ouen's Pond where it was found by A. Le Sueur in 1954. It remained in the area until at least the mid 1960s and though it has not been seen recently, it may reappear.
G rare; A rare; S Brecqhou.

O. azoricum C. Presl   **Small Adder's-tongue**

A specimen collected by J. Sidebotham in 1868 and labelled only 'Jersey' is in Hb Manchester.
G rare; S 1961.

Botrychium lunaria (L.) Swartz   **Moonwort**
G 1864.

OSMUNDACEAE

Osmunda regalis L.   **Royal Fern**

Locally common on the north coast cliffs and a few plants on Les Quennevais; formerly abundant in quarries at Mont Mado and La Saline, St John, before they were used as rubbish dumps in the 1960s and early 1970s; plentiful in the deep rock cleft and small quarry at La Rosière before they were used as part of the desalination plant in the mid 1960s, and occasionally planted and naturalised as near Valley House, Le Mourier. Many plants in inaccessible places in Jersey survived the fern craze of Victorian and Edwardian days, so that when the craze died away the species was able to spread back to most of its old areas. The other Channel Islands were not so fortunate and the present state of the Royal Fern is as follows:
G two plants of unknown origin; A rare; S rare; H planted.

ADIANTACEAE

Adiantum capillus-veneris L.   **Maidenhair-fern**
                               du ou d'la **capillaithe**

Recorded from Plémont Caves by J. S. Henslow in the *Phytologist* for 1858. There are no other records from the caves but in 1872 Dr M. M. Bull and Piquet found it in a gully near La Cotte à la Chèvre, Plémont, where it still grows. The only record from the south-west cliffs is Guiton's of 1910 from 'Mont Fiquet, in a little cave, close to high tide mark', (1934). There is no specimen which is surprising as he specialised in the pressing of plants and Maidenhair-fern would have made a good subject. The cave does not now contain it. According to Le Maistre, the Jersey-Norman-French name for Maidenhair-fern, Jersey Fern and Black Spleenwort may be the feminine *la capillaithe* if growing wild, but in cultivation it is always masculine, *le capillaithe*.
G rare escape; A 1865 and 1929; H ?1923.

PTERIDACEAE

Pteris cretica L.   **Ribbon Fern**

Self-sown and well-established under the small bridge by Trinity Manor pool. The spores of this south European species presumably came from plants cultivated some distance away in the Manor grounds.

GYMNOGRAMMACEAE

Anogramma leptophylla (L.) Link   **Jersey Fern**
(Gymnogramme leptophylla)   *du ou d'la* **capillaithe**

Local in sheltered pockets on stony hedgebanks, damp in winter but fairly dry in summer. Miss J. Marett of La Haule first found it in February 1852 and sent it to Dr Lindley at University College, London, for identification. When the presence in Jersey of this essentially south European and Mediterranean species was published in the *Gardeners Chronicle* for 29 January 1853, many botanists were originally sceptical of the claim that it was native to the island and the first mention of it in the *Phytologist* for 1853 reflected this: 'The President (E. Newman) had heard through the kindness of Mr Henry Hagen, that this pretty species had been found growing on a bank in Jersey. It appears that the late lamented Mr W. Christy, so well-known for his enthusiastic love of botany, resided for some months near the spot where this species occurs; and it is also a fact that Gymno-gramme *(Anogramma)* was a fern which Mr Christy took great pleasure in cultivating, raising it year after year from seed; but no evidence has yet been offered to show that he attempted to introduce it into the Channel Islands.' However in the same year 1853 a later entry in the *Phytologist* stated: 'The President observed that he had received several communications respecting the occurrence of Gymnogramme *(Anogramma)* in Jersey. All those from the island report the fern is widely distributed, growing on the banks of exposed lanes having a southern aspect, more especially those localities in which the moisture induces the growth of *Marchantia* . . . the accounts tend to establish the plant as a true native of the island . . .'. The distribution of the Jersey Fern in Europe as given in *Atlas Florae Europaeae* would appear to confirm its native status.

The map below, which contains all records since 1960, shows that the Jersey Fern is widely distributed. It grows so often in company with the liverwort *Lunularia cruciata* (L.) Dum. that Mrs E. M. Towers has found several new localities by looking first for this easy-to-see liverwort and then searching it for the less obtrusive fern. The aspect of the bank or wall need not be southerly as originally stated, and most often it is not, but as might be expected of a species of warm climates, Jersey Fern does better after a hot summer and mild wet winter. It was particularly fine and luxuriant in all its stations in the spring of 1978 when two mild, wet winters followed the 1976 summer which was one of the hottest and driest on record. It was perhaps this which enabled Miss F. M. Evans and Mrs E. M. Towers to refind it at St Martin after an interval of more than thirty years.

Jersey Fern, one of the island's specialities, was featured on the 3p stamp issued in 1972 by the Jersey Postal Authority and is included in the design on the face, the obverse, of the current £5 note issued by the States of Jersey. An illustration by Pandora Sellars is opposite page 6.

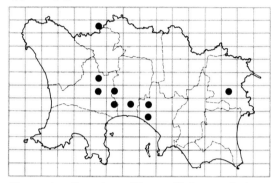

G one locality where Piquet, Guiton and Atten-borough always maintained it was introduced from Jersey.

HYPOLEPIDACEAE

Pteridium aquilinum (L.) Kuhn   **Bracken**
(Pteris aquilina)   *d'la* **feûgiéthe**

Subsp. *aquilinum* Common on uncultivated land, particularly on the cliffs and côtils. A *fugerum*, a parcel of land with Bracken growing on it, was sufficiently valuable in the past for Edward I in the *Extente* for 1274 to levy a charge for the use of one, e.g. Thomas La Rymache was charged four sols for a *fugerum* in the parish of St Brelade. Bracken remained so important for fuel and bedding that the Courts of the Fiefs had legislative powers to regulate its cutting on the Commons. These powers fell into disuse mainly last century. Bracken is still being occasionally cut for bedding for animals but its use in *le liet d'fouailles* or *la filyie*, day-beds filled with Bracken and used by country people, particularly knitters during autumn and winter evenings, lasted only up to the 1914–1918 War. Bracken is now known to cause cancer in animals.

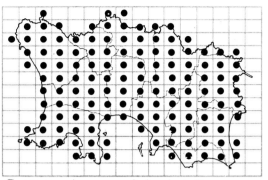

G common; A common; S abundant; H common.

HYMENOPHYLLACEAE

Hymenophyllum tunbrigense (L.) Sm.
     Tunbridge Filmy-fern

One doubtful record: the Talbot collection in the Manx Museum has a specimen labelled 'Jersey' and dated about 1866. The only Channel Island information on this species is that it was planted out in Guernsey in the 1880s but did not survive. It may have been similarly planted out earlier in Jersey. This single unsatisfactory specimen may have been the basis for the statement in Hooker's *Student's Flora* from 1870 to 1934 that the fern occurred in the Channel Islands.

THELYPTERIDACEAE

Oreopteris limbosperma (All.) Holub
(Thelypteris limbosperma)   **Lemon-scented Fern**

Though Piquet stated in the preamble to his 1896 list that Dr Bull had found Lemon-scented Fern in Jersey, he did not include it in his list, so presumably he considered it needed confirmation. Lester-Garland omitted it.
G error.

ASPLENIACEAE

Asplenium marinum L.   **Sea Spleenwort**

Locally frequent in crevices on the cliffs and outlying rocks within reach of the spray and in sea caves. It also grows high up on the walls of Seymour Tower.

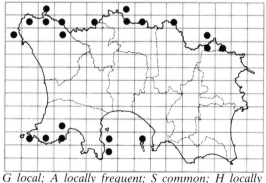

G local; A locally frequent; S common; H locally frequent.

A. trichomanes L.   **Maiden-hair Spleenwort**

Subsp. *quadrivalens* D. E. Meyer   Frequent in the mortar of old walls and sometimes in profusion as along the wall of a field on La Grande Route de St Ouen near the Parish Hall.

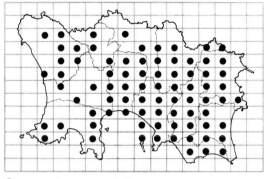

G scarce; A occasional; S rare; H rare.

A. fontanum (L.) Bernh.   **Rock Spleenwort**

A specimen labelled 'Jersey 1837' is in the T. Thompson collection in Hb Oxford. There are no local records and from its European distribution it is unlikely to occur in Jersey in the wild.

A. billotii F. W. Schultz   **Lanceolate Spleenwort**

Frequent on walls and stony hedgebanks. In 1689 Dr W. Sherard visited Jersey and recorded a fern, 'On the rocks on the north side.' From the Latin description it is presumed to be Lanceolate Spleenwort. See the Introduction. The species has undergone two name changes. It was formerly recorded as *A. lanceolatum* Huds. and then *A. obovatum* Viv. Recent work in Europe has shown that the name *A. lanceolatum* covered two closely related species: *A. obovatum* Viv. and *A. billotii* F. W. Schultz. The Jersey species is *A. billotii*. For 'var *Sinelii*', see under x *Asplenophyllitis*.

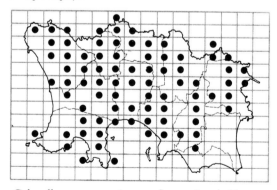

G locally common; A rare; S occasional; H occasional.

A. adiantum-nigrum L.   **Black Spleenwort**
                                          du ou d'la **capillaithe**

Common on walls and hedgebanks. See below for var. *acutum*.

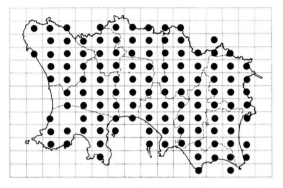

G common; A common; S common; H occasional.

A. x sarniense Sleep   **A hybrid Fern**
A. adiantum-nigrum x **A. billotii**

G scarce.

A. onopteris L.   **A Spleenwort**
(A. adiantum-nigrum var. *acutum* Moore)*

Piquet's record in his 1896 list was based on a specimen which was collected by a Mr Barter from Rozel in 1854. This was also the basis for the Jersey record in *The Wild Flowers of Guernsey* (1975). The specimen, originally in Piquet's herbarium but now in Hb Oxford, has recently been identified as *A. adiantum-nigrum*.

A. ruta-muraria L.   **Wall-rue**

Common on old walls, often in close association with Black Spleenwort.

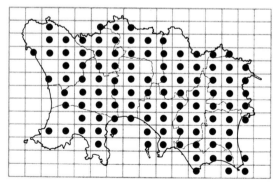

G, A, S and H rare.

Opposite, Plate 1   Jersey Fern *Anogramma leptophylla* with Ivy *Hedera helix* and Navelwort *Umbilicus rupestris*

6

x Asplenophyllitis microdon (T. Moore) Alston
A hybrid Fern
Asplenium billotii x **Phyllitis scolopendrium**

Under this heading A. H. G. Alston in 'Notes on the supposed hybrids in the genus *Asplenium* found in Britain' (*Proc. Linn. Soc. Lond.*, 1940 p. 141) mentions a problem fern *A. lanceolatum* var. *Sinelii* J. F. Robinson stated by Robinson (*Science Gossip*, 1880 p. 148) to have been found by J. Sinel at Bagot. In 1913 Sinel wrote to E. D. Marquand saying that the record was published without his knowledge. He found a single plant near Bouley Bay but though he searched repeatedly for many years he never saw another specimen. It was identified for him by Fraser and Moore, (Druce, B.E.C. 1912).
G scarce.

x A. jacksonii Alston **A hybrid Fern**
Asplenium adiantum-nigrum x
Phyllitis scolopendrium

One specimen collected from Grève de Lecq in November 1863 and initialled EHN is in Hb Moore. (Alston, A. H. G. As above.)
G not seen wild for over a century.

Ceterach officinarum DC. **Rustyback**
(*Asplenium Ceterach*)

Formerly rare but now well-established on many granite walls, sometimes over considerable lengths, as on the south-facing wall of a field in Val de la Mare, St Ouen, and at least once on shale. The increase seems to date from the 1930s, and has been such that Mrs E. M. Towers found Rustyback in about ten localities in a survey of the First Tower area, St Aubin's Bay, in the 1970s.

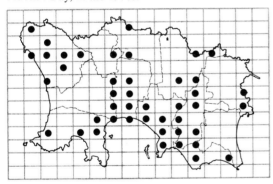

G rare; A occasional; H last seen 1972.

Phyllitis scolopendrium (L.) Newm. **Hart's-tongue**
(*Scolopendrium vulgare*) *d'la* **langue dé boeu**

Common in shady places and sometimes abundant as on the woodland floor on the west side of La Route de l'Aleval, St Peter. In Victorian and Edwardian days the many variations from the normal, long, tongue-shaped leaf were prized. Guiton (1934) mentions several of these oddities which occurred in Jersey, among them being *bifurcatum* where the tip of the frond is split in two; *multifidum* where the tip is split into many parts; *crispum* where the margins are crinkled and an extraordinary form where the frond is broader than long. Several specimens in the Société Jersiaise collection are of these curiosities which have no botanical significance.

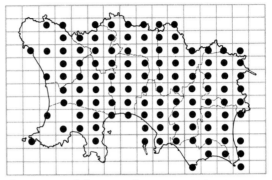

G common; A frequent; S common; H local.

ATHYRIACEAE

Athyrium filix-femina (L.) Roth **Lady-fern**

Frequent and often luxuriant in shady places inland. It is also by streams on the cliffs and in the reed-bed round St Ouen's Pond. Druce recorded var. *convexum* Newm. from Pont Marquet in 1906.

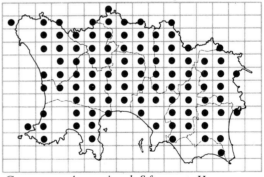

G common; A occasional; S frequent; H rare.

Cystopteris fragilis (L.) Bernh. **Brittle Bladder-fern**

Piquet stated in the introduction to his 1896 list that it was found by Dr Bull but no place or date is given, no specimen exists and Piquet did not include it in either his 1896 list or his supplementary list in 1898. A specimen in the Société's herbarium is labelled 'Very rare, July 1898, JP'. Dr A. Sleep has confirmed the identification but one would expect a locality to be given for such an extreme rarity and Lester-Garland who saw Piquet's specimens did not include it. There is therefore a possibility that the specimen is not from Jersey.

Attenborough stated in the botanical report of the Société for 1919 that Druce and he had found it in Le Mourier Valley in April, and in the botanical report for 1925 that Burdo had found it in good quantity near Vicart. Attenborough was not a collector but both Druce and Burdo were, yet again there are no specimens in the Société's, Druce's or Burdo's collections to support these records. In Hb Oxford there is a minute piece of a fern on a *Cystopteris fragilis* sheet with 'Near Crabbé, Apr. 1919, new to the Channel Islands. G. C. Druce' written against it. Crabbé is approximately a kilometre west of Le Mourier.

The fern is shown as absent from most of Normandy and Brittany in *Atlas Florae Europaeae*, and apart from some roots planted out unsuccessfully by Derrick in Guernsey in the 1880s there are no records from the other Channel Islands.

Onoclea sensibilis L.   **Sensitive Fern**

Two specimens are in Hb Oxford: one, undated, was collected at Le Creux de Vis, St Mary, by Piquet and the second from the cliffs at Plémont in August 1915 by Attenborough. Though the species was said to be well-established at Plémont it has not been refound. Sensitive Fern, an alien from America, is used as a ground stabiliser and in 1962 was growing freely where it was planted in the woods opposite La Chaire Hotel, Rozel.

ASPIDIACEAE

Polystichum setiferum (Forsk.) Woynar
(Aspidium angulare)   **Soft Shield-fern**
Now frequent and luxuriant in many woods and on hedgebanks but the quantity has varied considerably over the years: common in 1851, Piquet; rare in 1896, Piquet; rare in 1903, Lester-Garland; not uncommon in hedgerows throughout the island in 1934, Guiton. Piquet recorded var. *multifidum* from St Saviour.

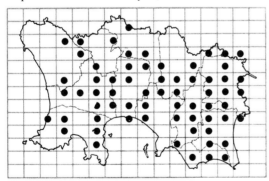

G local; A rare; S rare; H local.

P. aculeatum (L.) Roth   **Hard Shield-fern**
Babington's record (1839) was rejected by Lester-Garland (1903) and has not been confirmed.
G ?error.

Cyrtomium falcatum (L. fil.) C. Presl
               House Holly Fern
Self-sown on wall at Government House, 1975, Mrs M. L. Long.
G rare escape.

Dryopteris filix-mas (L.) Schott   **Male-fern**
(Aspidium Filix-mas)
Common in damp woods and valleys and sometimes on walls.

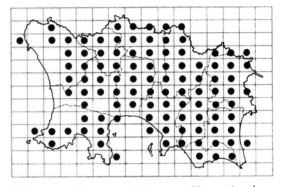

G frequent; A frequent; S frequent; H occasional.

D. affinis (Lowe) Fraser-Jenkins
     Common Golden-scaled Male-fern
Subsp. *borreri* (Newm.) F-J *(D. borreri)* Fairly frequent in heavier shade than the preceding species from which it was not separated in earlier Floras.

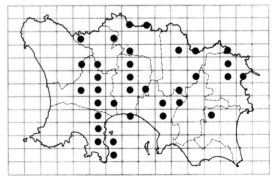

G occasional; A rare; S frequent; H rare.

D. dilatata (Hoffm.) A. Gray   **Broad Buckler-fern**
(Aspidium dilatatum)
Frequent and often luxuriant in woods and damp places.

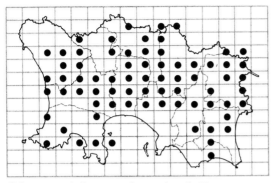

G frequent; A frequent; S occasional; H rare.

D. aemula (Aiton) O. Kuntze

Hay-scented Buckler-fern

This is listed in Moore's *Ferns of Great Britain and Ireland* (1857) as being found in both Jersey and Guernsey by J. James. The fern has a limited distribution in Europe, and the Channel Islands lie just within it, but there is no other record in spite of much searching.

BLECHNACEAE

Blechnum spicant (L.) Roth   **Hard Fern**

Widespread in damp places.

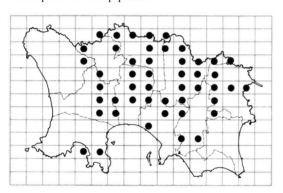

G scarce; A last record 1937; S rare.

POLYPODIACEAE

Polypodium interjectum Shivas   **Polypody**
(P. *vulgare* subsp. *prionodes*)

Common on walls, hedges and tree trunks.

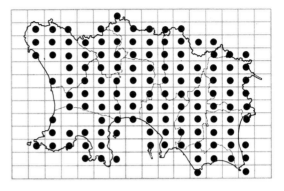

G common; A frequent; S frequent; H occasional.

P. cambricum L.   **Diploid Polypody**
(*P. australe*)

G rare and its hybrid with the above 1980.

MARSILEACEAE

Pilularia globulifera L.   **Pillwort**

A specimen collected by Rev. W. W. Newbould from St Peter's Marsh on 17 August 1842 is in Hb Cantab. Piquet, who in 1851 had listed it from St Peter's Marsh, stated in 1893 (Ansted & Latham Ed. 3) that it had disappeared when the marshes were drained. Though he again listed it in 1896 as in ditches in St Peter's Marsh, giving its status as very rare, he stated in the introduction to the list that it was extinct.

AZOLLACEAE

Azolla filiculoides Lam.   **Water Fern**

First noted in the wild in a pool in Bellozanne Valley in 1967 but it had gone by the following year, J. C. Fluck. In 1978 it was abundant in the watercress beds at Les Sts Germains, St Lawrence, but it had disappeared by 1982, Mrs M. L. Long. In 1983 it was so abundant in the large pool at Trinity Manor that no open water was visible and the pool looked like a green field.

    Aquarists sell Water Fern, a species from tropical America, to stock ornamental pools. While it may die out after a few years, it seems ineradicable in at least one garden pool in Jersey. Migrant waterfowl may have brought it accidentally to the Manor pool; it was not introduced by man.

G rare; A rare; S 1960.

9

SPERMATOPHYTA

GYMNOSPERMAE

Conifers have been much planted in wild woodlands and in open wild places. There are no signs that any but a very few species will regenerate. The trees include species and cultivars of *Abies, Picea, Larix, Cedrus, Pinus, Sequoia, Sequoiadendron, Taxodium, Cryptomeria, Cupressus, Chamaecyparis, Thuja* and *Juniperus*. Most are comparatively new to the island and only those species which have been here for some time are mentioned in the following general account.

Larix decidua Miller, European Larch, was planted last century. Now the choice tends to be Dunkeld Larch, the hybrid between *L. decidua* European Larch and *L. kaempferi* (Lamb.) Carrière, Japanese Larch. A few trees do well but they are a very small proportion of the number planted and no regeneration is known. *Pinus pinaster* Ait., Maritime Pine, was listed as frequent by Piquet in 1896. A few survive where they were planted, as on Les Quennevais dunes, but no seedlings have been noted. *P. radiata* D. Don, Monterey Pine, was frequently planted in the past, particularly in the south-west in the 1920s and 1930s, so that it is now the commonest pine in the island. In recent years it seems to have gone out of fashion and is no longer planted in any quantity. Seedlings are very occasionally seen. This is the pine of the Pine Walk at St Catherine's Bay, of the Pont Marquet area of St Brelade, of the heights overlooking Ouaisné Common and St Brelade and on part of the slopes of West Mount. *P. contorta* Douglas ex Loudon, Lodgepole Pine, seems to be taking its place now. *P. nigra* Arnold, Austrian Pine, mainly occurs as aged trees with no regeneration. *P. sylvestris* L., Scots Pine, was listed by Piquet in 1896 as frequent but planted. Pine pollen, presumably of this species, has been found in peat in Jersey but the present trees are not descendants of those in archaeological times. Scots Pine now occurs only occasionally, and is seldom replanted.

Cupressus macrocarpa Hartweg, Macrocarpa or Monterey Cypress, was commonly planted mainly for hedging in the first half of this century, particularly in the 1920s and 1930s. Many of the plants were allowed to grow to maturity so lines of trees now mark where hedgerows used to exist. Abundant seed is set and seedlings have been seen at the east end of St Brelade's Bay and on the slopes of West Mount. As a hedging plant, Macrocarpa proved unsatisfactory and was superseded by cultivars of *x Cupressocyparis leylandii* (A. B. Jackson & Dallimore) Dallimore, Leyland's Cypress, and *Chamaecyparis lawsoniana* (A. Murray) Parl., Lawson's Cypress. These were much planted in gardens and round fields in the 1960s and 1970s until they in their turn fell into disfavour and the States of Jersey no longer sold them at reduced prices. A specimen of *Taxus baccata* L., Yew, was collected by F. Piquet in 1871 in Waterworks Valley. Yew still grows there and seedlings are occasionally seen. It also occurs, probably planted, in the valley running down to St Catherine's Bay from Rosel Manor and at Bel Croute. (There is a magnificent row of Yews in Le Cimetière de l'Union beside St Martin's Arsenal. They were probably planted when Le Cimetière was formed in 1858.) Coniferous trees are planted in Guernsey, Alderney, Sark and Herm.

ANGIOSPERMAE – DICOTYLEDONES
SALICACEAE

Salix pentandra L.   **Bay Willow**

Planted at the top of the steps leading down to Portelet Bay and well-established by the 1960s.

S. fragilis L.   **Crack Willow**

Piquet (1896) recorded it as frequent along streams and in 1969 R. C. L. Howitt, an authority on willows, considered it common in Waterworks Valley where it still grows. Lester-Garland (1903) mentioned it only as a planted tree on Grouville Common and large single trees also occur elsewhere, always planted. Howitt reported that the only male var. *fragilis* tree which he had seen was in Jersey in 1969 (*Gardeners Chronicle*, 29 Dec. 1972). It was at Ponterrin Mill.

The name Crack Willow comes from the way small branches and twigs snap off easily at the joints. In the extraordinary ice-storm of February 1978, when over-cooled rain changed to ice on impact and branches of trees were covered with half an inch of ice or more, all the small branches of some Crack Willows snapped off at the joints because of the weight of ice on them. The trees were left as skeleton trees of trunk and main branches, with the base of the trunk surrounded by piles of broken-off small branches and twigs.

G, A, S and H planted.

S. alba L.   **White Willow**

Babington (1839) and Piquet (1896) recorded White Willow from St Saviour and Lester-Garland (1903) stated that it occurred as a planted tree. Howitt recorded it in Grands Vaux and from the holt in Waterworks Valley in 1969. A tree in Rue de Haut, St Lawrence, was destroyed when its site was developed for building in the 1970s, Mrs E. M. Towers.

G rare.

S. x rubens Schrank   **A hybrid Willow**
S. alba x **S. fragilis**

Most of the *fragilis* type willows probably belong here. *S.* x *basfordiana* Scaling, a derivative of this cross, was reported by Howitt to be 'all over the island'. In particular, it is the *fragilis*-like willow with coloured twigs in the willow holt in Waterworks Valley.

G rare.

S. triandra L.   **Almond Willow**

Subsp. *triandra* A short hedge of old but flourishing male Almond Willow occurs north-east of St Ouen's Pond and Howitt reported a few bushes in a willow holt in Waterworks Valley in 1969.

G 1900; S 1958.

S. x mollissima Hoffm. ex Elwert.   **A hybrid Willow**
S. triandra x **S. viminalis**
G 1900.

S. cinerea L.   **Common Sallow**

See the following species.

S. atrocinerea Brot.   **Pussy Willow** or
                           Common Sallow
                           du saux

The common, native Pussy Willow of Jersey, previously recorded as the above species, may belong here but it has recently been suggested that the majority of Channel Island material is the hybrid *S.* x *multinervis* and this is being investigated. Pussy Willow can be found on damp ground, by streams or as planted hedges well away from water. The leaves and stems of many bushes are covered with a black fungal mould determined as *Cladosporium herbarum* Link ex Fr. by the plant pathologists at the Howard Davis Farm.

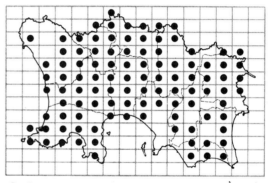

G ?common; A ?frequent; S ?frequent; H ?occasional.

S. x smithiana Willd.   **A hybrid Willow**
S. cinerea x **S. viminalis**

Hedge south of St John's Church, 1958, Mrs M. L. Long and Mrs J. Russell, det. R. D. Meikle.
G 1968; A 1900; S 1957.

S. aurita L.   **Eared Willow**
G rare; A 1900.

S. x multinervis Doell   **A hybrid Willow**
S. aurita x **S. cinerea**

See *S. atrocinerea*.
G 1957 and 1969.

S. x ambigua Ehrh.   **A hybrid Willow**
S. aurita x **S. repens**
G 1957.

S. caprea L.   **Goat Willow**

W. C. Trevelyan's record given by Babington in the *Addenda* to his Flora (1839) has always been doubted. Lester-Garland stated in 1903 that he had not met with it in Jersey. In 1961 Howitt made a particular search for it and found it in a quarry at La Crête Point. Subsequently it has been recorded elsewhere, mainly by J. C. Fluck. The lack of ridges under the bark of second year twigs has been used to confirm the identification. The map shows it widely distributed but most records are only of small groups or single bushes, and two areas, Miladi Farm and Le Squez, are now covered by housing estates.

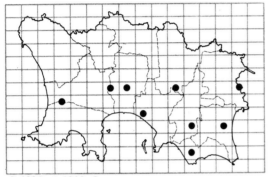

G 1897; A 1900; S error.

S. x reichardtii A. Kerner   **A hybrid Willow**
S. caprea x **S. cinerea**
S 1978.

S. x calodendron Wimmer   **A hybrid Willow**
S. caprea x **S. cinerea** x **S. viminalis**
G rare.

S. x sericans Tausch ex A. Kerner   **A hybrid Willow**
S. caprea x **S. viminalis**
A 1900.

S. repens L.   **Creeping Willow**

Subsp. *argentea* (Sm.) A. & G. Camus *(S. arenaria)* A native species of damp places, recorded from Les Quennevais by Babington (1839). Piquet (1851) recorded it from a bog near La Moye signal post and from Le Marais, Noirmont. Lester-Garland (1903) knew it only from the east side of St Brelade's Bay, i.e. from Piquet's locality, Le Marais, Noirmont, which is better known today as Ouaisné Common and where it is still locally abundant.

S. viminalis L.   **Osier**
d'l'ôsyi

Commonly planted in damp places. First recorded by Piquet in 1853 at St Catherine's Bay and mentioned, as planted, by Lester-Garland (1903).

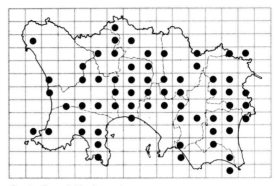

G, A, S and H planted.

S. x stipularis Sm.   **A hybrid Willow**
S. viminalis x ?
A 1838.

S. eleagnos Scop.   **A Willow**

Planted along a wild ditch north of St Ouen's Pond by J. Le C. Sumner in 1950, determined as this species by Meikle in 1957 and still there in 1983.

S. purpurea L.   **Purple Willow**

Purple Willow (male) was noted in 1957 as forming an old field hedge north-east of St Ouen's Pond (confirmed R. D. Meikle) and it was later found above Handois mudpond.
A planted, 1900.

S. daphnoides Vill.   **Violet Willow**

Planted along a wild ditch north of St Ouen's Pond by J. Le C. Sumner in 1950, determined as this species by Meikle in 1957 and still there in 1983.
G planted.

Populus alba L.   **White Poplar**
                                       un **blianc-bouais**

Planted, but recorded as common as long ago as 1839. It spreads by suckers and large areas, as at the north end of Les Mielles, St Ouen, and at Grouville are covered with it.

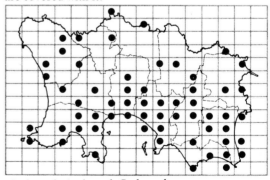

G planted; A planted; S planted.

12

P. x canescens (Aiton) Sm.   **Grey Poplar**
P. alba x **P. tremula**

La Gasca listed it in 1834 and it still occurs, rarely, as a planted tree, e.g. along the disused railway line near Pont Marquet.
G planted; A planted; H planted.

P. tremula L.   **Aspen**

Babington (1839) recorded it from St Lawrence Valley, now Waterworks Valley. Piquet, later last century, first stated that it was frequent in moist woods and then that it was in damp woods along mill streams. It is still in several places in Waterworks Valley, and also in damp areas at Grouville and St Catherine. Lester-Garland (1903) considered it native, as did Attenborough (1932) but some of the present trees, particularly those in dry places as in St Brelade, must be planted.
G rare.

P. *cf*. gileadensis Rouleau   **Balm of Gilead Poplar**

Aromatic poplars belonging to the Section *Tacamahaca* Spach are occasionally planted as in St Peter's Valley by La Hague Reservoir.
G planted.

P. nigra L.   **Black Poplar**

Stated by Piquet (1851 and 1896) to be frequent and by Lester-Garland (1903) to be common, but at that time the name '*P. nigra*' included the hybrid *P. deltoides* x *P. nigra* and the Jersey trees are this hybrid (see below) except for the Lombardy Poplar, a clone cv *Italica* of *P. nigra* which was frequently planted according to Lester-Garland and of which several aged trees remain.
G one tree of the type.

P. x canadensis Moench   **Black Italian Poplar**
P. deltoides x **P. nigra**

Frequently planted both now and in the past, see above.
G, A, S and H planted.

JUGLANDACEAE

Juglans regia L.   **Walnut**

Planted, usually as single trees on large properties. Several old-established farms are called Walnut Farm. No seedlings are known.
G planted.

BETULACEAE

Betula pendula Roth   **Silver Birch**
(*B. verrucosa*)   *un* **bouôlias**

Planted, both now and in the past, for decorative purposes and recorded by all botanists from La Gasca, 1834, onwards. Considering the numbers planted it seldom thrives and there are no records of

it spreading into wild areas.
G planted; A planted; S planted.

B. pubescens Ehrh.   **Downy Birch**

Planted in the inland valleys occasionally. Seedlings have been seen in the National Trust for Jersey's property, Le Don Powis, but Downy Birch seldom flourishes and several were killed in the drought of 1976.
G planted; S planted.

Alnus glutinosa (L.) Gaertn.   **Alder**

Though Babington (1839) thought Alder was probably planted, Lester-Garland (1903) stated unequivocally that it was a native tree and Piquet described it as frequent along mill streams last century. By 1932 Attenborough considered it 'rather uncommon', but it still flourishes in damp places, particularly in the interior of the island.

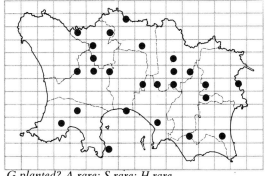

G planted? A rare; S rare; H rare.

A. cordata (Loisel.) Loisel.   **Italian Alder**

Recently rarely planted to replace elms, as in the National Trust for Jersey's property, Le Don Powis in St Peter's Valley.

CORYLACEAE

Carpinus betulus L.   **Hornbeam**

Planted. In the past Hornbeam was used as a hedging plant and it is still present in an old hedge in St Mary but it occurs more usually as fully grown trees e.g. in the National Trust for Jersey's property, Le Don Le Gallais in Vallée des Vaux. It is now being planted again to form hedges to replace elms.
G planted.

Corylus avellana L.   **Hazel**
                                   un **codriyi**

Native. Babington (1839) commented that it was scarcely to be found in a wild state though Piquet (1851 and 1896) described it as frequent in woods and hedges. Lester-Garland (1903) thought it decidedly rare but it still occurs in much of the interior of the island.

Hazel nuts have been found in the peat in St Ouen's Bay and below the Gas Works in Tunnell Street, St Helier. The Jersey-Norman-French name for Hazel occurred in place names in the past: a field called Le Codret was mentioned in a sale at St Ouen's Manor in 1539; Le Val du Codrey was described as near Vinchelez Millpond, also in 1539; a *codrey* of Ph. Le Cerf was mentioned in 1721 in a St Ouen's Church *Terrier des Dimes*. These place names, supplied by Charles Stevens, suggest that Hazel trees have a continuous history in Jersey. How much of the present population is derived from plantations in the past and how much is native is unknown.

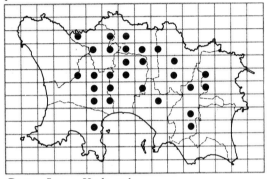

G rare; S rare; H planted.

FAGACEAE

Fagus sylvatica L.　　　　　　　　　**Beech**
　　　　　　　　　　　　　　　　　　　un **fau**

Mentioned in botanical records from La Gasca 1834 onward, and earlier, in 1808, Lyte had listed it with oak, elm, ash and chestnut as one of the 'woods' common to Jersey. Beech pollen has been found in peat, and seedlings and saplings have been seen recently. Nevertheless, Lester-Garland's comments in 1903 that most Beech trees are obviously planted is still true, and whether or not Beech has a continuous history in the wild in Jersey is unknown. Generally it occurs as single trees but occasionally there are small stands planted in inland valleys, as in the National Trust for Jersey's woodland, Le Don Gaudin, in St Peter's Valley. Beech suffered badly in the drought of 1976 and many fine trees had to be felled including some from the magnificent avenue opposite St Saviour's School. A few trees of the avenue had already been felled in 1944, during the Occupation, to make soles for shoes.

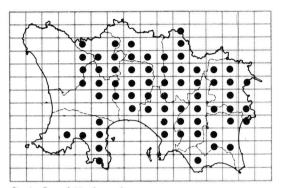

G, A, S and H planted.

Castanea sativa Mill.　　　　　　**Sweet Chestnut**
(*C. vulgaris*)　　　　　　　　　　*un* **chât'nyi**

Accounts of the island last century mention Sweet Chestnut as one of the commoner trees and this is still true. Seedlings and saplings occur in quantity and the species is thought to be native. Many trees felled for fuel during the Occupation (even though Sweet Chestnut is notoriously poor as fuel) have regrown and the stools have produced four or five growths, each now of full height. The chestnuts are frequently of edible size.

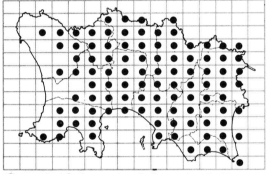

G occasional; A occasional; S occasional; H rare.

Quercus rubra L.　　　　　　　　　**Red Oak**

Planted rarely. Several mature trees were in Le Don Powis in St Peter's Valley when the National Trust for Jersey acquired the property in 1953. In 1969 there was a sapling which looked self-sown. Single trees are planted elsewhere. This tree is the floral emblem of the State of New Jersey of the United States of America.

Q. ilex L.　　　**Evergreen Oak** or **Holm Oak**
　　　　　　　　　　　　　　　　un **vèrt tchêne**

Jersey is at the northern end of the range of Evergreen Oak so, as Attenborough claimed, there is a possibility that it is native. Though planted round houses, it occurs frequently in woods where it regenerates freely. Stunted bushes, probably bird-sown, occur on the cliffs and occasionally on off-shore islets like La Grosse Tête, St Brelade. 'Les Chênes' or 'The Oaks' as a house name usually implies that this species is nearby and not Common Oak.

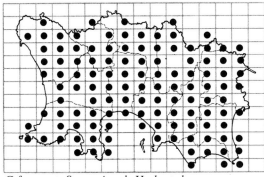

G frequent; S occasional; H planted.

Q. suber L.   **Cork Oak**

One tree still in a wood near La Haule where Mrs K. Le Sueur has known it for many years.
G in gardens.

Q. cerris L.   **Turkey Oak**

Many fine mature trees exist yet the first record seems to have been made during this survey, previous botanists tending to ignore non-native trees. Seedlings have been reported by D. Noble in the National Trust for Jersey's woodland on Mont Ubé, and both seedlings and well-grown saplings occur at Noirmont.

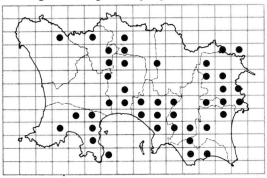

G, S and H planted.

Q. petraea (Mattuschka) Liebl.   **Sessile Oak**

This and *Q. robur* were stated by Attenborough in his article on the trees of Jersey to be equally common. No other botanist would agree. I know of but one mature tree.
G ?

Q. x rosacea Bechst.   **A hybrid Oak**
Q. petraea x **Q. robur**

Trees bearing short-stalked leaves and long-stalked acorn cups occasionally have tufts of hairs in the axils of the leaf veins. Though usually much nearer to

Q. robur they should perhaps be recorded as intermediates.

Q. robur L.   **Common Oak**
                         un **tchêne**

A native species, fine specimens being common in woods and hedges, while gnarled trees, sculptured by the wind, grow on exposed rocky coasts. Oak pollen occurs in peat, and church records indicate oak was present in Norman times. In 1090 St John's Church was called Sancti Johannis de Caisnibus and in c. 1140, Sancti Johannis de Quercubus, which implies that the church was in an oak wood according to C. Stevens (pers. comm.). In 1789, the 280 ton ship Elisha Tupper was built at Bel Royal from Oak grown in St Lawrence and enough extra oak was cut to build a somewhat smaller ship and a small boat. It was claimed that there was considerably more oak left in the Parish – more than a hundred times as much – and that other parishes were equally well wooded. A. Podger (1962) suggests in an article on ship building in Jersey that this may not have been true, and that it is more likely that the politics of the time dictated an exaggeration of the amount.

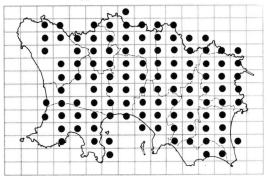

G frequent; A rare; S occasional; H occasional.

ULMACEAE

Ulmus spp.   **Elm**
                un ou eune **orme**

Elms are difficult to name. Hybridisation between the species is frequent and, because many of them sucker freely, they can easily be transported and grown away from their place of origin. Botanical records in the past claimed only two kinds as being common or frequent in Jersey and this is still true today but, with new scientific information, names have changed. Dr R. H. Richens, an authority on elms throughout western Europe, visited Jersey in 1976 to study the elm population and his work was supplemented by members of the Botanical Section of the Société Jersiaise who sent him elm specimens from every parish. The following account of elms in Jersey is based on Dr Richens' work. (See below for Jersey-Norman-French names and some points from the history of elms in Jersey.)

U. glabra Huds.   **Wych Elm**

Rare and all trees seen were obviously planted, usually in prominent places, but Dr Richens thinks that a detailed search might reveal some in native situations in sheltered valleys. The Wych Elm does not sucker and this alone sets it apart from the bulk of Jersey's elms.
G rare; A rare; S rare; H ?

U. minor Mill.   **Small-leaved Elm**

Common all over the island until Dutch Elm Disease began taking its toll. Two of the varieties listed by Dr Richens in 1977 within the *U. minor* complex (*Taxon* 26 p. 583) occur or occurred rarely in Jersey: var. *vulgaris* (Aiton) Richens (*U. procera* Salisb.) St Andrew's Park 1971, near Grainville Manor 1971, and near Almorah 1969, all determined Richens.
var. *sarniensis* (Loud.) Richens   Richens places the upright form of *U. minor* here. It is common in Guernsey where it is the only form of *U. minor*. Some trees of this form have been imported into Jersey from Guernsey. Their upright habit makes them easily identifiable. The elm trees of the magnificent avenue which once stood along La Grande Route de St Ouen, near St Ouen's Manor, were of this form. Unfortunately only two now remain. These elms were imported from a nursery in Guernsey about 1880 according to Dr F. Le Maistre, whose grandfather planted them. Similar elms were planted by Mr Le Cornu of Le Cornu's Nurseries on the west side of New Beaumont Hill sometime before 1889 for Mrs M. L. Long's great-grandfather. They also occur, rarely and always planted, elsewhere.
G only var. sarniensis; *Small-leaved Elms also occur in Alderney, Sark and Herm but quantity and variety are unknown.*

U. x hollandica Mill.   **A hybrid Elm**
U. minor x U. glabra

Common until Dutch Elm Disease began taking its toll. Past records of *U. glabra* belong here. From researches into the European distribution of *U. minor* and *U. glabra*, Richens and Jeffers (1975) suggest that the Small-leaved Elm *U. minor* did not spread northwards naturally after the last Ice Age but was brought north from the Garonne district of southern France by man in pre-Roman times, arriving in this area by a sea route. *U. glabra*, being a hardier tree, had already spread back to northern Europe. Where they met, hybrids were formed. The type of hybrid in the Channel Islands resembles that in the Cotentin, Bauplois and Coutances districts so closely that Richens and Jeffers suspect a common origin. One possibility is that when the island was enclosed in the sixteenth and seventeenth centuries, and apple orchards were planted, hybrid elm for

hedges came from France with cider apple material for the orchards.
G common; A, S, H recorded but quantity unknown.

Elm is used, or was until Dutch Elm Disease struck, for hedging round fields. The trees are lopped every few years so that shading is reduced and side shoots are produced to form a windbreak. This is not a new practice. Poingdestre mentioned it in 1682; Falle in 1694 wrote of trees in hedges being pruned to the very top once every seven or eight years, and Plees in 1824 of pollards being exceedingly numerous. Unfortunately in these accounts the trees pollarded were not specifically named but as oak, sweet chestnut and elm were the only trees described as common by Plees, they were almost certainly elms, like today.

The first known record of an elm, apart from elm pollen in peat, is in 1533. Mrs J. Stevens reports that a manuscript of that date mentions *l'horme du conseil* on the Fief des Arbres border. Internal evidence suggests that it is the same elm as *l'ancien Orme du Conseil* which Charles Le Brun felled in 1707 and which, because it marked a boundary, he was ordered to replace by the Sénéchal of the Court of the Fief des Arbres. The new tree was to be provided by the Seigneur of St Lawrence.

The Jersey-Norman-French names for elms follow standard French closely. The Small-leaved Elm *U. minor* is *rouoge orme*, cf the French *orme rouge*. The hybrid of *U. minor* with *U. glabra* is *blianche orme* cf the French *orme blanche* for *U. glabra*. *U. minor* produces better wood than its hybrid with *U. glabra* so, according to P. Le Gresley of L'Étacq Woodcrafts, *U. minor* is sometimes called *orme d'Jerri* and the inferior wood of the hybrid *orme d'Dgernesy*, this apparently being sufficient to indicate immediately, to a Jerseyman, which was the better wood.

This use of the island's names for the quality of the wood is not connected with the confused nomenclature in horticulture where the names Guernsey Elm and Jersey Elm are given for the upright form of the Small-leaved Elm, *U. minor* Mill. var. *sarniensis* (Loud.) Richens. This, as stated above, occurs naturally in quantity in Guernsey but is rare and always planted in Jersey. Its name should be the Guernsey Elm. It may be that the variety was sometimes distributed through Jersey or, more likely, that horticulturists of the past, like botanists, sometimes used the names Jersey and Guernsey indiscriminately, simply meaning that the variety came from the Channel Islands.

MORACEAE
Ficus carica L.   **Fig**
                                     un **fidgi**

Much grown in old gardens and producing good edible figs which contain no viable seeds because the

Blastophagus wasp required to fertilise the flower is absent. In spite of this, seedlings occur and Fig trees are occasionally seen in places where they were not planted. One grows on the rocks above Snow Hill car-park at the Hill Street end. These plants are presumed to have come from seed in imported figs. *G rare.*

CANNABACEAE

Humulus lupulus L.   **Hop**
                                              du **houbillon**

Babington in 1839 and Piquet in 1851 described Hop as common. By 1896 Piquet thought it uncommon and in 1903 Lester-Garland stated that it was rare. Today it is widespread in hedges, as the map shows, but nowhere is it common. Plees, writing in 1824, mentioned an unsuccessful attempt to grow Hops so this may account for the quantity early last century, followed by its decrease.

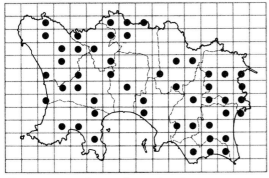

G uncommon; A rare; S occasional.

Cannabis sativa L.   **Hemp**
                                             du **cannevi**

Hemp used to be grown for fibre for ropes and canvas, essential to a maritime community. The name Les Quennevais is thought to come from the word *canneviéthe*, meaning the place where hemp is grown and several old field names are also variants of it. Hemp may have been in short supply in 1556 because the Rolls of the Royal Court for that year mention an Order forbidding the export of rope and canvas. Botanists of early last century regarded hemp as naturalised but by 1903, Lester-Garland thought it only an occasional casual. Its few appearances in recent years have been from bird seed, as a rare casual on rubbish dumps or on heaps of compost. *G rare; A 1901.*

URTICACEAE

Urtica dioica L.   **Stinging Nettle**
                                             d's **ortchies**

A common perennial on land which is not frequently disturbed and which does not dry out in summer. It is a good indicator of where poultry has been kept or rubble or rubbish deposited in the past.

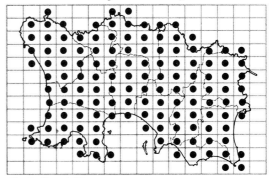

G, A, S and H common.

U. urens L.   **Small Nettle**
                                    d's **ortchies grégeaises**

A common annual weed in gardens and cultivated fields. Though a much smaller, more delicate plant than the above, its sting is as bad, as implied by the word *grégeaise*, meaning fierce, in its Jersey-Norman-French name.

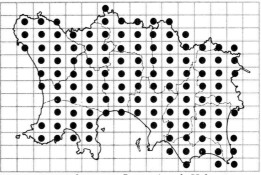

G frequent; A frequent; S occasional; H frequent.

Soleirolia soleirolii (Req.) Dandy
                              Mind-your-own-business

A garden plant first collected in the wild in 1927 near Tesson Mill, St Peter's Valley, by Burdo. The following year Ariste collected it at Beaumont and stated that it occurred at the foot of old walls and on hedgebanks. This suggests that it had been established outside gardens, but unrecorded, for some time. The extraordinary English name can cause problems. I remember A. J. Robinson, the geologist, botanist and retired schoolmaster from Victoria College, bringing a piece to a botanical meeting of the Société Jersiaise. On being asked what it was by Attenborough, he casually replied, without realising the effect it would produce on a forthright, equally elderly, gentleman, "Mind-your-own-business". The meeting was adjourned until the problem was sorted out. The species is now fairly frequent in the right habitat: somewhat damp, shady places near habitation.

Map overleaf

17

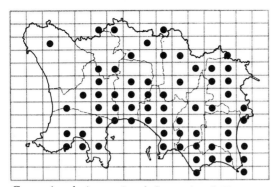

G occasional; A occasional; S occasional; H rare.

Parietaria judaica L. **Pellitory-of-the-wall**
(P. diffusa) *d'l'***apathitouaithe**

Common since records began and well-named since it is usually seen either on or at the foot of walls. The medicinal uses of this plant in the past are given in the *Dictionnaire Jersiais-Français.*

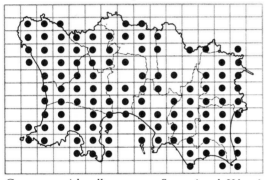

G common; A locally common; S occasional; H local.

SANTALACEAE

Thesium humifusum DC. **Bastard Toadflax**

Rare. This native, perennial hemiparasite grows on both Grouville Common and Les Quennevais where it was first found in the middle of last century.

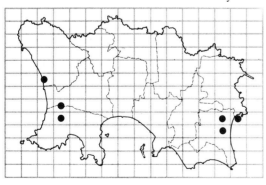

A occasional.

LORANTHACEAE

Viscum album L. **Mistletoe**
du **dgi**

Rare and not known genuinely wild. The Rev. E. Durell in his notes (1837) in Falle's *Account of Jersey* stated that Jersey orchards were entirely free of Mistletoe. Ereaut has a Jersey specimen dated 1847 but the host tree is not mentioned. It now occurs on a few apple trees in gardens and in 1968 it was well-established on two apple trees in an orchard at St Lawrence. The only other host tree known was a poplar at La Becquetterie, St Clement. Here, Mistletoe was planted on a tree which died, but not before the Mistletoe had seeded naturally on the poplar where it remained for many years until the tree was blown down in a gale in 1961.
G rare.

POLYGONACEAE

Polygonum maritimum L. **Sea Knotgrass**

Reported last century as occurring rarely in St Aubin's Bay and St Ouen's Bay but Lester-Garland (1903) dismissed the records as probably being *P. oxyspermum* subsp. *raii*, and specimens collected by Piquet in 1860 and by Burdo and Ariste in the 1920s, and labelled *P. maritimum*, were certainly in error. The Rev. W. W. Newbould claimed to have found it in 1841/2 but no supporting specimen is known. Attenborough reported it at Le Sauchet in 1917 and in St Ouen's Bay in 1925. No specimens seem to have been collected but in the 1960s he gave the writer a specimen which he said he had collected in St Ouen's Bay in 1921. The identification is confirmed by B. T. Styles (Hb Société Jersiaise). An undated Jersey specimen is in the N. B. Ward collection in the British Museum herbarium and four Jersey specimens: 1837 from the Hb W. W. Saunders; sands of St Aubin's Bay, 1859, Piquet; Petit Port, 1863, no collector; St Ouen's Bay, 1936, J. Chapple, are in the *P. maritimum* folder in Hb Oxford.
G last record 1891; H local.

P. oxyspermum Meyer & Bunge ex Ledeb.
Ray's Knotgrass

Subsp. *raii* (Bab.) D. A. Webb & Chater (*P. Raii*) R. M. Lingard collected a specimen near St Helier in 1837 and it was reported rarely from St Clement's Bay, Grève d'Azette, St Aubin's Bay and St Ouen's Bay last century. Lester-Garland stated that it was fairly plentiful in Grouville Bay in 1901. Since then the only records have been Burdo's from Bonne Nuit in 1925, determined Styles, and a sight record by D. McClintock in 1947.
G last seen 1961; A 1838; S 1838; H 1851.

P. aviculare L.   **Knotgrass**
                                                    d'la **s'nîle traînante**

Common on roadsides, disturbed ground and
cultivated land. Six names are given for Knotgrass in
the *Dictionnaire Jersiais-Français*, four of them being
based on *s'nîle* which by itself is *Chenopodium album*,
Fat Hen. The map includes records of Small-leaved
Knotgrass.

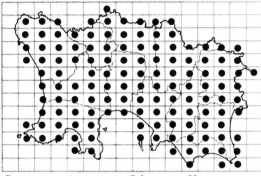

G common; A common; S frequent; H common.

P. rurivagum Jordan ex Boreau

                                        Narrow-leaved Knotgrass
G rare; S ?

P. arenastrum Boreau   **Small-leaved Knotgrass**

This has not always been separated from *P. aviculare*.
It occurs round the coast and can survive on trodden
areas or areas driven over by cars. The first mention
of it in Jersey (as *P. microspermum*) is in the third
edition (1863–1892) of Sowerby's *English Botany*
where the editor J. T. Boswell-Syme stated that he
had seen a specimen gathered in Jersey by the Rev.
W. W. Newbould who visited Jersey in 1841/2. In
1981 stunted plants grew on the eroded parts of Le
Rond Île, Le Pulec. When the National Trust for
Jersey excluded cars, the plants formed large flat
masses.

G rare; A frequent; S occasional.

P. minus Huds   **Small Water-pepper**

Small Water-pepper used to grow in the St Peter/St
Lawrence Marsh. Two specimens exist: St Peter's
Marsh, 1842, Rev. W. W. Newbould (Hb Cantab.); St
Lawrence Marsh, 1852, Piquet (Hb Oxford). Lester-
Garland (1903) considered it extinct in Jersey.

P. mite *Schr.*   **Tasteless Water-pepper**

Piquet noted this in his copy of Babington's Flora as
at Goosegreen but the only known Jersey specimen
labelled *P. mite* (1866, no collector but probably
Piquet, Hb Oxford) was determined as *P. aviculare
s.s.* by Styles.

P. campanulatum Hooker fil.   **Himalayan Knotweed**

A garden outcast, native in the Himalayas, noted in

the valley from Rosel Manor to St Catherine in 1973
by Mrs M. L. Long.

P. hydropiper L.   **Water-pepper**
                                                    du **tcheurrage**

Frequent iin wet areas. Le Maistre states that he was
given the name in all the parishes which suggests that
the species has been widespread for some time. It is
difficult to account for the name, which Le Maistre
says may be the French *'courage'*, unless it refers to
the plant's peppery taste and the courage required to
eat a leaf.

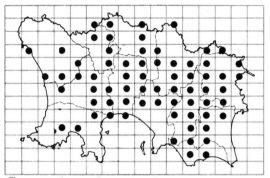

G scarce; A rare; S occasional.

P. persicaria L.   **Redshank**
                                                    du **paîvre à j'va**

Common on cultivated and disturbed land, and, as
Babington stated in 1839, white-flowered specimens
occur. The Jersey-Norman-French name, which was
checked against the plant, means 'horse-pepper' and
the seed is called *la canârie*.

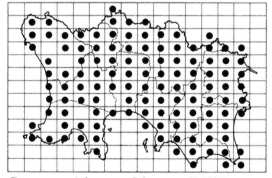

G common; A frequent; S frequent; H 1837.

P. lapathifolium L.   **Pale Persicaria**
(including *P. nodosum*)

Frequent on dampish land. A specimen collected by
Babington in 1837 near St Brelade, and labelled
'*P. laxum*', is in the *P. nodosum* folder in Hb Cantab.

Map overleaf

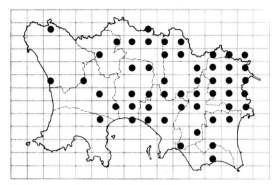

G frequent; A occasional; S 1872.

P. amphibium L.   **Amphibious Bistort**

Frequent in ponds and reservoirs and as Lester-Garland (1903) stated 'The terrestrial form (var. *terrestre* Leers) is not uncommon on stiff soils, and a most troublesome weed where it occurs.'

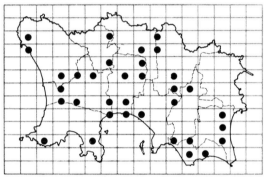

G locally frequent; A occasional; S rare.

P. amplexicaule D. Don   **Red Bistort**

A garden outcast, native in the Himalayas, first noted on Portelet Common in 1962 and still there. In 1971 K. E. Bull reported it in quantity in a car park at Rozel.
G rare.

Fallopia convolvulus (L.) Löve   **Black Bindweed**
(Bilderdykia convolvulus,   *du* **pèrsicarré**
Polygonum convolvulus)

Last century Black Bindweed was described as common or very common and in 1903 Lester-Garland thought it a frequent weed of cultivated land. It remained so until the 1960s but it appears to be decreasing. The English name, Persicaria, is sometimes used for Redshank, *Polygonum persicaria*, so differing from the Jersey-Norman-French use of *pèrsicarré* for Black Bindweed.

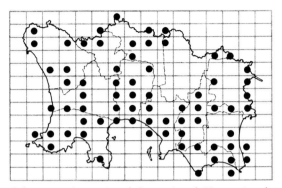

G frequent; A occasional; S occasional; H occasional.

F. aubertii (Henry) Löve   **Russian Vine**
(Bilderdykia aubertii)

A white-flowered garden relic or escape, native in west China and Tibet, which is planted to climb up and over outbuildings or fences. It spreads far and wide so that it is difficult to decide when to record it as a 'wild' plant and the map must be read with this in mind. It was well established by the early 1950s. The species was recorded in the past as *Polygonum baldschuanicum* but that name belongs to closely allied pink-flowered species now also in the *Fallopia* genus.

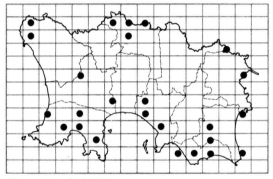

G occasional; S 1960.

Reynoutria japonica Houtt.   **Japanese Knotweed**
(Polygonum cuspidatum)

A garden escape, native in Japan, first known at Lowlands, Beaumont New Hill before 1915 when some was accidentally transferred to The Farm, Vallée des Vaux, with other garden plants and where it was soon a weed. Ariste collected it from Les Hautes Croix in 1925 and it was frequent on roadsides and disturbed ground until recently when it may be decreasing. As I write there are claims that a weed-killer can control it. Writers on gardens used to recommend it as an easy-to-grow plant suitable for a 'wild' garden or to give height at the back of a border, not realising its invasive character and that it is (or perhaps was) almost ineradicable.

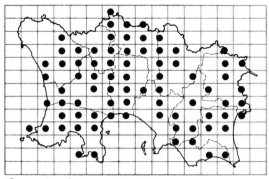

G occasional; A occasional; S rare.

Fagopyrum esculentum Moench **Buckwheat**
du **sarrasîn**

This has been recorded from La Gasca's time, 1834, onwards, the amount seeming to depend on how frequently it is cultivated as a crop.

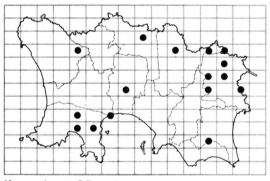

G rare; A rare; S Brecqhou 1902.

Rumex acetosella L. **Sheep's Sorrel**
d'la **p'tite suthelle**

A weed of fairly dry fields, gardens and uncultivated land and an indicator of acid soil. It has decreased on cultivated land since the States gave a lime subsidy to farmers but it is often abundant elsewhere.

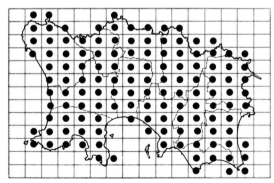

G, A, S and H common.

R. acetosa L. **Common Sorrel**
d'la **grand' suthelle**

Common in slightly damper habitats than the last species. Le Maistre says it used to be eaten as a salad; now it would be too acid for people's taste and French Sorrel *R. scutatus* is more likely to be cultivated.

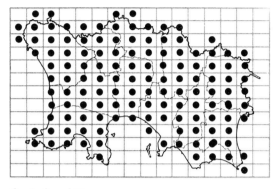

G, A, S and H common.

R. hydrolapathum Hudson **Great Water Dock**

Recorded by Babington (1839) from near Petit Port; by the Rev. W. W. Newbould in 1841/2 from Grouville; by Piquet in 1851 from 'St Peter's Marsh and other swamp places' and in 1896 Piquet stated that it was frequent in marshes. He may have been referring to last mid century, for by 1903 Lester-Garland stated that it was rare and gave 'St Ouen's Bay near the Pond' as the only place where he had seen it.

Ariste collected it from Grouville in 1925 and Mrs M. L. Long who has known it by the stream on the west side of New Beaumont Hill for more than forty years, found it in Beaumont Marsh in 1983. It used to grow by the side of the stream between the Co-op Freezer Department and the public car park at Beaumont until the stream was 'tidied up' in the late 1960s. A few garden species were planted in place of magnificent wild dock in spite of the *Dictionary of Gardening* of the Royal Horticultural Society saying of it, 'A good foliage plant for the side of ponds or slow streams, not spreading unduly'. The dock regrew but was removed again in the next clearance. R. W. S. Knightbridge found it in 1983 in the valley below Val de la Mare Reservoir, perhaps in Lester-Garland's old locality.
G rare.

R. crispus L. **Curled Dock**

Common on roadsides and a bad weed on farmland.

Map overleaf

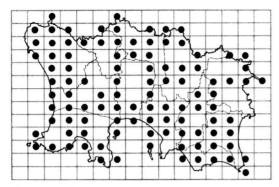

G, A, S and H common.

R. x pseudopulcher Hausskn.   **A hybrid Dock**
R. crispus x **R. pulcher**
A 1953.

R. x pratensis Mert. & Koch   **A hybrid Dock**
R. crispus x **R. obtusifolius**
Collected at Millbrook in 1961 by Mrs E. M. Towers
and determined by J. E. Lousley.

R. conglomeratus Murray   **Clustered Dock**
Frequent and widespread on disturbed ground and in
damper places than the following with which it can be
confused.

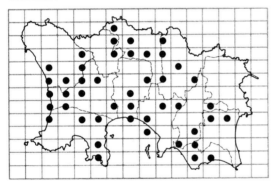

G frequent; A frequent; S occasional; H frequent.

R. sanguineus L.   **Wood Dock**
(R. nemorosus)   *d'l'***hèrbe à sang**
Frequent in hedges and on wooded côtils in the
interior of the island. There are two varieties: one is
green-veined and is the commoner; the other, the
type, has varying amounts of red in its veins, stem and
branches. The Jersey-Norman-French name presumably refers to the red-veined variety but whether
because of its colour or because of its use to staunch
blood is unknown. This variety may once have been
cultivated for medicinal and culinary use and escaped
into the wild.

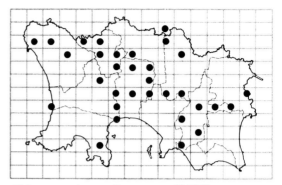

G frequent; A rare; S common; H 1958.

R. rupestris Le Gall   **Shore Dock**
Rare. Recorded from six places during the survey,
usually where fresh water runs down the cliffs onto
the shore. The north coast localities are difficult of
access and Shore Dock may well be in many more
similar situations, but only approachable by boat.
J. E. Lousley in the *Flora of the Isles of Scilly* pointed
out that this is one of the world's rarest docks occurring on only a few shores of north-west Europe. He
was concerned for its survival because of disturbance
of small seaside coves by holiday-makers and
commented on the importance of the Isles of Scilly
populations. Many of Jersey's plants would seem to
be safe from such disturbance though those at Le
Grouet, near La Corbière, have been lost because of
gardening of the low cliff on which it used to grow.
Early records (Hb Cantab.) are all from St Aubin's
Bay: 1842, Rev. W. W. Newbould; from a brick
waterway on the shore at Beaumont, 1876, T. B.
Blow; rocky shore, 1885, A. Ley. It presumably disappeared from Beaumont when the seawall was
built, but J. E. Lousley collected a specimen from the
shore west of St Aubin in 1950.

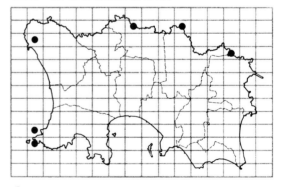

G rare; A rare; H rare.

R. pulcher L.   **Fiddle Dock**
Subsp. *pulcher* Common, particularly on road sides
round the coast.

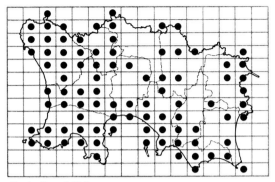

G, A, S and H frequent.

R. obtusifolius L.   **Broad-leaved Dock**
des **doques**

Common generally, and a bad weed of cultivated land.

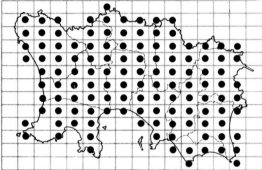

G common; A frequent; S common; H frequent.

R. x ogulinensis Borbás   **A hybrid Dock**
R. obtusifolius x **R. pulcher**
G 1953.

R. x dufftii Hausskn.   **A hybrid Dock**
R. obtusifolius x **R. sanguineus**

Collected in Le Mourier Valley in 1961 by Mrs M. L. Long, det. J. E. Lousley.

R. maritimus L.   **Sea Dock**

Between 1730 and 1740 the Rev. W. Clarke gathered Sea Dock for Dillenius' herbarium, Oxford, from either Jersey or Guernsey and in 1834 La Gasca listed it for Jersey. The first locality given is St Ouen's Pond (Babington, 1839) but most specimens are from Le Marais at La Moye: 1850, J. Piquet; 1871, F. Piquet; 1876, T. B. Blow. J. Piquet also noted it as growing in Le Marais à la Coque and though Lester-Garland (1903) considered it extinct in Jersey, J. Piquet collected a specimen from Grouville in 1904. The only other record this century is in the Société's botanical report for 1915 where Attenborough and Guiton claimed to have refound it in Jersey at Mont

Fiquet, but Guiton was a keen collector and no specimen exists.

Muehlenbeckia complexa (Cunn.) Meissn.
    Wire Plant

Garden escape or relic which, once established, smothers hedges both in and out of gardens with its black-brown wiry stems. Both male and female plants occur and seed is set but no seedlings have been noted.

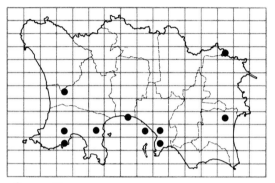

G rare; H rare.

CHENOPODIACEAE

Beta vulgaris L.

Subsp. *vulgaris*   **Beetroot** etc.

This subspecies is the basis for the garden vegetables beetroot, spinach-beet and chard, and for the field crops sugar-beet and mangolds. It is therefore occasionally seen on dumps.

Subsp. *maritima* (L.) Arcangeli   **Sea Beet**
    des **bettes**

Common round the coast and it occasionally occurs inland where vraic has been carted. The map shows the distribution only of Sea Beet.

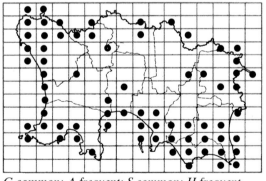

G common; A frequent; S common; H frequent.

Chenopodium botrys L.   **A Goosefoot**

A specimen in the Société Jersiaise herbarium labelled '*C. ambrosioides* L. 1902' and credited to Mr

Lester, i.e. Lester-Garland, in Piquet's handwriting, was determined as *C. botrys* by Professor J. P. M. Brenan who has given considerable help with *Chenopodium* species. An undated note in Babington's copy of his Flora states that H. C. Watson found it in St Brelade's Bay.

C. schraderanum Schultes **A Goosefoot**

A specimen collected by Burdo from the top of the steps at Hauteville, St Saviour's Road, in 1929 was determined as this by Brenan. The seed may have been brought into the island by Louis-Arsène.

C. bonus-henricus L. **Good King Henry**
d's **aulouoches**

Lester-Garland (1903) stated that Good King Henry was a relic of former cultivation. Last century it was recorded without locality by Babington (1839) and from Mont au Prêtre by Piquet in 1851 and 1896. There has been no record since Piquet collected a specimen at Mont au Prêtre in 1902.
G error.

C. glaucum L. **Oak-leaved Goosefoot**

Two specimens gathered by Piquet from 'Waste ground' in July 1911 and labelled *C. urbicum* were determined as *C. glaucum* by Brenan. In Piquet's notes in his copy of Babington, he makes no mention of *C. glaucum* but gives *C. urbicum*, with the locality of St John's Road, and likewise P. É. F. Perrédès in his *Obituary* of Piquet. It seems a reasonable assumption that the specimen now determined as *C. glaucum* came from St John's Road.
G rare.

C. rubrum L. **Red Goosefoot**

Unaccountably rare. Listed by La Gasca in 1834 and claimed by J. S. Gaskin in 1911 from First Tower. No specimens exist of these. A specimen collected by Miss E. H. du Feu, from a rubbish dump at Trinity in 1959, was determined as this by N. Sandwith and there were three plants where an old rubbish dump bordered a sandpit under excavation at St Ouen in 1981.
G local; S 1874.

C. botryodes Sm. **Small Red Goosefoot**

Piquet's specimen collected from shingle in St Ouen's Bay in 1900 was confirmed as this by Brenan.
G rare.

C. hybridum L. **Maple-leaved Goosefoot**

Though Piquet recorded this from Trinity in his 1898 *Supplementary List*, his three specimens are all from St Helier: 1898 confirmed Brenan, Hb Société Jersiaise; 1899 and 1902, Hb Oxford, and in his copy of Babington, he wrote against this species 'In a

garden at St Helier, rare'.
G ?

C. polyspermum L. **Many-seeded Goosefoot**
d'la **rouoge s'nîle**

Frequent on cultivated or disturbed land.

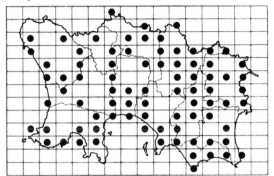

G frequent; A rare; S occasional; H occasional.

C. vulvaria L. **Stinking Goosefoot**

Listed by La Gasca in 1834 and stated by Piquet in 1851 to be common near the sea. From then onwards it appears to have been rare. Early records were from St Ouen's Pond, presumably from the shore nearby, Petit Port, St Helier, Mont Orgueil and Grands Vaux while in the past twenty years it has been seen at La Haule, Elizabeth Castle, Samarès Manor and Grouville. It does not seem to persist in any one place for more than a few years. A seeding specimen, brought to me for identification, was put outside overnight because of its nauseous, disgusting smell of putrefying fish. For about three years, plants of Stinking Goosefoot grew in our vegetable garden but it eventually died out naturally.
G rare; A ?1962.

C. urbicum L. **Upright Goosefoot**

Error for *C. glaucum*; see that species.

C. murale L. **Nettle-leaved Goosefoot**
d'la **vèrte s'nîle**

Common in fields and on disturbed ground.

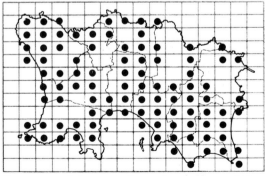

G common; A frequent; S occasional; H common.

C. ficifolium Sm.   **Fig-leaved Goosefoot**

Either rare or overlooked. La Gasca's record was ignored by Lester-Garland who does not mention the species, even in his ambiguities and errors list. Other records are: Anne Port, 1960, P. J. O. Trist; St Ouen's Bay, 1961; Trinity 1968, Mrs M. L. Long and Mrs E. M. Towers.

G frequent; A rare.

C. opulifolium Schrader ex Koch & Ziz

         Grey Goosefoot

G 1906 and 1953; A 1906.

C. album L.   **Fat-hen**
         d'la **blianche s'nîle**

Common in many areas, and often abundant in cultivated fields.

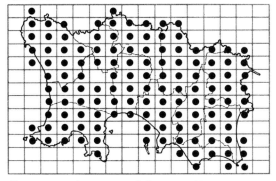

G common; A common; S frequent; H common.

Atriplex halimus L.   **Argentum** or **Shrubby Orache**
         *d'l'***argentinne**

Much planted for hedging near the sea as a wind break because it can withstand salt-laden winds and rain. Flowers and seeds are produced but no seedlings are known, the flourishing thickets apparently being formed by natural layering of the original plants. When it came into the island is unknown as early botanists ignored it, but it was well established last century.

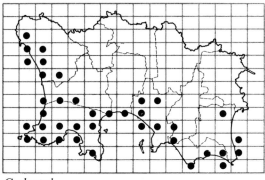

G planted.

A. hortensis L.   **Mountain Orache**

Local. Two early records: Le Hocq, 1885, A. Ley; var. *rubra* (L.) Roth, Bel Royal, 1906, Druce. In 1965 many plants of var. *rubra*, which is grown by flower arrangers for its dark purple foliage, appeared in waste ground above the sea wall near Le Bourg, and from then onwards it has been reported from various localities in the south-east. One large plant of the normal colour was on Les Landes, St Ouen, in 1981.

G rare.

A. rosea L.   **An Orache**

Piquet listed this as from St Ouen's Bay in 1851 and from St Aubin's Bay in 1853. Later he omitted the records. They probably belonged to *A. glabriuscula.*

H error.

A. laciniata L.   **Frosted Orache**
(A. farinosa)

Local on the shore where sand accumulates and is not swept away at high tide.

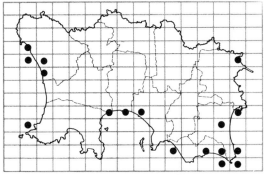

G local; A frequent; S last record 1892; H 1893 and 1975.

A. littoralis L.   **Grass-leaved Orache**

G local; A rare.

A. patula L.   **Common Orache**

Fields and disturbed ground. Widespread but only thinly distributed and considerably less common than the next species.

Map overleaf

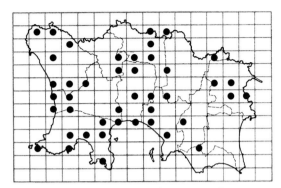

G common; A occasional; S frequent; H frequent.

A. prostrata Boucher ex DC.   Spear-leaved Orache
(A. hastata)

Common on disturbed ground and on the seashore, and sometimes abundant in fields.

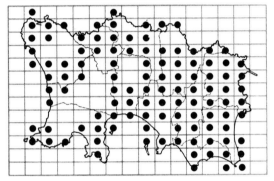

G common; A frequent; S occasional; H frequent.

A. glabriuscula Edmondston   Babington's Orache
(A. Babingtonii)

Recorded under various names from 1834 onwards where sand accumulates on the shore. Piquet's *A. rosea* probably belongs here.

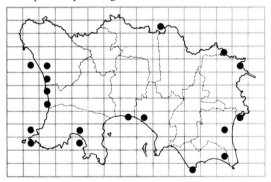

G local; A occasional; S rare; H scarce.

A. glabriuscula x A. prostrata   A hybrid Orache
A 1967.

Haliminione portulacoides (L.) Aellen   Sea-purslane
(Atriplex portulacoides)

Recorded as common by Babington in 1839 and listed by Piquet in 1851 from St Helier and St Clement without comment. By 1896 Piquet considered it rare and crossed out 'Common' in his copy of Babington's *Flora* putting 'NO' beside it. Lester-Garland, in 1903, was scathing of Piquet's record from St Ouen and considered the species extinct. From 1916 records began again but whether this was because of renewed botanical activity, including the formation of a botanical group within the Société Jersiaise, or represents a real increase in the species, is difficult to say. Attenborough reported it in St Catherine's Bay in 1916, in Grouville Bay in 1917 and in St Aubin's Bay in 1919. A. J. Wilmott reported it on ballast by the railway line, St Helier, in 1922. This is not so unusual habitat as it may seem because the railway used to run along the edge of the shore. (Trains were often delayed by seaweed and boulders being thrown across the lines at high tide.) In 1933 Attenborough wrote that it was increasing in the island and in 1946 it was found in abundance in small salt-marshes behind the sea wall at St Ouen. It is still locally abundant there, and tide-lines of dried seaweed and other debris, which show where sea water reached over the land behind the wall, are marked by living Sea-purslane.

Sea-purslane exists in a second habitat in the Channel Islands. Louis-Arsène found it in great abundance on the high cliffs of Le Val Rouget in 1925 and it is still there. McClintock, in his *Wild Flowers of Guernsey*, reported it from the same unusual habitat on the cliffs of Guernsey, a habitat so different from the usual mud and that he wondered if an investigation might prove the cliff-dwelling one to be a different form of Sea-purslane.

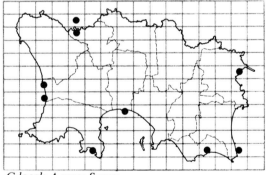

G local; A rare; S rare.

Salicornia europaea group   Glasswort

Saunders' record (1839) was rejected by Lester-Garland but glassworts have appeared, rarely, round the muddier parts of the coasts of the south and east from 1915 onwards, usually not lasting long in any one place. The exception was Elizabeth Castle where

Attenborough recorded it as plentiful in 1949 and it was still in good quantity until the area was 'tidied up' in the mid-1970s.
G both S. europaea s.s. and S. ramosissima rare.

Suaeda vera J. F. Gmelin   **Shrubby Seablite**
La Gasca listed this in 1834 and Piquet claimed to have found it on 'Waste ground at Havre des Pas' in his 1898 *Supplementary List*. Lester-Garland rejected both records.
G 1877.

S. maritima (L.) Dumort.   **Annual Seablite**
Recorded rarely last century, but, since the building of sea walls with the consequent formation of small salt-marshes behind them, Annual Seablite has increased considerably, e.g. Attenborough recorded it in 1946 in great plenty in St Ouen's Bay behind the sea wall and it is still common, even abundant, in places.

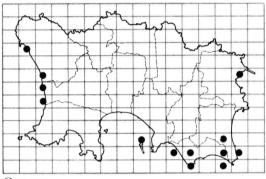

G scarce.

Salsola kali L.   **Prickly Saltwort**
     du **geon d'mielle**
Subsp. *kali* No longer common in sandy bays, as it was in the past, but some years it still appears, locally, in fair quantity.

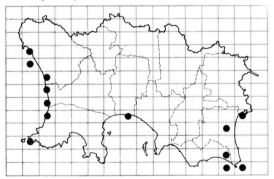

G rare; A rare; S 1838; H rare.

AMARANTHACEAE

Amaranthus caudatus L.   **Love-lies-bleeding**
In the 1950s and 1960s Love-lies-bleeding occurred, rarely, as a garden outcast or casual on rubbish dumps. Guiton's 1900 plant collected in a cultivated field near Gorey (B.E.C. *Report* 1900) was determined as the next species by Professor J. P. M. Brenan who has given considerable help with *Amaranthus* species.

A. hybridus L.   **Green Amaranth**
Subsp. *hybridus* East of the island, 1966, Mrs L. A. Morris, det. J. E. Lousley; Val de la Mare, St Ouen, 1983.
Subsp. *incurvatus* (Tim. ex Gren. & Godr.) Brenan Cultivated field near Gorey, 1900, Guiton, det. Brenan.

A. retroflexus L.   **Common Amaranth**
     du **chuchot**
Piquet collected a specimen in 1873 in St Clement from 'town sweepings and other refuse' and reported the species as rare in 1896. By 1903 Lester-Garland considered it common in potato fields at Samarès, Le Hocq and Pontac. In the post-war years it was common and widespread until the 1962/63 frost, after which it was rare for several years. It recovered but seems to have decreased recently, perhaps being susceptible to the weedkillers now used on farm fields.
For map see page 222

A. albus L.   **White Pigweed**
G 1958.

A. graecizans L.   **An Amaranth**
Subsp. *sylvestris* (Villars) Brenan Piquet's three specimens labelled *A. blitum* – 'Waste places, rare, 1899'; 'A casual weed, 1900' and 'Cultivated field, Bagot, 1900' – were all determined as this by Brenan, as were Lester-Garland's two specimens labelled *A. blitum* from Le Hocq in 1899 and near St Saviour's Church in 1902. It is therefore presumed that Lester-Garland's other records of *A. blitum* belong here. A specimen was collected from a rubbish dump in Grouville in 1957.

A. deflexus L.   **Perennial Pigweed**
Ariste has a specimen labelled *'Pied des Murs'* Jardin Botanique 1928 so the species was in the island more than fifty years ago, even if not in the wild. In 1960 Miss D. Mauger found it on disturbed ground at Grève d'Azette (det. J. E. Lousley) and in 1961 it was noted from several places in the south-east, usually at the foot of walls or in gardens where it is a weed difficult to eradicate. It easily survived the 1962/63 frost which considerably reduced *A. retroflexus*, and

it is now in quantity in some gardens of the south-east.

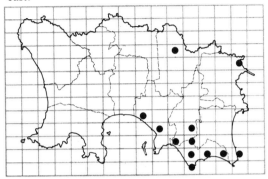

G rare.

A. lividus L.　　　　　　　　　**Grey Pigweed**
(A. blitum)
Lester-Garland (1903) claimed '*A. blitum*' from several places but see *A. graecizans.*
G rare.

NYCTAGINACEAE

Mirabilis jalapa L.　　**Marvel of Peru** or **Belle de Nuit**
This began to appear as a garden escape in the late 1950s and by 1962 it was well-established on most rubbish dumps of the island. It perished in the frost of winter 1962/3, when both mature plants and seedlings were killed. Since then only rarely have plants been seen outside gardens, perhaps because rubbish dumps no longer exist in their previous form, but it seeds itself so freely in gardens at Pontac and Beaufort Square as to be a nuisance.
G rare.

PHYTOLACCACEAE

Phytolacca acinosa Roxb. aggr.　　　　**Poke-berry**
In the 1960s Poke-berry was in a garden in Rouge Bouillon and one plant appeared spontaneously in Constable K. Baal's garden in Midvale Road. Several plants, not looking part of the garden, were in the grounds of Samarès Manor in the 1970s and were still there in 1983. One plant appeared spontaneously in Mr Prouten's garden at Le Lecq in 1975. All the plants were of the East Asian aggregate.

AIZOACEAE

Mesembryanthemums or iceplants have long been known in the gardens of Jersey and inevitably some have escaped or been deliberately planted out. They come mainly from South Africa and the climate of Jersey suits many of them, though exceptional frosts, like that experienced in the winter of 1962/63, can kill off huge areas of them.

Mesembryanthemums grow out in the wild in the Isles of Scilly and J. E. Lousley stated in his *Flora of the Isles of Scilly*, 'Mesembryanthemums are exceedingly difficult to name. They make poor herbarium specimens and are poorly represented in the national collections. They are still inadequately studied even in South Africa and new species are constantly being described.' In the following account, particularly of the *Carpobrotus* and *Lampranthus* genera, it will be seen that many identification problems remain.

The first record in Jersey is of a 'Mesem' species in St Brelade's Bay in 1868 by C. Bailey. By 1886 H. Epps could write in *Science Gossip* that a yellow-flowered 'Mesem' was growing freely in great abundance in the middle of St Aubin's Bay and at the Battery at La Moye Point. Bailey and Epps were both botanists from England, the early local botanists, Piquet, Lester-Garland and Attenborough, never recording so alien a plant.

Carpobrotus sp.
C. edulis (L.) N. E. Br.　　Hottentot-fig, usually with long dark green leaves and large yellow flowers which turn pink as they go over, is now growing in quantity on parts of the east, south and west coasts. Originally it was planted but Jersey's climate suits it and it has spread far and wide, particularly on the cliffs between Portelet and La Corbière where it smothers, and so kills, large areas of the other vegetation. It also occurs on off-islets like the Île Percée where pieces of broken-off, brown, dead-looking stems are taken by herring gulls as nesting material. The stems then take root in the guano-rich environment. An exceptionally hard frost kills the plant, or at least all the top green layer of it, leaving an ugly brown mass of decaying stems, sometimes a foot deep. If some of the lower stems have not been reached by the frost, they will put out new shoots. Seeds also may germinate. The result is that Hottentot-fig continues its smothering spread, eliminating Jersey's natural vegetation in its track. (The same problem occurs in Guernsey and on the Lizard Peninsula in south-west England where an attempt is being made to remove it, or at least to restrict it, in order to save some of England's rarer native plants.)

Hottentot-fig is also responsible for damaging the cliffs. Long streamers of it hang down over the cliff edge and eventually their weight is such that the plant falls, bringing the top part of the cliff with it. To see this, stand in Portelet Bay by the Île au Guerdain and look back to the mainland cliff-face. Bare areas, with piles of Hottentot-fig, soil and rocks underneath, show where the falls have been, and there will be few, if any, falls on areas covered by Jersey's native vegetation. The piles of Hottentot-fig, soil and rock are washed away on the next high spring tide.

As with most 'mesems' there is an identification problem. A look at some of the areas covered by Hottentot-fig will reveal that more than one large-flowered species, subspecies or variety is involved.

North of Kempt Tower in St Ouen's Bay, two kinds grow together. One has the typical large yellow flowers and large, dark-green leaves; the other has flowers paling to white at the very base and leaves of a slightly yellower green. In 1982 and 1983 they were mainly in separate patches but in the past they grew intermingled. The two kinds can be recognised, whether in flower or not. And at Bouilly Port, west of St Brelade, a pink-flowered *Carpobrotus*, also large-leaved, grows on the hillside among yellow and red-flowered plants.

A certainly different *Carpobrotus* species grows on rocks inland from Le Havre, L'Étacq, where it has been for at least twenty-five years. It has smaller leaves than *C. edulis* and smaller flowers with red petals conspicuously white at the base. P. Sell determined it as *C. glaucescens* (Haworth) Schwantes. *G, A and H. Carpobrotus sp. occur.*

Drosanthemum floribundum (Haworth) Schwantes
Drosanthemum

One record: near La Rocque Harbour, 1961, J. C. Fluck, conf. J. E. Lousley but the plants died in the 1962/63 frost.
G rare.

Aptenia cordifolia (L. fil.) N. E. Br. **Aptenia**

This had been known on a bank near Rozel Harbour for more than ten years before it was killed by the 1962/63 frost, J. C. Fluck. In 1979 it was found in local abundance, wild and dominant on the ground near and under conifer trees behind Le Château des Roches, St Brelade's Bay. Though almost certainly originally planted in a rockery behind the house, it was in such quantity that it must have been in the wild for a great number of years. Plants under trees in Mrs Lort-Phillips' garden at Gorey survived the great frost and it is thought that the Le Château des Roches population must have done so, as it would appear to pre-date the frost. In 1980 Mrs E. M. Towers found one plant on a shaded bank near Grouville Common. The St Brelade plants have pale-green heart-shaped leaves and small dark pink flowers. The Grouville plant has larger, darker-green leaves which are not always heart-shaped, and the flowers are slightly larger and a different pink. It is thought they are probably different clones of *Aptenia cordifolia*.
G rare.

Disphyma crassifolium (L.) L.Bolus **Disphyma**

Completely naturalised for many years under the trees on West Mount and hanging down in long strings over the wall on St Aubin's Road. It also occurs at Beau Port and in St Ouen's Bay. The species is locally abundant north of Le Braye Slip in St Ouen's Bay where salt water comes over the sea wall at high tide, so producing salt-marsh conditions. Its natural habitat in South Africa is salt-marsh, so this species, which survived the frost of 1962/63 with ease, is now likely to remain permanently part of Jersey's 'wild' flora.

Lampranthus sp. **Mesem or Iceplant**

This genus includes the 'mesem' which becomes totally covered with magenta or pink flowers in June. It is occasionally planted out in the wild but has difficulty in holding its own, permanently, in competition with Jersey's native vegetation. It is thought that more than one species is involved in Jersey, including perhaps *L. roseus* and *L. falciforme*, but more information is needed.
G rare; A rare; S 1924.

TETRAGONIACEAE

Tetragonia tetragonoides (Pallas) O. Kuntze
New Zealand Spinach

An occasional garden escape on rubbish dumps and where sand accumulates high on the shore, but decreasing as the number of rubbish dumps decreases.
G 1913.

PORTULACACEAE

Portulaca oleracea L. **Pot Purslane**
du **pourpyi**

Subsp. *oleracea* Now a frequent weed of sandy soil but it was not recorded until Piquet's *Supplementary List* in 1898 when he wrote of it, 'Sandy fields in St Aubin's Bay. Hardly a native.' A specimen in the British Museum herbarium, probably collected by Piquet, has a note attached saying, 'A late introduction to Jersey during the last 25 years. 1908'. Though an annual, it is surprisingly difficult to eradicate once established.

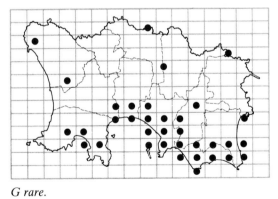

G rare.

Montia fontana L. **Blinks**

Subsp. *amporitana* Sennen Common in wet areas.
Subsp. *chondrosperma* (Fenzl) Walters Common on drier sandy areas.

The map includes both subspecies.

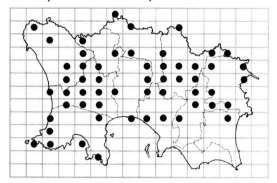

G common; A occasional; S frequent; H occasional.

M. perfoliata (Donn ex Willd.) Howell

Miner's Lettuce or **Springbeauty**

Though now locally common, Miner's Lettuce was not recorded until 1908 when Piquet found a plant at St Clement, Hb Oxford. The main increase seems to have been since the 1950s. Seeds germinate so early in the year that whole hedgebanks become covered with young plants before the native vegetation has started into growth after the winter. Other plants are therefore crowded out and eliminated but there is some evidence that after a few years in a particular place, Miner's Lettuce exhausts the soil of some essential constituent, and then begins to decrease. It used to be common in certain lanes at St Clement but has much decreased. It was abundant at the top of Mont Matthieu, St Ouen, in the 1950s and from there it spread down the hill so that it is now in Val de la Mare. But while it is still abundant on the lower parts of Mont Matthieu, it is dying out on the higher parts, and Navelwort, Sea Campion, English Stonecrop etc. are returning there. It has been in quantity under conifers at La Moye for some years; it is a garden weed occasionally, and it has recently colonised a gorse-covered côtil at St Ouen.

The name Miner's Lettuce was given to it because in the gold rush in North America last century, miners ate it to keep scurvy at bay, it being the first green plant to appear after winter. In spite of this few rabbits in Jersey ever seem to touch it.

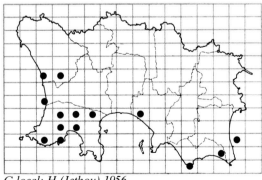

G local; H (Jethou) 1956.

M. sibirica (L.) Howell   **Pink Purslane**

This North American species was in good quantity on the west side of La Haule Hill and in the grounds of the house 'Grey Gables' in 1956. Though he did not record it, Attenborough said he had seen it there before the Occupation (1940–45). In 1964 there were several plants by the pool and in the woods at Rosel Manor. R. Dobson worked on garden projects at both Grey Gables and Rosel Manor so may have been an accidental carrier. The species was still present in both localities in 1982, and in the grounds of Le Coin, La Haule.

G rare.

Calandrinia ciliata (Ruiz & Pavon) DC.   **Red Maids**

Seedlings growing in sandy soil as garden weeds at Millbrook in autumn 1969 were identified as this when they flowered in 1970, and the species is still present, Mrs M. L. Long.

S 1957, now gone?

CARYOPHYLLACEAE

Arenaria balearica L.   **Mossy Sandwort**

A garden escape recorded by Ariste in 1927 from Grouville. In 1956 A. W. Holder found it on a wall in Rue de Haut, St Lawrence, where it persisted for about ten years.

S rare.

A. serpyllifolia L.   **Thyme-leaved Sandwort**

Locally frequent in sandy soil, including on walls. Lester-Garland recorded var. *macrocarpa* Lloyd (var. *Lloydii*) from Les Quennevais. See comments under *A. leptoclados* for the distribution map.

G frequent; A common; S 1879; H common.

A. leptoclados (Reichenb.) Guss.   **Slender Sandwort**

Recorded frequently for sandy soil but because of possible confusion with the above species, *A. serpyllifolia*, the records of both have been combined in the following map.

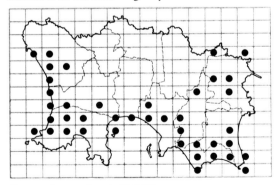

G rare; A occasional; H 1950.

Moehringia trinervia (L.) Clairv.

Three-nerved Sandwort

So frequent on shady hedgebanks and wooded côtils in Jersey that it is surprising to find it absent from the rest of the Channel Islands.

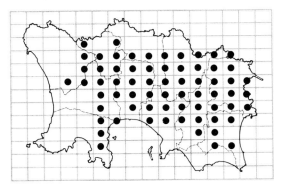

Minuartia hybrida (Vill.) Schischkin

Fine-leaved Sandwort

A specimen was collected by R. M. Lingwood near Petit Port in 1837 (Hb Cantab.). This is the source of Babington's record in his Flora. In 1969 Mrs D. L. Le Quesne found many plants in the joints of a wall along La Grande Route de St Clément. The plants were spread over a length of about fifty yards. The species appeared to have been there for some years and it still flourishes.

Honkenya peploides (L.) Ehrh.   **Sea Sandwort**
(Alsine peploides)

Locally frequent, sometimes abundant, on sandy soil at the edge of the coast.

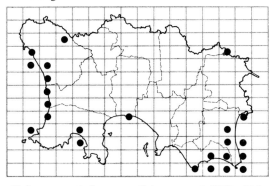

G frequent; A frequent; S last record 1872; H last record 1899.

Stellaria nemorum L.   **Wood Stitchwort**

Saunders claimed to have found Wood Stitchwort so Babington included it in his 1839 Flora. Lester-Garland rejected the improbable record and it remains unsubstantiated.

S. media (L.) Vill.   **Common Chickweed**
du **meurdron**

Subsp. *media* Common on roadsides and in fields and gardens, and on the dunes where rabbits are plentiful.

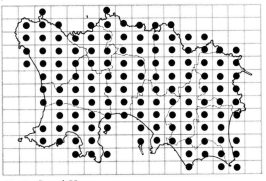

G, A, S and H common.

S. neglecta Weihe   **Greater Chickweed**

Lester-Garland (1903) recorded this as '*S media* var. *neglecta* = *S. major* Koch' and stated that it was not common in hedges and sheltered places and on Les Quennevais. It has not been refound. Large chickweeds exist but all those investigated have rounded tubercles on their seeds, not conical, and are therefore placed under *S. media* subsp. *media*.

S. pallida (Dumort.) Piré   **Lesser Chickweed**

Local on light sandy soil, the pale yellow-green plants often covering large areas in early spring. As in Guernsey, it may well be under-recorded. Lester-Garland (1903) thought it common in open sandy fields but in this survey it was recorded more from uncultivated open land.

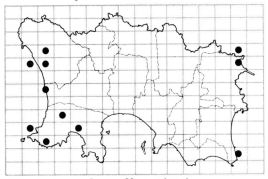

G local; A rare; S rare; H occasional.

S. holostea L.   **Greater Stitchwort**

Common on hedgebanks in the interior and near the cliffs yet surprisingly absent from the other Channel Islands.

Map overleaf

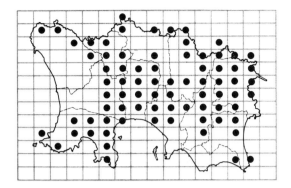

S. alsine Grimm   **Bog Stitchwort**

Frequent in wet places.

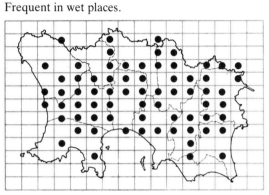

G local; S rare; H rare.

S. palustris Retz.   **Marsh Stitchwort**

Lester-Garland (1903) rejected Saunders' record which was published by Babington in 1839. In 1922 Attenborough stated that Mrs Robinson had found Marsh Stitchwort at Crabbé but there would not appear to be any suitable habitat there, either now or in 1921, and no specimen exists.

S. graminea L.   **Lesser Stitchwort**

Frequent in parts of the island. Why it should be largely absent from the south and west is unknown.

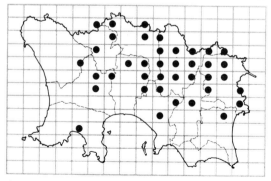

G rare; A rare; S 1874 and Brecqhou 1902.

Holosteum umbellatum L.   **Jagged Chickweed**

There is no confirmation of La Gasca's record of 1834 which was rejected by Lester-Garland (1903).

Cerastium biebersteinii DC.   **Snow-in-summer**
and **C. tomentosum** L.   *d'l'argent*

Snow-in-summer is frequently planted out on hedgebanks near habitation and then survives and spreads, even after the habitation has perhaps long disappeared, e.g. it was planted round some of the beach huts in St Ouen's Bay before the Occupation (1940–45) and is still there though the huts have gone. Ariste collected it from L'Hermitage on Elizabeth Castle in 1926. Two closely allied species are involved and it has not been possible to separate them in the field. The distribution map includes all localities where observers thought either of the two species was surviving in the wild unaided. Different observers may have different views on this. Nevertheless a map is given because it shows how widespread the two species are and it illustrates the random distribution of introduced species which persist where planted but do not produce seedlings in the wild.

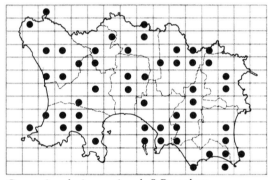

G occasional; A occasional; S Brecqhou.

C. arvense L.   **Field Mouse-ear Chickweed**

A specimen in the British Museum herbarium bears a label stating that it was collected at St Brelade in 1932 by R. Meinertzhagen. There is some doubt over the validity of the label so, as no other record is known either in Jersey or any other Channel Island, confirmation is needed.

C. fontanum Baumg.

      Common Mouse-ear Chickweed
          dé l'ouothelle dé souothis

Subsp. *glabrescens* (G. F. W. Meyer) Salman *et al.* *(C. triviale)* Common on cultivated land, roadsides, hedges and disturbed ground.

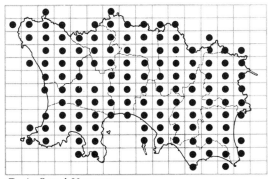

G, A, S and H common.

C. glomeratum Thuill.   **Sticky Mouse-ear Chickweed**
Common on cultivated land, roadsides, hedges and disturbed ground.

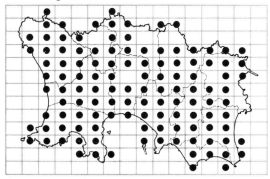

G common; A frequent; S common; H frequent.

C. semidecandrum L.   **Little Mouse-ear Chickweed**
Subsp. *semidecandrum*   Not as widespread round the coast as Sea Mouse-ear Chickweed but common where it occurs and sometimes abundant.

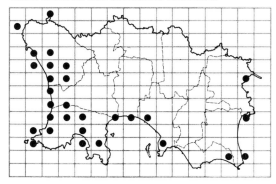

G local; A frequent; S error; H frequent.

C. diffusum Pers.   **Sea Mouse-ear Chickweed**
Subsp. *diffusum (C. tetrandrum)*   Common on the dunes and coastal heaths and sometimes locally abundant.

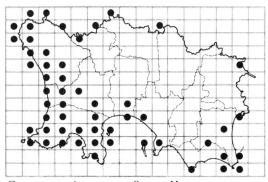

G common; A common; S rare; H common.

Moenchia erecta (L.) P. Gaertner, B. Meyer & Scherb.

Upright Chickweed
Subsp. *erecta*   Common, sometimes abundant, on the short turf of the dunes, cliffs and foothills.

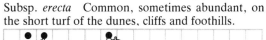
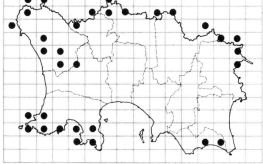

G locally common; A rare; S locally common; H local.

Myosoton aquaticum (L.) Moench   **Water Chickweed**
Some unknown seedlings were noticed among Common Chickweed seedlings in a greenhouse at Hérúpe, St John, in 1969 by Mrs M. L. Long and were left to flower. They proved to be Water Chickweed, an unexpected species for Jersey. All the soil in the greenhouse was obtained locally, and the origin of the plants is unknown. Every year since 1969 some plants have been in flower.
G 1979 and 1982.

Sagina nodosa (L.) Fenzl   **Knotted Pearlwort**
A rare species not seen recently. It was recorded from wet places on Les Quennevais and in St Ouen's Bay by all botanists last century. Lester-Garland did not find it and in 1903 queried whether or not it was extinct in Jersey but Ariste refound it on Les Quennevais in 1924. Louis-Arsène's specimens, a few days later in 1924, are labelled as from a quarry near Don Bridge. He told the writer that it was in great quantity in a dip in Les Quennevais to the east

of Don Bridge Station. Though this area would now seem to be built over, Knotted Pearlwort may well still exist on Les Quennevais.
G rare; A occasional; S 1903.

S. subulata (Swartz) C. Presl   **Heath Pearlwort**
Locally frequent on open heathland by the coast and perhaps under-recorded.

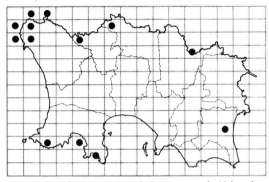

G occasional; A occasional; S occasional; H local.

S. procumbens L.   **Procumbent Pearlwort**
Subsp. *procumbens* Common on lawns, paths, walls and banks.

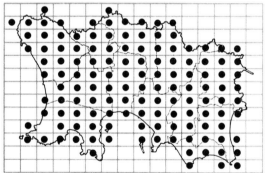

G common; A frequent; S frequent; H common.

S. apetala Ard.   **Annual Pearlwort**
The two pearlworts previously known as *S. apetala* and *S. ciliata* are combined in *Flora Europaea* into one species and then separated as two subspecies. Unfortunately, under the rules of nomenclature, the old species *S. ciliata* appears as subsp. *apetala* and the old species *S. apetala* as subsp. *erecta*. The criterion used for identifying the subspecies was spreading or appressed sepals but because of the difficulty involved, the species as a whole may be under-recorded. Nevertheless the following maps are given because they appear to indicate that the two sub-species require slightly different habitats. Compare J. E. Lousley's statement in the *Flora of the Isles of Scilly* that subsp. *apetala* seems to grow in drier places than subsp. *erecta*.

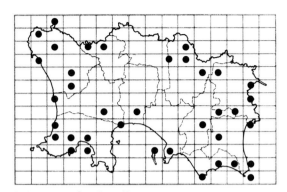

Subsp. *apetala* Locally common.
G common; A frequent; S occasional; H common.

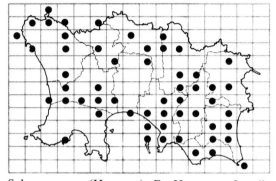

Subsp. *erecta* (Hornem.) F. Hermann Locally common.
G common; A frequent; S occasional; H occasional.

S. maritima G. Don fil.   **Sea Pearlwort**
Locally frequent on the coast but perhaps under-recorded.

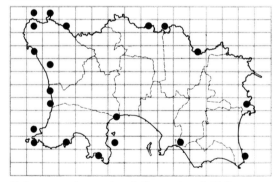

G frequent; A occasional; S occasional; H frequent.

Scleranthus annuus L.   **Annual Knawel**
Subsp. *annuus* This seems to have decreased over the years: common, Babington, (1839); common, Piquet, (1851); frequent, Piquet, (1896); local, Lester-Garland, (1903). It is now rarely found but

when it is, there are usually many plants over a small area.

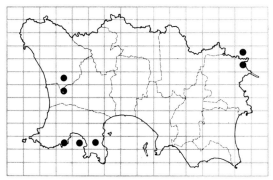

G last record 1904; A rare; S common; H local.

Corrigiola litoralis L.   **Strapwort**

Marked as an introduction to Jersey on the species distribution map in the *Atlas of the British Flora* but the record, which was from Louis-Arsène's herbarium, is now withdrawn.

Herniaria glabra L.   **Smooth Rupturewort**

Reported in the past from St Aubin's Bay and St Brelade's Bay but Dr L. C. Frost has shown that all ruptureworts in the Channel Islands are the next species.
G similar error.

Herniaria ciliolata Melderis   **Fringed Rupturewort**

Babington found a rupturewort, which has proved to be this species, in St Aubin's Bay in 1837 and the species was still present there until 1903 according to Lester-Garland, who considered it doomed. It is no longer there but when it disappeared is unknown. Piquet recorded it from Le Marais, Noirmont, i.e. Ouaisné Common, in 1851. In the early 1960s Ouaisné Common was suffering badly from erosion caused by cars driving over the area, and the destruction of the rupturewort colony seemed imminent. To prevent further erosion, a car park was formed in one corner of the Common in 1965. Part of the rupturewort colony, unfortunately, was where this car park now is, but the Public Works Committee assisted in every possible way and those plants about to be destroyed were moved to what seemed identical habitats on the Common nearby. Growing conditions were excellent at the time of the transplanting. Most of the work was done by the Botanical Section of the Société Jersiaise whose members included two professional gardeners, yet not one plant seems to have survived. On the other hand, the undisturbed rupturewort, growing naturally on the Common, was still present in 1983 though the severe drought of 1976 affected it severely and so has the number of people now using the Common. To human eyes there would

appear to be much suitable habitat left so it may increase.

H. W. Pugsley (1914), Dr A. Melderis (1957) and Dr L. C. Frost (1966) have studied Jersey's rupturewort, including its nomenclature, and their papers should be consulted. Dr Frost has shown that the Jersey plants have 108 chromosomes, as do those in Brittany, whereas those in Guernsey and Alderney and on the Lizard Peninsula have 72 chromosomes. There are also other significant differences. Dr Frost is still working on the species with a view to finding out whether the Jersey plants are endemic or reached Jersey from the mainland of Europe.
G rare; A last record 1956.

H. hirsuta L.   **Hairy Rupturewort**

A specimen collected by C. J. Tempère, and labelled as from 'Jersey' in 1876, is in the Birmingham University herbarium. Nothing is known of the species locally.

Illecebrum verticillatum L.   **Coral Necklace**

No satisfactory record. Saunders' record, published by Babington (1839), was rejected by Lester-Garland (1903), and Louis-Arsène's claim to have collected it in Jersey in 1926 was rejected by Le Sueur (1982). The only other claim is an undated note by Babington in his copy of his Flora that Dr Graham had found it on Gallows Hill. These records may be the basis for the Channel Island entry on the map in Hegi's *Flora von Mittel-Europa* (1961) but no *Illecebrum* is known in any Channel Island.

Polycarpon tetraphyllum (L.) L.

                    Four-leaved Allseed

One of Jersey's commonest weeds of light soil in gardens and fields and it also occurs on the dunes and cliffs. A specimen collected in Jersey by a Mr Clark between 1730 and 1740 is in the Dillenian herbarium, Oxford. The conditions under which Four-leaved Allseed grows seem greatly to influence its form. In a wet summer on good land, it will be large, green and bushy and its stems can be 25 cm. or more long, but in a hot dry summer it will be small and stunted with reddish leaves, particularly in the drier places like the sand dunes and roadsides. Its stem may then only be 2 cm. long when it flowers. Lester-Garland (1903) described two forms: (a) Panicle dense, foliage reddish or yellowish: dry situations exposed to sun and wind, (b) Panicle lax, foliage green: cultivated ground, especially where protected by the crop. These are the extremes and all stages in-between can be found. The conditions also seem to influence the leaves. One pair is often less well-developed than the other pair at the same node. Perhaps partly because of this, many botanists have been tempted to call the smaller plants *P. diphyllum*, Two-leaved Allseed, the next species.

Map overleaf

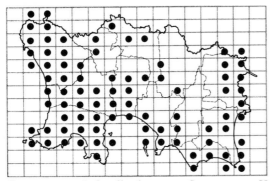

G common; A locally frequent; S common; H common.

P. diphyllum Cav.   **Two-leaved Allseed**

In spite of much searching, no Two-leaved Allseed is known in Jersey. Pugsley (1914) claimed to have collected it in St Aubin's Bay but specimens from there, in the British Museum herbarium, have been placed in the Four-leaved Allseed folder. Wilmott wrote in his notebook that he had seen only Two-leaved Allseed in 1922, which must have been a mis-identification considering the amount of Four-leaved Allseed in Jersey. A. O. Chater comments in *Flora Europaea* that experimental investigation of the genus *Polycarpon* is needed.
G errors.

Spergula arvensis L.   **Corn Spurrey**
                                   *d'l'**hèrbe à mille noeuds***

The Corn Spurrey of gardens and cultivated fields is common, occasionally abundant, except where the land has been well limed. The States lime-subsidy is probably responsible for its recent decline in some fields. The smaller spreading form, var. *nana* E. F. Linton, is common on the cliffs and flowers from January to March in bare patches in open turf.

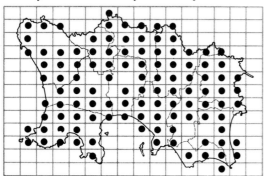

G common; A locally common; S common; H frequent.

Spergularia rupicola Lebel ex Le Jolis
(*S. rupestris*)   **Rock Sea-spurrey**
Common on rocks round the coast.

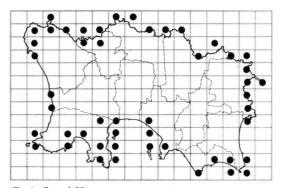

G, A, S and H common.

S. media (L.) C. Presl   **Greater Sea-spurrey**
Druce interpreted a record by Dr W. Sherard, given in the first edition of Ray's *Synopsis* (1960), as *Spergularia media* but the entry was withdrawn in later editions. See the Introduction. There is no satisfactory record of this locally common British coastal plant in any Channel Island.

S. marina (L.) Griseb.   **Lesser Sea-spurrey**
(*S. neglecta*)
Confined to a few areas where spray comes over the sea wall at high tide, but abundant where it occurs.

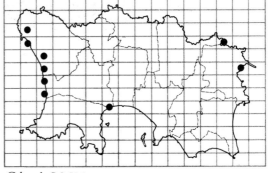

G local; S ? H ?

S. marina x **S. media**   **A hybrid Sea-spurrey**
This hybrid was reported as occurring in Jersey in *The Cambridge British Flora* (Moss, 1920) but it cannot exist since there is a sterility barrier between the species (J. A. Ratter in Stace, 1975).

S. rubra (L.) J. & C. Presl   **Sand-spurrey**
Frequent in dry places.

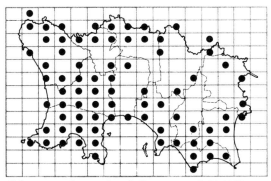

G frequent; A occasional; S occasional; H 1957.

S. bocconii (Scheele) Aschers. & Graebn.

Greek Sand-spurrey

Greek Sand-spurrey was not recorded until 1906 when Druce collected it in St Helier. Since then it has been recorded from many places from Gorey round the south coast to St Ouen's Bay, usually at the foot of walls, or on roadsides or disturbed ground. D. McClintock comments that, as it is apparently always in ruderal habitats in Guernsey, it is likely to be an introduction. The same is probably true for Jersey.
G occasional; S 1936.

S. bocconii x S. marina　　　**A hybrid Spurrey**

A plant collected by Lady Davy in 1935 was originally determined as this cross, but later work has shown the specimen to be large *S. bocconii* (J. A. Ratter in Stace, 1975).

Lychnis coronaria (L.) Desr.　　　**Rose Campion**

This occasionally occurred on rubbish dumps in the 1960s and 1970s but it is nowhere established.
G garden outcast.

L. flos-cuculi L.　　　**Ragged Robin**
du **coucou d'pré**

Subsp. *flos-cuculi*　Ragged Robin still occurs in most wet meadows as in the past.

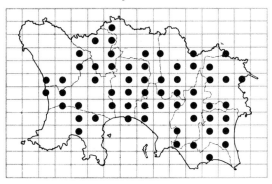

G frequent; A occasional.

Agrostemma githago L.　　　**Corncockle**
d'la **nêle**

All the early botanists from La Gasca in 1834 to Lester-Garland in 1903 recorded Corncockle from cultivated fields, though by 1903 Lester-Garland considered it rare. A garden form was at the top of Grands Vaux mudpond in 1961, J. C. Fluck, but previous to that, the last record was from a hen run on the west side of Beaumont Hill between 1935 and 1940, Mrs M. L. Long.
Last records: G 1934; A 1932; S 1902 and 1969.

Petrocoptis pyrenaica (J. C. Bergeret) A. Braun

Petrocoptis

Ariste collected a specimen from a wall at Grouville in 1927 and Louis-Arsène collected one, also from Grouville, in 1929.

Silene nutans L.　　　**Nottingham Catchfly**

Subsp. *nutans*　Past records give the distribution as north and west and Lester-Garland stated in 1903 that it was locally abundant. This is still true. In a paper on *Silene nutans* in *Watsonia* (1951) F. N. Hepper stated: 'Jersey specimens are very similar to var. *salmoniana* Hepper'.

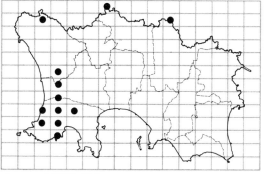

A rare; S 1902; H frequent.

S. vulgaris (Moench) Garcke　　　**Bladder Campion**
(*S. Cucubalus*)

Bladder Campion was recorded as rare by Piquet in 1851 and 1896 and by Lester-Garland in 1903. Normally it has continued to be rare with the 'dots' on the map representing only small groups of plants, but there have been extraordinary exceptions. It appeared in abundance, with Wild Mignonette, in the mid-1950s in a field along Le Chemin de l'Ouzière, St Ouen, when the field was ploughed for the first time for years. Similarly in 1970, when a nearby grassy field was ploughed, Bladder Campion appeared in abundance. It remains in the same areas elsewhere, with remarkable persistence, records today coming from roughly the same areas as those of last century.

Map overleaf

37

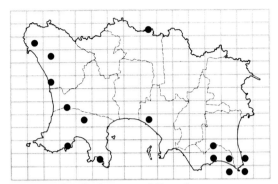

G rare; A locally frequent; S Brecqhou.

S. maritima With. Sea Campion
(S. vulgaris subsp. *maritima)* *d's* **iliets d'rotchi**

Common on the cliffs and on rocky or stony ground. A perennial plant, its roots often survive the fires which sweep through gorse-covered côtils, and the following year the côtils may be white in late spring with its flowers. See *The Bladder Campions* (Marsden-Jones & Turrill, 1951) for an account of Channel Island plants. Le Maistre (1966) gives five different names: *d's iliets d'rotchi, du blianc coucou, d'mouaîselles, blianches femmes* and *bouonnefemmes.* The last three are from a child's game where the calyx is turned inside out and the petals removed. A figure like a crinolined lady is left.

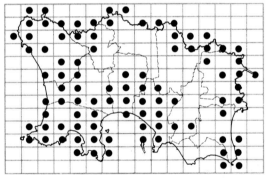

G, A, S and H common.

S. armeria L. Sweet-William Catchfly
Piquet recording finding this garden escape in 'the road leading from La Haule to St Peter' in 1851 and F. Piquet collected a specimen from St Saviour in 1869 but the species is nowhere established.

S. noctiflora L. Night-scented Catchfly
No specimen supports Babington's (1839) record from La Haule and Lester-Garland (1903) rejected it.
G 1968.

S. pratensis (Rafn) Godron & Gren. White Campion
(S. alba; Melandrium pratense) *des* **vieil'yes fil'yes**
Widespread but never many plants in any one place.

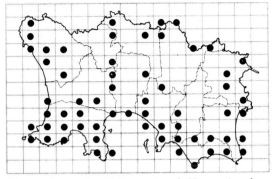

G rare; A occasional; S occasional; H occasional.

S. dioica (L.) Clairv. Red Campion
(Melandrium silvestre) *d's* **iliets d'fôssé**
Common and luxuriant, making many hedgebanks bright pink in early summer. Four different names are listed in the *Dictionnaire Jersiais-Français: d's iliets d'fôssé* (cf *S. maritima* as *d's iliets d'rotchi), du rouôge coucou, des vièrs garçons* and *d'la p'tite molène.*

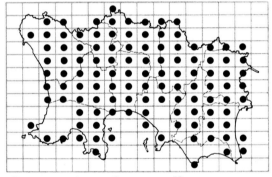

G common; A rare; S common; H common.

S. x intermedia (Schur) Philp A hybrid Campion
S. dioica x S. pratensis
Plants with apparently intermediate characters occur and presumably are hybrids. The first record is a specimen collected by Babington on 8th August 1837 at St Martin as *S. dioica* but which has been determined as the hybrid by Dr H. C. Prentice.
G rare; A common; S occasional; H rare.

S. cretica L. A Campion
Piquet collected two specimens: field near St Lawrence Church, 1857, and St Ouen, 1901, both in Hb Oxford.

S. dichotoma Ehrh. Forked Catchfly
Subsp. *dichotoma* Piquet collected a specimen, at

Dancaster's Farm at the north end of Les Mielles, St Ouen in 1901 (Hb Société Jersiaise). In notes in his copy of Babington's Flora he wrote, '. . . also at St Catherine's Bay. Rare'.
S 1902.

S. gallica L.   **Small-flowered Catchfly**
So many different species, forms and varieties of Small-flowered Catchfly have been described from Jersey that it is a relief to find them all now nestling under *S. gallica* L. For example, in the *Journal of Botany* for 1879, Melvill wrote '. . . It is rarely that so good a field for research on to these plants is found as in this locality (Westmount), for altogether five forms were observed, all merging into one'. Five species were then named and described. Later, J. W. White asked *re S. anglica* var. *rosea* in the B.E.C. *Report* for 1899, 'Is not this var. an ultra-sub-*anglica* hybrid with *quinque-vulnera?*' Small-flowered Catchfly still occurs frequently on light soil. Its petals vary from small dingy white to large pale rose, and the var. *quinquevulnera* (L.) Koch still flourishes in many of its old haunts like West Mount, Pontac and St Brelade. This striking variety, which has a blood-red spot on each of its five white petals, was first recorded, probably before 1782, by Captain J. Finlay (see the Introduction). In a copy of Ray's *Synopsis* at Kew, the owner, the Rev. J. Lightfoot, made various notes and they include under *S. quinquevulnera*, '*In insula Jersey inventa a Dom Finlay*'.

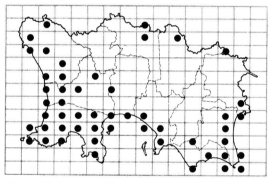

G rare; A frequent; S occasional; H occasional.

S. conica L.   **Sand Catchfly**
Subsp. *conica* Sand Catchfly is still common, sometimes locally abundant, in the main sandy areas. Earlier botanists recorded it from the south coast, e.g. from the sands of St Helier, 1851, Piquet, and on sandbanks past Bel Royal, 1890, A. J. Binet. These sands have gone and with them Sand Catchfly. Normally the species is pink-flowered but white flowers have been seen on Les Quennevais. The size of the plants varies with the conditions under which they are growing and they have been found from only a few centimetres in height to over fifty centimetres.

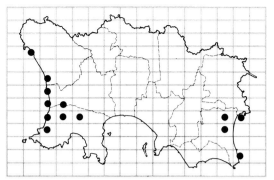

G local; A local; S ?1833.

S. conoidea L.   **Mediterranean Sand Catchfly**
This species has been repeatedly and erroneously described as established in Jersey. Plate 71 in *The Cambridge British Flora* (Moss, 1920) purports to be an illustration by E. W. Hunnybun of a Jersey specimen of *S. conoidea* but the plant would appear to be *S. conica* which can grow large and lush in good conditions. The original drawing, dated 2 June 1902, is in Cambridge. G. C. Druce attempted to clear up the confusion when he wrote in the *Journal of Botany* (1926), '*Silene conoidea* L. only appeared as a rare alien in Jersey, where Mr Piquet and myself gathered it on a rubbish heap at St Ouens with other aliens, and as such it has appeared now and then in Britain. . . . Moreover, the plant figured for it in the *Cambridge British Flora* is almost certainly *conica*'. There are no other records.
G error.

Cucubalus baccifer L.   **Berry Catchfly**
In 1851 Piquet stated that this had been found by a Mr Matthews on the heights above Bouley Bay and he repeated the record in his 1896 list. No specimen has been found and Lester-Garland rejected the record.

Saponaria officinalis L.   **Soapwort**
(*S. Vaccaria*)   *des* **mains jointes**
Garden escape naturalised since at least 1847 when it was collected by Ereaut. It persists remarkably in its known stations. The above-ground parts of the plant near L'Étacq are pulled off or weed-killed almost every year yet the plants have survived for thirty years at least. In 1851 Piquet stated that it was 'On the wall, Pier Rod, opp. the Military Hospital' and it was still in roughly the same area in the 1960s. Le Maistre states that in the past *des mains jointes* was used to heal wounds in cattle. The Jersey-Norman-French name would come from its jointed rhizome whereas the English name is from the lather which is produced when the leaves and roots are crushed and boiled in water, and which can be used for washing, particularly for washing delicate fabrics.
For map see page 222

Opposite, Plate 4   Sea Stock *Matthiola sinuata* with Sea Bindweed *Calystegia soldanella* and Marram
Ammophila arenaria

Vaccaria hispanica (Mill.) Räuschel   **Cow Basil**
(*V. pyramidata*)

Four casual records – two in 1898: Five Oaks Brick Kilns, Lester-Garland, and St Ouen's Bay, Piquet, and two probably from bird seed in 1967: Petit Port, St Brelade, Miss P. Donaldson and Pontac, Mrs D. L. Le Quesne.
G rare casual.

Petrorhagia nanteuilii (Burnat) P. W. Ball & Heywood   **Childing Pink**
(*Dianthus prolifer*)

Locally common on the dunes. Normally pink-flowered but McClintock reported a white-flowered plant in 1947. Recent work has shown that the name *P. prolifer (Dianthus prolifer)*, as used in the past, covered two species, a diploid with 2n = 30 which retains the name *P. prolifer* and a tetraploid with 2n = 60 now called *P. nanteuilii*. Jersey's Childing Pink is the latter, which is the Childing Pink of WSW Europe (Ball & Heywood 1962).

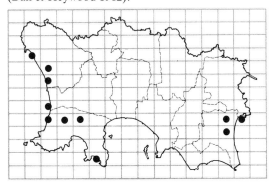

Dianthus gratianopolitanus Vill.   **Cheddar Pink**
(*D. caesius* Sm.)

The Jersey Pink, *D. gallicus*, was erroneously identified as the Cheddar Pink when it was first found and it appears under *D. caesius* in Piquet's *Supplementary List* of 1898.

D. caryophyllus L.   **Clove Pink**

La Gasca recorded this in 1834 putting '*Colitur*' against it, and in 1923 Major N. V. Rybot reported it growing in good quantity, apparently wild, on the outer walls of Elizabeth Castle. It was still there until the 1950s when the walls were cleaned and this interesting historical record of former cultivation was destroyed.

When aged between 72 and 85, an Englishwoman Mrs Delaney (1700–1788) created nearly 1,000 remarkable paper mosaics. One, of *Dianthus caryophyllus*, is labelled 'Jersey Pink' and is dated 8 September 1779. The pink was given to her by General Conway who, being Governor of Jersey from 1772 to 1795, occasionally visited the island.

Elizabeth Castle was the main military headquarters at that time.
G short-lived outcasts.

D. gallicus Pers.   **Jersey Pink**

Rare in short turf on the dunes. Piquet was thought to be the first finder in 1897. Therefore when Gathorne-Hardy in his *Wild Flowers in Britain* (1938) accused a botanist of 'wickedly and deceitfully' sowing it, that botanist was presumed to be Piquet. Piquet planted out several species in the wild but he made no secret of it and there is no justification whatever for this slur. Recently it has become known that A. J. Binet found it five years earlier, as the following extract from his diary shows: '24/7/92 Tram St Aub's. Walk Jubilee Road as far as Les Hanières. A great surprise as I was so certain of there being but one pink in Jersey. A large and beautiful bank of it opposite the 2nd round tower in St O's Bay counting from the N. Had Hooker with me but was obliged to fall back on Bentham to make sure of it. Very much delighted – probably not native.' Had Piquet introduced it so successfully, he would surely have listed it in 1896.

Binet originally wrote *D. caesius* Cheddar Pink against the entry but later he crossed out *caesius* and wrote *gallicus*. He also added that the patch was about three yards square when he found it. In August 1919 he added that the patch had increased very much. In the 1950s and 1960s the original, and then still the only, site was dug for sand and the *Dianthus* would have been destroyed so some of the turf was removed to a similar habitat nearby. Sand had already been dug from this site and it was unlikely to be disturbed again. The present population is from these transplants.

The species is native up the west coast of Europe to Brittany and a number of species with a similar distribution cross to Jersey and are considered native. On the other hand, if it were introduced, accidentally or otherwise, the short turf of St Ouen's Bay would provide an ideal place for it to become established. Though it appears to set seed, I do not recollect seeing a seedling, the increase being vegetative. An illustration by Pandora Sellars is opposite page 22.

D. deltoides L.   **Maiden Pink**

Two records only: rocks of Bouley Bay, 1881, Vaniot and made-up ground near Meadow Bank, St Lawrence, 1964, K. Le Sueur. It has disappeared from both sites. Piquet listed it in 1896 from Bouley Bay but his specimen is the next species.
G 1968; S 1953.

D. armeria L.   **Deptford Pink**

La Gasca listed this in 1834 as '*Colitur*' but it may be a rare native on short turf. In 1853 Piquet reported it from a lane near La Haule and in 1957 it was found near Belle Vue, La Haule, on the heights overlooking St Aubin's Bay, where it persisted for a few years.

Specimens were collected from Bouley Bay in 1881 by Vaniot and in 1903 by Piquet and Lester-Garland. Babington, in annotations in his Flora at Cambridge, stated that Dr M. M. Bull (d. 1879) had found it on the road to Fliquet Bay.
G rare; A last record 1900; S rare.

D. carthusianorum L.   **A Pink**
The Pink on the walls of Elizabeth Castle was identified as this, in error, when first recorded in 1923.

NYMPHAEACEAE
Nymphaea alba L.   **White Water-lily**
This, in its various forms and hybrids, is much grown in ornamental pools and occasionally it is planted in wild areas. Lester-Garland recorded it in the Old Reservoir, Waterworks Valley, in 1903. It is no longer there but it still survives in the South Canal, St Ouen's Pond, where it was planted about 1968, and in Dannemarche Reservoir and mudpond where it was first noted in the late 1970s by Mrs M. L. Long. Two colour forms are present at St Ouen, one with pure white flowers, the other white with the outer petals tinged pink.
G planted.

Nuphar lutea (L.) Sibth. & Sm.   **Yellow Water-lily**
Yellow Water-lily grew in La Hague Reservoir, St Peter's Valley, in the 1960s but has since disappeared. It was presumably planted.
S rare.

CERATOPHYLLACEAE
Ceratophyllum demersum L.   **Rigid Hornwort**
Recorded by Babington in 1839 but his specimens are the next species. Babington himself realised the error and altered the name of the species to *C. submersum* in his own copy of his Flora, now at Cambridge. Piquet listed it from 'Brooks in Samarès Miles' in an appendix to his 1851 *Catalogue* but did not give it in his published list of 1896, so presumably he decided it was an error.
G one record 1971.

C. submersum L.   **Soft Hornwort**
Babington's *C. demersum* from Grève d'Azette was this species as he himself realised later and as his specimens prove.
G rare.

RANUNCULACEAE
Helleborus lividus Aiton   **Corsican Hellebore**
Subsp. *corsicus* (Willd.) Tutin   Seedlings were seen flowering on a wall in 1973, McClintock.

H. viridis L.   **Green Hellebore**
One plant in a wood in St Martin in 1981, Miss F. M. Evans. The species is not native and this plant may have been a garden outcast. It was used medicinally for cattle in the past.

Nigella hispanica L.   **Spanish Love-in-a-mist**
Subsp. *hispanica*   One plant flowering and fruiting well in a gravel path near where birds had been fed at Tabor, St Brelade, in 1977, Mrs P. Attenborough.

N. damascena L.   **Love-in-a-mist**
Ariste collected a garden escape from 'La Route de St Martin' in 1926 and plants were seen on rubbish dumps, rarely, in the 1950s.

Caltha palustris L.   **Marsh-marigold**
Strangely rare in, or absent from, each of the Channel Islands. The first record in Jersey was in 1834 when La Gasca listed it as 'Culta'. On 24 October 1845, J. Atkins wrote to Babington reporting that he had seen Marsh-marigold in a marshy spot near St Catherine's Bay. Unfortunately there is no evidence as to how wild the plants were. Later Piquet introduced it in a 'Wet meadow at Trinity', from where there are specimens dated 1898 and 1899 in the Société herbarium. He also introduced it in Samarès Marsh where Lester-Garland saw it flowering in 1900. When the archaeological excavations were being carried out at Le Pinacle between 1930 and 1936 Major A. D. B. Godfray planted Marsh-marigold in Le Canal du Squez according to Père Burdo (pers. comm.). It survived for a few years, plants being found there in the late 1930s by N. Le Brocq and one plant in 1956 by Mrs G. Mackie. In 1965 J. C. Fluck reported Marsh-marigold abundant on a small area of a wet cliff/wall in the garden of a house above Ouaisné Common and it is thought that this may have been the original source of Major Godfray's Canal du Squez plants. N. Le Brocq also recorded it in the valley running down from Rosel Manor grounds to St Catherine's Bay in the late 1930s and it has been recorded from there at intervals ever since. Marsh-marigold is planted in Rosel Manor grounds near the pools, and the plants in the valley seem to be of the same large variety so they presumably come from there.
A 1966; H planted.

Aconitum napellus L.   **Monk's-hood**
'Cultum' according to La Gasca in his 1834 list. One plant was reported in a wood above Vicart Mill by J. C. Fluck in 1968.

Consolida ambigua (L.) P. W. Ball & Heywood
(Delphinium ajacis) **Larkspur**

The statement that '*D. ajacis* is not infrequent in Jersey' is in the third edition (1863–92) of Sowerby's *English Botany* and there are many specimens from last century in various herbaria. Babington (1839) originally recorded the following species, but at an unknown date he crossed it out in his own copy of his Flora and inserted; '*D. ajacis no consolida*. In many parts of Jersey on rubbish and in potato fields.'

In the 1950s, 1960s and early 1970s any load of light garden soil tipped on a dump or on disturbed ground was likely to have Larkspur growing on it the following summer. When trenches were dug between Bel Royal and Beaumont in the 1950s and 1960s and near Longueville, St Clement, Larkspur grew in quantity on the piles of earth by the trenches. Larkspur is not now grown in gardens in sufficient quantity to account for the plants as new escapes. It may be that the seeds were present in the soil from gardens in the past and germination was triggered off by the disturbance. Seeds were collected about 1965 from plants on one of the piles of soil and sown in a garden near Mont Matthieu, St Ouen. Every year since then, Larkspur has been present in fair quantity, seeding itself, even though it is almost 'weeded out' occasionally.

C. regalis S. F. Gray **Branching Larkspur**

Subsp. *regalis* (*D.consolida*) Lester-Garland (1903) mentions only this species so some confusion is suspected. All known specimens labelled '*D. consolida*' are the above species.
G, A and S 'Larkspurs' have occurred rarely.

Anemone nemorosa L. **Wood Anemone**
d's **anémônes du bouais**

Le Maistre states that the Jersey-Norman-French name *anémônes du bouais* referred to *Anemone nemorosa* grown as a garden flower. This is in line with the fact that the only specimen from the past is of a double form collected by Ereaut in 1847 and a double form occurs in Le Cimetière de l'Union at St Martin.

Records of single-flowered forms begin in the 1920s. Madame de Gruchy of Noirmont Manor told me that she had first noticed Wood Anemone, with surprise, in the grounds of the Manor in the early 1920s. She had not planted it and it was in an area of the woods which she knew well, so that it could not have been overlooked earlier. Attenborough recorded it in 1923 from St Peter's Valley but later found that it had been planted there some years previously. Miss D. C. Mauger can remember picking it in the wood in Grève de Lecq Valley in the early 1930s and Mrs L. A. Morris knew it in the wood opposite La Chaire, Rozel, at about the same time.

Wood Anemone is still in the above places and it continues to spread. All records, planted or otherwise, are on the map.

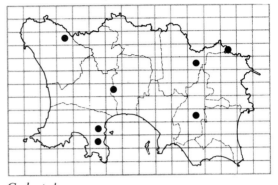

G planted.

Clematis vitalba L. **Traveller's-joy**
d'la **barbe d'vièr bouonhomme**

This is now widespread in hedges and on disturbed ground but there are few early records. In 1853 Piquet reported it from a hedge in St Aubin's Bay; in 1881 Vaniot collected a specimen and in 1896 Piquet listed it as from a hedge opposite Mont Orgueil Castle. By as late as 1903, Lester-Garland could only write that it was occasionally planted in gardens. The increase began in the 1930s according to Attenborough (pers. comm.).

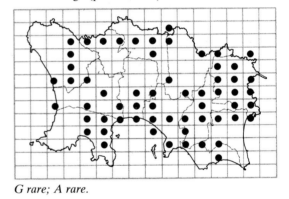

G rare; A rare.

Adonis annua L. **Pheasant's-eye**

A rare casual: 1834, La Gasca; St Helier, 1858, Piquet; La Pulente, 1929, Mrs Godfray and there is an undated specimen labelled 'Jersey, G. A. Holt' in the Manx Museum. Holt lived 1852–1921.
G last record 1923.

Ranunculus repens L.   **Creeping Buttercup**
du **pipot**

Common particularly in rather moist habitats.

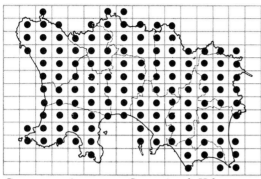

G common; A common; S occasional; H frequent.

R. acris L.   **Meadow Buttercup**
du **pipot**

Common in damp meadows.

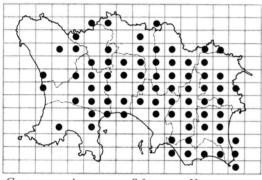

G common; A common; S frequent; H rare.

R. bulbosus L.   **Bulbous Buttercup**
du **pipot**

Subsp. *bulbosus* Locally common in short turf on light soil. In *The Cambridge British Flora* (Moss, 1920) '*R. aleae* Willk.' was claimed for Jersey. Druce and Attenborough searched in the 1920s for plants which might be this but failed to find any and A. J. Wilmott wrote in his 1922 diary '*Ranunculus aleae* – all over.' In a paper in *Watsonia* (1973) Dr S. M. Coles considered '*R. aleae* Willk.' to be an intermediate between subsp. *bulbosus* and subsp. *adscendens*. All known Bulbous Buttercups are the normal hairy bulbous plants of coastal districts and are subsp. *bulbosus*.

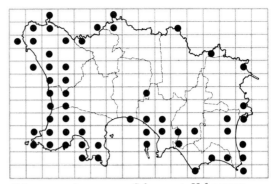

G frequent; A common; S frequent; H frequent.

R. sardous Crantz   **Hairy Buttercup**
(*R. hirsutus*)   *du* **pipot**

Occasional but still an expected plant in wet places.

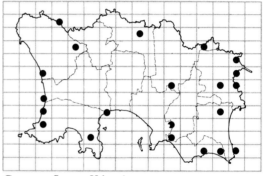

G scarce; S rare; H local.

R. arvensis L.   **Corn Buttercup**

A rare casual, probably always from poultry food as the last two records were: hen run at Les Vagues, Pontac, 1962, Mrs D. L. Le Quesne; Government House compost heap, 1968.
G last record 1929.

R. parviflorus L.   **Small-flowered Buttercup**

Small-flowered Buttercup seems always to have been rare, Lester-Garland (1903) giving no records of his own, merely stating five places where it was found by other botanists. It has gone from last century's inland sites at Mont Neron, St Peter's Marsh and Vallée des Vaux and also from Georgetown but it is established in the north-east and south-west.

Map overleaf

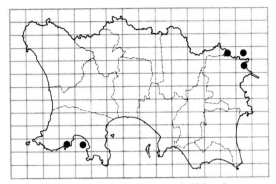

G rare; A occasional; S occasional, H local.

R. paludosus Poiret   **Jersey Buttercup**
(R. chaerophyllus)

First found by Dr M. M. Bull above St Aubin on 13 May 1872. In the *Journal of Botany* for that year (X: 175) H. Trimen, to whom it was sent for confirmation, quoted Dr Bull: 'Brébisson's "Flore de la Normandie" gives as one of its stations the cliffs of Carteret, separated from this island by not more than twenty miles of sea. This determined me to look for it here. Passing over a dry rocky slope of small extent where grows *Hypochaeris glabra* and the quinque-vulnerate form of *Silene anglica*, my attention was caught by what seemed to be the flower of *Ranunculus repens* on an upright stem. The leaves were concealed by an intervening obstacle, but when I got near I found that the foliage resembled that of *R. bulbosus*, but that the calyx was not reflexed. Pulling up the plant to look at the root, I saw at once what it must be. I gathered only the two specimens sent, but observed other plants on the same slope. They were mostly if not all single-flowered. It is not unlikely that, now attention will be directed to it, it will be found in other localities.'

The plants begin growth in winter, flower in May and have usually disappeared by about the third week in May, if not much earlier. The number of flowers varies considerably from year to year, e.g. some years there are hundreds on a côtil in Val de la Mare; other years, and this is the more usual, there are few, even none. This has led botanists who could not find the Jersey Buttercup in its well-known locality above St Aubin, to declare it extinct. Between 1872 and 1958, a few localities, other than that above St Aubin, were discovered and Piquet planted it on West Mount. Louis-Arsène knew it in at least four places in the 1920s and stated that it was not as rare as commonly believed, but he did not mention the habitat in which he had found the plants, so botanists continued to search dry banks, the habitat given in British literature.

In May 1958 it was found on a dry côtil in Val de la Mare. When Mrs J. Russell was shown it in March 1959 she commented on the unexpected wetness of the ground. This led to an appreciation that the wrong habitat was being searched, and that though sun-baked in summer, it should be soaking wet in winter. Jersey Buttercup was then found in a number of places along the south and west coasts. It was almost possible to survey a stretch of coast, looking for areas wet in winter but dry in summer, and predict, correctly, that Jersey Buttercup would be growing there.

Jersey Buttercup, one of the island's specialities, is included in the design on the face, the obverse, of the current £1 note issued by the States of Jersey in 1976.

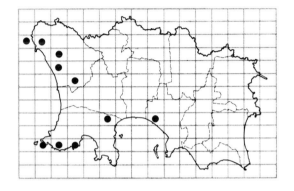

R. auricomus L.   **Goldilocks**

Saunders' record given by Babington (1839) was rejected by Lester-Garland but Piquet gathered a specimen in a meadow north of St Ouen's Pond in 1890 (Hb Oxford). Babington noted in his copy of his Flora that the Rev. W. W. Newbould had found it at St Brelade in 1841/2 but this has not been confirmed.

R. sceleratus L.   **Celery-leaved Buttercup**

Subsp. *sceleratus* Usually rare in wet places but in the last few years it has increased considerably at St Ouen.

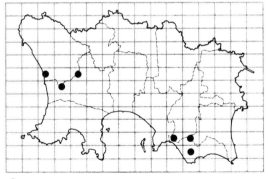

G rare.

R. ficaria L.   **Lesser Celandine**
du **morrhouiton**

Subsp. *ficaria* Abundant on many hedgebanks in spring. Lester-Garland (1903) described a large form as being 'about half-way between the English plant and the S. European var. *grandiflora*' and in 1915 Attenborough and Guiton suggested that it be compared with subsp. *ficariiformis* Rouy & Fouc. Plants from La Haule were used in *The Cambridge British Flora* (Moss, 1920) to illustrate f. *luxurians*. Dr B. M. G. Jones, an authority on *R. ficaria*, considers all specimens he has seen to be forms of subsp. *ficaria*. In recent searches, particularly in the La Haule region, it has seemed that the size of a plant varies with its habitat.

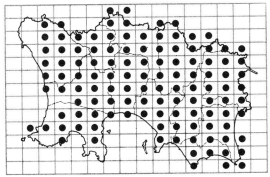

G abundant; A common; S abundant; H frequent.

R. flammula L.   **Lesser Spearwort**
des **maillettes**

Subsp. *flammula* Common in wet places.

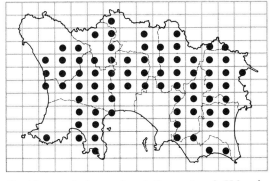

G widespread; A occasional; S occasional; H local.

R. lingua L.   **Greater Spearwort**

Babington (1839) recorded Greater Spearwort in St Peter's Marsh and in a marsh near Grève d'Azette but collected no specimens. Lester-Garland (1903) rejected both records. J. Lloyd claimed to have seen it with *R. ophioglossifolius* (*Phytologist* 1853). Piquet did not list it and the only specimen he collected is unlocalised and labelled simply, 'Marshes and

ditches. June 1900'. In the late 1930s N. Le Brocq and Dr W. J. Le Quesne claim to have found it by the side of a wild pond at Saut Faluet.
G planted; A last record 1906.

R. ophioglossifolius Vill.   **Adder's-tongue Spearwort**

Babington first noted Adder's-tongue Spearwort in St Peter's Marsh in 1838. A specimen gathered there by him before breakfast on 6 June 1838 was used to illustrate the species on Plate 2833 of Sowerby's *English Botany* Vol. III Sup. 1843 and it was stated that the species 'has only been noticed in one place namely St Peter's Marsh where it occurs in the greatest profusion'. Though Lester-Garland (1903) considered it extinct and stated that J. C. Melvill failed to find it in 1876, there is a specimen in Hb Carlisle dated 1884.

Parts of the marsh are still there and perhaps there is yet hope that it will be refound because in 1851 W. Borrer wrote to Babington, 'Dr Dickson told me *R. Ophioglossifolius* had been quite lost for some years. The Marsh too was mown – but I found 2 v. small specimens' (Ms Hb Cantab.).

R. hederaceus L.   **Ivy-leaved Crowfoot**

Ivy-leaved Crowfoot has decreased considerably since last century when it was considered frequent by Babington (1839) and Piquet (1851). Lester-Garland (1903) considered it not common. Today it is decidedly rare, only four localities being known: in wet patches by the side of the road on Mont Rossignol; in a small valley on the south side of Val de la Mare reservoir; by the pool on Ouaisné Common and in a swampy meadow in the south of St John.
G, A, S and H rare.

R. tripartitus DC.   **Three-lobed Crowfoot**

Piquet listed this in 1896 from shallow ditches but Lester-Garland (1903) rejected the record and there is no specimen.

R. baudotii Godron   **Brackish Water-crowfoot**

Vaniot collected a specimen from near St Ouen's Pond in 1881 and Lester-Garland (1903), whose specimen from a quarry pool at Portelet was confirmed by A. Bennett, considered it rare. It has not been found recently, but see the following hybrid *R. x segretii*.
G rare; S rare.

R. x segretii A. Félix   **Hybrid Water-crowfoot**
R. baudotii x **R. trichophyllus**

Specimens of water crowfoot sent to Professor C. D. Cook from a small pool north-east of St Ouen's Pond in 1956, from a sandpit pool north of Le Chemin de l'Ouzière, St Ouen in 1957 and from the pool on Ouaisné Common in 1958 were determined by him as

the hybrid *R. baudotii* x *R. trichophyllus*. This hybrid is sterile, and annual, so unless seeds were brought in on, say, the feet of wading birds, both parents must have been present in Jersey though neither has been recorded for some time.
G 1958.

R. peltatus Schrank Large-flowered Water-crowfoot
Not recorded recently but perhaps overlooked as there are several records from the past: St Peter's Marsh, 1854, Piquet (Hb Oxford); Waterworks Valley and La Moye Marsh, Lester-Garland (1903) confirmed A. Bennett; three localities, 1914 (*Cambridge British Flora* 1920); Ouaisné Common Marsh, 1925, Ariste; Waterworks Valley, 1933, A. J. Wilmott.
G local; S ?1874.

R. aquatilis L. Common Water-crowfoot
A specimen labelled '*R. heterophyllus*' was collected by Babington in St Peter's Marsh on 6 July 1838 (Hb Cantab.).
G local.

R. trichophyllus Chaix
(R. Drouetii) Thread-leaved Water-crowfoot
Vaniot collected a specimen from Samarès Marsh in 1882; Piquet listed it as common in running streams in 1896; Lester-Garland considered it local in 1903 giving localities at Samarès and St Ouen, and Ariste collected it in 1925 at Samarès. Though there is no recent record see the hybrid *R.* x *segretii*.
G local; A rare; S unconfirmed; H rare.

Myosurus minimus L. Mousetail
Saunders' record (Babington, 1839) of Mousetail 'In fields at St Saviour' was rejected by Lester-Garland (1903) and there has been no confirmation.
G 1957.

Aquilegia vulgaris L. Columbine
des **vièrs garçons**
Columbine occasionally occurs as a garden escape but it does not persist more than a year or two.
G garden escape; S 1953; H 1957.

BERBERIDACEAE
Berberis vulgaris L. Barberry
*d'l'*êpinne-vinnette
Barberry was listed for Jersey by La Gasca in 1834 without being labelled '*Culta*'. Babington (1839) published Saunders' comment that it was naturalised in Jersey. Piquet listed it in 1851 stating that he had been shown a specimen gathered by Ereaut in a wood near St Ouen's Manor and there is a later entry, 'I have since found it growing in a valley at Rozel'. An undated specimen of Piquet's in Hb Oxford is labelled 'St Martin'. In his 1896 list Piquet stated it was 'In woods occasionally but probably planted'. Lester-Garland (1903) banished the records to his *Ambiguities and Errors* stating, 'I have never seen it, not even in a garden'. Whatever its status last century, it has not been recorded wild this century.
G last century, planted.

B. darwinii Hooker Darwin's Barberry
Planted in a hedge in Mourier Valley.
G 1969.

LAURACEAE
Laurus nobilis L. Bay Tree
Commonly placed near houses because of the use of its leaves in cookery. It sets abundant seed and seedlings are frequent. Ereaut has a specimen dated 1847.
G rare.

PAPAVERACEAE
Papaver somniferum L. Opium Poppy
Subsp. *somniferum* Opium Poppy has been here since at least 1834 when it was listed by La Gasca. It fluctuates in quantity from year to year depending to a certain extent on the amount of available habitat, usually disturbed ground. Sometimes it is abundant over small areas. Seeds may come from gardens, if the plant is fashionable, or from bird seed. Copious seed is set but it does not necessarily germinate the following year and seems able to lie dormant for some time, though this has not been fully investigated.
Subsp. *setigerum* (DC.) Corb. was collected by Druce in 1906 from Millbrook.

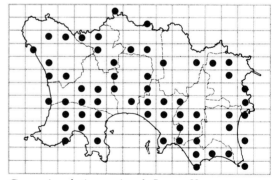

G occasional; A occasional; S rare; H rare.

P. rhoeas L. Common or Round-headed Poppy
des **roses à tchian**
Piquet described Round-headed Poppy as common both in cornfields (1851) and in waste places round the coast (1901, on a specimen sheet in his herbarium). Cornfields are no longer as common as

they were, and seed is cleaner, but Round-headed Poppy still occurs frequently on disturbed ground, and it is sometimes abundant over small areas. As with Opium Poppy, there is evidence that seed can remain dormant for some time.

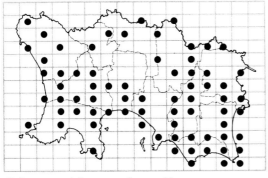

G frequent; A frequent; S rare; H rare.

P. dubium L.   **Long-headed Poppy**
des **roses à tchian**

Still frequent in sandy soil, as reported by Piquet last century.

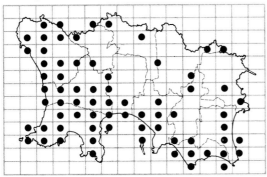

G scarce; A frequent; S last record 1907; H rare.

P. lecoqii Lamotte   **Yellow-juiced Poppy**
A note in W. Hillhouse's copy of Babington's Flora states, 'Sept. 1879. *Papaver lamotii* Quenvais – S of Quenvais, (1 fine specimen only)'. There is no confirmation of this and no other record.
G ?1859.

P. argemone L.   **Prickly Poppy**
La Gasca listed Prickly Poppy in 1834 and it has been reported, at intervals, ever since. Records since the Occupation are: a few plants north of St Ouen's Pond in 1956; in the field making the corner of Le Chemin du Moulin and Mont Matthieu in 1958; near Green Island in 1962, Miss P. Donaldson, and many plants in a flower-bed near the Bowling Club on West Mount in 1962, Miss P. Donaldson.
G ?

P. hybridum L.   **Rough Poppy**
Rare in the past and not seen recently. La Gasca listed it, without locality, in 1834. Both Babington (1839) and Piquet (1896) stated that it was near St Peter's Barracks, and Piquet has a specimen from there in 1871. He has another from La Rocque in 1904. Attenborough (1940) stated in *The Calcareous Flora of Jersey* that Rough Poppy was not uncommon in cornfields. I am unable to account for this as the only record since 1904 seems to be D. McClintock's in the late 1950s, on which the 'dot' in the *Atlas of the British Flora* (1962) is based.
G last record 1894; A occasional.

P. orientale L.   **Oriental Poppy**
In 1978 a patch, a few metres long, was found on the edge of an old consolidated rubbish dump in the north of St Ouen's Bay. The clump was still there in 1982, flourishing in competition with the natural vegetation of the area.

Meconopsis cambrica (L.) Vig.   **Welsh Poppy**
Welsh Poppy is not native but it has twice been reported from wild parts of gardens at Samarès and Rozel where it was spreading quickly and unaided.
G as in Jersey.

Roemeria hybrida (L.) DC.   **Violet Horned-poppy**
Recorded in error in the Société's Botanical Report for 1977.
A 1956.

Glaucium flavum Crantz   **Yellow Horned-poppy**
des **jaunes pavots**
Still on the sands of the seashore as recorded by Babington (1839) but decreasing because of the pressure of holidaymakers who enjoy the same habitat. It still exists in good quantity at La Rosière, near La Corbière. An illustration by Pandora Sellars is opposite page 38.

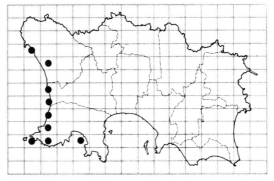

G local; A frequent; H rare.

G. corniculatum (L.) J. H. Rudolph

Scarlet Horned-poppy

Piquet collected a specimen from Mr Dancaster's farm, St Ouen's Bay in 1907 (Hb Oxford) and plants grown from Jersey seed were used to illustrate *The Cambridge British Flora* (Moss, 1920). One plant grew in a garden at La Rocque in 1965, probably from bird seed, B. Harrison.
G 1936–41; A 1903.

Chelidonium majus L.

Greater Celandine
*d'l'***hèrbe à véthues**

Occasional on old walls, but widespread. The Jersey-Norman-French name means 'herb for warts'. Several species which discharge coloured juice from a a cut stem are given this name because the juice is supposed to cure warts over which it is spread. The juice of the Greater Celandine is bright orange.

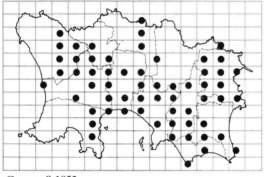

G rare; S 1852.

Eschscholtzia californica Cham.　**Californian Poppy**

Ereaut collected a specimen for his *Hortus Siccus* in 1847 but its origin is unknown; C. Bailey reported seeing it in St Brelade's Bay in 1868 and J. C. Melvill who collected a specimen from La Haule in 1879 considered it naturalised. It has been a garden weed at Millbrook since the mid 1970s, Mrs M. L. Long, and it occasionally persists for a year or two along roadsides or on rubbish dumps as a garden escape.
G casual; A occasional; H 1958.

Corydalis claviculata (L.) DC.　**Climbing Corydalis**

Subsp. *claviculata* Collected by Guiton from La Crête Point in 1900 and by Ariste from the valley running down to St Catherine's from Rosel Manor in 1926. It is still in both places, spread over a wide area.

C. lutea (L.) DC.　**Yellow Corydalis**

Yellow Corydalis was not certainly recorded until 1927 when Ariste found it on a wall at St Martin. Though widespread, it is still scarce.

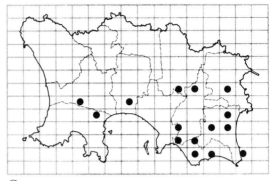

G rare.

Fumaria species

Early records of fumitories are exceedingly confused and few specimens are available for checking. The following account is based mainly on records this century.

F. capreolata L.　**White Ramping Fumitory**

Subsp. *babingtonii* (Pugsley) P. D. Sell　Occasional on both cultivated and disturbed land. Neither Lester-Garland nor Pugsley mention it yet it is the only fumitory, other than *F. muralis* subsp. *boraei*, to occur often enough to be mapped. Perhaps it has increased this century. Specimens are in the Société's herbarium.

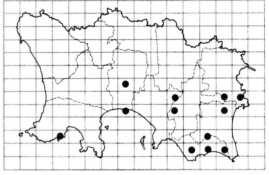

G occasional; A rare; S rare.

F. bastardii Boreau　**Tall Ramping Fumitory**

Druce claimed to have found *F. bastardii* frequently in 1906 and 1907 and H. W. Pugsley gave *F. bastardii* var. *Gussonei* Pugsley for Jersey in his paper *Fumaria in Britain* 1912. Pugsley visited Jersey in June 1914 and later that year wrote of the species in the *Journal of Botany* (LII: 328): 'About Beaumont and here and there west of St Aubin's, but much less abundant than the subsp. *boraei* and rarely seen except in cultivated ground'. The species is still rare.
G scarce; A last record 1938; S last record 1906; H 1894.

F. bastardii x **F. muralis** subsp. *boraei*

A hybrid Fumitory

G 1914.

F. martinii Clavaud   **Martin's Fumitory**

G 1914, 1928.

F. muralis Sonder ex Koch   **Ramping Fumitory**

d'la **finnetèrre**

Subsp. *muralis* Recorded with reservations by Lester-Garland (1903) and not confirmed. This taxon has probably never occurred in the British Isles.
Subsp. *boraei* (Jordan) Pugsley Much the commonest fumitory in the island and it seems to have been continuously so for more than a century at least. H. Trimen visited Jersey in 1871 and later in the *Journal of Botany* (IX: 200) wrote, 'I think the common Channel Island plant, which has large pink flowers, bears more resemblance to *F. Boraei* than to any other British variety'. In 1903 Lester-Garland considered it abundant. In 1914 Pugsley wrote that it was 'very abundant in the SW of Jersey'. It is still widespread and in places abundant.

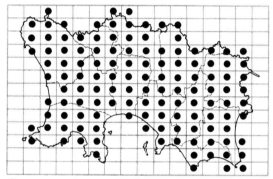

G common; A common; S common; H frequent.

F. muralis subsp. *boraei* x **F. officinalis**

A hybrid Fumitory

G 1900.

F. officinalis L.   **Common Fumitory**

Subsp. *officinalis* As in Guernsey, the name, Common Fumitory, is a misnomer in Jersey. Lester-Garland (1903) thought it frequent and apparently spreading but it has seldom been seen in the last twenty years and is now thought to be rare.
G occasional; A occasional; S 1852 and 1906; H rare.
Subsp. *wirtgenii* (Koch) Arcangeli Collected by W. Fawcett in St Helier c. 1873, det. H. W. Pugsley.

CRUCIFERAE

Sisymbrium irio L.   **London Rocket**

Saunders' record of London Rocket given by Babington (1839) was rejected by Lester-Garland (1903) and it has not been confirmed.
G one ? record.

S. altissimum L.   **Tall Rocket**

(S. pannonicum)

Lester-Garland recorded Tall Rocket at L'Étacq in 1900 and Piquet collected a specimen from St Ouen's Bay – so perhaps from the same place – also in 1900. Another specimen was collected in St Ouen's Bay in 1912 by a member of Le Collège de Bon Secours.
G one ? record.

S. orientale L.   **Eastern Rocket**

A specimen collected by Piquet in 1900 in St Ouen's Bay, and originally wrongly labelled '*Erysimum* sp.', is in Hb Oxford. The next record was not until 1956 when it was found on a rubbish dump at the head of the North Canal, St Ouen's Pond. Since then it has usually been present on disturbed sandy ground or along roadsides in Le Chemin du Moulin district of St Ouen and near Red Houses. Elsewhere it is more of a a casual.

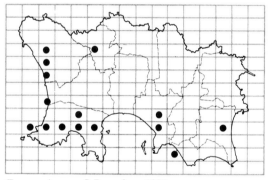

G rare; A rare; S Brecqhou 1957.

S. officinale (L.) Scop.   **Hedge Mustard**

du **pid-d'ouaîsé**

Common on roadsides, hedges and in cultivated fields. The Jersey-Norman-French name which means 'bird's foot' comes from the shape of some of the first leaves. Le Maistre said the species was well-known to country people in the past because its wiry stems blunted scythes and sickles (pers. comm.).

Map overleaf

49

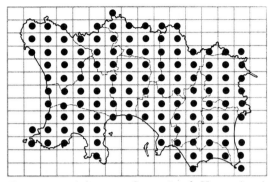

G common; A frequent; S occasional; H occasional.

Descurainia sophia (L.) Webb ex Prantl   **Flixweed**
(Sisymbrium Sophia)
Piquet who collected a specimen from St Ouen's Bay in 1898 considered that it was probably introduced with foreign seed.

Alliaria petiolata (Bieb.) Cavara & Grande
(A. officinalis)   **Garlic Mustard**
All previous botanists have described this common English species as rare in Jersey and it has only been found very occasionally in recent years. Most 'dots' on the map represent only a single locality in that area.

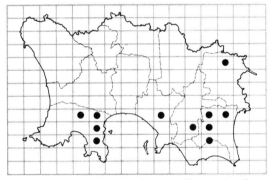

G not common; A locally frequent; S occasional.

Arabidopsis thaliana (L.) Heynh.   **Thale Cress**
(Sisymbrium Thalianum)
Common in dry places, particularly on walls.

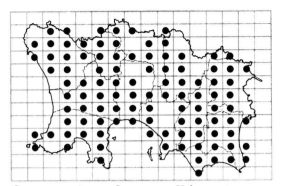

G common; A rare; S common; H frequent.

Bunias erucago L.   **Crested Bunias**
A casual; Piquet and Guiton collected specimens from West Mount in 1900.

B. orientalis L.   **Warty Cabbage**
G 1899.

Erysimum hieracifolium L.   **A Treacle Mustard**
In a list of *Additional Casuals* in his Flora, Lester-Garland (1903) gives '*E. strictum* DC?' as being found in St Ouen's Bay in 1900, but there is no *Erysimum* specimen in his herbarium at Kew.

E. cheiranthoides L.   **Treacle Mustard**
A specimen in the Société's herbarium gathered in St Ouen's Bay in August 1900 by Piquet and labelled *E. cheiranthoides* was stated by J. E. Lousley not to be this but otherwise to be indeterminate. This is presumed to be the source of P. É. F. Perrédès' note in the *Journal of Botany* for 1912 (L: 373).
G last record 1968.

Hesperis matronalis L.   **Dame's Violet**
In the 1960s a plant by a St Ouen farm entrance lasted a few years. This was probably planted but a large plant on the Archirondel side of La Crête Quarry in 1966, one in the sandpits north of St Ouen's Pond in the late 1960s and one which appeared on rough ground by Mr Bisson's vegetable garden at Les Ormes, St Peter in 1975 were not.
A 1962; S rare.

Malcolmia maritima (L.) R. Br.   **Virginian Stock**
An occasional garden escape near houses or on rubbish dumps but decreasing, probably with the vagaries of gardening fashion, and not seen recently.
G casual; A 1973; S rare.

Cheiranthus cheiri L.   **Wallflower**
d'la **violette sauvage**
Frequent on old walls. Wallflowers have survived, seeding themselves, on the walls of Mont Orgueil

Castle since at least 1841/2 when the Rev. W. W. Newbould told Babington of them. In 1862 Le Hericher could write of *les belles touffes de violiers* which grew there. Wild wallflowers, *violettes sauvages*, were given many different names in the past according to Le Maistre: *jaunes violettes* to distinguish them from the newer, differently coloured introductions; *violettes d'hivé* to distinguish them from stocks which were *violettes d'été*, and in some parts of the island *d'la ravenelle*.

Newer kinds of wallflower, as well as the long-established *violettes sauvages*, also appear on walls occasionally. They were called *violettes de gardîn* or, unaccountably, *la baume dé la résurrection*.
G occasional; A occasional; S occasional; H 1957.

Matthiola sinuata (L.) R. Br. **Sea Stock**
d'la **violette dé mielle**

The French botanist J. Gay listed this from La Plage, Havre des Pas, in 1832 and in the past it was also in St Catherine's Bay, St Aubin's Bay and St Brelade's Bay. For many years now, it has been confined to the south of St Ouen's Bay and to the sandier parts of the dunes of Les Quennevais. Its quantity varies. At times it seems to be in danger of extinction, then with a change of conditions and more open sand, it appears in quantity again, growing luxuriantly. An illustration by Pandora Sellars is opposite page 39.

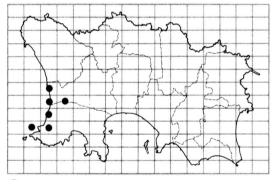

G now very rare.

M. incana (L.) R. Br. **Hoary Stock**
d'la **violette d'été**

A garden escape on the walls of St Aubin's Fort and Fort Regent and occasionally elsewhere.
G local; A locally common.

Barbarea vulgaris R. Br. **Winter-cress**
Babington (1839) and Piquet (1851) described Winter-cress as common but Lester-Garland gives only six localities for it in his Flora of 1903 and it has only been recorded four times since. It may be that this species was confused with other winter-cresses but F. Piquet's specimen from near St John's Church in 1871 was confirmed by J. E. Lousley, and Vaniot

collected a specimen from the road to Grouville in 1881.
G last record 1928; S rare.

B. stricta Andrz. **Small-flowered Winter-cress**
This is recorded for the Channel Islands in the *Flora of the British Isles* (Clapham *et al.* 1952, 1962) but there is no local knowledge of it.

B. verna (Miller) Ascherson **American Winter-cress**
Piquet described American Winter-cress as frequent in 1851 and 1853 but rare in 1896. Lester-Garland (1903) gave five localities. Since then it has only been seen rarely, the last record being from St Mary's Churchyard by Dr J. G. Dony in 1970, where it survived for several years, but was not there in 1982.
G last record 1957; A rare; S 1906.

B. intermedia Boreau
Medium-flowered Winter-cress
The first specimen was collected by Vaniot in 1881 and, though still rare by 1903, it is now widespread over the island and is the most likely winter-cress to be encountered.

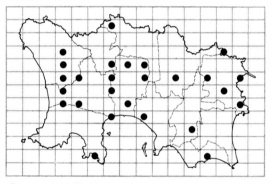

G rare; A 1963; S occasional.

Rorippa sylvestris (L.) Besser **Creeping Yellow-cress**
Subsp. *sylvestris* (*Nasturtium silvestre*) First collected by Piquet from Grands Vaux, near Town Mills Pond, in 1896 and now occasionally seen as a persistent weed, e.g. it has been in the grounds of Highlands College for more than fifty years.

Map overleaf

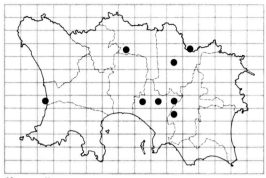

G rare; S rare.

R. palustris (L.) Besser   Marsh Yellow-cress
(Nasturtium palustre)

Specimens were collected from St Lawrence Marsh in 1854 and near Town Mills Pond in 1876 by Piquet, det. B. Jonsell (Hb Oxford). It was also recorded last century from St Peter's Marsh, Grouville Marsh and St Brelade. In 1983 R. W. S. Knightbridge found it in a wet ditch south-east of St Ouen's Pond and at the foot of Queen's Valley.
G 1981; S error.

Armoracia rusticana P. Gaertner, B. Meyer & Scherb.
(Cochlearia Armoracia)   **Horse-radish**
d'la **radiche à j'vaux**

Horse-radish often persists in corners of fields or on waste ground, as a relic of cultivation, and once established it is difficult to eradicate.

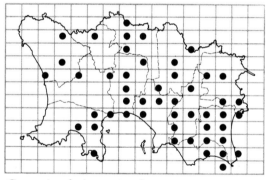

G occasional; A occasional.

Nasturtium officinale R. Br.   Water-cress
du **cresson**

Water-cress is common in wet places. *N. officinale* is probably the species mainly involved, but no map is given since most recorders have not separated this species from the next.
G frequent; A local; S locally frequent; H local.

N. microphyllum (Boenn.) Reichenb.   Water-cress

Druce recorded this water-cress in 1907; W. B. Turrill, in an address to the British Ecological Society in the 1950s, claimed to have seen it in Jersey; a specimen was collected near Val de la Mare Reservoir in 1968 and another near Mont Matthieu, St Ouen in 1982. It may well be commoner than these few records suggest because, though leaf colour gives an indication of its possible presence, a lens is needed to see the essential differences in the seed coat. The species is therefore not easily identified in the field until ripe fruits are present.
G rare.

N. x sterilis (Airy-Shaw) Oefelein
N. microphyllum x N. officinale   Hybrid Water-cress

Vaniot collected a specimen from Vallée des Vaux in 1881 and it was in quantity in a damp area by the old railway line near Pont Marquet in 1960. It remained there until recently when the area was 'tidied up'. It was probably a relic of cultivation.
G 1958; A rare; S locally frequent.

Cardamine pratensis group   Cuckooflower
du **coucou**

Common in damp meadows. Most plants are single-flowered though double-flowered clones exist in a few places, e.g. St Martin's Churchyard where they were probably planted, and Samarès Marsh, apparently wild.

Druce in 1907 stated that he '. . . only saw the var. *palustris* Peterm. in the islands'. No attempt has been made recently to separate the *C. pratensis* group into its possible members or subspecies and no chromosome numbers are known.

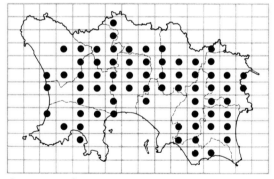

G common; S rare.

C. flexuosa With.   Wavy Bitter-cress

Wavy Bitter-cress is strangely unrecorded by the early botanists, Vaniot in 1881 being apparently the first to collect it. Lester-Garland (1903) considered it not very common in damp shady places and though now frequent in these habitats, it is seen much less often than the following species.

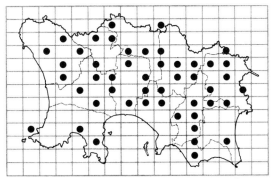

G occasional; A last record 1900; S occasional.

C. hirsuta L.   **Hairy Bitter-cress**

Common, even abundant some years, and apparently so since records began.

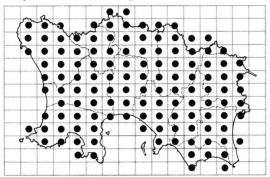

G, A, S and H common.

Arabis hirsuta (L.) Scop.   **Hairy Rock-cress**

Recorded by Druce as 'Rather plentiful on the sand-hills' of Les Quennevais in 1906/7 (*Journal of Botany* XLV: 398). He does not say it is a new island record, which he normally would do, nor did he collect a specimen. Les Quennevais had been well investigated botanically by then and it seems unlikely that other botanists would not have found a species recorded as plentiful. Could it be a slip for, say, *Hornungia petraea*, because Druce comments on the lime content of the soil?
G scarce; A locally frequent.

A. caucasica Schlecht.   **Garden Arabis**
S Brecqhou 1957.

Aubreta deltoidea (L.) DC.   **Aubretia**

Aubretia, a species from Greece and the Aegean, is much planted in rock gardens. It can seed itself and as a result it is sometimes found, though rarely, well away from gardens. While it is never fully established, it can survive for a time unaided, e.g. plants (self-sown?) on a rocky hedgebank of a field on Mont Matthieu survived for about ten years.
G rare.

Lunaria annua L.   **Honesty**

Subsp. *annua* Honesty used to be one of the expected plants on rubbish dumps, where it would persist for a few years, but with the virtual disappearance of rubbish dumps, Honesty is now a rare casual.
G casual; A 1957; S 1978.

Berteroa incana (L.) DC.   **Hoary Alison**

Piquet collected an unlocalised specimen in 1898 and Lester-Garland, who considered it a scarce casual from ballast, collected a specimen at Samarès in 1901.
G 1889 & 1899.

Lobularia maritima (L.) Desv.   **Sweet Alison**
                                      d'l'alysson

Listed by La Gasca in 1834 and by all botanists since. Though Sweet Alison is of garden origin, it was naturalised and well-established by the beginning of this century, if not before. It is particularly plentiful on walls by the sea, as along La Route de L'Étacq.

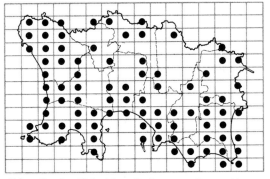

G locally plentiful; A locally frequent; S rare; H rare.

Draba muralis L.   **Wall Whitlowgrass**

A copying error in the Armorican Flora of 1971 led to this being recorded for Jersey, Guernsey and Alderney. The species intended was *Diplotaxis muralis* L.

Erophila verna (L.) Chevall.   **Whitlowgrass**
(*Draba verna*)

Whitlowgrass is frequent, sometimes locally

abundant, in short open turf round the coast, on rocky banks and on the top of low walls.

Over the years there has been considerable difficulty in assigning specimens to the various species, subspecies or varieties within the complex. As Lester-Garland stated in 1903, the plants are almost entirely short-fruited forms. He goes on to say that they are 'presumably referable to *E. praecox* DC.'. The same plants by today's nomenclature would be called *E. verna* subsp. *spathulata* (A. Lang) Walters. He also mentions a long-podded form at La Rocque. These forms occasionally occur, and the pods of some such plants at Les Hâtiveaux, Val de la Mare, St Ouen, each 6–7 mm long, contained well over forty seeds. They may be subsp. *verna*.

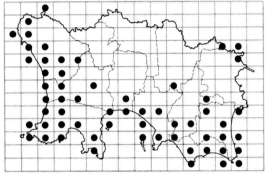

G frequent; A frequent; S 1930; H 1976.

Cochlearia danica L.   **Danish Scurvygrass**
                                          d'l'escorvie

Common and often abundant especially near the coast. Scurvygrass is one of the first plants to appear in the new year and sailors making land after a long winter voyage would eat its heart-shaped green leaves because they prevented scurvy. The Jersey-Norman-French and English names both refer to this. Like Whitlowgrass it is not a grass in the strict botanical sense. The name comes from the use of the word grass for herbage in general.

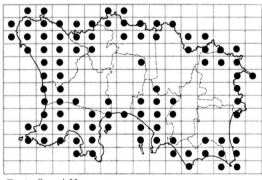

G, A, S and H common.

C. officinalis L.   **Common Scurvygrass**

No confirmed record known. La Gasca listed it in 1834, but with a query, and Babington (1839) gave only Saunders' record which has always been doubted and was probably *C. danica*.
G 1841 and ?1852; A locally frequent.

C. anglica L.   **English Scurvygrass**

No confirmed record. Babington (1839) gave only Saunders' record and, like his *C. officinalis*, it has always been doubted.
G Gosselin, 1780s.

Camelina sativa (L.) Crantz   **Gold-of-pleasure**

Piquet, 1851, gave a record of Ereaut's from St Saviour's Valley and later added in his notes that he himself had found a plant at Millbrook in 1855. A specimen in Vaniot's collection came from L'Étacq in 1891 and the last record is Piquet's var. *pilosa* collected from St Ouen's Bay in 1896.
G 1904, 1970.

Capsella bursa-pastoris (L.) Medicus

Shepherd's-purse
d'la **bourse**

Common and so highly variable that botanists have tried to split the species into smaller groupings. Druce searched Jersey for examples of Almquist's 1921 splits and specimens of *Bursa batavorum* Almq. from St Helier in 1924, *B. druceana* Almq. from Pontac in 1923 and *B. turoniensis* Almq. from La Corbière in 1923 are in the Druce herbarium at Oxford. Whether these are of any significance or not, remains to be seen.

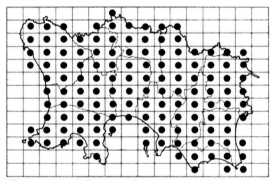

G common; A frequent; S common; H frequent.

C. rubella Reuter   **Pink Shepherd's-purse**
Meadow Bank, St Lawrence, 1979, D. McClintock.

Hornungia petraea (L.) Reichenb.   **Hutchinsia**
Hutchinsia, a plant of lime-rich habitats, was recorded on Les Quennevais by Piquet in 1851 and it is still locally plentiful there, early in spring, in open turf on the sandier parts. There are no limestone

rocks in Jersey, the lime content of Les Quennevais sand coming from mollusc shells.
G error?

Teesdalia nudicaulis (L.) R. Br.　　**Shepherd's Cress**
Common on the foothills and coastal cliffs. As the map shows, it was not found in the south-east in the recent survey and this agrees with previous records, all of which, if localised, are from the west or north.

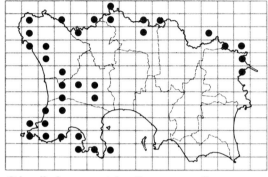

G locally frequent; A locally common; S common.

Thlaspi arvense L.　　**Field Penny-cress**
Attenborough stated in 1940 that Field Penny-cress was common in cultivated land. This is difficult to understand unless its numbers expanded rapidly and then decreased with the same speed. This is possible since the increase in Guernsey was in the 1930s.

Babington did not see it and in 1839 published Saunders' record from St Saviour. Piquet, who listed it from St Saviour in 1851, omitted it in 1896, but in 1897 he found it near St Peter's Barracks in a cultivated field. Lester-Garland (1903) thought it a rare colonist and Druce (1907) also considered it rare. Since the Occupation (1940–45) there have been few records and nowhere is it established.

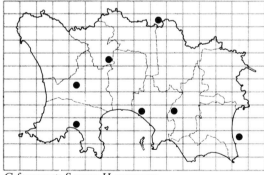

G frequent; S rare; H common.

Iberis sp.　　**Candytuft**
Piquet collected three specimens which he labelled *I. amara* L.: St Saviour 1852, but Druce thought it *I. umbellata* L. (1920); an unlocalised casual 1866,

which Lester-Garland (1903) accepted as *I. amara* and a specimen from 'sandbanks in St Aubin's Bay' 1902, which J. E. Lousley dismissed as a garden *Iberis*. This is probably true of all the specimens, no *Iberis* being native.

Lepidium campestre (L.) R. Br.
　　Common Pepperwort
G 1892.

L. heterophyllum Bentham　　**Smith's Pepperwort**
(*L. Smithii*)
Recorded as common last century and still so in dry fields, on hedgebanks, walls and roadsides.

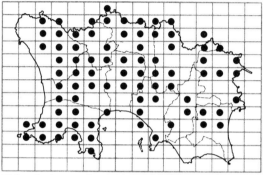

G local; A rare; S common; H 1904.

L. sativum L.　　**Garden Cress**
A rare garden escape, being the Cress of 'Mustard and Cress', but it can occur in unexpected places, perhaps from bird seed, and cause confusion.
G rare; A 1903; S rare.

L. virginicum L.　　**An American Pepperwort**
Three specimens collected about the turn of the century and originally identified as *L. ruderale* belong here: rubbish heap, Samarès, 1899, Lester-Garland (Hb Kew); St Peter's Valley, 1901, Piquet (Hb Oxford det. A. Thellung and Hb Société Jersiaise).

L. ruderale L.　　**Narrow-leaved Pepperwort**
Three specimens originally labelled this by Lester-Garland and Piquet are of the above species and the 1970 record was *L. sativum*.
G 1889–1899; A 1899; 1900; S Brecqhou 1902 (? above species).

L. perfoliatum L.　　**A Pepperwort**
One record: Dancaster's Farm, St Ouen's Bay, 1897, Piquet (Hb Oxford).

L. latifolium L.　　**Dittander**
Saunders' record of Dittander given by Babington (1839) was rejected by Lester-Garland and there has

55

been no confirmation.
G local.

Cardaria draba (L.) Desv.   **Hoary Cress**
(Lepidium Draba)

Local. Piquet collected a specimen in 1869, and by 1896 he still considered Hoary Cress rare. It tends to be along road sides and the edges of fields rather than in cultivated ground, and to persist in the same areas rather than spread widely. F. Piquet found it in Almorah Cemetery in 1871 and it is still there. Lester-Garland (1903) recorded it from several places including beside the railway line near Bel Royal where it was abundant. The railway line has gone but Hoary Cress is still along Victoria Avenue, near Bel Royal.

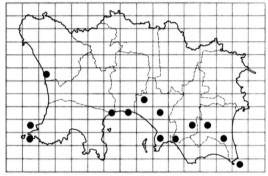

G occasional; A occasional; S 1907.

Coronopus squamatus (Forsk.) Ascherson
(C. Ruellii)
                       Swine-cress
                 d'la **cône dé chèr**

Swine-cress, a native species, was described as frequent by Babington (1839) and as common by Piquet (1851). It seems to have decreased considerably, for by 1896 Piquet could only call it rare and Lester-Garland (1903) used the vague term 'not common'. Most of the map records are from the early 1960s when it was occasionally found on roadsides and paths rather than on cultivated land. In more recent years it seems to have decreased yet further. That such an apparently insignificant plant should have a Jersey-Norman-French name suggests that it was indeed common in the past. The name was queried when the *Dictionnaire Jersiais-Français* was being compiled so Le Maistre brought a plant for confirmation.

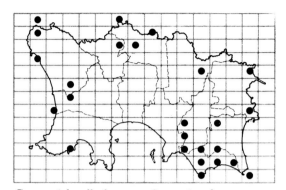

G rare; A locally frequent; S occasional.

C. didymus (L.) Sm.   **Lesser Swine-cress**
                 du **cresson à couochons**

A common weed, thought to be South American in origin, of cultivated land, roadsides and disturbed ground. When it first arrived in Jersey is unknown, but Babington (1839) reported it as frequent and the Frenchman, Le Hericher, in his book *Jersey Monumental et Historique* (1862) commented that Lesser Swine-cress *'couvre les chemins'* and *'On rencontre dans presque toute d'ile une plante plus rare encore en Normandie, la senebiere pinnatifide'*.

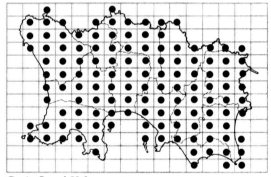

G, A, S and H frequent.

Conringia orientalis (L.) Dumort.

                     Hare's-ear Mustard

Three records: Lester-Garland (1903) cites a Piquet specimen from St Ouen's Bay; by the old railway line west of Don Bridge, 1956, Mrs J. Russell; garden weed, Petit Port, 1968, Miss P. Donaldson.

Diplotaxis tenuifolia (L.) DC.   **Perennial Wall-rocket**

Frequent in light soil round the coast and locally abundant in St Ouen's Bay.

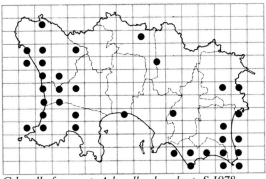

G locally frequent; A locally abundant; S 1978.

D. muralis (L.) DC. Annual Wall-rocket

Frequent on light soil. Though more widespread than
the above species, it is less likely to be encountered,
except as a garden weed. Druce recorded var.
caulescens Kittel from Bel Royal in 1907.

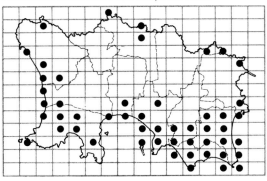

G occasional; A occasional; H Jethou.

Brassica oleracea L. Wild Cabbage

Truly wild *Brassica oleracea*, growing naturally on the
cliffs, is unknown in the Channel Islands. All records,
including one in the Société's botanical report for
1955, have been of cultivated forms, growing in the
wild. Enormous numbers of derivatives of Wild
Cabbage are grown in the island. Cabbages, cauliflowers, Brussel sprouts, greens, etc. have been
important crops for many years and can appear
temporarily on dumps. Until recently, *chour* or Long
Jack, a cabbage which can grow ten feet high or
more, was widely grown. The stem leaves were
stripped off as the plant grew and were fed to cattle;
the top was eaten by the farmer's family and the stalk,
after treatment, was sold as a 'Jersey Cabbage walking stick'. Such sticks are still made.
G, A, S and H not known wild.

B. napus L. Swede, Rape
des **suidiches**

Recorded by all botanists from La Gasca, 1834,
onwards as an escape from cultivation and it is still
found occasionally on dumps, perhaps from bird food
or because it is the 'mustard' of 'Mustard and Cress'.
Le Maistre (1966) stated that *suidiches* were not used
as a crop until the end of last century and that their
popularity lasted only until the Second World War,
since when it has decreased considerably. Rape is not
normally used as a green manure in Jersey, as it is
elsewhere.
See *Sinapis alba*, White Mustard.
G rare; A locally frequent; S rare; H 1958.

B. rapa L. Wild Turnip
des **navets**

A rare escape from cultivation both now and in the
past. Le Maistre mentions '*Des navets 'Jèrriais pouor
les bêtes*' which he says is a species of unknown origin
peculiar to Jersey. He also states that *le navet* was
grown at Noirmont in 1620.
G uncommon; A 1962; S (Brecqhou) 1957.

B. juncea (L.) Czern. Chinese Mustard

Recorded in error in the Société's botanical report
for 1979. See the following species.
G 1980.

B. nigra (L.) Koch Black Mustard
(Sinapis nigra)

Local. Babington (1839) recorded Black Mustard
from 'St Brelade, St Helier, &c.' as though he had
seen it frequently, and Piquet described it as frequent
in 1851 and common in 1896, chiefly on the coast on
sandy ground. Lester-Garland (1903) recorded it in
abundance at Gorey, where it still grows by the
Castle, and in Samarès Meadows. It was in quantity
on disturbed sandy soil at La Collette during the
initial stages of work on the new harbours etc. and
was still there, though only locally common, in 1983.
Also in 1983 several plants were on banks formed
round car parks and along track sides on Les Landes,
St Ouen, near Le Chemin des Landes.
G local; A 1969; S 1908; H 1837.

Sinapis arvensis L. Charlock
du **bréha**

The names *bréha* and Charlock seem to be used in
Jersey to cover several different yellow crucifers.
Sinapis arvensis, the species to which the name
Charlock refers in England, is only occasionally
found in Jersey and seems to have decreased
considerably since last century when it was
apparently common. Babington (1839) reported a
hairy-podded form as well as the normal glabrous.
The following *Sinapis* species is met with much more
frequently.

Map overleaf

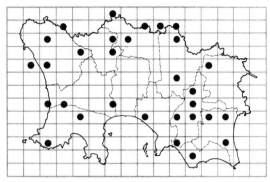

G frequent; A common; S rare; H rare.

S. alba L.   **White Mustard**
Subsp. *alba*   White Mustard is used in quantity as a green manure after early potatoes are dug and it frequently escapes. It seldom persists but its numbers are replenished each year. This *Sinapis* is much more likely to be found than Charlock.
G casual; A rare; S rare; H rare.

Eruca vesicaria (L.) Cav.   **Rocket**
Subsp. *sativa* (Miller) Thell.
A 1980.

Rhyncosinapis cheiranthos (Vill.) Dandy
(Brassica Cheiranthus)   **Wallflower Cabbage**
Subsp. *cheiranthos*   Wallflower Cabbage was first noted by J. Gay, a French botanist, on 8 August 1832 at St Helier, '*sur la Plage*'. It is still locally frequent on roadsides or disturbed sandy ground particularly in the west of the island. In some areas it is peculiarly constant, for example in Waterworks Valley it has seeded itself along a certain stretch of roadside for upwards of fifty years.

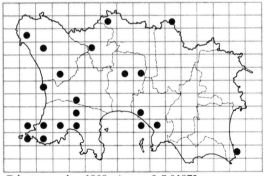

G last record c. 1909; A error? S ?1872.

Hirschfeldia incana (L.) Lagrèze-Fossat
(Erucastrum incanum)   **Hoary Mustard**
Babington (1839) recorded Hoary Mustard from Les Quennevais and Piquet (1851) recorded it from 'St Ouen's Bay, beyond the Pond'. By 1896 Piquet

considered it abundant in St Ouen's Bay and some years it is still so, particularly as he said, to the north of the Pond. Away from the west, it tends to be more of a casual.

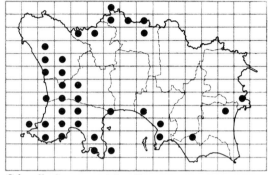

G locally frequent; A locally common.

Cakile maritima Scop.   **Sea Rocket**
                                                  d'la **julienne**
Subsp. *maritima*   Records of last century tell of Sea Rocket being common along the sands of the sea shore. It is still widespread but is now only occasionally found and seems to be decreasing except at La Rosière and in St Ouen's Bay where some years it is locally common.

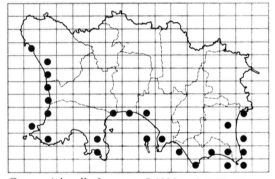

G rare; A locally frequent; S 1838 and 1879; H rare.

Rapistrum rugosum (L.) All.   **Bastard Cabbage**
Two records: rubbish tip behind La Moye School, 1957, Miss M. McC. Webster; disturbed ground between Bel Royal and St Aubin, 1958. The fruits on the specimens are different. The first is subsp. *rugosum* and the second is subsp. *orientale* (L.) Arcangeli.
G rare.

Crambe maritima L.   **Sea-kale**
                                                du **chou-mathîn**
Sea-kale was first recorded by Piquet in 1851 on shingle in St Ouen's Bay and this was its only known locality for more than fifty years. It has increased

considerably this century as the many localities on the distribution map show.

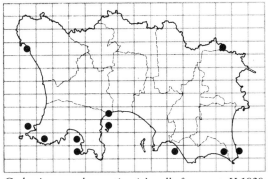

G also increased recently; A locally frequent; H 1939, 1976.

Raphanus sativus L.   **Garden Radish**

An occasional escape on rubbish dumps.
G escape; A 1962; H 1958.

R. raphanistrum L.
Subsp. *raphanistrum*   **Wild Radish**

Wild Radish was collected from near Grève de Lecq by Miss M. McC. Webster in 1957 (confirmed Dandy) and it was reported from Trinity by Dr J. G. Dony in 1970. There has been difficulty in separating this subspecies from some forms of the following so its status and distribution are unknown. This difficulty was perhaps also encountered in the past. Piquet in 1896 described it as common yet Lester-Garland, only seven years later, stated that it was very rare.
G frequent; A rare; S frequent; H 1958.

Subsp. *maritimus* (Sm.) Thell.   **Sea Radish**
                        du **bréha**

Common, sometimes abundant, round the coast and frequent along roadsides just inland from the sea. The flowers are occasionally white but the great majority is the usual yellow-flowered form which some years produces enormous sheets of yellow in St Ouen's Bay in June.

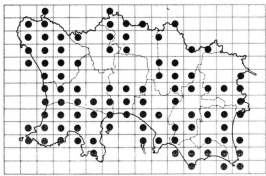

G common; A locally common; S? 1841; H frequent.

RESEDACEAE

Reseda luteola L.   **Weld**
                *d'l'***hèrbe à teindre**

Still frequent on roadsides and disturbed ground. Piquet in 1851 thought it common, principally on high ground. As the map shows, the present distribution is somewhat different.

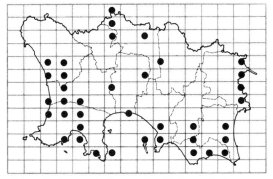

G locally frequent; A occasional; S locally frequent; H rare.

R. alba L.   **White Mignonette**

Piquet found White Mignonette on Gorey Common in 1898. Since then there have been about ten records from the sandier parts of the island but the species is nowhere established. The last plants were at La Collette in 1979 during work on the Harbour.
G five records.

R. lutea L.   **Wild Mignonette**

Wild Mignonette is usually rare, and most records, both now and in the past, are from the west of the island. Exceptionally, it has been locally abundant on at least two occasions as follows. In his 1851 list, Piquet originally noted it as rare as St Ouen but at a later date added 'Abundant on the hillsides at the northern extremity of St Ouen's Bay near the road leading to the marais'. In the mid-1950s a field along Le Chemin de l'Ouzière, St Ouen, was ploughed for the first time for many years. The following year Wild Mignonette flourished there abundantly but it disappeared as soon as the field reverted to grazing in the third year.

Map overleaf

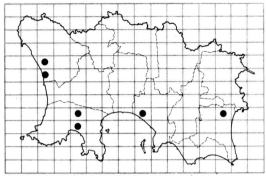

G three records; A rare; H two records.

DROSERACEAE

Drosera rotundifolia L.   **Sundew**

Sundew was recorded by Babington (1839) from a marshy spot between La Moye and Corbière. When it disappeared from there is unknown but it is still on the north coast between Bonne Nuit and Bouley Bay, from where Piquet reported it in 1851.
G ?

CRASSULACEAE

Crassula tillaea Lester-Garland   **Mossy Stonecrop**

Locally frequent on heaths and paths damp in winter. As the soil dries out in summer, the plants turn red and are sometimes in sufficient numbers to make the ground look red.

Lester-Garland is cited as the authority for the name *Crassula tillaea* because when he was engaged in writing the *Flora of Jersey* (1903) he was unable, for reasons he explains, to use the previous scientific name *Tillaea muscosa* L. He therefore made a new name, the one above, which was first used in the *Flora of Jersey* and is still in use today.

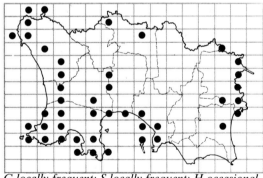

G locally frequent; S locally frequent; H occasional.

C. aff. radicans (Haw.) Dietr.   **A Crassula**

An alien *Crassula*, found growing on Les Quennevais in 1970 by a visitor G. P. B. Martin, was provisionally identified *(in litt.)* by J. E. Elsley and A. C. Leslie in 1972 as '. . . close to *Crassula radicans*', a South African species, and this provisional determination still stands. One problem is that the plant would appear to be growing in the wrong habitat because, in its South African home, it grows in woody places near the Zwartkops River. Its Quennevais site is very different, and was particularly so in the drought year of 1976. For a full account of the *Crassula*, see *B.S.B.I. News* No. 29. E. J. Clements has helped considerably with this puzzling alien which still grows in its original place.

C. helmsii (T. Kirk) Cockayne   **A Crassula**

One small plant of this Australasian waterweed was found on damp ground in the valley south of St Mary's Church in 1983 by R. W. S. Knightbridge.

Umbilicus rupestris (Salis.) Dandy
(Cotyledon Umbilicus)   **Pennywort** or **Navelwort**
                                des **cratchillons**

Common, sometimes abundant, on rocks, banks and walls in both full sun and shade.

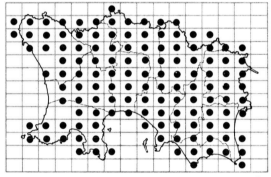

G common; A common; S common; H occasional.

Sempervivum tectorum L.   **Houseleek**
                                         d'la **jombarbe**

Babington (1839) recorded Houseleek as naturalised on walls and house tops. Piquet repeated this in 1851 but by 1896 considered it rare. Lester-Garland (1903) said he had not seen it and there is no record this century other than in the *Dictionnaire Jersiais-Français* (1976) where Le Maistre states that in his youth he sometimes used to see it on the roofs of old houses. There is a long tradition that the plant wards off thunderbolts and to grow it on a roof would seem a very necessary precaution for superstitious householders in the days of thatch. It may be that as thatch disappeared as a roofing material in Jersey, *jombarbe*, a corruption of *joubarbe*, Jove's beard, and not of *jaune barbe*, yellow beard, was considered unnecessary.
G as in Jersey.

Sedum praealtum A. DC.   **Greater Stonecrop**

In 1920 Druce found a patch of a large Mexican

yellow-green stonecrop, a garden escape, on the rock face of the quarry behind St Catherine's breakwater. The amount then is unknown but Burdo (pers. comm.) said it was just as large a patch in 1924 as it was in the late 1950s. It must therefore have been on the rock, unrecorded, for some considerable time. When in flower the large area of brilliant yellow, high on the cliffs, was visible from miles out to sea until a rock fall in 1963, probably caused by the previous winter's hard frost, removed it from its high position. The plant still grows in quantity on the lower rocks of the quarry face and smaller pieces are on the rocks nearby. The species was originally named *S. arboreum* and later, in error, *S. dendroideum*, before finally being named *S. praealtum* A. DC., Greater Stonecrop. More recently, it has occasionally been planted on banks outside houses.
G occasional.

S. confusum Hemsley   **A Stonecrop**
G 1980 (a garden plant from Mexico).

S. telephium L.   **A Stonecrop**
A 1900.

S. stoloniferum S. G. Gmel.
       Slender Caucasian Stonecrop
Specimens, collected near a house in Grève de Lecq Valley in 1924 by Ariste and Louis-Arsène, were originally labelled *S. telephium* but were determined as *S. stoloniferum* by J. E. Lousley and D. McClintock.
G 1968; A 1963.

S. spurium Bieb.   **Caucasian Stonecrop**
Caucasian Stonecrop is sometimes planted out on walls or banks well away from houses and persists for a few years. It has also been seen on rubbish dumps.
G rare; A 1963.

S. ochroleucum Chaix   **A Stonecrop**
Subsp. *ochroleucum (S. anopetalum)* The editor, Boswell-Syme, included this in the third edition of Sowerby's *English Botany* (1863–92) because of a specimen said to have been sent by W. Borrer to H. C. Watson from Jersey about 1850. But Boswell-Syme goes on to say that there may have been a confusion of localities, in which case the record cannot be accepted.

S. reflexum L.   **Reflexed Stonecrop**
La Gasca included Reflexed Stonecrop in his list dated 1834 and it has been seen occasionally, out of a garden, ever since. Mrs E. M. Towers states that it is still on the rocks by the side of Mont Cochon where Lester-Garland reported it looking native in 1903.
G rare.

S. forsteranum Sm.   **Rock Stonecrop**
Babington considered Rock Stonecrop to be naturalised on the walls at Grouville (1839) and Piquet who collected a specimen from St Helier in 1851 listed it as 'On the wall Pier Road, opposite the Military Hospital'.
G one record.

S. acre L.   **Biting Stonecrop**
       du **jaune pain à crapauds**
Common on walls and dry places but most plentiful on sandy soil near the sea. This species and English Stonecrop share a number of Jersey-Norman-French names including *pèrche-pierre, corînthe à poules, hèrbe ès tuilles.*

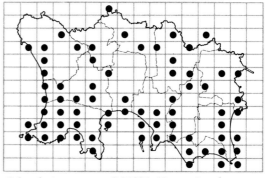

G local; A common; S ?1897; H occasional.

S. album L.   **White Stonecrop**
An undated specimen of Piquet's in the Société's herbarium has 'Rare' written against it, and Lester-Garland, who in 1903 was the first to record White Stonecrop, mentioned it only from Grand Val and Le Hocq. An alien, it is now thoroughly naturalised and is widespread on banks, walls and uncultivated land.

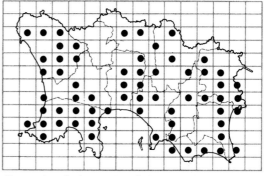

G occasional; A occasional; S rare; H local.

S. anglicum Hudson   **English Stonecrop**
       du **pain à crapauds**
Subsp. *anglicum* Common on dry banks and hill-sides. Some years it is so abundant that it carpets

huge areas with pale pink. See Biting Stonecrop for its other Jersey-Norman-French names.

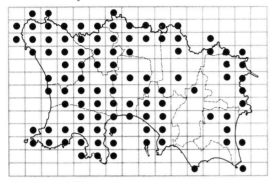

G, A, S and H common.

SAXIFRAGACEAE

Saxifraga x urbium D. A. Webb   **London Pride**
S. spathularis x **S. umbrosa**

La Gasca recorded *S. umbrosa* as 'Colitur' in his 1834 list. It is thought he intended only one of the *S. umbrosa* group, of which London Pride *S. x urbium* is a member. Ereaut collected a specimen in 1847 and Mrs M. L. Long found it on a dump at St Ouen in 1969.
A 1963.

S. tridactylites L.   **Three-fingered Saxifrage**

Common, sometimes abundant, in open turf on sandy ground and frequent on wall tops.

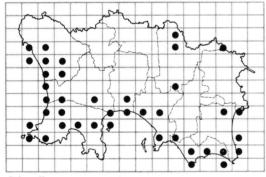

G locally common; A frequent; H frequent.

S. granulata L.   **Meadow Saxifrage**

In May 1955 Meadow Saxifrage was found growing on a hedgebank and in a field near La Hougue Bie. It was reported later in Trinity Churchyard by Miss E. H. du Feu, in Almorah Cemetery in 1962 by Miss P. Donaldson, in Mont à l'Abbé Cemetery in 1963 by Mrs E. M. Towers and in St Mary's Churchyard in 1969 by Miss Luce who said it had been there for many years. All these plants were double-flowered which suggests that they were of garden origin,

though all were growing completely wild. In 1981 B. Brée found one flowering plant, which was single-flowered, on the Grouville golf course, where it did not survive.

Bergenia sp.   **Bergenia**

A Bergenia of garden origin was reported to be growing by the stream through Egypt Valley in 1969 by Mrs N. Stuart-Williams and it was still there in 1982.
G two records.

Chrysoplenium alternifolium L.
     Alternate-leaved Golden-saxifrage

La Gasca listed this in 1834 and Babington gave Saunders' record in 1839. Lester-Garland (1903) rejected both and there has been no confirmed record. They are assumed to be errors for the following species.

C. oppositifolium L.
     Opposite-leaved Golden-saxifrage

Opposite-leaved Golden-saxifrage occurs plentifully in its right habitat, damp shady places by shallow streams along the inland valleys and on the cliffs.

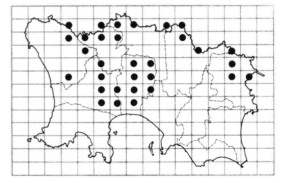

G very local.

HYDRANGEACEAE

Hydrangea macrophylla (Thunb.) Ser.   **Hydrangea**

Subsp. *macrophylla* Hydrangeas are obviously all planted in Jersey but they tend to be left, and then to persist, when a building is demolished and the rest of the garden destroyed. For example for many years there were Hydrangeas growing in competition with native vegetation by the side of one of the airport approach roads in St Peter. Hydrangeas were much planted in the past in gardens and they flourished exceedingly in Jersey's climate, Samuel Curtis mentioning one at Rozel with 2,700 blooms (*Phytologist*, 1853, IV: 1091). Though still planted they seem to have gone slightly out of fashion.
G, A, S and H similarly planted.

ESCALLONIACEAE

Escallonia macrantha Hooker & Arnott   **Escallonia**

Escallonia has been used as a hedging plant in gardens for many years but is still only rarely seen as a windbreak elsewhere.

G planted and seedlings seen; A planted; S planted; H planted.

GROSSULARIACEAE

Ribes sanguineum Pursh   **Flowering Currant**

Flowering Currant, an introduction from North America, is used rarely as a field hedge as at the north end of Val de la Mare, St Ouen.

G rare.

R. rubrum L. and **R. nigrum** L.
      Red Currant and **Black Currant**
      des **gradiles**

Both Red Currant and Black Currant occur in a few inland copses, usually remote and well away from habitation, and are probably from bird-sown seeds. Unfortunately a record was not always kept of the species involved so the map is an aggregate one. Both were on La Gasca's 1834 list.

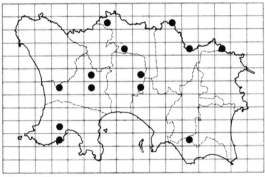

G rare; S rare.

R. uva-crispa L.   **Gooseberry**
      des **grouaîsiles**

Gooseberry is a rare garden escape, presumably bird-sown. La Gasca listed it in 1834 and F. Piquet collected a specimen from Swiss Valley in 1869. This century the only record is from a wooded thicket on Les Quennevais where D. Attenborough found it in 1946 and where it was still present in the late 1950s.

G, A, S and H rare.

PITTOSPORACEAE

Pittosporum crassifolium Putterlick   **Karo**

A seedling was found growing through a crack in the tarmacadam by the side of the road up Mont Cochon in 1970 by Mrs E. M. Towers. It was presumably bird-sown. Though a field hedge of Karo has recently been planted in St Lawrence, there is no Karo 'presence' in the Channel Islands as there is in the Isles of Scilly where it is commonly planted as a windbreak and where it has recently begun seeding itself in cracks in the granite and among boulders.

PLATANACEAE

Platanus x acerifolia (Aiton) Willd.   **London Plane**

London Plane, thought to be a hybrid between Oriental Plane and Western Plane, is occasionally planted, as in St Helier Churchyard, and there is an old tree of unknown origin in a long-established hedge in Waterworks Valley.

ROSACEAE

Spiraea latifolia (Aiton) Borkh.   **Spiraea**

Growing freely in 1982 and 1983 on the site of the old Bouley Bay Hotel, La Rue de la Petite Falaise, Trinity, det. Dr A. C. Leslie. It was probably in the garden before the hotel was demolished in the 1950s.

In the past botanists in Jersey lumped spiraeas together under the broad covering name of *S. salicifolia*. La Gasca (1834) listed it as 'Culta' and how wild Ereaut's 1847 or Piquet's 1898 plants were is unknown. During the survey 1960–70 'Spiraea' was recorded four times as a garden relic or outcast.

Filipendula vulgaris Moench   **Dropwort**

La Gasca listed Dropwort as 'Culta' in 1834; Ereaut has an unlocalised specimen dated 1847 and Ariste and Louis-Arsène both collected specimens from St John's Cemetery on 2 September 1924.

A rare.

F. ulmaria (L.) Maxim.   **Meadowsweet**
(Spiraea Ulmaria)

Still in a field by the stream in Vallée des Vaux from where it was first recorded by Piquet in 1898. Earlier La Gasca had written 'Culta' against it in his 1834 list and Babington (1839) had given Saunders' record from St Saviour's Valley.

G last record 1928.

Rubus idaeus L.   **Raspberry**

Raspberry is not native but is much cultivated, so bird-sown seedlings of garden origin occur, usually single plants. The only area where it is established is near Millbrook Reservoir, Waterworks Valley, Mrs M. L. Long.

G as Jersey; A last record 1900.

R. loganobaccus L. H. Bailey   **Loganberry**

One bush grew on a rubbish dump at St Ouen for about ten years after first being noticed in the mid-1950s.

G rare.

R. fruticosus L. agg. **Bramble; Blackberry**
eune **ronche;** *des* **mouaithes**

Brambles (*Rubus* species of the subgenus *Rubus*) are exceedingly difficult to name. A botanical textbook should be consulted for a detailed explanation of the problems but, briefly, most brambles set seed without fertilisation, so their minor strains reproduce themselves exactly. New strains arise as a result of rare, successful crosses and these in turn reproduce themselves indefinitely. The result is that within the broad covering name of *Rubus fruticosus* L. there are about 2,000 species in Europe differing only slightly, but permanently, from one another – and the number is increasing. A specialist is needed to name all but a very few.

Jersey's brambles were first investigated by the Rev. W. M. Rogers in 1897. His findings, which were published in the *Journal of Botany* for 1898, were used by Lester-Garland in his *Flora of Jersey* in 1903. Since then there has been a great increase in the knowledge of brambles and this has resulted in many changes in nomenclature. D. E. Allen, who has recently begun a study of Jersey brambles, points out that they are probably more like those of Normandy and Brittany than England and a detailed knowledge of the bramble flora of those regions will be necessary before Jersey's bramble flora can be fully elucidated.

Recent records are given first under each species in the list below followed by older records which are presumed to belong to that species, together with the name under which they were first recorded for Jersey. Any species recorded in the past, but not seen recently, is square-bracketed and, if there has been a name change, the new name is used where there is no ambiguity, though the old name is also given. In some old records, where the name is ambiguous, that name has had to be retained until further information is obtained.

This is an interim list only, based on the work of D. E. Allen, who has many more bramble specimens awaiting identification. Allen has also given guidance with the difficult nomenclature and provided the notes on some of the species.

Rubus briggsianus (Rogers) Wats. (*R. affinis* Weihe & Nees var. *briggsianus* Rogers) In one spot near the Waterworks Valley, 1897, Rogers; Corbière, 1906, Druce det. Rogers. The specimens collected in Guernsey by Rogers are correctly named, so these records may safely be accepted.

R. sublustris Lees agg. A form with broader petals than the true type, Mont Rossignol side of Val de la Mare Reservoir, 1978, Allen. (*R. corylifolius* var. *sublustris* (Lees) Rogers) Bouley Bay, 1897, Rogers.

R. conjungens (Bab.) Wats. (*R. corylifolius* var. *cyclophyllus* Lindeb.) Bouley Bay, 1897, Rogers. Allen confirms that the specimen in Hb Rogers appears correctly named.

R. balfourianus Bloxam ex Bab. Head of the Vallée des Vaux, 1897, Rogers. Allen has traced the specimen in the British Museum (Hb Rogers) and confirms its correctness.

R. dumetorum Weihe & Nees agg., including a form corresponding to No. 49 of Rogers' 'Set of British Rubi'. A colony on a brackeny area inland from L'Âne, 1978, Allen. Generally distributed, 1897, Rogers. [Var. *tuberculatus* Bab. Between Les Marais Station and Fauvic, 1897, Rogers. Allen comments that this name could apply to a fair number of the *Triviales* Section.]

R. questieri Muell. & Lefèv. Abundant along wood margins and among gorse scrub on hillsides in the Vallée des Vaux, 1978, Allen. Vallée des Vaux, 1897, Rogers – and originally found there by A. Ley in the 1880s.

R. laciniatus Willd. Garden relic on Mont du Vallet, L'Étacq, where it was in good quantity when found in the 1950s but almost perished in the drought of 1976; self-sown plants at Le Val House, Le Ouaisné, 1979, Sir Colin Anderson.

[**R. lindleianus** Lees In several places, 1906, Druce.]

[**R. macrophyllus** Weihe & Nees Deep lane, Bouley Bay, 1897, Rogers. Allen suggests that this may be *R. boulayi* Sudre, a widespread N. French species.]

[**'R. villicaulis'** sensu Wats, non Koehl. ex Weihe & Nees Claimed by Watson (1958) on unknown evidence.]

[**R. riddelsdellii** Rilst. Allen believes the 'very handsome plant' found in good quantity in Waterworks Valley by Rogers in 1897 to be this species but this awaits confirmation. It is represented by a specimen in the British Museum (Hb Barton and Riddelsdell 8044).]

R. polyanthemus Lindeb. Brackeny area inland of L'Âne, 1978, Allen. (*R. pulcherrimus* Neum.) Trinity Hill and Waterworks Valley, 1897, Rogers.

[**R. rubritinctus** W. C. R. Wats. Claimed by Watson (1958) on unknown evidence.]

[**R. rhombifolius** Weihe ex Boenn. (*R. incurvatus* Bab.) St Aubin's Bay, 1897, Rogers. Allen comments that it is clear from Rogers' remarks that his St Aubin's Bay plant was the distinct entity later separated as var. *subcarpinifolius* Rogers & Riddelsd. and not the true *R. incurvatus*.]

R. prolongatus Boulay & Letendre One bush, bottom of St Peter's Valley near Tesson Mill, 1978, Allen.

R. cardiophyllus Muell. & Lefèv. A patch of the normal form at La Ville des Quennevais and one clump on roadside in St Peter's Valley, 1978, Allen. (*R. rhamnifolius* Weihe & Nees) Small-leaved forms at Rozel and Pont Marquet, 1897, Rogers; Portelet and St Aubin's, 1906, Druce det. Rogers.

R. dumnoniensis Bab. Jardin d'Olivet in quantity, 1978, Allen conf. Newton. Said by Rogers to be one of the most frequent brambles in 1897 and his specimen from Waterworks Valley ('abundant') was confirmed by Miles.

[**R. altiarcuatus** Barton & Riddelsd. Fliquet Bay, Druce det. Watson (B.E.C. *Report* for 1930), but Allen comments that many of these early determinations of Watson's later proved unsustainable.]

R. ulmifolius Schott. Abundant, 1978, Allen. (*R. rusticanus* Merc.) Very common, 1897, Rogers.

'R. argentatus' sensu Rogers Abundant, Vallée des Vaux; Jardin d'Olivet, 1978, Allen. Locally abundant, 1897, Rogers; Plémont, Druce.

R. procerus P. J. Muell. La Ville des Quennevais and St Peter's Valley, just north of Victoria Hotel, 1978, Allen. A garden escape.

R. sprengelii Weihe Jardin d'Olivet, in plenty, 1978, Allen. Anneport (confirmed Miles) and Bouley Bay, 1897, Rogers; St Helier, 1906, Druce.

R. adscitus Genev. St Peter's Valley in National Trust woodland and a patch beside stream just north of Victoria Hotel, 1978, Allen conf. Newton. (*R. micans* Gren. & Godr.) Gorey and Anneport, 1897, Rogers; Grosnez, Druce det. Watson (B.E.C. *Report* for 1931).

[**R. leucostachys** Schleich. Abundant 'but usually untypical', 1897, Rogers. Var. *angustifolius* Rogers Pont Marquet, Anne Port, Rozel, 1897, Rogers; Gorey, 1906, Druce det. Rogers. Allen considers all these records doubtful.]

R. boraeanus Genev. Generally distributed and particularly common in Les Quennevais district, including on fixed dunes, and abundant on the Mont Rossignol side of Val de la Mare Reservoir, 1978, Allen. General, 1897, Rogers; Bouley Bay and Grosnez, 1906, Druce det. Rogers.

R. dentatifolius (Briggs) Wats. Patch halfway down valley leading to Bouley Bay and one clump in Jardin d'Olivet, 1978, Allen. (*R. borreri* Bell Salt.) Bouley Bay, 1897, Rogers.

[**R. radula** Weihe ex Boenn. A weak form at Fauvic and nearby Les Marais, 1897, Rogers. This doubtful record was not given by Rogers until 1920 in the *Journal of Botany*.]

[**R. adenanthus** Boul. & Gill. Gorey Bay, in some quantity, 1897, Rogers but Miles was unable to name the specimen in the British Museum herbarium.]

R. echinatus Lindl. One bush on brackeny area inland of L'Âne, 1978, Allen, conf. Newton.

R. bloxamii Lees Colony on edge of fragment of oakwood north of the Harvest Barn Inn, Vallée des Vaux, 1978, Allen det. Newton.

R. leightonii Lees ex Leighton Abundant among gorse at Grosnez; Rue du Manoir, St Ouen; plentiful inland of L'Âne; Jardin d'Olivet; above Mourier Valley; the Mont Rossignol side of Val de la Mare Reservoir; two places in St Peter's Valley; edge of oakwood, top of Vallée des Vaux, 1978, Allen. (*R. radula* var. *anglicanus* Rogers) In good quantity, 1897, Rogers; Grosnez, 1906, Druce det. Rogers.

[**R. furvicolor** Focke St Ouen, 1923, Druce det. Watson (B.E.C. *Report* 1930). Allen comments that, as this is a North England endemic, it is most unlikely.]
About thirty species have been recorded in R. fruticosus *agg. in Guernsey and smaller numbers in Alderney, Sark and Herm.*

R. caesius L.   **Dewberry**
Les Marais and La Corbière, 1897, Rogers, but confirmation is required.
G occurs? A occurs?

Rosa species   **Garden Roses**
Garden species occur occasionally, growing in competition with the natural vegetation. No serious attempt has been made to name them. Some are the result of deliberate planting, as are the red roses near the desalination plant at La Rosière and the pink roses spilling over the cliffs near a car park at Bonne Nuit. More often they are relics from gardens which have disappeared. For example, in the north-west, a small double-flowered beautifully scented white rose

grows by the stones of a demolished building on Le Mont du Vallet; a rose, which never seems to flower, is in the remnants of a very old hedge on the cliffs of Le Mont ès Ânes, overlooking Le Pulec, and American Pillar grows on the top of a disused quarry at L'Étacq and hangs down over the quarry face. In 1945 some of the German bunkers on the Noirmont headland and at La Moye were found to have Dorothy Perkins and American Pillar roses growing round the entrances and sprawling over the nearby rocks. Some were still there until at least 1981.
*G occasional; A rare; H rare (*R. multiflora *x* rubiginosa).

R. pimpinellifolia L.   Burnet Rose
d'la **rose à sablion**

H. D. Inglis (1834) wrote that the shores of St Brelade's Bay were everywhere covered with a small ground rose, of the finest colour, and emitting all the fragrance of the *rose-d'amour*. This is presumably the Burnet Rose which Lester-Garland (1903) stated was locally abundant and filled the whole air with fragrance on hot days. Though Burnet Rose is no longer in St Brelade's Bay in quantity, it is still abundant elsewhere, as on Les Quennevais.

In 1978 var. *pimpinellifolia* with smooth pedicels and var. *hispidula* Rouy with hispid pedicels were determined from Les Quennevais by Dr R. Melville who commented that most of the latter were of the form *hispidissima* Rouy with pedicels densely hairy and a very dense armature on the stem.

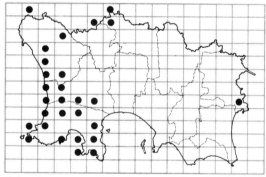

G local; A rare and R. pimpinellifolia *x* R. sherardii *claimed 1900; S locally common; H locally common.*

R. rugosa Thunb.   Japanese Rose

Japanese Rose was found on Ouaisné Common by Dr H. J. M. Bowen in 1956 and it was reported in quantity in a rough field close to the pond there in 1971 by K. E. Bull. Mrs M. L. Long and Mrs E. M. Towers have known it from at least 1965 onwards on Mont Cochon, and there are three records of single plants: sandpits north of St Ouen's Pond, 1962; Egypt Valley and Portelet, 1964, J. C. Fluck. Dr Melville comments that this is often used as a stock for garden roses and as it suckers freely, it can outlive the cultivar grafted on it, and so survive on the sites of old gardens. It is also bird-sown and so may appear in out-of-the-way places.
G rare; A rare.

R. stylosa Desv.   Columnar Dog Rose
A (?)1900; S 1897.

R. canina L.   Dog Rose
d'la **rose sauvage**

Wild roses are not common in Jersey, or in any of the other Channel Islands, and they are not a feature of the island's hedges in June, as they are in England. The map shows that they are widespread but each 'dot' probably represents only one bush in that area. The only place where Dog Roses occur in any quantity is near the rock at St Catherine. That they have never been common is confirmed by La Gasca not listing them after living in Jersey for three years (1831–1834), and succeeding botanists have recorded them as rare or not common.

The wild roses in the hedge opposite Les Crochenoles, Mont Matthieu, St Ouen, were bought from an English nursery c. 1960 and planted. This may have happened elsewhere. Earlier the two political parties, the Rose and the Laurel, which flourished last century, may well have affected the distribution of the wild rose. See the Introduction.

Dr R. Melville has identified the following varieties:
var. *dumalis* W. Dod   Les Quennevais, 1978, and Lester-Garland (1903) thought this was the prevailing form.
var. *spuria* (Pug.) W. Dod f. *syntrichostyla* (Rip.) Rouy   Mont de la Mare, St Peter, 1964.
var. *sylvularium* (Rip.) Rouy   St Catherine and the road to La Coupe from Rosel Manor, 1964.

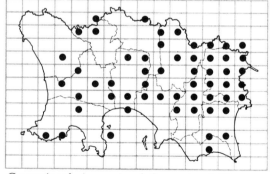

G occasional; A occasional; S occasional; H rare.

R. obtusifolia Desv.   A Dog Rose
Recorded by Druce (1906/7) from Pont Marquet.
G 1900.

R. tomentosa Sm.   **A Dog Rose**
A 1900.

R. rubiginosa L.   **Sweet Briar**
                                        d'la **rose sauvage**
Sweet Briar, *R. rubiginosa*, was listed by La Gasca in
1834 and subsequent records are: Gorey, 1897, Rev.
W. M. Rogers; Fiquet Bay, Lester-Garland (1903); in
quantity at Verclut, 1917, Guiton; above Le
Colombier, near Bonne Nuit, 1965, J. C. Fluck, det.
Melville. Other bushes of 'Sweet Briar' have been
reported, rarely, from the north-east but without
differentiation between this and the following
species.
G last record 1900; A occasional; S rare; H local.

R. micrantha Borrer ex Sm.   **Sweet Briar**
Sweet Briar, *R. micrantha*, seems confined to the
south-west (but see *R. rubiginosa*): var. *micrantha*
Pont Marquet, 1897, Rev. W. M. Rogers, conf.
Melville; St Brelade and St Aubin, Lester-Garland
(1903); old quarry Don Bridge, 1926, Ariste; top of
Les Quennevais, 1964, J. C. Fluck, det. Melville; f.
trichostyla R. Kell. Beauport, 1964, J. C. Fluck, det.
Melville.
G 1892; A 1900; S last record 1896; H 1879 and 1968.

Agrimonia eupatoria L. and **A. procera** Wallr.
                Agrimony and **Fragrant Agrimony**
Records of these species are inextricably mixed.
When herbarium specimens are available they are
often immature. Also most plants found during the
survey were immature so they were often recorded
only as '*Agrimonia*', a later check not being made. A
joint map is given to show that the aggregate occurs
occasionally and is not as rare as the individual
records would suggest.

There are many past records of both species but
because of the confusion, only those supported by
specimens are given below. Strangely both species
have been collected from Gorey Castle.

A. eupatoria: near Gorey Castle, 1854, Piquet
(Hb Oxford); Jersey, 1883, Fawcett, det. A. Melderis
(Hb Brit. Mus.); Les Quennevais, 1899, Piquet, near
Pont Marquet, 1983, R. W. S. Knightbridge, La
Coupe 1957 and at foot of outer wall of Gorey Castle,
1983 (Hb Société Jersiaise). This may be the
commoner species but more information is needed.

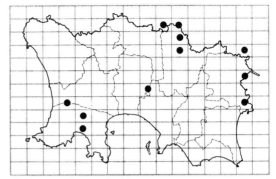

G ?errors; A rare; S 1892 and 1979.

A. procera: behind Gorey Castle, 1851, Piquet
(Hb Oxford); Beaumont, Rev. W. W. Newbould, and
Jersey, 1847, ex Hb S. H. Bickham (Hb Cantab.).
G rare, last record 1978; S 1958; H frequent.

Sanguisorba officinalis L.   **Great Burnet**
Records by La Gasca (1834), Saunders (Babington
1839) and Piquet (1896) were all rejected by Lester-
Garland (1903) and there has been no confirmation.

S. minor Scop.   **Salad** and **Fodder Burnet**
Both subsp. *minor*, Salad Burnet, and subsp.
muricata Briq., Fodder Burnet, have been reported,
rarely, but there has been difficulty over the years in
separating them. If the records are correct, both have
occurred on West Mount and on Les Quennevais,
near Don Bridge. All identifiable specimens are
subsp. *muricata*, Fodder Burnet, as is the first record,
Ereaut's from Les Quennevais in 1847, but many are
too young for determination and these may include
subsp. *minor*. The map is a composite one as most
records were merely of the species.

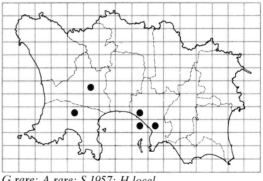

G rare; A rare; S 1957; H local.

Geum urbanum L.   **Wood Avens**
                                       *d'l'*hèrbe b'nêt
Frequent on wooded côtils and hedgebanks.

Map overleaf

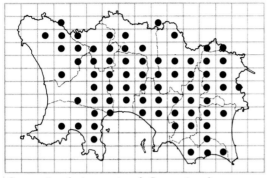

G occasional; A occasional; S occasional.

Potentilla palustris(L.) Scop.　　　**Marsh Cinquefoil**
G rare.

P. anserina L.　　　**Silverweed**
　　　d'la **t'naisie**

Subsp. *anserina* Common in damp places. A specimen in the Dillenian herbarium, Oxford, was collected by a Mr Clark in Jersey between 1730 and 1740.

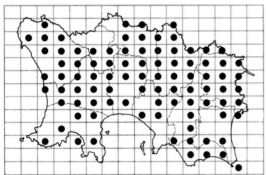

G frequent; A frequent; S rare; H local.

P. argentea L.　　　**Hoary Cinquefoil**
Rare in the past and not seen recently but it may still occur. Babington (1839) recorded it from St Brelade and St Clement. Other records are more detailed: near St Brelade's Church, 1847, Ereaut; Le Val, St Brelade, 1870, F. Piquet; sunny rocks in a valley behind the Rifle Range, St Peter (i.e. on Les Quennevais), 1899, Lester-Garland; dry bank beside the road between St Aubin and St Peter, 1902, Lester-Garland; near Beauport Battery, 1926, Burdo, Louis-Arsène and Ariste, and this was Attenborough's 1926 locality which he called 'near St Brelade's Church' (pers. comm.). In 1928 Attenborough found it 'in good quantity near Don Bridge' and he said later (pers. comm.) that this was Lester-Garland's old site on Les Quennevais. Louis-Arsène collected it from Les Quennevais in 1952 and when he took me to see the locality in 1958 it again

proved to be Lester-Garland's old site. No plants could be found but the area was overgrown. This may be the reason for its disappearance. On the other hand there are fifteen rooted specimens dated 1952 from Les Quennevais in Louis-Arsène's herbarium and he may have distributed others to collectors. *S self-sown in La Seigneurie Gardens 1976.*

P. recta L.　　　**Sulphur Cinquefoil**
Two records: several fine plants on made-up ground leading to Cap Verd, St Lawrence, in 1961, J. C. Fluck, where they survived for about ten years; several clumps on top of the hill north-east of Petit Port, St Brelade, in 1966, Miss R. Kilby. *S 1953.*

P. hirta L.　　　**A Cinquefoil**
Lloyd (1853) gave Piquet's record of this 'On a wall near Millbrook' but Piquet omitted it from his own list in 1896.

P. tabernaemontani Aschers.　　　**Spring Cinquefoil**
Attenborough recorded Spring Cinquefoil from two areas in 1927 but he and Burdo worked together and Burdo's specimen, dated 1927, is in error for *P. anglica* x *P. reptans*, determined Dr B. Harold.

P. erecta (L.) Räusch.　　　**Tormentil**
(P. silvestris)　　　*d'l'* **hèrbe à paralysie**
Common on the cliffs.

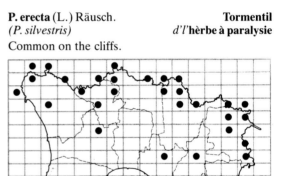

G common; A frequent; S common; H frequent.

P. anglica Laichard　　　**Trailing Tormentil**
(P. procumbens)
'Not uncommon' in 1903 according to Lester-Garland who listed six widely separated localities. This species is now known to hybridise with *P. erecta* and *P. reptans*. The hybrids bear a fairly close resemblance to *P. anglica* and are not easy to separate. They and *P. anglica* are therefore at present under-recorded. Only those specimens determined by Dr B. Harold, an authority on the *Genus*, are given here: St Saviour, 1850, and no locality, 1898,

Piquet; near Val de la Mare Reservoir, 1962, J. C. Fluck. More information is needed on this and its hybrids.
G rare; S rare.

P. x suberecta Zimm.　　　**A hybrid Tormentil**
P. anglica x P. erecta
One certain record: Mont Cochon, 1957, det. Dr B. Harold. See above.
G local.

P. x mixta Nolte ex Reichenb.　　**A hybrid Tormentil**
P. anglica x P. reptans
Two certain records: near Sion Chapel, 1881, Vaniot; near Bouley Bay Hotel, 1927, Burdo, both determined Dr B. Harold. See above.
G frequent; A frequent; S rare.

P. reptans L.　　　**Creeping Cinquefoil**
Frequent in richer, damper habitats than *P. erecta*. Though some hybrids may have been included in the records, it is thought that the following distribution map is substantially correct.

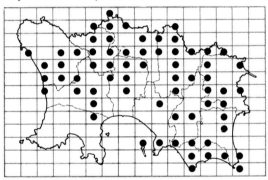

G frequent; A common; S occasional; H occasional.

P. sterilis (L.) Garcke　　　**Barren Strawberry**
(P. Fragariastrum)
Frequent on hedgebanks and on old roadside walls in the interior.

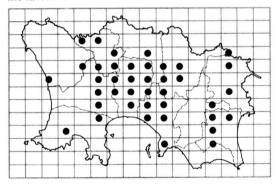

G frequent; A occasional; S rare.

Fragaria vesca L.　　　**Wild Strawberry**
des **frâses sauvages**
Frequent on hedgebanks in the interior.

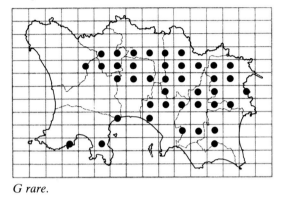

G rare.

F. x ananassa Duchesne　　　**Garden Strawberry**
des **frâses**
A rare escape from gardens: Elizabeth Castle, 1957, but eliminated when the Castle grounds were tidied; frequent in one small area of Beaumont Valley, 1962, J. C. Fluck.
G rare; A occasional.

F. chiloensis (L.) Duchesne　　　**A Strawberry**
S subsp. lucida *since 1933.*

Duchesnea indica (Andr.) Focke
　　　Yellow-flowered Strawberry
Yellow-flowered Strawberry has been known in the grounds of Highlands College for almost forty years. Though originally probably planted, it was growing like a weed in the old quarry in 1977 and was flowering and fruiting well, J. C. Fluck. It is still there. In 1981 Mrs M. L. Long found it as a garden relic in La Rue de Haut, St Lawrence.
G one locality.

Aphanes arvensis L.　　　**Parsley-piert**
(Alchemilla arvensis)
Plants recorded as *Aphanes arvensis*, Parsley-piert, in the past, were shown by Dr S.M. Walters in 1949 to be separable into two species. For one, the name *A. arvensis* was retained. This is not the common one in Jersey, indeed it is comparatively rare, but it has been recorded often enough to be mapped. Specimens, confirmed J. E. Lousley, are in the Société's herbarium.

Map overleaf

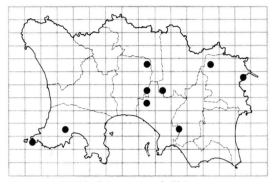

G rare; A ?1933; S ?occasional; H ?

A. microcarpa (Boiss. & Reuter) Rothm.

Slender Parsley-piert

Past records of *A. arvensis* generally belong here. The species is still abundant in open turf on the drier parts of banks, cliff heaths and côtils.

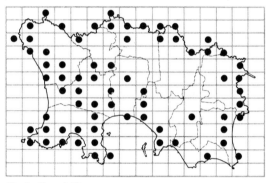

G, A, S and H common.

Alchemilla 'vulgaris'   **Lady's-mantle**

Lester-Garland (1903) rejected Babington's (1839) record from St Lawrence Valley and it has not been confirmed.
G error.

Chaenomeles speciosa (Sweet) Nakai   **Japonica**

A bush, presumably planted, was noted in a wild hedge along les Ruettes, St Peter, in the early 1970s and it is still there.

Cydonia oblonga Miller   **Quince**

Three bushes which had been in a field hedge on the top of Mont Rossignol for many years were removed during alterations in the 1980s, Mrs M. L. Long.

Pyrus sp.   **Wild pear**
un **paithyi sauvage**

Pear trees occur occasionally growing wild on the cliffs and in hedges or on wooded côtils. Their history is obscure.

The first mention of pears growing in Jersey is an incidental one by Drouet Le Hardy when giving testimony in 1463 about events during the French occupation of Jersey (1461–1468). Poingdestre, writing in 1682, stated that, though cider was then the principal drink, earlier it had been perry. If this was made on the island, as presumably it was, there must have been pear trees in quantity in those earlier years.

Later, particularly in the nineteenth century, pear-growing for high quality dessert fruit became both fashionable and lucrative. So many pears of such quality were exported that some varieties became so associated with Jersey that they underwent name changes: Bonne Louise d'Avranches became Louise Bonne de Jersey and Belle de Thouars became Belle de Jersey. As to size, the third *Annual Report* (1835: 55) of the Jersey Agricultural & Horticultural Society stated that two Belle de Jersey, weighing together 96 oz, were sent, with other kinds equally large for their variety, to William IV in 1834. New varieties were produced, for example Poire Beurré Langelier about 1845. In Leroy's *Dictionnaire de Pomologie* (1859) a nurseryman from London is quoted as saying in 1849 that the best Chaumontel pears grow in the isle of Jersey, from where they are exported to London each year at a very good price, and Leroy goes on to say that the soil of Jersey is so favourable for the growing of this pear that growers from Jersey each year buy considerable numbers of young trees from the Angers region of France. That there was a considerable influx of young trees from France is also evident from the advertisements in the local papers, for example in the *Gazette* for 30 October 1790 there was a notice that a consignment of young fruit trees, for sale, was expected from Orléans at the end of November, and twenty-eight different varieties of pear were listed. Most large gardens still contain a few pear trees but they are no longer grown in the quantity they were last century, when in 1872, for instance, Sir John Le Couteur grew eighty-one named varieties.

The above is given as background information because the present wild population of pear trees may be reversions or derivatives of those cultivated in the past. Two species may be involved but more botanical research on pears in Europe is needed.

P. pyraster Burgsd.   **Round-fruited Wild Pear**

(*P. communis* L. var. *achras* Wallr.). Rare. A tree on a wooded slope of Les Quennevais has been called *P. achras* since before the First World War (1914–18). In 1916, when the wood was about to be felled for fuel, representations were made to the Army authorities that this tree be left and, through the intervention of Major Naish R.E., it was preserved. There are now several trees in this neighbourhood. Other such trees occur behind La Moye School, at

Opposite, Plate 6 Sea-holly *Eryngium maritimum* with Sea Sandwort *Honkenya peploides*

the top end of Waterworks Valley and in Swiss Valley. Fruit brought to me by E. C. Newman in 1967 from a tree in Swiss Valley was sent to Dr R. Melville at Kew who replied: 'The round-fruited wild pears come under *Pyrus communis* var. *pyraster* and that is the best name I can give you at present. Your fruits are more flattened than any other form I have seen and more so than the one originally figured by Gaertner as '*P. achras*'. Related round-fruited pears appear to be distributed through central France, Germany and Austria. Whether this pear is native in Jersey is very difficult to judge. It may have been introduced centuries ago or it might have been brought in as a stock for grafting.'
A rare.

P. communis L. Normal-fruited Wild Pear
(Pirus communis)

The Normal-fruited Wild Pear occurs, rarely, in hedges and on the cliffs. Its origins are unknown.

The map shows the distribution of Wild Pears regardless of species.

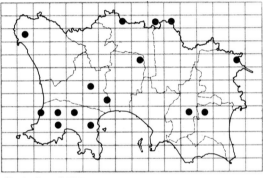

G, A, S and H Pyrus *sp. occur rarely.*

Malus sylvestris Miller Crab Apple
(Pirus Malus)

It is doubtful whether truly wild Crab Apples, as opposed to 'feral' domestic apples, have occurred in Jersey. All specimens seen have been the following species. Attenborough, who had earlier reported Crab Apples, stated in the Société's botanical report for 1956 that Jersey plants are apparently the following species and in a discussion he told me that he had never seen a true Crab Apple tree in Jersey.
G, A, S and H as Jersey.

M. domestica Borkh. Apple
un **pommyi**

Apple trees occur occasionally in hedges and on the cliffs where they were not planted. They are not as common as might be expected, considering the vast numbers of apples grown in the past for cider. Falle in 1694 described the island as looking like an entire

forest because of the many hedges and orchards. From about the middle of last century, the orchards have gradually given way to potatoes and other crops. No map is given because many recorders had difficulty in deciding how 'wild' a tree was.
G rare; A rare; S rare; H 1922.

Sorbus sp. Whitebeam; Service-tree

It ought perhaps to be put on record that no Whitebeam or Service-trees are now growing wild in the island. Until recently there were very few indeed in gardens but they are being planted in increasing numbers and may in future be found in the wild.

Sorbus aucuparia L. Rowan

Subsp. *aucuparia* Rowan has been known in gardens for many years but no records of it in the wild were given by Piquet, Lester-Garland or Attenborough. A few trees occur in a wood on Les Quennevais, well away from habitation or cultivation so they are presumed to be bird-sown, one grows in Waterworks Valley and there used to be one on Fort Regent. Rowan is being increasingly planted and may appear in greater quantity.
G one record; S 1960.

Amelanchier lamarckii F.-G. Schroeder
A Snowy Mespilus

Three localities: long-established trees, saplings and seedlings on a côtil north of Gargate Mill, St Peter's Valley, Mrs M. L. Long and on a côtil north of Dannemarche mud-pond, Waterworks Valley, Mrs E. M. Towers; two old trees near Quetivel Mill, below Handois reservoir.

Cotoneaster sp. Cotoneaster

Though many different species of cotoneaster are grown, and their berries appear equally attractive to birds, the only stones which germinate frequently, and produce seedlings in gardens or on garden walls, are *C. horizontalis* and *C. simonsii*. These two species, and *C. microphylla*, have been reported outside gardens, on nearby walls, but only rarely, as given below, and not in the quantity one might expect:

C. horizontalis Decne Fish-bone Cotoneaster

Two records: Beaumont, 1968, Mrs M. L. Long; near St Brelade's Church, 1971, K. E. Bull.
G rare.

C. simonsii Baker
Himalayan Cotoneaster; Khasia Berry

Two records: south of La Hague, St Peter's Valley, 1971, Mrs M. L. Long; near Les Raisies, St Martin, 1971, Mrs E. Whiteside.
G rare; A rare.

C. microphyllus Wallich ex Lindley
Wall Cotoneaster
Two records: between Plémont and L'Étacq, 1928, Ariste; near St Brelade's Bay Hotel, 1961, D. McClintock.
G occasional.

Mespilus germanica L.
Medlar
un **meïlyi**
Probably introduced in the distant past and now thoroughly naturalised. Though thorny, its south-eastern distribution in Europe would seem to prevent it being considered native in Jersey. G. Henslow writing in the *Phytologist* (1858) described it as abundant in many hedges, especially in St Martin. While this is no longer true, it is still frequent and widespread in the north-east.

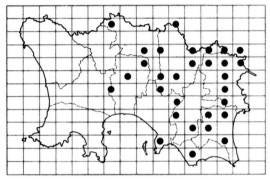

G rare; S rare 1960.

Crataegus laevigata (Poiret) DC.
Midland Hawthorn
No confirmed record is known. In the past the name 'Mespilus oxyacanthoides', as used by Lester-Garland (1903), covered both this species and *C. monogyna*. The native Channel Island species is *C. monogyna*, and not *C. laevigata* which was given in the Armorican Flora (1971).
G, A, S and H as Jersey.

C. x media Bechst.
Hybrid Hawthorn
C. laevigata x **C. monogyna**
Some bushes in a newly planted hedge on La Route des Laveurs, near the foot of Mont Pinel, St Ouen, are this hybrid Hawthorn but so much Hawthorn is being planted to replace elm trees that it may well be present elsewhere. Flowers on new hedges should be examined to see whether there are 2–3 styles (Midland Hawthorn), 1 style (Hawthorn) or a mixture 1–2 styles (the hybrid) and the leaves should be compared with those of the native species.
G, A, S and H as Jersey.

C. monogyna Jacq.
Hawthorn
(Mespilus oxyacanthoides
d'la **blianche êpîngne**
var. *monogyna)*
Subsp. *nordica* Franco Hawthorn, a native species of both cliffs and inland areas, has been used as a hedging plant for centuries. Poingdestre, in his *Caesarea* written in 1682, gives a detailed account of how it was grown and planted to make massive hedges. The Société Jersiaise published *Caesarea* in 1889. This is now out of print but his account of how the islanders used Hawthorn is in *A Natural History of Jersey* (Le Sueur 1976). This century, Hawthorn fell slightly out of favour, perhaps because of the many newer hedging plants available. Now, with the death of so many elms, it is once again being planted in quantity.

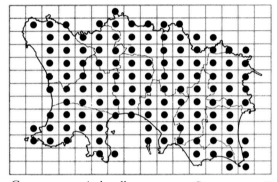

G common; A locally common; S common; H occasional.

Prunus spinosa L.
Blackthorn; Sloe
d'la **néthe êpîngne**; *eune* **preunelle**
'Blackthorn' is usually considered to be native on the cliffs and hillsides. It was used extensively for hedges in the past and was one of the hedging plants mentioned by Poingdestre in 1682, together with hawthorn and willow.

It still occurs in quantity but there are problems over its precise botanical 'make-up'. *P. spinosa* in England has numerous, rigid, stout, black side shoots which later become the thorns from which it gets its name. Jersey's Blackthorn sometimes has a few thorns, but nothing approaching the quantity on Blackthorn elsewhere. On the other hand, its white flowers appear well before the leaves, smothering the dark, naked branches. Petal lengths fall within the *P. spinosa* range and the fruit, the sloes, from three typical hedges, averaged just below the upper limit for *P. spinosa* in one case and just above it in the other two. It would therefore appear that Jersey's 'Blackthorn' is nearer *P. spinosa* than any other *Prunus*, though there may have been some hybridisation years ago. A detailed investigation of the *Prunus spinosa/domestica* complex in the Channel Islands is required.
G, A, S and H all have similar 'problem' Blackthorn.

P. x fruticans Weihe   **A hybrid Prunus**
P. spinosa x **P. domestica**

Bushes in a short hedge in Val de la Mare, St Peter, have greenish, thornless pliable branches. Their small white flowers always appear with the leaves and for the last twenty-five years, at least, they have produced no fruit. They are presumed to be of hybrid origin.
G occurs; A ? S ? H ?

P. domestica L.   **Plum** and **Bullace**

Subsp. *domestica* The only plum trees known are obviously planted, but see *P. spinosa*, Blackthorn.
Subsp. *insititia* (L.) C. K. Schneid. Lester-Garland (1903) stated that there were no Bullaces in Jersey but in the Société Jersiaise botanical report for 1921, Attenborough reported that a Mr Godfrey had found it in fine fruit at Fliquet Bay. There is no specimen and J. C. Fluck has heard Medlars being called Bullaces in Jersey so the record needs confirmation.
G, A, S and H occurs.

P. avium L.   **Wild Cherry**

Not recorded until 1910 when C. E. Salmon found a tree near 'Grand Val Mill' (*Journal of Botany* LI: 18). Many inland woods now contain fully grown trees with well-defined trunks. See the following species.
G, S and H planted.

P. cerasus L.   **Morello** or **Dwarf Cherry**
eune **badgiole**

Recorded by La Gasca and Piquet last century and stated by Lester-Garland (1903) to be thinly distributed over the interior of the island. A good stand is on the hillside near the Guard House east of Grève de Lecq. The Jersey stock may be derived from hedging plants in the past or from Morello cherries in cultivation. More information on cherries in Jersey is needed. During the survey 1960–70 this and the above species were recorded fairly frequently but were often not separated being recorded simply as 'wild cherry' so no map is given.
G rare; S 1953.

P. cerasifera Ehrh.   **Cherry Plum**
G rare.

P. laurocerasus L.   **Cherry Laurel**
du **louothie d'Espangne**

The garden shrub Cherry Laurel, a native of the Balkans, grows apparently wild and seeding itself in several wooded areas. It is widespread and there is more than might be expected. This may be connected with the Rose and Laurel political parties of last century. See the Introduction.

LEGUMINOSAE

Cytisus scoparius (L.) Link   **Broom**
Subsp. *scoparius*   *du* **genêt**

Still locally common as it has been since records began. Many place names contain the word *genêts* and with reason. For example some years a field called Le Clos de Genêts, along La Route des Genêts, St Brelade, is yellow with flowering broom.

Subsp. *maritimus* (Rouy) Heywood
Prostrate Broom
du **genêt d'falaise**

Locally abundant on exposed parts of the south-west cliffs in St Brelade and on the north-west cliffs in St Ouen. The plants are prostrate and keep close to the soil or rock over which they grow so that in spring they blanket the area with yellow. Lester-Garland stated that this was merely a form produced by the exposed position in which the plants grew and that in a sheltered position they would revert to normal. This has been disproved. The difference is genetic and plants come true from seed.

The map includes both subspecies.

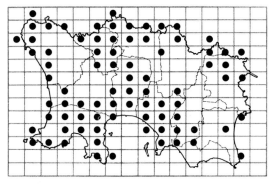

G local; A locally common; S common; H only subsp. scoparius.

Genista tinctoria L.   **Dyer's Greenweed**

Dyer's Greenweed grows on a restricted stretch of the north coast cliffs, roughly from Havre Giffard to Vicart, from where Piquet first recorded it (at Belle Hougue) in 1851. The quantity has varied over the years, sometimes the species being recorded as rare and at other times as abundant. Fires seem to affect it badly as none was found on the west side of Belle Hougue Point in 1979 when other species had begun to regrow after a serious fire.

In 1918 Attenborough reported that it had not been found elsewhere in spite of careful search but in 1925 Mrs Robinson claimed to have found it in quantity at Ronez. This record remains unconfirmed.

Ulex europaeus L.   **Gorse**
         du **geon**

Subsp. *europaeus* Locally abundant. Most years, Gorse flowers well. In 1981, a sea of unbroken yellow stretched northwards from Mont du Vallet across Les Landes, almost as far as the eye could see. Only very occasionally does it do badly. Flowers can be found in all months of the year but each spring it has a peak flowering time. This varies slightly from year to year, as can be seen from the following rough notes made each year since 1972 on 10 May about Gorse flowering on a côtil overlooking St Ouen's Bay:

   1972 over; has been only fair.
   1973 in full bloom; excellent.
   1974 in bloom; very poor.
   1975 nearly over; has been very good.
   1976 fading; very good.
   1977 failure.
   1978 nearly over; has been very good.
   1979 just out; poor.
   1980 full bloom; very good.
   1981 just over; has been magnificent.
   1982 just over; has been excellent.
   1983 nearly over; grazed hard by horses, so poor.

The 1977 failure was probably because of the long, severe drought of 1976, one of the worst on record.

In the past Gorse played an important part in the island's economy, being used for fuel and as food for horses. Strict regulations governed its cutting on the commons. See the Introduction.

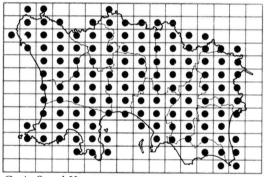

G, A, S and H common.

U. europaeus x U. gallii   **A hybrid Gorse**
On 9 October 1978, specimens of *U. europaeus*, *U. gallii* and a suspected hybrid, all from Grosnez, were sent to Dr M. C. Proctor, the authority on *Ulex*, who confirmed the hybrid and suggested that another specimen, one of those sent as *U. gallii*, was probably also of hybrid origin, a back-cross to *U. gallii*.
G occurs.

U. minor Roth   **Dwarf Gorse**
(*U. nanus*)

Only one correct record is known: Plémont, 1859,

Piquet, Hb Oxford, conf. Proctor. Dwarf Gorse was recorded as frequent last century but Lester-Garland (1903) said he had never seen it and thought the following species was the one intended. It has not been refound in spite of much searching.
G 1892; A ?

U. gallii Planch.   **Western Gorse**
    d'la **grappue**

Western Gorse is a low growing species flowering in August at the same time as Heather, with which it grows intermingled. Though local, as the distribution map shows, it can be abundant as on the south-west cliffs near La Corbière and near Grosnez. As with Gorse, strict regulations governed its cutting on the commons. See the Introduction.

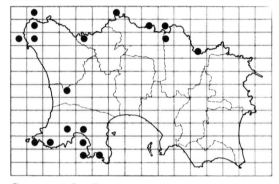

G scarce; A locally common; S occasional.

Lupinus luteus L.   **Yellow Lupin**
Yellow Lupin was used as a green manure in the late 1950s in the nurseries at the top of Beaumont Hill and for a few years it seeded itself nearby.

L. polyphyllus Lindley   **Garden Lupin**
Garden Lupin appears on rubbish dumps, rarely, and may persist for a time but it is not established in Jersey as it is in other parts of Europe.
G rare.

L. arboreus Sims   **Tree Lupin**
    *d'l'***arbre à lupîns**

Tree Lupin, an introduction from California, is completely naturalised in Jersey. When it first arrived is unknown, but Attenborough (pers. comm.) said he remembered seeing it by the railway line between St Helier and St Aubin during the First World War (1914–18). Jersey's sandy soil and mild climate are ideal for it and by 1981 it was spreading over the dunes at St Ouen so rapidly, eliminating local species, that measures to control it had to be taken.

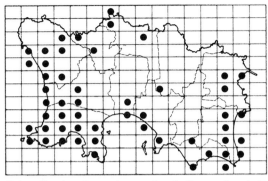

G locally abundant; A occasional; S occasional; H rare.

Robinia pseudacacia L.   **False Acacia**

False Acacia, a North American tree widely naturalised on the continent, is surprisingly rare and always seems planted. Seedlings have been reported in unexpected places but they may be suckers from distant trees.
G rare.

Vicia cracca L.   **Tufted Vetch**
                                     du **véchon**

Frequent in hedges, and sometimes so beautiful and prolific in its flowering that it is left uncut in the *branchage*.

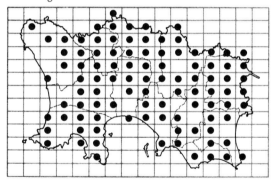

G frequent; A rare; S occasional.

V. villosa Roth   **Winter Vetch**

Three records: St Clement, note by Piquet in his copy of Babington's Flora; thinly scattered in stubble betwen St Aubin and St Brelade, 1929, I. A. Williams; subsp. *varia* (Host) Corb. Le Hocq Common, St Clement, 1958 and still there 1962, but the site is now destroyed.
G 1971; A 1902 and 1932.

V. hirsuta (L.) S. F. Gray   **Hairy Tare**
                                     du **véchon**

Frequent in grassy places.

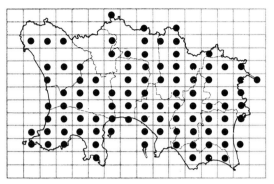

G frequent; A frequent; S common; H 1957.

V. tetrasperma (L.) Schreb.   **Smooth Tare**

Babington (1839) did not see Smooth Tare on his visits to Jersey and had to use Saunders' record. Piquet (1896) considered it rare and it has remained so. Each 'dot' on the distribution map represents only one locality each time and the plants at Le Squez vanished in the 1970s when Le Squez housing scheme was built.

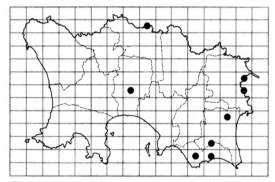

G rare; A rare; S frequent.

V. sepium L.   **Bush Vetch**

Always rare and becoming rarer. Three localities: near Don Bridge, 1892, A. J. Binet – still there in the 1970s but now gone; St Peter, 1927, Ariste; corner of wet meadow, Jambart Lane, St Clement, 1962, Mrs D. L. Le Quesne, and still there in the 1970s.
G rare; S Brecqhou.

V. pannonica Crantz   **A Vetch**

D. McClintock stated (pers. comm.) that the Jersey record given in *The Wild Flowers of Guernsey* is of a plant found by I. A. Williams in a stubble field at St Brelade in 1930. No more information is available.

V. sativa L.   **Vetch**
                                     d'la **vèche**

Subsp. *sativa* Common, Babington (1839) and Piquet (1851); frequent, scarcely wild, Piquet (1896);

much planted for fodder, Lester-Garland (1903). Vetch has not been seen planted as a fodder crop for decades and true subsp. *sativa* may no longer exist in Jersey though intermediates with the following subspecies are common in late spring and summer.

Subsp. *nigra* (L.) Ehrh. *(V. angustifolia)* This narrow-leaved subspecies is common and would appear to be native. In spring its brilliant rose-purple flowers are conspicuous in hedgebanks and in grassy places. Early botanists attempted to separate the complex into varieties *Bobartii, Garlandii* and *canescens* but these are no longer sustained.

As spring changes into summer, plants become more difficult to assign to either subspecies. This is assumed to be because of hybridisation in the past.

The map includes all records of *V. sativa*.

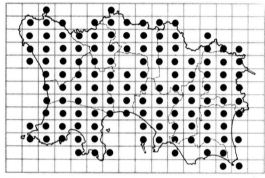

G common; A common; S common; H occasional.

V. lathyroides L.   Spring Vetch

Locally frequent in spring and early summer in open turf on sandy areas.

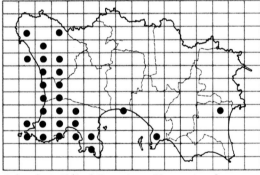

G local; A 1952; S Brecqhou; H occasional.

V. lutea L.   Yellow Vetch

Subsp. *lutea* Dr M. M. Bull (d. 1879) found Yellow Vetch on Fort Regent, according to an undated entry by Babington in his own copy of his Flora. In 1885 it was on Mont Orgueil (A. Ley) where it persisted until at least 1907. Attenborough mentioned it at Mont Orgueil in the 1939 botanical report of the Société Jersiaise but it is not clear when he himself

saw it. In 1922 Lady Davy found it near La Corbière and it is still on the hillside north of La Corbière towards Le Grouet. In 1928, a third locality was found by Louis-Arsène in the valley between St Brelade's Church and La Moye School, and this was confirmed by Mrs Godfray of La Moye School who saw the plants in fine flower in 1929.

G scarce.

V. hybrida L.   A Vetch

There has been no confirmation of La Gasca's 1834 record which was ignored by Lester-Garland (1903).

V. bithynica (L.) L.   Bithynian Vetch

G rare; A 1963.

Lathyrus niger (L.) Bernh.   Black Pea

Several plants near Mont Cambrai, 1962 and 1963, Mrs J. Brooks.

L. pratensis L.   Meadow Vetchling

Frequent on grassy hedgebanks except in the far west and south.

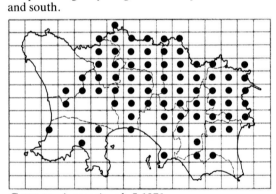

G scarce; A occasional; S 1971.

L. latifolius L.   Broad-leaved Everlasting-pea

First noted by Piquet as 'scarcely wild' in Pier Road in 1851. It is no longer commonly grown in gardens, but it seems well able to survive occasionally as a flourishing garden outcast or relic.

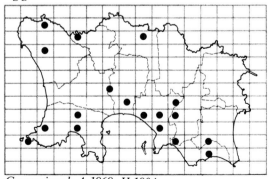

G occasional; A 1969; H 1904.

L. cicera L.   **Lesser Chick-pea**

First found by Guiton in 1905 on Les Quennevais near Don Bridge Station. It remained in the region for some time, being reported occasionally. The last record seems to be Mrs E. M. McAllister Hall's from the railway-side between Les Quennevais race-course and Blanches Banques Station (B.E.C. *Report* 1935).

L. hirsutus L.   **Hairy Pea**

J. P. O. Trist collected a specimen in a field on the north side of the old railway line from Pont Marquet Station to Don Bridge Station in 1960.
G 1923; S 1930.

L. ochrus (L.) DC.   **A Lathyrus**

Garden weed at the north end of La Route des Mielles, St Ouen, in 1965, A. Lister.

L. aphaca L.   **Yellow Vetchling**

A rare casual recorded by Piquet from near the Town Mills Pond and Bouley Bay (1851), from St Peter and Trinity (1853) and from Trinity (1896). Lester-Garland (1903) added two more: Five Oaks Brick Kilns, 1898, Miss D. Higginson; Samarès, 1900, Miss A. Goate.
G 1894; A rare.

Pisum sativum L.   **Pea**

Subsp. *sativum* In the mid-1960s pea plants, small and with purple flowers, came up in the most unexpected places: Mount Bingham, in cracks between the stones near the harbour, in Val de la Mare near the site of the old mill and in gardens in St Helier and at Bel Royal. Eventually it was realised that small boys with pea-shooters were responsible. When the craze died away, so did the supply of new seedlings.
G rare.

Ononis reclinata L.   **Small Restharrow**

A specimen labelled 'Jersey, 1871', det. F. A. Lees, is in Hb Oxford. Small Restharrow is a very rare plant of Guernsey and Alderney and, as there is no locality named in Jersey on the specimen sheet, confusion of island names is suspected.
G last seen 1956; A rare.

O. spinosa L.   **Spiny Restharrow**

The record given in the B.E.C. *Report* (1936) has since been withdrawn, as an error, by the recorder.

O. repens L.   **Common Restharrow**
                             du **ricolisse en bouais**

Still common on the sandier parts of the coast, as it was last century. In spite of Lester-Garland (1903)

stating 'Only var. *inermis* quite devoid of spines', the stems do, rarely, have soft spines.

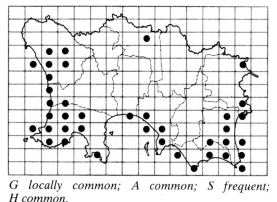

G locally common; A common; S frequent; H common.

Melilotus altissima Thuill.   **Tall Melilot**

Lester-Garland recorded Tall Melilot as an occasional casual from Millbrook and Samarès in 1896 and from Le Hocq in 1900 but he collected no specimen. The B.S.B.I. Atlas 'dot' is based on an unconfirmed report in 1957 from Les Quennevais. No other records exist, the following being the usual species.
G 1890; A rare.

M. officinalis (L.) Pallas   **Ribbed Melilot**
(M. arvensis)   *du* **mélilot**

Ribbed Melilot has been an occasional casual since 1851 when Piquet recorded it from behind Saunders' Nurseries and from near Town Mills Pond.

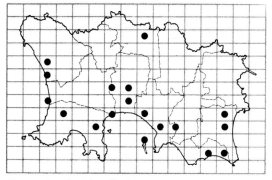

G occasional; A locally frequent.

M. alba Medicus   **White Melilot**

An occasional casual on light soil, first recorded by A. J. Binet in 1891.

Map overleaf

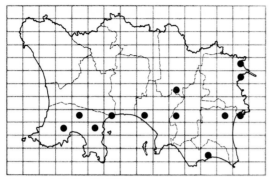

G rare; A 1906; H 1876.

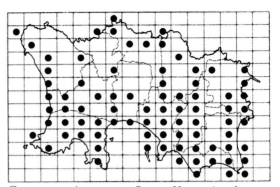

G common; A common; S rare; H occasional.

M. indica (L.) All.   **Small Melilot**
(M. parviflora)

Not recorded until 1903 when Lester-Garland commented that Small Melilot was the commonest of the four species. This is still true and in some areas, for example the north end of St Ouen's Bay, Small Melilot is locally common.

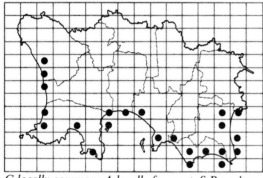

G locally common; A locally frequent; S Brecqhou.

Trigonella hamosa L.   **A Trigonella**

One record: potato field, Jersey, July 1876, Dr M. M. Bull (Hb Brit. Mus.).

Medicago lupulina L.   **Black Medick**
du **trêfl'ye à moutons**

Common and recorded as such, or as frequent, in dry sunny places, since records began.

M. sativa L.
Subsp. *sativa*   **Lucerne**
d'la **lûzèrne**

Lester-Garland (1903) stated that Lucerne had been much planted as a fodder crop for more than a hundred years. It continued to be used in quantity until about the First World War (1914–18) but is now only rarely sown. Jersey's climate and light soil suit it with the result that it remains well established in the wild, principally in the sandier areas.

Subsp. *falcata* (L.) Arcangeli   **Sickle Medick**
d'la **lûzèrne en faûcil'ye**

Only one record, from the back of Bel Royal Station, August 1878, Piquet. Le Maistre (1966) states that he was told by elderly people that Sickle Medick used to be cultivated long ago. This is perhaps confirmed by the fact that it has a Jersey-Norman-French name.
Subsp. *sativa* x subsp. *falcata*. The only past record of the hybrid (*M.* x *varia* Martyn) is one by Druce from West Mount. But if plants with greenish or blackish flowers, or pods not spiralling well, are of hybrid origin, then many records of subsp. *sativa* should belong here. The map contains all records.

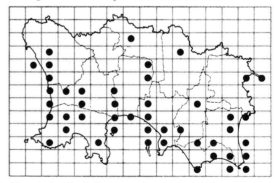

G occasional; A frequent; S occasional.

M. arabica (L.) Hudson   **Spotted Medick**
(M. maculata)   *du* **trêfl'ye d'Jérusalem**

Common in grassy places since records began.

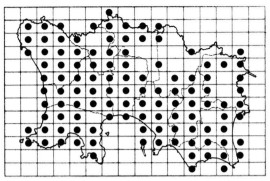

G common; A frequent; S rare; H occasional.

M. polymorpha L.   **Toothed Medick**
(*M. denticulata*)

Frequent in dry sandy areas and it still occurs in many of the places, South Hill, West Mount etc., mentioned in the past. Var. *microdon* (Ehrenb.) Urban, with small fruits with short spines, has been recorded from South Hill, Grouville Common and St Aubin's Bay.

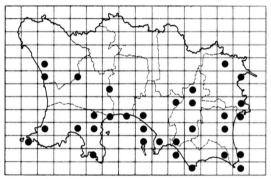

G occasional; A rare; S error; H 1957.

M. minima (L.) Bartal.   **Bur Medick**

Locally frequent in dry sandy soils and still sometimes abundant in St Ouen's Bay, as A. Ley reported in 1897.

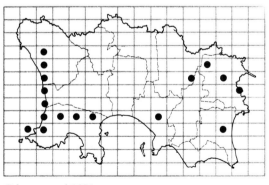

G last record 1953.

Trifolium ornithopodioides L.   **Fenugreek**
(*Trigonella ornithopodioides*)

First noted by La Gasca in 1832 from St Helier and since then frequently from various places round the coast. Though attractive, it is an unassuming little clover and may well have been under-recorded during the survey, particularly along the north coast. In 1983 it was locally abundant and dominant on a côtil in Val de la Mare.

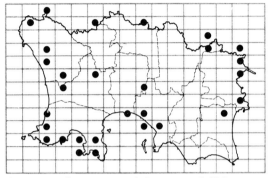

G occasional; A occasional; S occasional; H frequent.

T. strictum L.   **Upright Clover**

In Sowerby's *English Botany* Supplt Vol. IV 1843, W. Borrer stated that Upright Clover 'has been repeatedly gathered near St Brelades in Jersey where it was first discovered in 1836 by Mr Woods'. Unfortunately, simply because it was rare, it continued to be gathered for the next century and more. That it still exists, still rare, in St Brelade, illustrates how tenacious some annual species are if the habitat is unchanged. Only one locality is now known, but specimens came from several different localities in the past in St Brelade, and it may still be present in some of the others.
G last seen c. 1933.

T. repens L.   **White Clover**
du **trêfl'ye d'natuthe**

Subsp. *repens* Common since records began. Lester-Garland recorded var. *proliferum* S. F. Gray from Samarès in 1899. It has leafy flower heads caused by mycoplasma.

Map overleaf

79

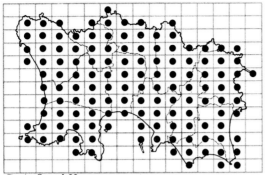

G, A, S and H common.

T. occidentale D. E. Coombe   **Atlantic Clover**

In *Watsonia* (1961) D. E. Coombe described *T. occidentale*, Atlantic Clover, a new species so superficially resembling *T. repens*, White Clover, that it had previously been included, unrecognised, with *T. repens*, though distinct from that species. Among the localities listed for the new clover, which has now been found from S. Ireland to N. Portugal, were La Grosse Tête, 1959, and Le Pinacle, near L'Étacq, 1960. A careful search will probably reveal other localities in Jersey.
G locally frequent; A locally frequent; S occasional; H occasional.

T. hybridum L.   **Alsike Clover**

Subsp. *hybridum* Alsike Clover was not listed by any botanist until 1903 when Lester-Garland described it as a not common escape from cultivation. Perhaps in earlier years it was considered not sufficiently wild. Recorders in the survey also had difficulty in deciding its status, wild or cultivated, so it was not mapped, though it was seen fairly frequently.
Subsp. *elegans* (Savi) Aschers. & Graebn. One record from near the Airport car park, 1954, D. McClintock.
G locally frequent; A rare; S rare (All only subsp. hybridum*).*

T. glomeratum L.   **Clustered Clover**

Common on dry light soil and on the tops of walls near the coast. Clustered Clover was present as part of the natural turf on a côtil at St Ouen when observations on the côtil began in 1958 and it remained in roughly the same quantity, listed as fairly frequent, until 1979 when it suddenly became dominant. Apart from the vegetation being cut early each summer, there was no interference by man. The sward of Clustered Clover in 1979 was about 12 in. high and so thick as to exclude all else. The stems were so tough it was impossible to mow or sickle the area and by late summer the ground was covered with a layer of fruiting heads. In 1980, numbers were back to normal.

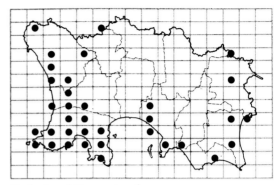

G, A, S and H occasional.

T. suffocatum L.   **Suffocated Clover**

Suffocated Clover, first reported by J. Gay from St Helier in 1832, was rare last century according to Piquet (1896), and it was listed from only six places by Lester-Garland (1903). This century it has increased so that it is now locally frequent.

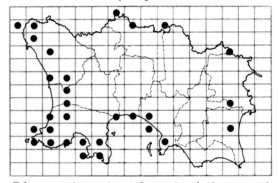

G frequent; A occasional; S occasional; H occasional.

T. fragiferum L.   **Strawberry Clover**

Local. Strawberry Clover seems to have decreased since last century when Babington (1839) described it as common and Piquet (1896) as frequent. Its main areas were Grouville Marsh, the wet areas of St Clement and St Ouen's Pond. It has not been seen at Grouville since last century; it disappeared from Samarès Marsh when the Le Squez Flats were built but it is still in the Rue des Près region and at St Ouen's Pond.

A specimen gathered by Piquet from St Ouen's Pond in 1850 (Hb Oxford) is labelled subsp. *bonannii* (C. Presl) Soják but the specimens in the Société's herbarium appear to be intermediate between this and subsp. *fragiferum*.
G local; A rare.

T. resupinatum L.   **Reversed Clover**

Reversed Clover used to be 'more or less naturalised beside the road along the shore in St Ouen's Bay' according to Lester-Garland (1903) but it is no longer

there, probably because of road-widening. There are three other records of casuals: south side of Lower People's Park, 1889, Binet; First Tower, 1898, Lester-Garland; Samarès, 1926, Ariste.
G last record 1944.

T. aureum Poll.   **Large Hop Trefoil**
Claimed from Bel Royal by Miss A. B. Cobbe (B.E.C. *Report* 1925) but unconfirmed.
S claimed.

T. campestre Schreb.   **Hop Trefoil**
(T. procumbens)
Frequent in sunny, dry places.

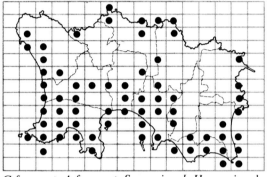

G frequent; A frequent; S occasional; H occasional.

T. dubium Sibth.   **Lesser Trefoil**
Common in grassy places.

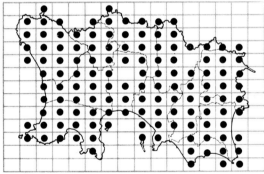

G, A, S and H common.

T. micranthum Viv.   **Slender Trefoil**
(T. filiforme)
Locally frequent in open turf.

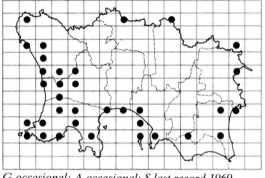

G occasional; A occasional; S rare; H rare.

T. striatum L.   **Soft Clover**
Common round the coast most years.

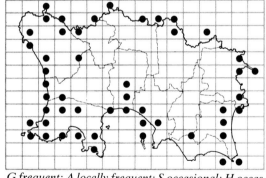

G occasional; A occasional; S last record 1969.

T. arvense L.   **Hare's-foot Clover**
Piquet (1896) and Lester-Garland (1903) stated that Hare's-foot Clover was frequent all round the coast. This is still true. Var. *perpusillum* DC. was collected on Les Quennevais in 1924 by Ariste and Louis-Arsène.

G frequent; A locally frequent; S occasional; H occasional.

T. bocconei Savi   **Twin-flowered Clover**
A rare native in two localities, both in short turf in the south-west. It was found in the first locality by Lady

Davy in 1934, and refound by Mrs J. Russell in 1956, but it has not been seen there since myxomatosis swept through the area in the early 1960s when it was crowded out by rank vegetation no longer kept in check by rabbits. Otherwise the area has not altered and it may reappear. It is still in the second locality found by Miss K. Gorringe and Mrs G. Williams in 1960.

T. scabrum L.   **Rough Clover**

Common near the coast since records began, and in some years locally abundant.

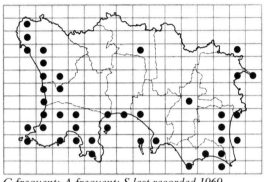

G frequent; A frequent; S last recorded 1969.

T. stellatum L.   **Starry Clover**
A 1933.

T. incarnatum L.

Subsp. *incarnatum*   **Crimson Clover**
                                      des **soudards**

In the first annual *Report* of the Jersey Agricultural and Horticultural Society (1834: 6–7) the Honorary Secretary Col. J. Le Couteur stated that Crimson Clover, a new clover to Jersey, 'has proved so profitable . . . as to be encouraged by all breeders . . . of cattle . . . Can a finer crop be suggested to the Jersey Farmer, who considers his cow the great object of his care, and the great source of his profit?' After this testimonial, it was much grown for fodder last century and was frequently found as an escape from cultivation. This century its use has largely died out but it still occurs, rarely, in sown leys for example in St Mary in 1964, and in rough pasture for example near Oaklands, Trinity, in 1965. As an escape, it is now correspondingly rare.

The Jersey-Norman-French name, which also means 'soldiers', may have been given because of the plants' resemblance to the red-coated Jersey Militia on parade.
G last record 1963; A last record 1937; S rare; H 1904.

Subsp. *molinerii* (Balbis ex Hornem.) Syme
                                 Long-headed Clover
Piquet added later to his 1851 list that *T. molinerii* was

abundant in June 1863 on the islet in Portelet Bay. This was the first record and the clover is still there, though threatened by Hottentot Fig in recent years. Some seasons there is little, and fears are expressed for its continued existence, but in 1977 and 1978 it appeared in abundance and there was more than in all the previous ten years put together. The heat and drought of summer 1976 may have been responsible for its sudden increase. In 1926, Attenborough found it in good quantity on the cliffs on the north coast and from his directions it was refound on the steep west-side slopes of Rouge Nez in the 1950s and 1960. Attenborough also stated (pers. comm.) that he had once found one plant on the Île Percée.
H error.

T. pratense L.   **Red Clover**
                                   du **rouoge trêfl'ye**

Common on roadsides and in cultivated fields where it tends to be large and lush and is probably an escape from cultivation, but smaller forms occur, looking native, elsewhere.

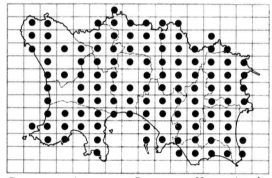

G common; A common; S common; H occasional.

T. medium L.   **Zig-zag Clover**
G two doubtful records; A 1953.

T. alpestre L.   **Mountain Zig-zag Clover**
G 1974.

T. ochroleucon Huds.   **Sulphur Clover**
Saunders' record from St Saviour's Valley, given by Babington (1839) and rejected by Lester-Garland (1903), has never been confirmed.

T. squamosum L.   **Sea Clover**
(T. maritimum)
The only records are from the end of last century: First Tower and St Ouen's Bay, 1898, Piquet; Bellozane Valley, 1899, Lester-Garland, who thought the species might be a survival from the south coast salt marshes which had been drained and cultivated. If so, it seems strange that there are no records from earlier last century.
G rare.

T. subterraneum L.   Subterranean Clover

Common on light soil, but it tends to occur a little further inland than *T. striatum* and *T. scabrum*. The name comes from the way the flower stalks lengthen and bend towards the soil as the fruit begins to form. The calyces then turn backwards, lengthen and pull the fruit underground. Babington noted in his own copy of his Flora that Druce had found Subterranean Clover growing 12 in. to 18 in. high about St Aubin in 1877.

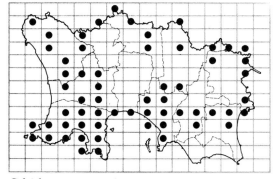

G fairly common; A frequent; S occasional; H occasional.

Lotus tenuis Waldst. & Kit. ex Willd.
Narrow-leaved Bird's-foot-trefoil

Several plants were found on Le Hocq Common in 1958 but the habitat was later destroyed.
G rare.

L. corniculatus L.   Common Bird's-foot-trefoil
des p'tits chabots

Common, with var. *crassifolius* Pers. near the coast.

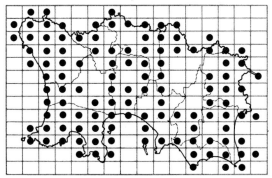

G, A, S and H common.

L. uliginosus Schkuhr   Greater Bird's-foot-trefoil

Common and often luxuriant in damp places.

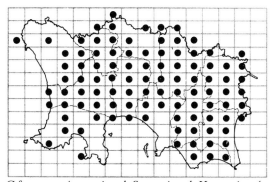

G frequent; A occasional; S occasional; H occasional.

L. subbiflorus Lag.   Hairy Bird's-foot-trefoil
(L. hispidus)

Subsp. *subbiflorus*   Frequent in open turf.

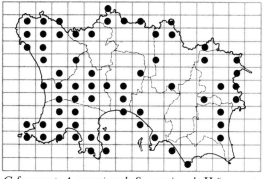

G frequent; A occasional; S occasional; H frequent.

L. angustissimus L.   Slender Bird's-foot-trefoil

This species of heaths and côtils near the sea has undergone dramatic changes in numbers over the last thirty years, for no known reason.

J. Gay first listed it in 1832 from Les Quennevais and both Babington (1839) and Piquet (1896) reported it as frequent. Lester-Garland (1903) thought it 'not very common' and stated that *L. subbiflorus* was commoner. Attenborough (1919) wrote that it was curious that this species should be so much rarer than *L. subbiflorus*.

In the mid-1950s, it was decidedly rare, only very few plants being seen over several years, then suddenly in 1958, there was a resurgence of it, so that it was common, sometimes abundant, in many places. The resurgence died away almost as quickly as it came and, within a year or two, *L. angustissimus* was again rare. No member of the Société Jersiaise Botanical Section saw it between 1971 and 1981 but in 1982 and 1983 a few plants were found in one area.
G, A, S and H rare.

Anthyllis vulneraria L.   **Kidney Vetch**

Plentiful on the north-west and south-west cliffs. J. Cullen has determined all the specimens he has seen from the Jersey cliffs as subsp. *vulneraria* var. *langei* Jalas which in *Flora Europaea* he states to be intermediate between subsp. *vulneraria* and subsp. *iberica* (W. Becker) Jalas. Subsp. *maritima* (Schweigger) Corb., which in theory grows only round the Baltic, was recorded in the Armorican Flora and should be checked.

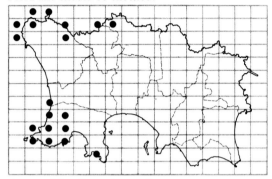

G rare; A locally common; S rare.

Ornithopus compressus L.   **A Bird's-foot**

In July 1958 more than thirty plants of this southern European bird's-foot were found on the headland above Beauport in close turf which appeared not to have been disturbed for at least a generation, if ever. A few plants were found in 1961 but none has been seen since.

O. perpusillus L.   **Bird's-foot**

Common on dry banks and côtils.

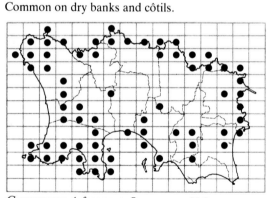

G common; A frequent; S common; H frequent.

O. pinnatus (Miller) Druce   **Orange Bird's-foot**

This was thought to be a Bailiwick of Guernsey speciality until 1979. The only certain records until then had been a specimen collected by a Miss Guille at Noirmont in 1850 and Piquet's from St Ouen in 1854. F. W. Hanbury's specimen of 1884 is labelled

simply 'Jersey' with no locality and a 1924 record from La Corbière was in error for the above species. In 1979 hundreds of plants were found by Mrs M. L. Long on an old tennis court and in the surrounding area when the grounds of Le Val, St Brelade, were open to the public. The land at Le Val borders Ouaisné Common, which officially is La Commune de Bas du fief et seigneurie de Noirmont, and botanists last century used to refer to Le Ouaisné as part of Noirmont. It is therefore thought that Orange Bird's-foot may have had a continuous history in the area and that it is a native species.
G local; A locally frequent; S rare; H 1899 and 1904.

Hippocrepis comosa L.   **Horseshoe Vetch**

Horseshoe Vetch was first found by F. Piquet at Plémont in 1869 and was recorded by Attenborough (1940) as being abundant from L'Étacq round Grosnez to Le Creux Gros. Most years this is still true but in 1978 only a few plants were found after a thorough search. This may be connected with the heat and/or drought of 1976. By 1981, the population was back to normal.

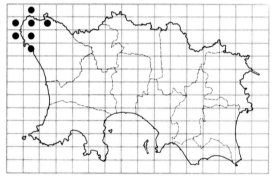

Onobrychis viciifolia Scop.   **Sainfoin**

Piquet collected a specimen of this fodder plant in 1857 and noted that it was occasionally seen in fields.
G 1790; A pre-1908.

OXALIDACEAE

Oxalis corniculata L.   **Yellow Sorrel**

Most *Oxalis* species which now appear as weeds in fields or gardens came to Jersey only this century mostly from South or Central America or South Africa. By contrast, *O. corniculata* is a south European species which was here in La Gasca's time, 1831–1834. Piquet listed it as common in gardens in 1851 and it is still so, particularly in rock gardens where the stems, which root at the nodes, are difficult to remove. Out of gardens, it is not so common, though, as Lester-Garland (1903) stated, it appears naturalised in hedges and on roadsides near houses. The South African var. *repens* (Thunb.) Zucc. with smaller leaves and var. *atropurpurea* van Houtte ex Planchon with purple leaves also occur.

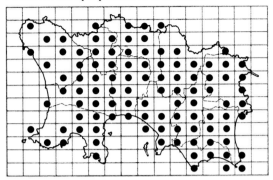

G common; S occasional; H local.

O. exilis A. Cunn.   **Least Yellow Sorrel**

This extremely small-leaved and small-flowered Australasian *Oxalis* occasionally grows as a greenhouse weed or outside in sheltered gardens. Its leaves are always less than 6mm and its fruit capsules are less than 7mm.
G rare; S rare; H occasional.

O. stricta L.   **A Yellow Sorrel**

This was found at Belcroute in 1916 by Guiton, according to Attenborough in the Société Jersiaise botanical report for that year but the plant was probably wrongly identified. There is no specimen, which is strange because Guiton was a collector, and a specimen which Burdo gathered as *O. stricta* in 1926 from, he thought, the same place, is *O. pes-caprae*, Bermuda Buttercup.
S rare.

O. europaea Jordan   **Upright Oxalis**
G two records; H 1958.

O. articulata Savigny   **Pink Oxalis**

Pink Oxalis, a native of South America, is much planted in gardens, as opposed to occurring as an unwanted weed like the bulbous species. How long it has been in the island is unknown. It occurs frequently planted on hedgebanks outside gardens, sometimes very thickly, and its stout rhizomes help it to become established if thrown away with garden rubbish. Apart from its root, the simplest way to recognise it, is by the orange dots, pin-prick size, round the underside of its three leaflets. It was not mapped because of the difficulty in deciding how 'wild' the plants were, but it is widespread in every parish.
G frequent; A locally frequent; S occasional; H occasional.

O. acetosella L.   **Wood-sorrel**
     du **pain d'coucou**

Wood-sorrel is the only native *Oxalis*. It was first reported by Saunders from Rozel (Babington 1839) and its delicate flowers can still be found in spring in the valley running down to St Catherine from Rozel. It is a plant of dampish, shady places so woodlands are its normal home but it also occurs on the north coast cliffs where bracken presumably provides the shade.

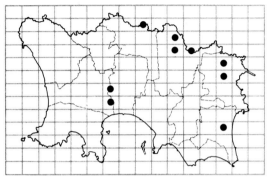

G error; S error.

O. corymbosa DC.   **Small Pink Oxalis**
     du **trêfl'ye à ouognons**

First recorded only in 1956 but it was probably in the island earlier. In the 1960s and 1970s it increased considerably, being introduced with peat. It comes from South America and is one of the bulbous species almost impossible to eradicate. In *O. corymbosa* the bulb itself splits up into innumerable bulblets when ripe and any attempt to remove it scatters the bulblets in the soil. The leaves of this species can easily be distinguished from those of *O. articulata* by the dots on the underside of the leaves being red, closer to the edge and being so small that they are not readily seen with the naked eye. The leaves can be distinguished from those of *O. latifolia* by their rounded, not pointed, leaflets.

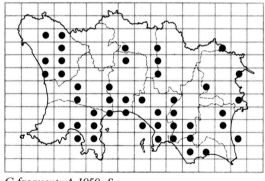

G frequent; A 1959; S rare.

O. latifolia Kunth   **Mexican Oxalis**
                          du **trêfl'ye à ouognons**

In Louis-Arsène's collection there is a specimen of
O. latifolia labelled that it was gathered on 15 July
1925 in Bellozanne Valley. Ariste collected one from
the same place on 20 August 1927. Since then it has
increased tremendously. Small bulblets are produced
on short runners off the parent bulb and any disturbance of the soil, for example by rotary cultivators,
spreads the new bulblets far and wide. Each one
seems to grow. The lobes of each of the three leaflets
are pointed, giving a fish-tail effect but in some plants
the leaflets are more rounded. The species comes
from Mexico and tropical South America.

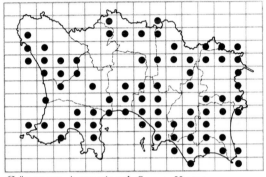

G frequent; A occasional; S rare; H rare.

O. tetraphylla Cav.   **Four-leaved Oxalis**
                          du **trêfl'ye à ouognons**

Four-leaved Oxalis, another bulbous species, is not
as widespread as the two previous ones, but it can be
locally abundant and an equal nuisance.

Its first record was from a field at La Haule in 1917
when it was taken to the Ladies' College by Miss P.
Donaldson. Her friends, doing the then equivalent of
O-levels, took it to be Four-leaved Clover and
wanted more of it for good luck. Miss Donaldson was
able to supply all that was needed – and more, it was
in such good quantity. The fact that every leaf on
every plant had four leaflets made her query the
identification, as well as the general look of the
plants, but none of this bothered her contemporaries.
It was not until some forty years later, at a meeting of
the Botanical Section of the Société Jersiaise, that
Miss Donaldson discovered what her 'Four-leaved
Clover' was. Meanwhile Louis-Arsène and Ariste
had found it in the same cultivated field at La Haule
in the 1920s. It remained there until the mid-1960s
when the field was allowed to revert to grass. Leaving an area to grass for a few years is one way of
ridding it of Oxalis, but it is obviously impractical if
the area is arable land or a garden.

Four-leaved Oxalis spreads by the main bulb producing several bulblets on underground stolons up to

10cm long. If the parent bulb is dug up, the small ones
may drop off and remain in the soil.

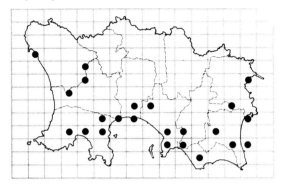

O. deppei Loddiges ex Sweet   **Deppe's Oxalis**

This four-leaved oxalis with brick-red flowers is as yet
only known by Jersey botanists as a garden/house
plant but in 1933 it was recorded by A. Chevalier, a
French botanist: 'Mauvaise herbe commune dans
quelques jardins à Jersey et à Guernesey' (*Bull.
Mens. de la Soc. Linn. de Normandie* 1933). D. P.
Young, the authority on *Oxalis*, stated (*in litt.*) that
Chevalier in a paper on *Oxalis* said he considered
O. tetraphylla and *O. deppei* to be the same. In the
absence of a specimen, this record must therefore be
taken as *O. tetraphylla* which does occur in Jersey.
G same error?

O. pes-caprae L.   **Bermuda Buttercup**

This oxalis, neither a buttercup nor a native of
Bermuda, was collected by Burdo from Belcroute in
1926 as *O. stricta* and, in the absence of a specimen,
there is a strong possibility that Guiton's *O. stricta*
from Belcroute in 1916 was also this. It was still there
until 1982 but was not found in 1983 because the
roadside gutter in which it used to grow had been
concreted. A field below La Valeuse, St Brelade's
Bay, was badly infested in 1960, Dr D. H. Phillips.
Only a few plants were in the neighbourhood by 1967
but some were still there in 1982. Elsewhere it has
been more transitory, as a garden weed: Gorey Hill,
1957, A. Le Sueur; Mont Sohier, 1959, D.
McClintock; Brig-y-don, 1967, Mrs J. Brooks;
Pontac House Hotel, 1983, Mrs D. L. Le Quesne.

Bermuda Buttercup is bulbous, but not a nuisance
in Jersey perhaps because the plants are frost-tender.
Though it comes from South Africa, it is now a pest in
many warm-temperate countries, including
Bermuda. This, together with its yellow flowers the
size of a buttercup, account for its English name,
Bermuda Buttercup.
G occasional; S 1951; H rare.

       Opposite, Plate 7   Spotted Rock-rose *Tuberaria guttata*

O. incarnata L.   **Pale Oxalis**

A specimen of Pale Oxalis is labelled as collected by Louis-Arsène from a hedge at Rozel in 1925 and another from St Peter's Valley in 1926. Ariste collected a specimen from Bagatelle in 1928. By the 1950s it was in great quantity in some areas, usually on shady banks or under trees. It is difficult to eradicate because new bulbils form on the stems, in the axils of the leaves, and drop back into the soil when the plant is disturbed. Fortunately, it is not likely to be an agricultural nuisance because of its habitat preference.

This relatively unknown species, which is fairly common in Jersey, looks like Wood Sorrel and all sightings of 'Wood Sorrel', rare here, should be checked. The flowers are somewhat similar but Pale Oxalis has a bulbous root and bulbils, and the backs of its leaves tend to be purple.

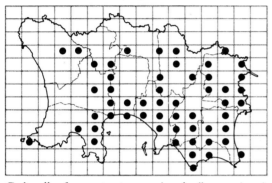

G locally frequent; A occasional; S occasional; H occasional.

O. rosea Jaquin   **An annual Oxalis**

Mrs E. M. Towers noticed this in a rockery on La Marquanderie, St Brelade, in 1970 where it was later eliminated by weedkiller. The following year it was growing in the gravel drive and at the foot of a privet hedge next door. It has not been seen since in St Brelade but in 1981 it was a garden weed on Les Grupieaux, St Peter, Mrs M. L. Long.

O. tuberosa Molina   **Oca**
(O. crenata)

There are now so many Oxalis species growing wild in Jersey that the following note is of interest. It appeared in the first *Report* of the Jersey Agricultural and Horticultural Society (1834: 12): 'The *Oxalis crenata* is said to surpass the Potatoe in weight of produce; and to equal it in value; being moreover a perennial plant; a trial of it is in progress, which will be duly reported to the Society.' Nothing more was heard of it. Oca is cultivated for its tubers in South America but they are 'of no very pleasant taste' (*Sturtevant's Notes on Edible Plants* 1919 Ed. Hedrick).

GERANIACEAE

Geranium sanguineum L.   **Bloody Crane's-bill**

Three records of garden escapes only: lane at St John, 1898, Piquet; one plant in rough grass below a wall, Petit Félard, 1964, Mrs E. M. Towers; Hautes Croix, St John, 1967, Mrs P. Green.
G two records; A rare.

G. pratense L.   **Meadow Crane's-bill**

Planted at the top of Ouaisné Hill, where it was first noted in 1966.
G two records; A rare; S ?1944.

G. versicolor L.   **Pencilled Crane's-bill**
(G. striatum)

Pencilled Geranium, a plant of mountain woods in the eastern Mediterranean, probably came to Jersey as a garden plant and escaped. J. Gay recorded it first from St Aubin and St Helier in 1832 and altogether it was seen in six different parishes last century. It tends to occur over a restricted length of a grassy hedge-bank and some localities, like the one on the road from Rozel Mill to La Chaire and that near Fontaine St Martin in St Lawrence, have been known for well over fifty years. They may be much older than that, but the localities given in early records are not detailed enough to be sure.

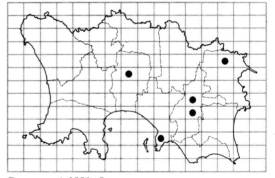

G scarce; A 1881; S rare.

G. pyrenaicum Burm. fil.   **Hedgerow Crane's-bill**

Rare, with few records until 1978: near Pontac, Babington (1839); Hautmont, undated note by Piquet; Vallée des Vaux, 1881, Vaniot; near Victoria College, no date, Dr M. M. Bull, (Lester-Garland 1903); Mont Misère, 1957, Miss McC. Webster; relic of planting in botanic garden, Highlands College, 1958. In 1978 Mrs K. Le Sueur found it by the roadside north of Kempt Tower where it still occurs and it is now in Les Mielles opposite.
G rare.

G. rotundifolium L.   **Round-leaved Crane's-bill**

This seems to have been strangely rare early last

century, considering how frequent it is now. Babington did not see it himself but had to rely on a record from W. Christy, and Piquet did not list it. By 1903 it was becoming less scarce so that Lester-Garland listed it as 'Not common', though he only gave five localities.

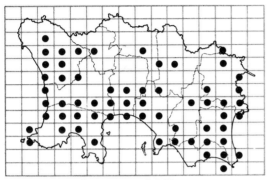

G rare; A locally frequent; S 1930.

G. molle L.   Dove's-foot Crane's-bill
Common in many different habitats.

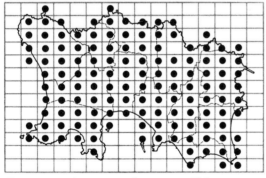

G common; A common; S common; H frequent.

G. pusillum L.   Small-flowered Crane's-bill
Small-flowered Crane's-bill, which looks like Dove's-foot Crane's-bill but has smaller, rather dingy purple flowers and hairy fruit, is rare and probably only a casual. There are four records from last century: 1839, 1866, 1882 and 1898, and six from this: 1930, 1933, 1960, 1964(2) and 1983. All are from widely separated localities.
G rare; A rare; S 1958; H rare.

G. columbinum L.   Long-stalked Crane's-bill
Long-stalked Crane's-bill was found in 1958 at Highlands College near the site of the old botanic garden. Louis-Arsène and Ariste both have specimens labelled as from Les Quennevais in 1929 but Ariste's is not mounted in the same way as all his other specimens, one of which is of this species from the botanic garden in 1928. There must therefore be

some doubt about the 1929 records. The only other record is Saunders', given by Babington (1839) and rejected by Lester-Garland (1903).
G rare; A last record 1900.

G. cf submolle Steudel   Alderney Geranium
The 'Alderney Geranium' which has been known in Guernsey from 1926 and in Alderney from 1938, was growing in a corner of a field at La Becquetterie, St Clement, Jersey in 1966. It is one of several closely related South American species which still require elucidation, but though the precise identity of the species is not certainly known, it is agreed that the Jersey specimens are the same as the 'Alderney Geranium'.
G rare; A occasional.

G. dissectum L.   Cut-leaved Crane's-bill
Common but less so than Dove's-foot Crane's-bill.

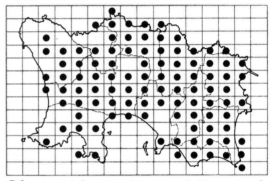

G frequent; A frequent; S occasional; H occasional.

G. lucidum L.   Shining Crane's-bill
Rare: La Haule, 1872, Dr M. M. Bull, Hb Oxford, and 1925, Ariste; bank west of Beaumont Hill, 1953, Mrs M. L. Long; wild part of garden, Faldouet, 1963, Mrs D. L. Le Quesne; garden weed at Hérupe, St John, 1973, Mrs M. L. Long. It is still present in the last three localities and was seen in a garden in St Saviour's Road in 1983.

G. robertianum L.   Herb-Robert
                                    du **rouoget**
Common on hedgebanks not in full sun. A white-flowered form was seen on Bulwarks Hill, St Aubin, in 1963, J. C. Fluck.

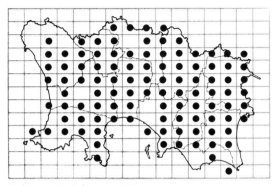

G frequent; A frequent; S rare.

G. purpureum Vill.   Little-Robin

Dr W. Sherard's list of species which he saw in Jersey in 1689 (Ray's *Synopsis* 1690) contained a species which, from its Latin description, Druce considered to be *G. purpureum*. See the Introduction. Lester-Garland (1903) described it as locally abundant on dry banks and it is still common in sunny places particularly in the west.

In the past there was considerable discussion on the relationship between this species and *G. robertianum*, Herb-Robert, and on the splitting of both species into subspecies. *Flora Europaea* has been followed in this account but if *G. purpureum* is split, then Jersey and Alderney have subsp. *purpurea* only and Guernsey has this and subsp. *forsteri* (Wilmott) Baker, though the latter may only be a habitat form.

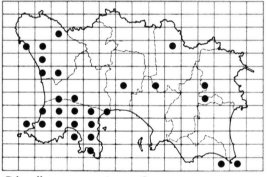

G locally common; A rare; S rare.

G. rubescens Yeo   Greater Herb-Robert
G rare.

Erodium maritimum (L.) L'Hér.   Sea Stork's-bill

Sea Stork's-bill grows in low open turf in exposed places on the cliffs and it is usually plentiful where it occurs. In the past it was considered rare, so either it has increased or, as the whole plant is small and the flowers often have no petals, it was overlooked.

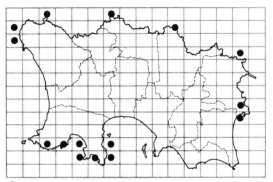

G rare; A occasional; S frequent; H common.

E. cicutarium (L.) L'Hér.   Common Stork's-bill
des **piègnes**

Subsp. *cicutarium* Common Stork's-bill or *des piègnes* is aptly named. It is indeed common in Jersey which is not necessarily true of a species with the word 'Common' in its English name. Its fruits, fancifully, are like storks' bills and they can also be likened as in the Jersey-Norman-French name to a comb, the beaks being the teeth of the comb. In early spring its flowers stud low open turf round the coast and on the foothills with rose-purple. White-flowered plants are occasionally seen.

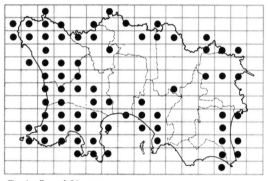
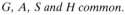

G, A, S and H common.

Subsp. *bipinnatum* Tourlet Specimens from Ouaisné Common in 1956 were confirmed by Professor T. G. Tutin and were used for the *British Flora Illustrations* (1957) which accompany the *Flora of the British Isles* (1952). It also occurs on Les Quennevais and at the north end of St Ouen's Bay. No satisfactory record of the hybrid between the subspecies exists but they grow together so it may occur.
S 1967.

E. moschatum (L.) L'Hér.   Musk Stork's-bill
d's **êpîles à chorchièrs**

Frequent and in some years, for example 1967, locally luxuriant and abundant. It seems to prefer a richer, moister soil than the preceding species. Musk Stork's-bill used to be cultivated in Elizabethan times for its pleasant scent though now it seems odourless or to have a slightly disagreeable smell. *D's épîles à chorchièrs* means 'sorcerers' pins' referring like the English name to the long beaks of the fruit. The Jersey-Norman-French names for this and the previous species are used for both, and several others are given by Le Maistre (1966).

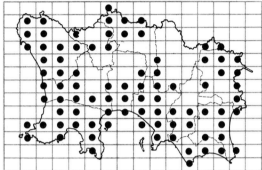

G frequent; A occasional; S occasional; H frequent.

TROPAEOLACEAE

Tropaeolum majus L.   **Nasturtium**

A garden escape occasionally seen on rubbish dumps where it may seed itself for a year or two but it soon dies out. Nowhere is it established.
G occasional; A occasional.

LINACEAE

Linum bienne Mill.   **Pale Flax**
(L. angustifolium)

Pale Flax is native in open grassland near the sea. In 1851 Piquet recorded it as common but by 1903 Lester-Garland thought it only frequent. Most of the records on the map were made in the early 1960s and Pale Flax seems to be getting progressively rarer.

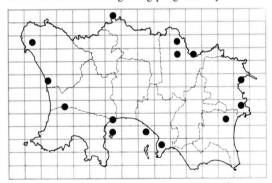

G local; A locally common; S frequent; H 1838.

L. usitatissimum L.   **Flax**

Lester-Garland (1903) considered this to be an escape from cultivation. He only knew of one record – J. Piquet's of 1866 – but F. Piquet collected a specimen from Samarès Lane in 1869. The only record this century is one from a paddock near Mont Les Vaux, St Aubin, in 1970.
G three records; A last record 1902; S sown wild 1953.

L. catharticum L.   **Fairy Flax**

Recorded from Les Quennevais by Babington (1839) and from near St Ouen's Pond by Lester-Garland (1903). It still occurs in both places, sometimes in good quantity. Vaniot collected a specimen from 'Les Landes de Boulay Bay' in 1881.
G rare; A occasional; H common.

Radiola linoides Roth   **Allseed**

Allseed occurs in open damp turf round the coast. It has not been recorded often, perhaps being overlooked, but it was abundant where noted.

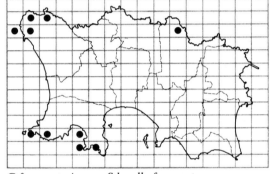

G frequent; A rare; S locally frequent.

EUPHORBIACEAE

Mercurialis annua L.   **Annual Mercury**
                                               d'la **tête**

A common, sometimes abundant, weed of cultivated land. Each plant is either male, with the flowers on long axillary spikes, or female, with the flowers in the axils of the leaves, so that to a non-botanist gardener they can appear as two different weeds. Plants bearing both male and female flowers have not been seen in Jersey.

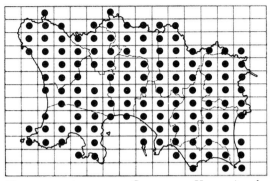

G common; A common; S common; H occasional.

M. perennis L.   **Dog's Mercury**

Dog's Mercury is very much rarer than Annual Mercury as the distribution map shows. Piquet (1896) listed it as common but Lester-Garland (1903) as rare. In different ways both statements are true. It only occurs in damp thickets but where they occur it is often in abundance. Unfortunately damp thickets are becoming scarcer through man's activities.

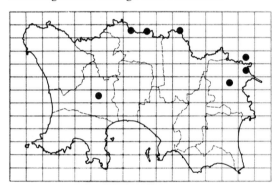

Ricinus communis L.   **Castor Oil Plant**

Seven scattered records from 1957 onwards, usually of single plants, but in 1971 several plants appeared in a field near Val de la Mare, St Peter, where cattle had been fed on Castor Oil Plant meal.

Euphorbia peplis L.   **Purple Spurge**

This prostrate spurge which was always rare used to grow high up on the beaches of St Ouen's Bay, St Aubin's Bay and Grouville Bay. A specimen in the Dillenian Herbarium, Oxford, is labelled, 'From Jersey, Mr Clark.' and was collected between 1730 and 1740. Piquet's specimen of July 1860 is labelled, 'Sands of St Aubin's Bay, near Mr Clarke's Shipyard, very rare.' There were two Clarke's shipyards in St Aubin's Bay, one west of St Aubin's Fort and the other extended from where Kensington Place is now

to West Park. The building of the sea walls round the island probably destroyed its habitat. The last record (*in litt.*) was by Père de Bellaing in 1902 and 1903 from 'Piquet's place' in Grouville Bay (probably the south end) from where Père de Bellaing said he did not think it was on the point of disappearing. Search should be made for it on any beach where sand and shingle accumulate.

G last good record 1861; A last record 1976; S 1838; H last record 1968.

E. helioscopia L.   **Sun Spurge**
                                  d'l'hèrbe à véthues

Widely distributed but thinly spread in cultivated fields and gardens where it is easily separated from Jersey's other spurges by its attractive ruff of serrated ray-leaves. The stems exude a caustic white milky juice when cut, as do all spurges, and this was supposed to cure warts if rubbed on them – hence the Jersey-Norman-French name.

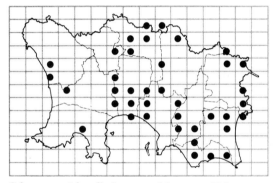

G frequent; A locally frequent; S frequent; H frequent.

E. lathyris L.   **Caper Spurge**
                                  d'l'hèrbe d'chorchi

Caper Spurge is occasionally seen as a garden escape usually on a rubbish dump or near where gardeners have tried to use it to deter moles. Some people swear by it as a mole deterrent but it has never been effective in our garden. On the other hand, a well-grown plant is so sculptural and decorative that it makes an excellent house plant. Abundant seed which germinates easily is produced. The seeds are somewhat poisonous and should not be confused with the capers used for flavouring which are the pickled flowerbuds of *Capparis spinosa*, a Mediterranean shrub. The origin of the English name Caper Spurge is unknown; it was *hèrbe d'chorchi* to a Jerseyman because a plant in the garden provided protection against witches.

Map overleaf

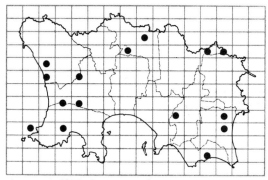

G rare; A 1977; S occasional; H occasional.

E. exigua L.   **Dwarf Spurge**

Dwarf Spurge has either decreased very considerably or was wrongly recorded last century. Lester-Garland (1903) was obviously puzzled by previous estimates of its quantity, common or frequent, and stated that it was very rare in his experience. As he cites no places, he may only have seen a specimen collected by F. Piquet from Le Cornu's Nurseries in 1870. The only records this century are two unlocalised specimens, dated 1901 and 1911, labelled 'cultivated fields. Rare' by J. Piquet.
G last record 1951; S last record 1930.

E. peplus L.   **Petty Spurge**
                                                        *d'l'***hèrbe à véthues**

Frequent rather than common, according to Lester-Garland (1903), and this is still true though in some years, like 1980, it was in greater supply than usual. It tends to be a garden weed rather than a plant of fields.

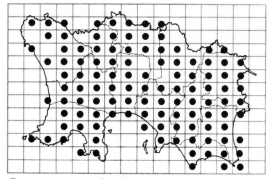

G common; A locally common; S occasional; H occasional.

E. portlandica L.   **Portland Spurge**

Portland Spurge is still in quantity on Les Quennevais from where J. Gay reported it in 1832, and it is still common in many coastal areas as Babington stated in 1839. It is a plant which often seems to be misnamed. It grows within sight of the sea so, when in good

blue-green leaf in spring and early summer, it tends to be misidentified as Sea Spurge. In late summer its stem often changes colour from blue-green to reddish purple with the result that it is recorded as Purple Spurge.

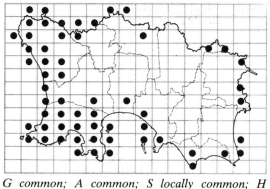

G common; A common; S locally common; H common.

E. paralias L.   **Sea Spurge**

Sea Spurge is now extremely rare and still decreasing. At various times it has been recorded from Grouville round to Le Hocq, St Aubin's Bay, St Brelade's Bay and St Ouen's Bay and in 1871 as locally abundant on Les Quennevais. All that seems to remain is a small quantity in St Ouen's Bay, and the Spurge Hawk-moth, whose caterpillar feeds on Sea Spurge and which used to occur on Les Quennevais, has not been recorded this century. Development along the coast was probably responsible for Sea Spurge's disappearance from the bays but why it should have gone from Les Quennevais is unknown.
G scarce and decreasing; A locally frequent; S last record 1872; H rare.

E. esula L.   **Leafy Spurge**

Listed by La Gasca in 1834 but rejected by Lester-Garland in 1903 and not confirmed.
S 1958.

E. x pseudovirgata (Schur) Soó   **A hybrid Spurge**
E. esula x **E. uralensis**

Above La Pulente, St Ouen's Bay, 1956, D. McClintock and still there 1962, J. C. Fluck. The nomenclature of Benoit and Stace in Stace (1975) has been followed.

E. cyparissias L.   **Cypress Spurge**

The roots of Cypress Spurge tend to roam and plants have been found as roadside escapes from gardens at Petit Port, St Brelade, at Rozel and at the Tas de Geon, Trinity.
G one ? record.

E. amygdaloides L.   **Wood Spurge**

Subsp. *amygdaloides*   Common in woods, on shady hedgebanks and on the north cliffs.

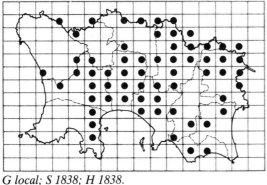

G local; S 1838; H 1838.

E. maculata L.   **A Spurge**

One plant making a circular mat about 60cm across in a quarry at Frémont in 1966, J. C. Fluck, det. J. E. Lousley. The species is an American succulent nursery weed established in south Europe.

SIMAROUBACEAE

Ailanthus altissima (Mill.) Swingle   **Tree of Heaven**

Rarely planted, for example, in the grounds of the old Government Office on Mount Bingham and in the area behind Churchill Memorial Park, St Brelade.

POLYGALACEAE

Polygala vulgaris L.   **Common Milkwort**

Local on the calcareous dunes of Les Quennevais and in St Ouen's Bay. Early botanists lumped all milkworts together under this specific name but the great majority of Jersey plants belong to the next species. Plate 2827 in Sowerby's *English Botany* Supplt III 1843 was drawn from a plant collected as var. *oxyptera* by Babington in St Aubin's Bay on 26 June 1838.

G rare; A rare; S common; H frequent.

P. serpyllifolia J. A. C. Hose   **Heath Milkwort**
(P. serpyllacea)   *d'la* **stchinnancie**

Common on heaths, cliffs and part of the dunes.

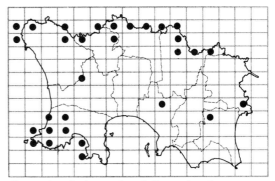

G occasional; A occasional; S occasional.

ACERACEAE

Acer campestre L.   **Field Maple**

Recorded as frequent by Babington (1839) in both Jersey and Guernsey but perhaps in error because there is no specimen to confirm the statement and in 1975 it was unknown in Guernsey (McClintock 1975). Piquet (1896) thought it rare in Jersey and Lester-Garland (1903) described it as very rare, doubtless planted, and indeed there are records of it being imported. It is still rare and most 'dots' on the map represent only one tree, but it is now being planted increasingly to replace the elms.

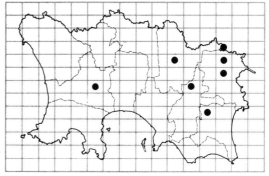

G two unsupported claims last century.

A. platanoides L.   **Norway Maple**

A Norway Maple grows in a field hedge in the north of St Lawrence.
G rarely planted.

A. pseudoplatanus L.   **Sycamore**
                                    un **sycomôre**

Babington (1839) stated that Sycamore was naturalised in several places and Lester-Garland (1903) stated briefly that it was 'A planted tree'. It is now common in many woodlands, seeding itself abundantly to the detriment of the other trees in those woodlands, and so many saplings are produced that few, if any, can attain major tree size. A form with the underside of the leaves a rich purple, f.

purpureum (Loudon) Rehder, originated in Saunders' Nursery in Jersey in 1828.

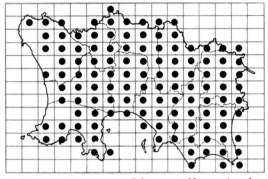

G frequent; A common; S frequent; H occasional.

HIPPOCASTANACEAE
Aesculus hippocastanum L.   **Horse Chestnut**
                                                  un **chât'nyi à j'va**

Frequently planted. Seedlings have been seen but only rarely do they reach sapling size.

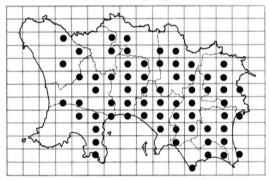

G rare; A rare; S rare; (otherwise as in J.)

BALSAMINACEAE
Impatiens glandulifera Royle   **Himalayan Balsam**

Casual, 1901, Piquet; garden weed, Le Colombier Manor, St Lawrence, 1971, Mrs M. L. Long; one plant growing on a heap of bannelais (road sweepings), Rue des Alleurs, St Martin, 1979, Mrs E. Whiteside.
G local; S local.

AQUIFOLIACEAE
Ilex aquifolium L.   **Holly**
                                                  un **housse**

Holly seems to have increased considerably in the wild since last century when Babington (1839) stated that he had found it in several parts of the island but it appeared planted, and Piquet (1896) stated that it was rare in woods and copses. Lester-Garland (1903) commented that it was planted in hedges and

shrubberies. It is not so much in hedges now, as in woodlands, and in many it is regenerating freely.

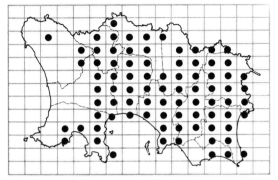

G widespread; S occasional; H planted.

CELASTRACEAE
Euonymus europaeus L.   **Spindle**

Rare. Spindle has been known on the mound at La Hougue Bie since at least the beginning of this century, at Beauport for over fifty years and Ariste has a specimen dated 1927 from an unknown locality in St Catherine. The first two were almost certainly planted.
G planted.

E. japonicus L. fil.   **Euonymus**
                                                  du **vèrt-bouais**

Common as a hedging plant. No seedlings have been seen in the wild though they do appear in gardens, rarely. Euonymus looks as though it has been in Jersey for centuries but the first plants were only brought from South Japan to Britain in 1804.
G commonly planted; S occasional.

BUXACEAE
Buxus sempervirens L.   **Box**
                                                  du **bouisque**

Much planted in the past. Guiton collected a specimen from St Peter's Valley in 1900 but how wild it was is unknown. Ariste labelled his specimens 'Cultivée et subspontanée' from Waterworks Valley in 1924 and J. C. Fluck found about six plants, probably relics, in Coin Hâtain, near Waterworks Valley in 1963.
G planted.

RHAMNACEAE
Frangula alnus Miller   **Alder Buckthorn**

One bush planted, apparently many years ago, in a hedge in Mourier Valley.

VITACEAE

Vitis vinifera L.   **Grape**
du **vèrjus**

Subsp. *vinifera*   Rare. Cultivated Vines can survive long after the gardens in which they were originally planted have disappeared and a few such Vines exist in Jersey. The Vines seen in hedges are presumably from discarded pips. Some Vines produce small but edible Grapes.

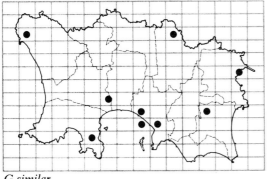

G similar.

Parthenocissus quinquefolia (L.) Planchon
Virginian Creeper

A North American species still growing where planted many years ago in a wild hedge below Mont Fallu in St Peter's Valley. This and related species used sometimes to occur on rubbish dumps where they would persist for a few years.
G planted; S planted.

TILIACEAE

Tilia x vulgaris Hayne   **Lime**
T. cordata x **T. platyphyllos**   *un* **tilleul**

Lime was recorded as a planted tree in Jersey in the 1830s and as such it is still fairly common, mainly in St Helier and in gardens, but it does occasionally occur planted in a field hedge. Unfortunately aphids are often present in such quantity on the leaves that honey-dew, a sticky liquid produced by the aphids, is in sufficient quantity to drip off the trees. Because of this, other species of lime are now being planted. In July 1941, during the Occupation, the Germans suggested using lime tree blossom as tea substitute.

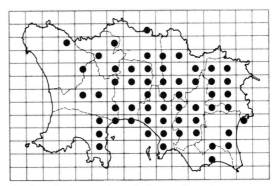

G planted; A rare planted; S rare planted.

MALVACEAE

Malva moschata L.   **Musk Mallow**

A beautiful plant of open grassy areas, still rare and uncertain in its appearance, as stated by Lester-Garland (1903) and Attenborough (1919), and still plentiful where it occurs, as further stated by Attenborough.

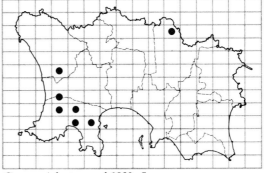

G rare; A last record 1932; S rare.

M. sylvestris L.   **Common Mallow**
d'la **p'tite mauve**

Still common, as Piquet described it last century. Rarely, *la p'tite mauve* is to be seen with white flowers.

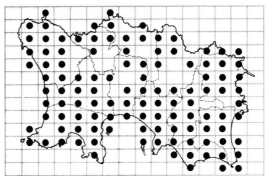

G common; A common; S frequent; H occasional.

95

M. parviflora L.   **Least Mallow**

In his 1898 *Supplementary List* Piquet claimed to have found Least Mallow on St Peter's Common but the record has not been confirmed.

M. pusilla Sm.   **Small Mallow**

One record: La Pompe, St Mary, 1960, Miss J. F. Arthur, det. J. E. Lousley.

M. neglecta Wallr.   **Dwarf Mallow**
(M. rotundifolia)

Frequent on disturbed ground and at the foot of walls, as it has been since last century.

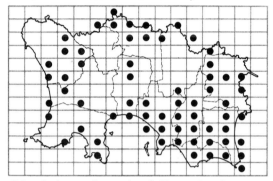

G local; A rare; S occasional; H occasional.

M. verticillata L.   **Chinese Mallow**

One record: St Peter's Common, 1900, Piquet (Hb Oxford and Société Jersiaise).

Lavatera cretica L.   **Smaller Tree-mallow**

In 1879 J. C. Melvill collected a specimen from St Aubin where the species continued to be known for about twenty years. There were four records, perhaps all casuals, between then and 1962 when it was found by the side of La Rue de l'Est, Mount Bingham, by Mrs D. M. England. It is still there in quantity, by the tunnel entrance. The species survived in the grounds of Highlands College on the site of the old botanic garden from at least 1927 to 1958, more or less unaided. The first year it was found, 1879, Professor W. Hillhouse stated that it was 'common'. This is difficult to believe unless he meant very locally common as it is today on La Rue de l'Est.
G locally common; S 1978.

L. arborea L.   **Tree-mallow**
                                        eune **mauve**

Luxuriant locally round the coast and on many off-islets including Les Écréhous and Les Minquiers but less frequent inland. Lester-Garland's comment 'Perhaps native once' is difficult to explain, as Tree-mallow would seem so obviously a native species. He also stated that it was much cultivated in cottage gardens on the coast. This also seemed strange until an elderly Jersey gentleman delicately pointed out that, in the past, the 'privy' tended to be at the bottom of the garden and Tree-mallows were strategically placed, because of their leaves. Children used to eat the fruits, *des p'tits pains*.

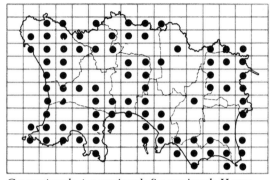

G occasional; A occasional; S occasional; H rare.

Althaea hirsuta L.   **Rough Marsh-mallow**

One record: St Ouen's Bay, July 1902, Piquet (Hb Oxford and Hb Nat. Mus. Wales).

A. officinalis L.   **Marsh-mallow**

Piquet (1851) stated that Ereaut had found Marsh-mallow in St Clement, near the sea, and this presumably refers to Ereaut's unlocalised specimen dated 1847. F. Piquet's 1869 specimen from Samarès Meadows may be from the same place. Later it was found between Pontac and La Rocque and it was still in both localities in 1903. Attenborough thought it was last seen about 1909.
G one record 200 years ago.

Alcea rosea L.   **Hollyhock**

An occasional garden escape on rubbish dumps.
G casual.

Hibiscus trionum L.   **Bladder Ketmia**

Bladder Ketmia, an annual from bird seed, was first noted in a garden at First Tower in 1977 and has seeded itself regularly since then, Mrs E. M. Towers.

THYMELAEACEAE

Daphne laureola L.   **Spurge Laurel**
                                        du **sênné**

Subsp. *laureola* Spurge Laurel is local on the north coast cliffs and in woodlands, being most plentiful in a wood on Les Quennevais. On the north coast it grows in the shade of trees usually towards the bottom of the cliff. It has been known at Mont Ubé for over a hundred and fifty years and at La Hougue Bie for over fifty years. It may have been planted in the latter localities but it appeared spontaneously, presumably bird-sown, in a garden at St Saviour, Mrs P. Stone.

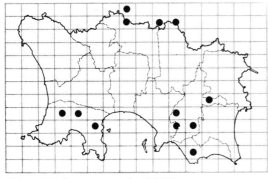

G two ?bird-sown records; S 1976.

ELEAGNACEAE

Hippophae rhamnoides L.　　　　**Sea Buckthorn**

Not native in Jersey and only two records: near Don Bridge Farm from pre-1956 until recently when the habitat was changed; on rocks at La Collette where it still grows.

GUTTIFERAE

Hypericum androsaemum L.　　　　**Tutsan**
　　　　　　　　　　　　　　　d'la **toute-saine**

Locally frequent on the north coast where it usually grows just above the cliff edge and is best seen from the beach, as at La Saline, St John. Rare elsewhere in woods, as in Le Don Gaudin in St Peter's Valley.

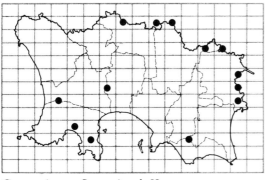

G rare; A rare; S occasional; H scarce.

H. inodorum Miller　　　　**Tall Tutsan**
G rare; S 1953; H 1957.

H. pulchrum L.　　　　**Slender St John's-wort**

A beautiful plant, well-named in Latin, frequent now rather than common as recorded last century. It grows on dry lime-free côtils and rough grassland.

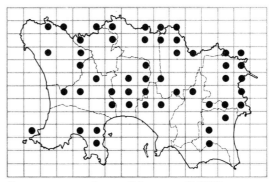

G not common; A rare; S frequent; H 1838.

H. montanum L.　　　　**Pale St John's-wort**

Listed by La Gasca (1834), rejected by Lester-Garland (1903) and not confirmed. Highly improbable.
G error?

H. elodes L.　　　　**Marsh St John's-wort**

Marsh St John's-wort is disappearing as the marshy places which are its habitat are drained or become overgrown because of lack of grazing animals. There are old records from above Bouley Bay and Giffard Bay but post-1960 it was only seen in the west of the island. In two of the localities shown on the map, behind St Ouen's Pond and east of the desalination plant at La Rosière, it has not been seen recently though it may return.

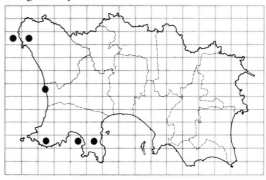

G rare; A last record 1900.

H. linarifolium Vahl　　**Flax-leaved St John's-wort**

Hypericum linarifolium has an extraordinary history in Jersey. Until about the mid-1960s this rare English species was comparatively easy to see here. It was first collected by Babington in 1837 and he listed it from five different places in his Flora (1839). In the following years it was found in many coastal areas, usually the coastal cliffs, and occasionally inland. Dr N. K. B. Robson has confirmed enough specimens, both post-war and dating back over the years, to indicate that the species was well-established and, in general, correctly identified. In post-war years it was found at Rozel, La `Crête, Noirmont, by the old railway line to La Corbière and it was locally frequent on the coast between La Corbière and St Brelade. Gradually, from about the mid-1960s, pure *Hypericum linarifolium* became increasingly difficult to find, most plants seeming to have some admixture of *Hypericum humifusum*. Now, in 1982, Jersey seems to have lost a species because of its (presumed) hybridisation with a closely related species, though that second species is still to be found commonly in a pure state. As yet not sufficient experimental work has been done to confirm hybridisation.

G very rare; A rare; S 1901.

?H. humifusum x H. linarifolium
A ?hybrid St John's-wort

This hybrid is suspected but is as yet unproved experimentally. In Sowerby's *English Botany*, 3rd Ed. (1863–92) J. T. B. Syme mentioned plants at Noirmont which were 'strangely intermediate' between the two species and Pugsley suggested in the *Journal of Botany* for 1915 that Syme's plants might be hybrids. Intermediates, or suspected intermediates, continued to be reported, both last century and this, and of the specimens in Jersey herbaria, Robson determined:

H. linarifolium ad *H. humifusum* verg. Mont Fiquet, 1900, Guiton; by deep quarry pool near La Corbière, 1956; road leading to Le Col de la Rocque, 1961, Mrs J. Brooks.
H. humifusum ad *H. linarifolium* verg. Landes humides de Boulay Bay, 1881, Vaniot; Noirmont, 1961, J. C. Fluck.
Intermediates are still being reported, see *H. linarifolium*.
G local.

H. humifusum L.   Trailing St John's-wort
Frequent on dry banks and côtils.

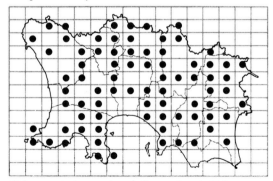

G frequent; A occasional; S occasional; H frequent.

H. tetrapterum Fr.   Square-stalked St John's-wort
Frequent in damp places.

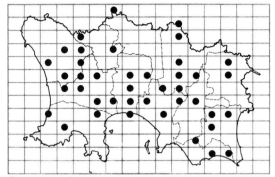

G occasional; A frequent; S locally frequent; H rare.

H. perforatum L.
Common or Perforate St John's-wort
du cache-dgiâbl'ye

Not as common as its English name might suggest and not widespread. The Jersey-Norman-French name probably covers the somewhat similar *H. pulchrum*, Slender St John's-wort, also. If not, it is difficult to see how the islanders could get enough to put round their windows on St John's Eve to keep out evil spirits. See Le Maistre, 1966.

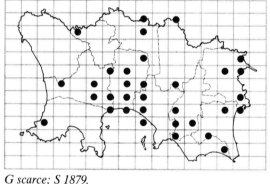

G scarce; S 1879.

VIOLACEAE
V. odorata L.   Sweet Violet
du coucou

A frequent garden escape which is now naturalised in several places, usually near houses. Both violet and white flowered forms are known.

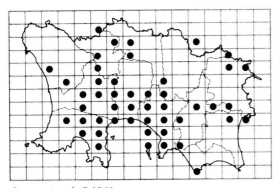

G occasional; S 1961.

V. riviniana Reichenb.　　　Common Dog-violet
　　　　　　　　　　　　　　　　　du **coucou**

This, the common wild violet of Jersey, is widely
distributed on hedgebanks and côtils, as the distribution map shows, and it can be unexpectedly abundant. The northern part of Les Landes, near
Grosnez, sometimes has sheets of violet on it after a
fire has swept through the heathland.

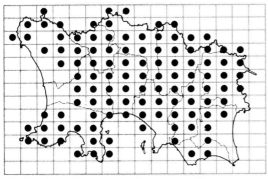

G abundant; A common; S common; H common.

V. canina L.　　　　　　　Heath Dog-violet

Rare. In the past this species and the previous one
were lumped together under the name *V. canina* and
any old records giving *V. canina* as common now
belong to *V. riviniana*. Specimens of *V. canina* were
collected from La Moye in 1906, Druce, and from the
western slopes of Les Quennevais in 1961, 1962 and
1964, confirmed Dr S. M. Walters.

V. lactea Sm.　　　　　　　Pale Dog-violet

Babington, in annotations in his own copy of his
Flora (1839), withdrew Saunders' record which he
had given. Dizerbo in the *Bull. Soc. Sc. de Bretagne*
(1970) stated that it had occurred in Jersey, using the
above record, unaware then that it had been withdrawn. Nevertheless a specimen collected by 'Mrs
Rothwell' on Les Quennevais was determined and
later confirmed as this by A. J. Wilmott (Hb Brit.
Mus.).　　　　　　　　　　　　　*G 1790.*

V. tricolor L.　　　　　　　　Wild Pansy

Both Babington's and Piquet's records of this refer to
the next two species. The only *V. tricolor* plants seen
have been no more than very temporary garden
escapes.
G ? S ?rare; H rare.

V. arvensis Murr.　　　　　　Field Pansy
　　　　　　　　　　　　　　　　　du **coucou**

If Piquet's records from last century are correct,
common 1851 and very common 1896, then Field
Pansy has decreased considerably. Guiton in 1901
thought it frequent and Lester-Garland used the
vague term, not common, in 1903. It was still locally
common in St Aubin's Bay in the mid-1960s. Now it is
only occasionally seen. See the next species.

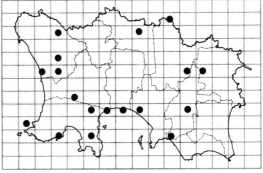

*G occasional; A occasional; S common and hybrid
with above 1929/30; H frequent.*

V. kitaibeliana Schult.　　　　Dwarf Pansy
(V. arvensis var. *nana)*

This beautiful miniature, the Dwarf Pansy, occurs in
open turf on sandy soil in St Ouen's Bay and on Les
Quennevais. The whole plant is often only about 2 to
3 cm high. The flower, only about 5 mm vertically, is
pale cream sometimes with a little blue-purple in it,
though as its face is not held out flat to the sun, the
pale colour of its petals does not show until one looks
at it closely. But its sepals and spur are a dark blue-
purple in exposed places, and Dwarf Pansies sometimes occur so abundantly on Les Quennevais that
the open turf has a blue-purple sheen on it.

　　The first published record seems to be Trimen's in
1871 from St Ouen's Bay (*Journal of Botany* 1871),
but it is more than likely that Piquet's 1851 record of
Field Pansy being common on the coast referred in
part to this species. An illustration by Pandora Sellars
is opposite page 54.

Map overleaf

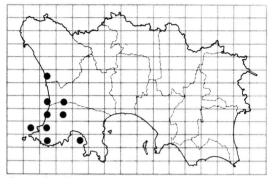

G very local; H rare.

CISTACEAE

Tuberaria guttata (L.) Fourr.   **Spotted Rock-rose**
(Helianthemum guttatum)

In 1689 Dr W. Sherard saw the Spotted Rock-rose, a Mediterranean annual very rare in Britain, near Grosnez. See the Introduction. Spotted Rock-roses still grow near Grosnez almost three hundred years later and they are locally common along the coastal cliffs of the south-west. Normally each of the five yellow petals has a dark brown blotch at its base but sometimes the blotch is missing. The petals fall shortly after mid-day so, to see this species at its best, a visit on a sunny morning is necessary. An illustration by Pandora Sellars is opposite page 86.

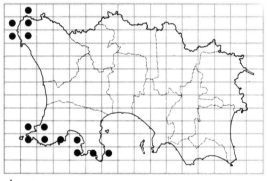

A rare.

TAMARICACEAE

Tamarix gallica L.   **Tamarisk**
    du **tamathìn**

Tamarisk, *T. gallica* including *T. anglica*, a shrub of south-west Europe, has been much planted for hedges by the coast for many years. Saunders (Babington 1839) called it naturalised, but though it holds its own against the native vegetation and thrives, no seedlings have been seen and all known bushes, however old, look planted.
G frequent; A occasional; S rare; H occasional.

FRANKENIACEAE

Frankenia laevis L.   **Sea-heath**

Sea-heath still grows in a gulley near Plémont where it has been known since last century, though one locality appears to have been lost, for Attenborough stated in the Société's botanical report for 1932 that it had 'unfortunately been exterminated in one of its two localities at Plémont'. A large amount of material, considering the rareness of the species in Jersey, is in Louis-Arsène's herbarium and is labelled as from Plémont. The only other recorded localities are 'Near the Grève d'Azette', Saunders, given by Babington (1839) and one plant was seen among rocks near Platte Rocque Point in 1980 by M. Ingrouille.
G last record 1865; A rare.

ELATINACEAE

Elatine hexandra (Lapierre) DC.

    Six-stamened Waterwort

Recorded in the past from Town Mills Pond, Waterworks Valley reservoir, Vicart Mill reservoir, and a pond at Le Marais, La Moye, but it seems not to have stayed in any area for any length of time. At the end of an exhaustive search of the ponds and reservoirs, and with the help of J. E. Lousley, the species was eventually found in abundance on the edge of La Hague reservoir in 1961, and it is still there.
G unconfirmed, 1862.

CUCURBITACEAE

Ecballium elaterium (L.) A. Richard

    Squirting Cucumber

Squirting Cucumber appeared as a garden weed in Beaufort Square for a few years in the late 1950s, J. C. Fluck, but it was eradicated. It was next seen on South Hill, St Helier in the early 1960s, K. Le Sueur, also for only a few years. From the early 1970s it has been a regular weed in several gardens at Pontac, Mrs D. L. Le Quesne.

A specimen, dated 1860 but labelled cultivated, is in Ereaut's collection.

Bryonia dioica Jacq.   **White Bryony**
(Bryonia cretica subsp. *dioica)*

Babington (1839) gave Saunders' record from 'Near Bagatelle'. This and Piquet's record 'Hedge at Trinity' in his *Supplementary List* (1898) were rejected by Lester-Garland (1903). In the Société herbarium there are two specimens gathered by Piquet: St Helier, very rare, 1898; hedge at Trinity, very rare, 1904. Attenborough often said that Piquet planted White Bryony and that he made no secret of it (pers. comm.). The only other records are: St Mark's Road, 1967, Mrs J. Brooks and still there 1982, Mrs E. M. Towers; St Saviour's Road between the Hôtel de France (Maison St Louis) and Highlands

College where it has been known for many years and was probably planted by either the Jesuits or the Frères de l'Instruction Chrétienne.

LYTHRACEAE

Lythrum salicaria L.   **Purple Loosestrife**

Locally frequent in wet areas. Lester-Garland (1903) stated that it was rare, and only St Ouen's Pond and St Peter's Valley were mentioned in the past, so it seems to have spread a little this century. A pink-flowered form used to occur in the millpond of Quetivel Mill, St Peter's Valley, Dr A. E. Mourant, but it has not been seen since the mid-1970s.

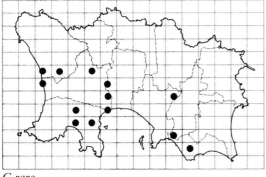

G rare.

L. junceum Banks & Solander   **Greater Grass-poly**

A bird-seed alien first noted near a quarry at Fauvic, 1969, Mrs E. M. Towers, and elsewhere since, always near where birds have been fed.
G 1924.

L. hyssopifolia L.   **Grass-poly**

Grass-poly, a rare species in Britain, has been known at St Catherine's Bay since 1841 when it was collected from there by the Rev. W. W. Newbould. The quantity varies considerably from year to year, as Attenborough noted as far back as 1917 – which was a 'good' year for it. So was 1982. *Flora Europaea* states that it needs disturbed and seasonally flooded ground, and this it has at St Catherine's Bay. Babington (1839) recorded it first from Grouville and it was collected from there again in 1894. Piquet knew it at Le Marais, St Ouen, from 1851 to 1911, and it was recorded from near Les Quennevais in 1876 and 1957 and from Ouaisné Marsh in 1950. Mrs E. M. Whiteside found it in 1967 in a field at St Martin and it has since appeared nearby in a garden, a most unusual habitat.
G last record 1898.

L. portula (L.) D. A. Webb   **Water-purslane**
(Peplis portula)

Still rare in wet places as recorded in the past, but perhaps overlooked. The first record was by J. Gay

from St Brelade in 1832.

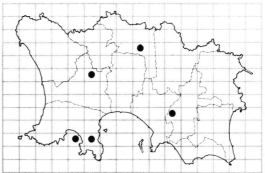

G rare; S rare.

ONAGRACEAE

Fuchsia sp.   **Fuchsia**

The only pre-war record is by A. Chevalier who stated in the *Bull. Mens. Soc. Linn. Norm.* (1933) that Fuchsia was *'si bien naturalisée dans les îles anglo-normandes qu'on l'emploie pour faire des haies vives'*. This is a surprising statement because until comparatively recently there were very few fuchsia hedges in Jersey and even now, in 1982, when they have become highly fashionable in gardens, there is no evidence of any naturalisation. Rarely are they seen on rubbish dumps, as garden throw-outs, and then they persist only for a short time. A similar situation prevails in the rest of the Channel Islands.
G planted and can self-seed; S planted; H planted.

Circaea lutetiana L.   **Enchanter's-nightshade**

Enchanter's-nightshade occurs in shady woods and as a weed in shady gardens. Though each 'dot' on the map may represent only one locality, the species is usually in abundance where it occurs. It seems to me worthy of space in a garden, but I am told that it is a persistent weed difficult to eradicate once established.

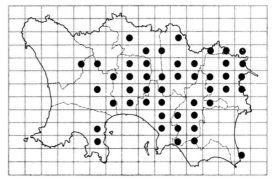

G local; A occasional.

Oenothera biennis L.   **Common Evening-primrose**

In the past the name '*O. biennis*' covered *O. biennis* and *O. erythrosepala*. None of the past records of '*O. biennis*', where a specimen is available, is of that species as it is known today. The only possible record is a plant gathered at La Hougue Bie in 1957 which Dr K. Rostański, an authority on the genus, queried as perhaps being *O. biennis*. Evening-primroses are common in Jersey but not this one which unfortunately has been given the English name, Common Evening-primrose.

G three records.

O. cambrica Rostański   **Welsh Evening-primrose**
des **roses d'un jour**

Evening-primroses, with flowers smaller than those of the two common Jersey species and with the general appearance of the whole plant very different from those two, were noticed in several localities in the early 1960s. It was impossible to assign them to any species given in the *Flora of the British Isles* (Clapham *et al.* 1952) so that members of the Société's Botanical Section were forced to list them as *Oenothera* 'new' or *Oenothera* 'small' during the survey and the plants continued to remain a problem.

In 1977 Dr K. Rostański investigated Evening-primroses in Britain. Plants which D. McClintock found frequently in Wales were put into a new species *O. cambrica* Rostański. Its description fitted this unidentified Evening-primrose of Jersey and Rostański has now determined specimens from various localities in Jersey from 1867 to 1973 as *O. cambrica*. The essential botanical characters are its small flowers compared with the other Evening-primroses in Jersey, its green sepals and its pink veins on the lower leaves. It still occurs here but not in the quantity of the 1960s. Why there should have been the sudden increase in the 1960s is unknown. The plants usually grow on light soil which has been disturbed.

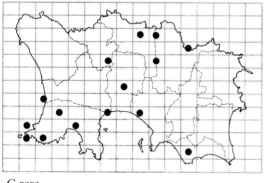

G rare.

O. biennis x **O. erythrosepala**
A hybrid Evening-primrose

One record: St Brelade's Bay, 31 July 1871, Bailey, Hb Manchester, det. B. M. Davis (*Proc. Am. phil. Soc.* 1926).
G 1941.

O. erythrosepala Borbás
Large-flowered Evening-primrose
des **roses d'un jour**

Locally frequent on light soil. It seems to have arrived in the island only about the end of last century because though Lester-Garland (1903) considered it naturalised near First Tower, he stated that it was rare.

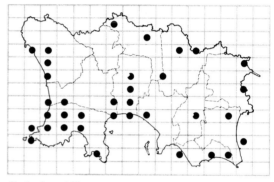

G, A, S and H rare.

O. stricta Ledeb. ex Link
(*O. odorata*)   **Fragrant Evening-primrose**
des **roses d'un jour**

Ereaut collected a specimen of this South American species in 1847, and Melvill by 1879 could describe it as abundant at St Aubin. Lester-Garland (1903) stated that it was locally abundant and thoroughly naturalised. This is still true. Its flowers attract night-flying insects so they open about dusk and close the following morning. The species is most plentiful on Les Quennevais and is in quantity along the sides of the lower parts of Mont à la Brune. An illustration by Pandora Sellars appears opposite.

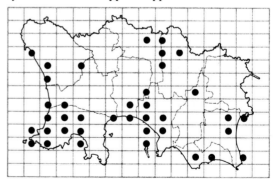

G locally frequent; A occasional; H rare.

Opposite, Plate 9   Fragrant Evening-primrose *Oenothera stricta*

Ludwigia palustris (L.) Elliott **Hampshire-purslane**
(L. apetala)

This used to be abundant in the St Peter/St Lawrence marshes from where it was first reported in the 1830s. It disappeared with the draining of the marshes in the 1870s. Piquet then found it in the marsh on Gorey Common where it remained until at least 1920 when Attenborough saw it. There has been no record since, though Burdo told me that he had brought some back from France and planted it in Le Marais at St Ouen and in the marsh at Gorey in 1927.

Chamerion angustifolium (L.) J. Holub
(Epilobium angustifolium) **Rosebay Willowherb**

This well-known plant of wartime bomb-sites and railway embankments in England is only occasionally seen in Jersey and it seldom persists in one place for any length of time. Babington (1839) gave a record by Saunders, but the first confirmed record is A. J. Robinson's from La Crête, St John, in 1923. The map would appear to indicate that it occurs frequently but this is not so. It was recorded only once in some of the marked areas and then died out there.

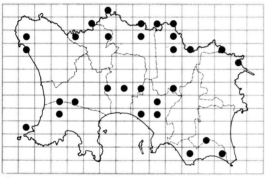

G scarce; A occasional; S rare.

Epilobium species **Willowherb**

Knowledge of Jersey's willowherbs is incomplete. Few hybrids have been reported, yet they probably exist and are complicating identification. Also, a new species *E. ciliatum* American Willowherb arrived in the late 1960s. The main problems arose with this new species and with *E. tetragonum* Square-stalked Willowherb and *E. obscurum* Short-fruited Willowherb so these are not mapped.

Epilobium hirsutum L. **Great Willowherb**

Frequent, often locally plentiful, in damp places and much increased since last century. Ereaut collected a specimen in 1847 and A. J. Binet recorded it three times: in gardens, including his own at 55 Val Plaisant, in 1877; in abundance in mud behind two targets in a quarry at St Catherine in 1891 and just past Don Bridge Station also in 1891. Piquet listed it

in 1896 as in 'Ditches and wet places, St Clement. Frequent' but Lester-Garland (1903) contradicted him, stating that it was 'Very rare' and 'Certainly not frequent there (i.e. St Clement) now.' Piquet regularly used to visit Mrs L. A. Morris' father's house in St Clement and Mrs Morris has always known Great Willowherb in quantity nearby. She considers it must have been there by the turn of the century and probably earlier.

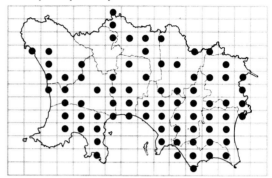

G frequent; A frequent; S rare; H rare.

E. parviflorum Schreber **Hoary Willowherb**

Occasional in damp places.

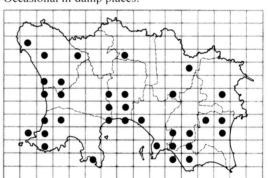

G frequent; A occasional; S occasional; H rare.

E. parviflorum x **E. tetragonum**
  A hybrid Willowherb

G 1971.

E. montanum L. **Broad-leaved Willowherb**

Frequent on dry banks and walls.

Map overleaf

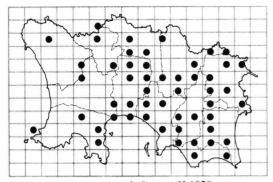

G frequent; A occasional; S rare; H 1958.

E. montanum x **E. obscurum**   **A hybrid Willowherb**
H 1958.

E. lanceolatum Seb. & Mauri
                    Spear-leaved Willowherb
Frequent on walls and roadsides.

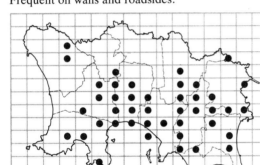

G occasional; A occasional; H 1958.

E. lanceolatum x **E. tetragonum**
                    A hybrid Willowherb
G 1971?

E. tetragonum L.   **Square-stalked Willowherb**
Occurs and thought to be frequent but see *Epilobium*
sp. above.
G frequent? A occasional; S rare; H occasional.

E. tetragonum x **E. obscurum**   **A hybrid Willowherb**
St Aubin, 1906/7, Druce (*Journal of Botany* 1907).

E. obscurum Schreber   **Short-fruited Willowherb**
Occurs and thought to be frequent but see *Epilobium*
sp. above.
G common; A 1958; S occasional; H occasional.

E. obscurum x **E. parviflorum**
                    A hybrid Willowherb
G 1971.

E. roseum Schreber   **Pale Willowherb**
Lester-Garland rejected La Gasca's record of 1834
and the 1968 record given in *The Wild Flowers of
Guernsey* was withdrawn.

E. palustre L.   **Marsh Willowherb**
Claimed at various times from Grouville, St Saviour's
Valley and Trinity but no specimens exist in the
Société's herbarium, in Hb Oxford or Hb Cantab.
The record given by Attenborough in the 1955
botanical report of the Société was in error. The
specimen is not Marsh Willowherb but is otherwise
indeterminate (Hb Société Jersiaise).
G one locality.

E. ciliatum Rafin.   **American Willowherb**
(E. adenocaulon)
In 1968 and 1970 Dr J. G. Dony reported American
Willowherb from several places in Jersey. It
continued to spread and by 1980 was well-estab-
lished.
G rare.

E. ciliatum x **E. parviflorum**   **A hybrid Willowherb**
G 1971.

E. brunnescens (Cockayne) Raven & Engelhorn
(E. nerterioides)   **New Zealand Willowherb**
This New Zealand species which is spreading rapidly
in Britain still survives in a garden at Hérupe, St John
where it was first seen among *Eryngium tripartitum*
bought in England in 1979, Mrs M. L. Long.
G similar occurrence but among heathers.

Gunnera species   **Giant Rhubarb**
Giant Rhubarb has been known in Jersey since last
century. More recently water gardens have become
highly fashionable so that many owners of large
properties have gardened the stream-sides of small
valleys. Giant Rhubarb, a much favoured species for
such plantings, is so large that it is likely to remain
long after the rest of the garden has been engulfed
again by natural vegetation. The species have only a
superficial resemblance to, and no botanical
connection with, culinary rhubarb which is a member
of the dock family. Two species are involved:
Gunnera tinctoria (Molina) Mirbel, a Chilean
species, the smaller of the two but still gigantic, seems
the less common. The small branches on the huge
inflorescences are stubby and flask-shaped, very different from the thin cylindrical ones of the next
species. Also, once the enormous size of the leaves of
both species ceases to overwhelm, and it is possible to
look objectively at them, it will be seen that the leaf
stalk joins the leaf differently in each species. Seedlings have appeared at Maison Charles, Bel Royal,
and in a valley running down to Dannemarche

Reservoir at Domaine des Vaux, St Lawrence. At least three other Jersey gardens are known to contain this species which can easily be seen where it was planted, from Maison Charles, in a wild wet area by the side of Mont les Vaux, St Aubin, near the junction (Seven Oaks) with Mont des Longchamps.
G naturalised; S naturalised; H occurs.

G. manicata Linden ex André, the larger of the two species, comes from South Brazil. The first record of a Gunnera in Jersey was in 1878 when Desmagny stated in *Cinq Jours de Fête à Jersey* (1878) that *G. scabra* was growing in the grounds of Rosel Manor. *G. 'scabra'* is usually equated with the previous species but here it is more likely to be this one, which is growing in Rosel Manor grounds now and has been throughout living memory. It has also been reported in the valley running down to St Catherine from the Manor. No seedlings are known though more clumps of this species have been noted than of *G. tinctoria*. It can easily be seen in the grounds of Samarès Manor or the Howard Davis Park and in the upper part of the valley on the west side of Beaumont New Hill.
G one locality.

Myriophyllum verticillatum L.
Whorled Water-milfoil
Recorded in the past but in error for *M. alterniflorum* DC.
G 1790?

M. spicatum L. **Spiked Water-milfoil**
Recorded by Piquet in 1851 from St Ouen's Pond and St Peter's Marsh. Lester-Garland (1903) knew it only in St Ouen's Pond where it has not been seen for at least forty years.
G extinct in the wild; A rare.

M. alterniflorum DC. **Alternate Water-milfoil**
Last century Piquet found Alternate Water-milfoil in the pool on the cliffs at Noirmont but he misidentified it as Whorled Water-milfoil. It is still there in quantity and in 1983 it appeared suddenly filling a pool at Ville à L'Évêque, Trinity. Its origin is unknown.
G rare.

M. aquaticum (Velloso) Verdc.
(M. brasiliense) **Brazilian Water-milfoil**
An alien from Brazil found by R. W. S. Knightbridge in July 1983 growing plentifully on mud in a farm reservoir at Trinity. It had perhaps spread from Augrès Manor, Trinity where he noted it planted in a pool belonging to the Jersey Wildlife Preservation Trust. Later in 1983 R. Long found it in quantity in St Catherine's Reservoir.

HIPPURIDACEAE
Hippuris vulgaris L. **Mare's-tail**
In 1961 Mrs E. M. Towers found five spikes in a wild wet area at the foot of the valley on the west side of La Haule Hill, but the plants were not seen there again. They may have come from an ornamental pool in the grounds of Le Coin, higher up the valley, where the species was well-established in 1982, and looked as if it had been so for some years. In the early 1960s it was planted in three small pools in the Corbière region and in 1982 it was noticed in a tiny planted-out roadside pool in a ditch above Handois dam.
G 1790; A locally frequent.

CORNACEAE
Cornus sanguinea L. **Dogwood**
Subsp. *sanguinea* Dogwood, in spite of much searching, has not been found in the wild since 1927. The localities, if given, have always been on a small stretch of the north coast: on a hedge near the granite quarry at La Saline, St John, Piquet (1851); near Mont Mado quarries and at Le Câtel de Lecq, Piquet (1896); on the cliffs between Le Mourier Waterfall and La Plaine, 1917, Attenborough; near Le Val Rouget, 1927, Attenborough, and with the 1927 record, Attenborough added 'formerly found on Le Câtel de Lecq'. The first records were by La Gasca (1834) and Saunders in Babington (1839) but no localities were then given.

C. alba L./**sericea** L. **Red-osier Dogwood**
G local garden escape.

ARALIACEAE
Hedera helix L. **Ivy**
du **dgèrrue**
Abundant. Recent work has shown that there are two chromosome races of Ivy, one with 20, the other with 40 chromosomes. So far all Ivy in Jersey critically examined is reported to be the one with 40 chromosomes, subsp. *hibernica* Kirchner sometimes raised to specific rank as *H. hibernica* (Kirchner) Bean but more information on Ivy in Jersey is needed and subsp. *helix* may exist. The Ivy Broomrape is exceedingly rare.

In 1858 de la Croix wrote in *Jersey Ses Antiquités* that ivy *'dans plusieures localités forme des bouquets d'une beauté peu ordinaire, couronnant les arbres et les murs qui lui servent d'appui, et qu'il tapisse d'une éternelle verdure.'* This was followed in 1874 in Hill's *Historical Directory of the Channel Islands* by 'There is one picturesque feature which is intermixed, with most of the views in Jersey; the trunks of the trees, are covered with ivy, to a great extent, which not only adds to the beauty of the scenery when the trees are in leaf, but greatly softens the sterility of a winter prospect, and lends a greenness to the landscape throughout the year; Nor is the luxuriant growth of the ivy in Jersey confined to the trees; it covers the banks by the wayside; creeps over the walls, and even climbs upon the rocks by the sea shore.'

Subsp. *canariensis* (Willd.) Coutinho was reported in error for Jersey, Guernsey and Sark by A. Chevalier in 1933 and others, for example Fournier, because of a confusion of names.

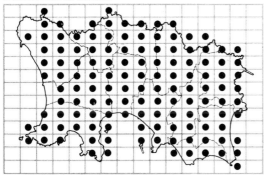

G common; A frequent; S frequent; H frequent.

Aralia elata Seeman   **Angelica Tree**
This has flourished among the natural vegetation on the west side of Dannemarche mudpond for more than twenty years – and probably much longer. It survives severe hacking from time to time with ease.

UMBELLIFERAE
Hydrocotyle vulgaris L.   **Marsh Pennywort**
Still frequent in marshy places.

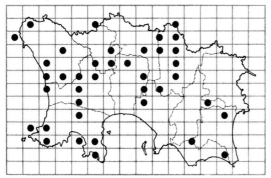

G frequent; A occasional; S frequent; H local.

Eryngium maritimum L.   **Sea-holly**
            du **housse dé mielle**
Locally frequent on the sandier parts of the coast and on the dunes. An illustration by Pandora Sellars is opposite page 70.

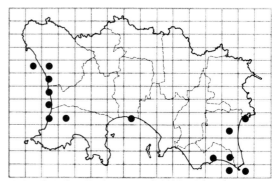

G local; A locally frequent; S 1838; H local.

E. campestre L.   **Field Eryngo**
Lester-Garland rejected La Gasca's (1834) record but a specimen gathered by Piquet in St Ouen in 1902 is in Hb Oxford.
G rare; A rare.

Chaerophyllum temulentum L. **Rough Chervil**
Thinly widespread and no longer frequent as Piquet described it in both 1851 and 1896.

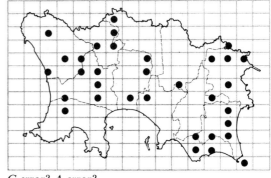

G error? A error?

Anthriscus sylvestris (L.) Hoffm. **Cow Parsley**
This common English roadside umbellifer is extremely rare on the mainland of Jersey. The only record when Lester-Garland wrote his Flora in 1903 was one of Trevelyan's given by Babington in 1839, and as Lester-Garland stated, it was unconfirmed. This century it was found well-established in Queen's Road in 1961 by Miss E. H. du Feu and it remained there until 1973 when the habitat was destroyed during building development. In 1964 one plant was found in a hedge in the upper part of St Peter's Valley and in 1983 one plant grew at Les Hâtivieaux, St Ouen. But cross to Les Écréhous, and while Cow Parsley does not now form 'nearly all the herbage' there, as Piquet wrote in 1851, it is still plentiful.
G rare; A locally common.

A. cerefolium (L.) Hoffm.   **Garden Chervil**

No recent record. La Gasca listed Garden Chervil in 1834; Ereaut has a specimen dated 1847 and Piquet wrote in 1851 'On cultivated ground but scarcely wild'.

A. caucalis Bieb.   **Bur Chervil**
(A. vulgaris)

One of the commoner early umbellifers of the sandier soil of the south and west.

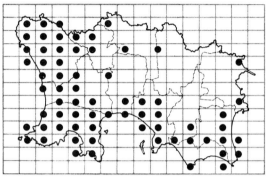

G local; A frequent; S 1944; H common.

Scandix pecten-veneris L.   **Shepherd's-needle**

Subsp. *pecten-veneris* Always a rare casual but perhaps becoming even scarcer. There are about half a dozen records from 1834 onwards, the last being by Dr D. H. Phillips of the States Experimental Farm in the late 1950s, perhaps from bird-seed.
G last record 1978; A last record 1900; S 1903 and Brecqhou 1957.

Coriandrum sativum L.   **Coriander**

Recorded by La Gasca in his 1834 list but not seen again until A. Lister found it near a restaurant at the north end of St Ouen's Bay in 1965.
G 1877.

Smyrnium olusatrum L.   **Alexanders**
                    *d'l'***alisandre**

J. Gay, a French botanist, saw Alexanders on Mont Orgueil in August 1832 and Babington (1839) recorded it from 'Pontac and other places'. Lester-Garland (1903), who considered it locally abundant, stated that it was at Gorey, Pontac, the slopes of Fort Regent, St Aubin's Bay and St Ouen's Bay. It still grows in all these, as the map shows, and it seems to have moved inland a little, where the soil is light. An alternative Jersey-Norman-French name is *céléri sauvage*. It may well be that Alexanders was introduced as a vegetable and then spread outside gardens. Its large, almost spherical flower-heads made up of countless small cream flowers are abundant in some lanes near the sea in early spring.

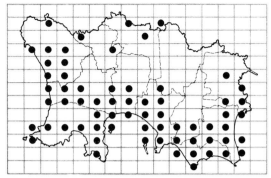

G locally abundant; A rare; S common; H common.

Conopodium majus (Couan) Loret   **Pignut**
(C. denudatum)

Occasional on hedgebanks and in woods. The present distribution pattern follows closely that of earlier years: in the north east, Babington (1839); St Saviour's Valley, Piquet (1851); shady woods, St Peter, Piquet (1896); St Brelade's Bay, wood near Trinity Manor, frequent in the north, Lester-Garland (1903).

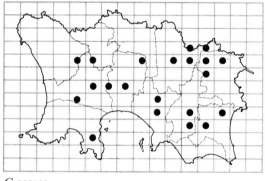

G scarce.

Pimpinella major (L.) Hudson
                    Greater Burnet-saxifrage
G rare.

P. saxifraga L.   **Burnet-saxifrage**

Lester-Garland (1903) rejected Saunders' record given in 1839 and it has not been confirmed.
G unconfirmed.

Aegopodium podagraria L.   **Ground-elder**

Common particularly as a garden weed where its long slender rhizomes can get under walls and among other plants, and are then almost inextricable.

Map overleaf

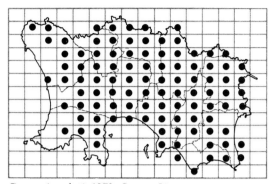

G occasional; A 1972; S rare; H rare.

Sium latifolium L.   **Greater Water-parsnip**

Saunders' record from St Saviour's Valley (1839) was rejected by Lester-Garland (1903). Mrs E. M. Towers found one plant at Millbrook in 1967 among Hemlock Water-dropwort.

Berula erecta (Huds.) Coville **Lesser Water-parsnip**
(S. angustifolium)

Babington (1839) recorded this for Jersey, Guernsey and Alderney. No other botanist has noted it in any Channel Island so in the absence of a specimen it must be presumed an error.

Crithmum maritimum L.   **Rock Samphire**
d'la **pèrche-pièrre**

Common on rocks round the coast.

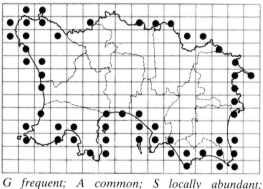

G frequent; A common; S locally abundant; H common.

Oenanthe fistulosa L.   **Tubular Water-dropwort**

Occasional in wet areas. It was recorded from St Peter's Marsh, St Ouen's Pond, Grouville and Samarès Meadows by Lester-Garland (1903) and it was still in all these areas, and others, in 1960–70 as the distribution map shows. It has not been seen recently in St Peter's Marsh, though it may still be there, but it has gone from Samarès Marsh now that the land has been drained for a housing estate. In

1983 R. W. S. Knightbridge found it in a new area in Waterworks Valley.

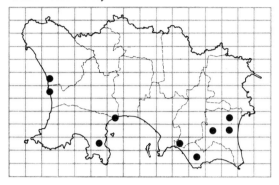

G rare.

O. pimpinelloides L.   **Corky-fruited Water-dropwort**

Recorded in the past but the name then covered the following species also, and all specimens seen have been of that.

O. lachenalii C. C. Gmel.   **Parsley Water-dropwort**

Rare. Babington noted in his own copy of his Flora that the Rev. W. W. Newbould had found this at St Clement in 1841/2. It is still in St Clement in the wet area south-east of the Rue des Prés Trading Estate, R. W. S. Knightbridge, but it has gone from Samarès Marsh where it survived until the housing estate was built in the early 1970s. Babington also noted that H. C. Watson had found it 'In a small swamp on the high ground near Petit Port' though which Petit Port is not clear. F. Piquet collected it at St Ouen's Pond in 1870 and it is still there. Lester-Garland recorded it at La Pulente from where Ariste collected a specimen in 1927.
G rare.

O. crocata L.   **Hemlock Water-dropwort**
d'la **chue**

Abundant in wet places. The green parts of the plant seem to be edible as cattle frequently graze on them but if a wet ditch is redug or cattle trample down the sides of a ditch, the tuberous roots may be exposed and eaten, and these roots contain one of the most virulent poisons of any plant. Fairly regularly there are reports of cattle and horses dying through eating them. On 27 February 1942, during the German Occupation, L. P. Sinel wrote in his diary, 'Several foreign labourers die from poisoning after having eaten hemlock under the impression that it was edible; these poor men are half starved and eat anything resembling food irrespective of where it is found'. Attenborough, who like so many botanists of old was also a well-known local chemist, was called in and he identified the plants as *Oenanthe crocata*, Hemlock Water-dropwort. This long name is often erroneously shortened to Hemlock, another extremely poisonous plant but one which has nothing obviously edible about it. The source of trouble with Hemlock Water-dropwort is its dahlia-like tubers which look almost as edible as parsnips.

There is no Hemlock Water-dropwort in Alderney which is strange. Marquand in his *Flora of Guernsey* (1903) explained it by stating that it was probably exterminated by farmers because of its danger to cattle. Perhaps, but if so Alderney must have had much less than Jersey. Eradication here would be impossible.

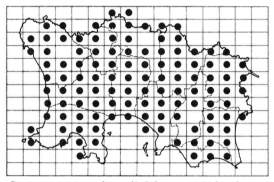

G common; A eradicated? S frequent; H local.

O. aquatica (L.) Poiret **Fine-leaved Water-dropwort**
(*O. Phellandrium*)
Lester-Garland rejected both Saunders' record in Babington (1839) and Piquet's from Marais à la Coque which he gave in his 1896 list and there has been no confirmation.
G error.

Aethusa cynapium L.   **Fool's Parsley**
d'la **p'tite chue**
Subsp. *cynapium* Still as Lester-Garland (1903) described it, thinly distributed as a weed in cultivated places.
Subsp. *agrestis* (Wallr.) Dostál Cultivated field, Mont à l'Abbé, 1983, Mrs M. L. Long.
Subsp. *cynapioides* (Bieb.) Nyman A specimen collected by Piquet in St Saviour's Valley is in Hb Oxford.

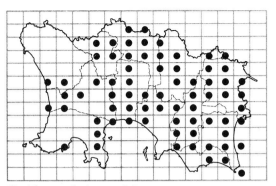

G widespread; A rare; S frequent.

Foeniculum vulgare Miller   **Fennel**
du **fanon**
Frequent on the sandier parts of the coast, and inland on roadsides and disturbed ground. In the past Fennel leaves were commonly used to make a sauce particularly for mackerel.

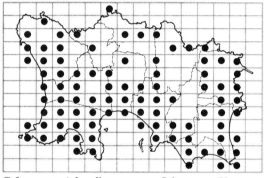

G frequent; A locally common; S frequent; H rare.

Anethum graveolens L.   **Dill**
A specimen collected at St Ouen in 1857 by Piquet is in Hb Oxford.

Conium maculatum L.   **Hemlock**
d'la **bênarde**
Frequent in hedges and on disturbed ground. Where there are many plants together their disagreeable smell of mice becomes noticeable, particularly on damp days. It seems extraordinary that the Jersey-Norman-French name of this poisonous plant which contains the alkaloid conine, and which may have been the plant whose juice killed Socrates, should be the same as that of Hogweed which is completely harmless when eaten by man or beast.
Map overleaf

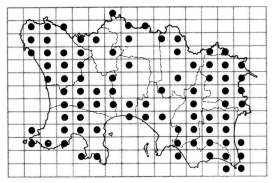

G occasional; A locally frequent; S occasional; H frequent.

Bupleurum subovatum Link   **False Thorow-wax**
(B. lancifolium)

A specimen in the British Museum herbarium was collected by T. B. Blow from sands near the sea in St Aubin's Bay in 1873. There was no further record until 1954 when Miss E. H. du Feu found a plant, probably from bird-seed, in her garden in Chevalier Road. Since then there have been several records, all from near where birds have been fed or near rubbish dumps.

G bird-seed casual.

B. baldense Turra   **Small Hare's-ear**
(B. aristatum)

Subsp. *baldense* Still locally frequent on Les Quennevais where Babington (1839) found it, and in St Ouen's Bay. The minute plants, sometimes only an inch high, need open turf on fixed dunes. Very exceptionally in Jersey are plants more than about two inches high but an 1894 Jersey specimen in the British Museum herbarium is ten inches high.

G locally frequent; A locally frequent; H local.

Apium graveolens L.   **Wild Celery**
du **céléri sauvage**

In the past Wild Celery was reported from St Catherine's Bay, Grouville, Samarès, St Peter, St Ouen's Pond and L'Étacq, and Lester-Garland (1903) stated that it was frequent. It is now known from only two places: by the stream on the north side of Mont Pinel, St Ouen, a locality known to Attenborough from before the 1914–1918 war, and from Jambart Lane, St Clement, where it was found by Mrs L. A. Morris.

G rare; A rare.

A. nodiflorum (L.) Lag.   **Fool's Water-cress**
d'la **bêle**

Common in wet places. Lester-Garland (1903) reported var. *ochreatum* (DC.) O. Kuntze from

L'Étacq, and Babington var. *minus* (Koch) Godron from Grouville.

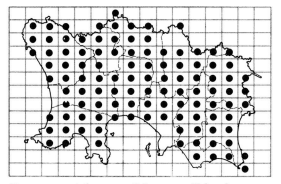

G common; A frequent; S frequent; H local.

A. repens (Jacq.) Lag.   **Creeping Marshwort**

Claimed only in the mid-nineteenth century and thought to be from a confusion of names. The plants were almost certainly the var. *minus* (Koch) Godron, previously the var. *repens* Hook. f., of *A. nodiflorum*.

G error.

A. inundatum (L.) Rchb. fil.   **Lesser Marshwort**

Still abundant in the small pool at Noirmont in 1983 from where Babington recorded it nearly a hundred and fifty years previously. It is also in the wet area on Ouaisné Common and until recently it used to be by the side of the road on La Pulente Hill but it seems to have vanished during roadworks there. Past records came from Town Mills Pond, the old reservoir Waterworks Valley, St Peter's Marsh and St Ouen's Pond, and it may yet linger in some of these.

G rare; S 1838.

Petroselinum crispum (Mill.) A. W. Hill
Garden Parsley
du **pèrsi**

Occasionally naturalised, usually near the coast, as at L'Étacq where it may well have been for centuries. More recent garden escapes f. *crispum* are to be seen on dumps.

G local; A occasional; S rare.

P. segetum (L.) Koch   **Corn Parsley**

Five records, probably all from the same place: lane near St Ouen's Watermill, 1858, H. C. Watson (Babington in notes in his own copy of his Flora); casual, not far from St Ouen's Pond, 1886, J. Crossfield (Lester-Garland 1903); Val de la Mare, St Ouen, 1957, Miss M. McC. Webster, and found in the same locality in 1969 and 1981.

Sison amomum L.   **Stone Parsley**

Lester-Garland (1903) rejected Saunders' record given in 1839. Piquet, who added it in an Appendix (1852) to his previous list, later omitted it. A specimen in the Carlisle herbarium was gathered by Dr J. Leitch at 'Les Marais Station' in 1882.
G 1790.

Cicuta virosa L.   **Cowbane**

Saunders' record given by Babington (1839) was rejected by Lester-Garland and it has never been confirmed.

Ammi visnaga (L.) Lam.   **A Bullwort**

A bird seed alien: Old Beaumont Hill, 1971, Mrs K. Le Sueur.

A. majus L.   **Bullwort**

A bird seed alien: garden, St Andrew's Road in 1977, Mrs E. M. Towers; garden, Millbrook, 1981, Mrs M. L. Long.
G rare.

Falcaria vulgaris Bernh.   **Longleaf**
(F. Rivini)

Three localities: field near Don Bridge Station, 1901, Piquet, and still there until the field, behind the present Quennevais Parade shopping centre, was developed as a playing field in the late 1960s; field north of La Saline Slip, St Ouen, where it was first noted by Le Maistre in the late 1940s and where it still grows; South Canal, St Ouen's Pond, 1957, Mrs J. Russell, where it also still grows.
G rare; A rare.

Carum carvi L.   **Caraway**

Two large clumps by the side of the track north of Grands Vaux Reservoir, 1969, Mrs L. A. Morris.
G one record.

C. verticillatum (L.) Koch   **Whorled Caraway**

Whorled Caraway has been known in some of the wetter areas of Trinity since records began, and in a few it grows abundantly.

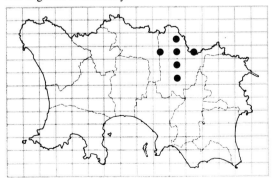

Angelica sylvestris L.   **Wild Angelica**
                      du **graslard**

Piquet (1896) described Wild Angelica as frequent in damp shady woods near streams and Lester-Garland (1903) thought it 'not common' in boggy places on the cliffs, adding Waterworks Valley and Trinity Manor. As the map shows, it is widely distributed along the north cliffs and in the central valleys. In some areas it is plentiful; in others only one or two plants may be growing. Strangely, it appears to be absent from the other Bailiwick.

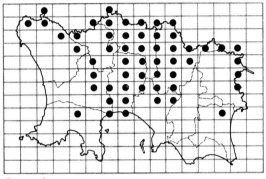

G error?

Peucedanum officinale L.   **Hog's Fennel**

Lester-Garland rejected Saunders' record given by Babington (1839) and it has not been confirmed.

Pastinaca sativa L.   **Wild Parsnip**
               d'la **pânnais sauvage**

For six centuries or more Parsnips were cultivated extensively. See Le Maistre (1966). Its decrease in the wild parallels its decline as a crop: common, Piquet (1851); frequent, Piquet (1896); rare, Lester-Garland (1903) and there have only been two recent records.
G rare escape; A occasional; S rare.

Heracleum sphondylium L.   **Hogweed**
                    d'la **bênarde**

Subsp. *sphondylium* Common and sometimes so well-grown and luxuriant that it has been mistaken for the next species. If cut on a very hot summer's day the stems exude a juice which can severely blister the skin. Several young pupils of Trinity School were found to have huge blisters on their bodies and legs during a medical inspection in June 1973. They had gathered ordinary, but extremely large, Hogweed for their rabbits during a heatwave and had carried the luscious plants home, holding them against their bodies. They were wearing only bathing trunks. No permanent harm resulted though the blisters required hospital treatment. Mr P. McGarry, the then headmaster of Trinity School, took me to the field to identify the plants and provided the rest of the information above. Professor G. Henslow (1901) drew attention to the danger of cutting Hogweed in hot weather but his warnings have largely been ignored perhaps because of the greater problems caused by the following species.

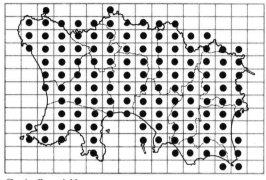

G, A, S and H common.

H. mantegazzianum Sommier & Levier
Giant Hogweed

First recorded from the foot of La Haule Hill in 1959, but on reading the record J. Le C. Sumner of Belle Vue, La Haule, said that he had known it there for many years previously. The colony is decreasing and there was only one plant in 1982 and 1983. Ariste collected a specimen in 1929 from 'Route de la Trinité', and there was one plant in a town garden in 1981.

Torilis nodosa (L.) Gaertn. Knotted Hedge-parsley

Knotted Hedge-parsley has decreased considerably: common, Babington (1839); frequent, Piquet (1896); not common, Lester-Garland (1903); uncommon, late 1930s, N. Le Brocq. By 1983 it was rare, though abundant over a small area on the dunes north of La Pulente.

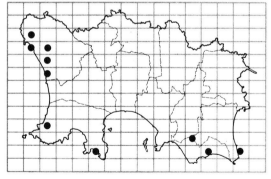

G scarce; A frequent.

T. japonica (Houtt.) DC. Upright Hedge-parsley
(T. Anthriscus)

Upright Hedge-parsley, though more plentiful than Knotted Hedge-parsley, is only occasionally found and must have decreased this century considering that Piquet recorded it as frequent in 1896 and Lester-Garland as common in 1903.

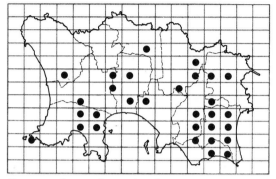

G scarce; A rare; S occasional.

Caucalis platycarpos L. Greater Bur-parsley
(C. daucoides)

A casual, recorded without proof by La Gasca in 1834 but collected by Piquet in St Ouen's Bay in 1898. *G 1900.*

Turgenia latifolia (L.) Hoffm.
(Caucalis latifolia) Broad-leaved Hedgehog-parsley

A casual collected in St Ouen's Bay by Piquet in 1900. *G 1898, 1900, 1902.*

Daucus carota L. Wild Carrot
d'la cârotte sauvage

Subsp. *carota* and subsp. *gummifer* Hook. f. Both subspecies occur but over much of the area, particularly just inland from the coast, it is impossible to allot plants to one or the other with certainty. The aggregate is always common but in 1978 there was a sudden, enormous increase in flowering plants so that in some areas, for example L'Étacq and Les Landes, it was dominant and the sward appeared to be flowering Wild Carrot. The increase, which may well have been connected with the hot dry summer of 1976, was paralleled by an increase in the Carrot Broomrape. By 1981 Wild Carrot was back to its normal status, common.

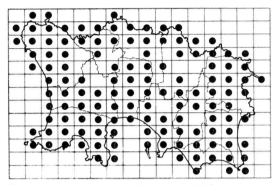

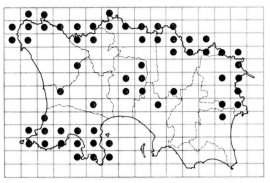

G common; A common; S common; H frequent.

G common; A common; S locally abundant; H common.

PYROLACEAE

Pyrola rotundifolia L.　　　**Round-leaved Wintergreen**
G established until about 1901.

ERICACEAE

Erica ciliaris L.　　　　　　**Dorset Heath**

The Armorican Flora, misquoting Lester-Garland, erroneously reported Dorset Heath to be in Jersey.

E. tetralix L.　　　　　　**Cross-leaved Heath**
　　　　　　　　　　　　　　　d'la **bruëthe**

Cross-leaved Heath was first reported by Babington (1839) from bogs near Petit Port, St Brelade. Piquet (1851) listed it from Le Marais, Noirmont, i.e. Ouaisné Common, where it still grows in good quantity, and from a marsh near La Moye Signal Post. It was last seen in the La Moye region in the mid-1970s, but the area, behind La Moye School, was later deprived of its water so the heather disappeared.
G error.

E. cinerea L.　　　　　　　　**Bell Heather**
　　　　　　　　　　　　　　　d'la **bruëthe**

Locally abundant on the coast and occasionally found on inland côtils and by roadsides. White-flowered forms have been reported from 1833 onwards, and the cultivar 'Jersey Wonder' which has golden-tipped leaves, was propagated and named by D. McClintock from cuttings taken from a plant on the Jardin d'Olivet in 1978.

E. vagans L.　　　　　　　　**Cornish Heath**
S garden escape.

Calluna vulgaris (L.) Hull　　　　**Heather**
(C. Erica)　　　　　　　　　　　*d'la* **bruëthe**

Common on the cliffs and coastal heaths. White-flowered forms occur.

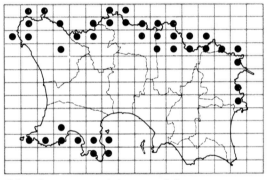

G locally common; A frequent; S frequent.

Rhododendron 'ponticum'　　　**Rhododendron**

Rhododendron has occasionally been planted but is seldom seen in any quantity. It used to be commonest in Noirmont Manor woods but it has recently been removed, or at least considerably thinned. A fair amount grows in the wild parts of Rosel Manor woods. Though still given the covering name *R. 'ponticum'* all established plants in the wild are hybrids between *R. ponticum* L., which comes from the Iberian peninsula and the eastern Mediterranean and is named after the Pontus Mountains near the Black Sea, and other garden species.
G, S and H rare.

Arbutus unedo L.　　　　　　**Strawberry Tree**

In 1961 J. C. Fluck reported that Strawberry Trees planted many years ago in Noirmont Manor woods were seeding and regenerating freely. They were established outside the woods, even on the beach, one fine tree being just above high water mark. This tree was killed in the extreme frost of winter 1962/63 but other Strawberry Trees are still present in the area. The only other record is La Gasca's in 1834. He did not write either *culta* or *colitur* after it, as he did to some garden plants, nor did he say where he found the trees. If they were at Noirmont, have they been there 150 years?

Gaultheria shallon Pursh   **Shallon**
Mrs M. L. Long reported this at Bel Croute in the 1960s. It had probably spread from the grounds of Noirmont Manor where it is established.

Vaccinium myrtillus L.   **Bilberry**
Bilberry was found on the slopes above Bonne Nuit in 1904 by Père de Bellaing who wrote to Lester-Garland saying there was 'a fair amount' of it. Two small plants were found in the late 1950s but none in the 1970s. The area is difficult to search intensively and de Bellaing's exact place is unknown so Bilberry may still survive.

PRIMULACEAE

Primula vulgaris Hudson   **Primrose**
(P. acaulis)   *des* **pip'soles**
Subsp. *vulgaris*   Locally common on the cliffs and inland côtils but seldom on hedgebanks with the result that many people think Primroses are scarce in Jersey. In 1958 a few dingy purple-pink Primroses were noticed among the normal wild yellow ones in the grounds of Noirmont Manor and Mme de Grucy of Noirmont stated that the Primroses on the front lawn at the Manor began to turn pinky-purple during the German Occupation (1940–45). Gradually they increased in relation to the yellow ones, in all the area round about. At the end of the Occupation there was a gradual return to normal yellow, almost – as Mme de Gruchy put it – as if they had been in mourning. Such plants also occur, rarely, elsewhere and are thought to be the result of some hybridisation with garden *Primula* species.

Le Maistre gives many different names, or different spellings of the same name, for Primroses: *pip'sole, pip'solle, pip'thole, pip'role, preunole, prunole, prunm'nole, pieunm'thole, prînmerole, prînm'thole, prînm'sole, pâqu'role, pâqu'thole* and *coucou.* For the districts and parishes in which these were used, see the *Dictionnaire Jersiais-Français.*

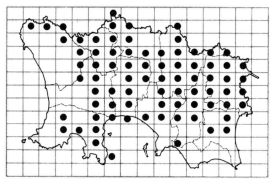

G common; A occasional; S locally abundant; H common.

P. veris L.   **Cowslip**
                                                 du **jaune coucou**
Subsp. *veris*   Rare as a native species on a small area of the north coast, but introduced plants occasionally occur elsewhere, as on the heights above the east side of St Peter's Valley, and plants from seed taken from the north coast about 1935 grow at Petit Port, near La Corbière.

Cowslips have a peculiar fascination for many people and a charisma which leads to their being picked, dug up and removed, or their seeds being collected. Jersey's small colony has survived satisfactorily for about a hundred and fifty years as far as is known and probably for much longer. I would like to appeal to anyone who sees a Cowslip to leave it where it is, to set and sow its seed *in situ.*
G no established colony; A rare.

P. x tommasinii Gren. & Godron
P. veris x P. vulgaris   **A Primrose-cowslip hybrid**
Cowslips (see above) were sown in 1935 in an area at Petit Port, St Brelade, where Primroses were already growing naturally. Plants thought to be hybrids soon appeared. Both parents and several intermediates were present by 1962. Earlier, Guiton had collected an intermediate in 1916 near the Cowslip colony on the north coast.

Cyclamen hederifolium Aiton   **Autumn Cyclamen**
Autumn Cyclamen is frequently planted in the wild parts of large gardens and there are several reports of it becoming naturalised in those gardens but in the 1970s there were five records of it growing in wild woodlands or on hedgebanks well away from cultivation: Vallée des Vaux, 1970, E. C. Newman; hedgebank above Gargate Mill, St Peter's Valley, 1971, B. J. Le Brocq; valley from Rosel Manor to St Catherine's Bay, 1971, Miss A. Le Cozannet; by quarry, top of St Peter's Valley, 1974, F. L. Duquemin; wooded slope of Grands Vaux, 1974, D. Cottrill.
G rare, two localities.

C. coum Miller   **Spring Cyclamen**
G Saumarez Park.

Lysimachia nemorum L.   **Yellow Pimpernel**
Yellow Pimpernel still grows in the valley from Rosel
Manor down to St Catherine's Bay where it was first
found by Ariste in 1925. The only other record is
from the roadside in St Peter's Valley in 1922, Miss J.
Luce, given in the Société's botanical report for 1922.
S occasional.

L. vulgaris L.   **Yellow Loosestrife**
One record: on a bank by the side of a pond on
Samarès Marsh, 1962, J. C. Fluck.
G rare.

L. nummularia L.   **Creeping Jenny**
Creeping Jenny does so well in some gardens it is
treated as a weed but it is seldom seen outside in the
wild. Saunders' record from St Saviour's Valley was
given by Babington (1839) and Lester-Garland found
it, presumably wild, in a meadow between
Longueville and Samarès in 1900. The only post-war
wild record is from the valley running down from
Rosel Mill to La Chaire where it was well-established
in the 1950s and 1960s.
G garden outcast.

L. punctata L.   **Dotted Loosestrife**
Two records: in 1966 Mrs D. L. Le Quesne found one
plant by the edge of a heap of tomato haulms in a field
at St Clement; in 1979 there were about a dozen
flowering spikes in the quarry on La Pulente Hill and
plants are still there.

Glaux maritima L.   **Sea Milkwort**
Sea Milkwort was first listed by La Gasca in 1834 but
Lester-Garland thought in 1903 that it was on the way
to extinction. This is decidedly not so, as
Attenborough stated as long ago as 1917 in the
Société's botanical report. It occurs where fresh
water runs off the land to the sea and it may well
occur in more places along the north coast, places
difficult of access. It is in good supply where it has
been recorded.

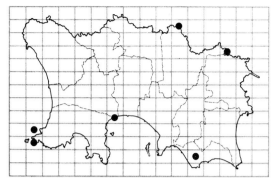

G rare; A rare; S 1847; H rare.

Anagallis minima (L.) E. H. L. Krause   **Chaffweed**
(Centunculus minimus)
Chaffweed is so small (A. J. Wilmott's 1922 speci-
mens from Noirmont, Hb Brit. Mus., are about $\frac{1}{5}$ in.
high) that it is impossible to say whether it is rare or
merely overlooked. The last record was in 1958 from
Ouaisné Common but few of the places from which it
was recorded in the past have changed a great deal so
it may well still be in some of them – and elsewhere:
Fliquet, Bouley Bay, Egypt, Bonne Nuit, Vallée des
Vaux, Noirmont, Portelet, Ouaisné Common, Les
Quennevais, St Ouen's Pond.
G rare; A rare; H 1894.

A. tenella (L.) L.   **Bog Pimpernel**
Local in wet areas. Bog Pimpernel, a slender plant,
spreads by rooting at the nodes and sometimes covers
the vertical sides of a ditch cut through marshy
ground with its delicate pink flowers. Records during
the survey 1960–70 were roughly from the same areas
as last century and early this, but R. W. S. Knightbridge found it, rare, in a wet meadow in St Clement
and in another in Grouville in 1983.

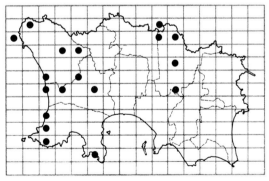

G, A, S and H local.

A. arvensis L.   **Scarlet Pimpernel**
               la **baronmette ès pouôrres gens**

Scarlet Pimpernel, sometimes called Poor-man's-weather-glass because its flowers close at the approach of wet or humid weather, is common all over the island. Normally the flowers are red but three other forms are fairly frequent: f. *carnea* (Schrank) Hyl. with flesh-coloured flowers; f. *lilacina* (Alefeld) Hyl. (*vinacea*) with blackberry-coloured flowers and f. *azurea* Hyl. with blue flowers. This last form should not be confused with the following species which also has blue flowers. If the petals are gland-fringed and the flower stalks are longer than the subtending leaves then a blue-flowered pimpernel is just a colour form of Scarlet Pimpernel.

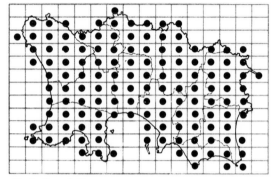

G, A, S and H common.

A. foemina Miller   **Blue Pimpernel**

Three confirmed records: St Helier, 1837, Babington; Grève d'Azette, 1847, Taylor; St Clement's Bay, 1908, Lester-Garland. Attenborough gave a record by H. J. Baal in 1917 but later (pers. comm.) said he considered it to have been the blue form of *A. arvensis* and that he himself had never seen *A. foemina*. *G 1890; S ?1879.*

Samolus valerandi L.   **Brookweed**

Local in wet places near the coast.

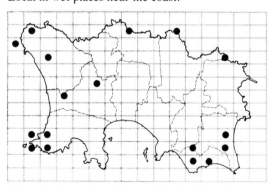

G local; A occasional; S occasional; H local.

PLUMBAGINACEAE
Armeria maritima (Miller) Willd.   **Thrift**
            d's **iliets d'falaise**

Subsp. *maritima* Common round the coast, sometimes locally abundant, producing sheets of pink in May. White-flowered plants are occasionally seen.

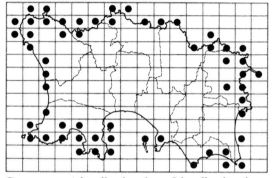

G common; A locally abundant; S locally abundant; H common.

A. maritima x **A. alliacea**   **A hybrid Thrift**

In 1867 J. T. B. Syme in the third edition of Sowerby's *English Botany* (7: 159–160) described a putative hybrid between the common Thrift and Jersey Thrift from St Brelade's Bay and it was illustrated on Plate 1155. Following botanists were unable to re-find it until recently. The common Thrift's peak flowering time is several weeks before Jersey Thrift's but the main difficulty is to find an area where the two grow together, their habitat requirements being sufficiently different normally to keep them apart. In 1957 they were found growing together in two areas in the middle of St Ouen's Bay and in both areas there were plants intermediate between them. The areas contained concrete and brick bases of beach huts pulled down during the German Occupation (1940–45) and these seemed to give *A. maritima* a habitat in an area otherwise occupied by *A. alliacea*. The two populations are still there. Professor Lawrence of Cornell University *in litt.* reports finding a similar population in St Ouen's Bay in 1951.

A. alliacea (Cav.) Hoffmans. & Link   **Jersey Thrift**
(*A. plantaginea*)   *d's* **iliets d'mielle**

Jersey Thrift is locally abundant in the west and south-west, forming sheets of colour in late July and August when the common Thrift has finished flowering. In the past there are records of it in quantity in St Aubin's Bay and from St Brelade's Bay right across Les Quennevais to St Ouen's Bay. It does not grow on the edge of the coast within easy reach of sea spray or on rocks, as the common Thrift does, but slightly further back on stabilised dunes or, more rarely, on cliff headlands. A species of central and south Europe, it comes up the mild west Atlantic coast of Europe to the Loire-Inférieure in fair quantity and then has a few outposts further north, of which Jersey is one. It does not occur in the other Channel Islands or on the mainland of Britain.

Jersey Thrift was depicted on the 5p stamp issued by the Jersey Postal Authority in 1972, and Pandora Sellars' illustration is opposite page 87.

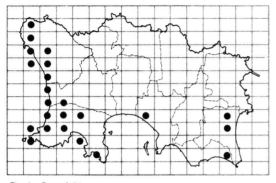

G, A, S and H common.

Limonium vulgare Miller   Common Sea-lavender
(Statice Limonium)

Subsp. *vulgare* This may have been common in Jersey before the salt marshes were drained but it is now rare. Babington (1839) gave a Saunders' record but he later crossed it out in his own copy of his Flora and it was rejected by Lester-Garland (1903). In 1946 it appeared in St Catherine's Bay just above the sea wall below the 'Pine Walk' and it is still there. In 1980 M. Ingrouille determined a sea-lavender which J. C. Fluck had found growing at Petit Port, Trinity, some years previously, as *L. vulgare*. As Ingrouille states, the habitat, where fresh water is trickling over rocks, i.e. not the normal salt marsh, is unusual for this species. The plants – or it may be one large plant spreading vegetatively – are still there.
G last record 1850.

L. binervosum (G. E. Sm.) Salmon
(Statice binervosa)   **Rock Sea-lavender**

Subsp. *sarniense* Ingrouille Dr Jermyn collected Rock Sea-lavender from L'Hermitage, Elizabeth Castle, in 1835 (Hb Brit. Mus.) and it is still in quantity along the base of the walls of the Castle. Except for the plants at Plémont, all records both now and in the past come from the south coast rocks. From research work done by M. Ingrouille in the early 1980s, Channel Island plants are now known to be slightly different from those elsewhere in Britain and they have been placed in this new subspecies (Ingrouille & Stace 1983).

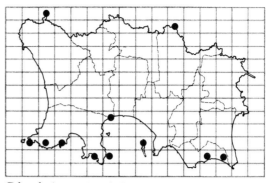

G local; A occasional; S occasional.

L. auriculae-ursifolium (Pourr.) Druce
    Broad-leaved Sea-lavender
(L. lychnidifolium; Statice lychnidifolia)

Rare. Broad-leaved Sea-lavender was first found in Jersey in 1916 by Attenborough and Guiton when they were climbing with ropes on a nearly inaccessible cliff at Rouge Nez, near Crabbé. Though they reported the species to be in good quantity it has not been refound but no difficult rock-climbing has been attempted. The habitat would appear to be unchanged so it may well still exist. The following year, 1917, they found it at Plémont where it still survives. M. Ingrouille who visited Jersey in 1980 considers specimens from Rouge Nez and the plants at Plémont to be *L. auriculae-ursifolium* in its strict sense and therefore to be extreme geographical outliers since the species is otherwise known only on the western Mediterranean coast of France, in the Balearic Islands and on the Biscay Atlantic coast of France. In the past the following species, for which the English name Alderney Sea-lavender has been kept, was included in *L. auriculae-ursifolium*.
G errors; A see next species.

L. normannicum Ingrouille nov. sp. inedit.
    Alderney Sea-lavender
('L. auriculae-ursifolium'; 'Statice lychnidifolia')

Locally common. In 1919 Père Morin collected a sea-lavender at Ronez and similar plants were collected there by Ariste and Louis-Arsène in the 1920s. According to Attenborough it grew on the large rock projecting out to sea down on the quarry floor, not high up on the cliffs (pers. comm.). How long the species remained there is unknown; the habitat had gone by the 1950s. In the Société's botanical report for 1946 Attenborough stated: '*Statice lychnidifolia* Kuntze This species, previously only known from the north of the island, has appeared in plenty in St Ouen's Bay. This is probably due to conditions created by the building of the Atlantic wall.' i.e. the sea defences built during the German Occupation 1940–45. The species still grows in good quantity behind the sea wall on the more open areas exposed to salt spray on normal tides and drenched by sheets of salt water on spring tides.

Louis-Arsène sent specimens of the north coast sea-lavenders to C. E. Salmon. In 1927 Salmon determined those gathered at Ronez as *L. lychnidifolium* var. *corymbosum* C. E. Salmon and commented on one that it exactly matched specimens from Portbail, Manche. He was less happy with the Plémont specimens and considered them untypical. Ingrouille has now shown that the St Ouen's Bay and Ronez plants are the same and differ significantly from those of Plémont and Rouge Nez, see the above species (*Watsonia* in press).

The Germans strengthened and extended the sea wall in St Ouen's Bay mainly with crushed stone from Ronez, using so much that a special railway was constructed to bring material direct to St Ouen's Bay. The railway joined a north-south line near the foot of La Rue de la Marette and it was just to the north of this, on what is now the National Trust for Jersey's property La Caumine à Marie Best, that the largest expanses of Alderney Sea-lavender occurred in the early years after the Occupation. Ingrouille suggests that the St Ouen's Bay population was probably founded by seed from Ronez and he is raising the variety to specific rank as *L. normannicum* Ingrouille (*Watsonia op cit.*). Its distribution is limited to Jersey, Alderney and the opposite coast of France from near St Malo north to Cherbourg.

The frontispiece is an illustration of Alderney Sea-lavender by Pandora Sellars.

A rare.

OLEACEAE

Fraxinus excelsior L.   **Ash**
                                                          un **frêne**

Subsp. *excelsior* Frequent in hedgerows and on the edge of woods.

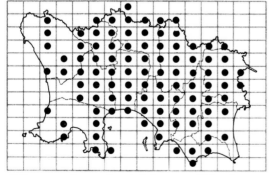

G frequent; A occasional; S frequent; H local.

Syringa vulgaris L.   **Lilac**
                                                      du **lilas**

Lilac has been used, rarely, as a hedge and it persists by suckering. One such hedge is at the top of St Peter's Valley.
G rare; S Brecqhou.

Ligustrum ovalifolium Hassk.   **Japanese Privet**

Hedges of Japanese Privet have been common in the island for many years. When it first came is unknown but it was probably in use by late last or early this century.
G common; A frequent; S Brecqhou.

L. vulgare L.   **Privet**
                                                    d'la **troène**

This native Privet still grows in quantity on the hill slopes in the south of St Ouen's Bay and on the Île Agois as reported last century. It also occurs occasionally in smaller quantity elsewhere along the north coast and inland. Lester-Garland (1903) stated that it was used frequently for hedging so some of the present population may be relics of former plantings.
G local; A rare; S occasional; H local.

GENTIANACEAE

Cicendia filiformis (L.) Delarbre   **Yellow Centaury**
(Microcala filiformis)

Yellow Centaury, a rare plant of damp open places, has only been recorded in three localities since the 1940s: Grosnez, marsh above Egypt and La Moye. In the past it was also recorded from Bouley Bay, Les Quennevais, St Brelade and St Ouen. Each plant is so small and slender that it is difficult to find unless its tiny yellow flower is open. It therefore may well be under-recorded.
G rare.

Exaculum pusillum (Lam.) Caruel
                                      Guernsey Centaury
G rare.

Blackstonia perfoliata (L.) Huds.   **Yellow-wort**

Subsp. *perfoliata* An undated specimen labelled Jersey gathered by Thomas Clark (1793–1864) is in Birmingham University herbarium. The next record was not until 1911, from Anneport by J. S. Gasking. In 1912 Attenborough found it at Gorey Castle where it was on the north side (pers. comm.) and may have been in Gasking's locality. It remained in this region until the late 1960s but in spite of much searching it has not been seen since. It probably disappeared in the 'tidying up' of the area. In 1922 Attenborough recorded two or three plants on the cliffs at Noirmont. Plants were still in the area in the 1960s.

Centaurium erythraea Rafn   **Common Centaury**
(Erythraea Centaurium)   *d'l'***hèrbe d'St Martîn**
Subsp. *erythraea* Common in dry places, and in
some recent years, for example 1978, in glorious
abundance locally. Babington's specimens labelled
C. latifolium and *C. littorale* and Druce's *C. capitatum* are all this species.

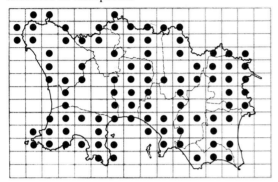

G, A, S and H frequent.

C. latifolium (Sm.) Druce   **Broad-leaved Centaury**
(Erythraea latifolia)
Recorded in error for Common Centaury by
Babington (1839) who later crossed out the entry in
his own copy of his Flora.
G error; A error.

C. littorale (D. Turner) Gilmour   **Seaside Centaury**
(Erythraea 'linarifolia')
Recorded in error for Common Centaury by
Babington (1839).
G same error.

C. pulchellum (Sw.) Druce   **Lesser Centaury**
(Erythraea pulchella)
Rare. Babington's specimen is the following species
but there are five other records: St Ouen's Pond,
1873, F. Piquet, but not there by 1903; 'La Frette',
1884, Rev. J. Leitch (Hb Carlisle); Samarès
Meadows, 1897, Lester-Garland, but the fields were
ploughed by 1903; south end of St Ouen's Bay, 1947,
D. McClintock and 1955 Dr J. Mills.
G rare; A rare.

C. tenuiflorum (Hoffmans. & Link) Fritsch
                   Slender Centaury
One record: Babington's specimen labelled
Erythraea pulchella from Les Quennevais in 1837 has
been determined as this species (Hb Cantab.).
G 1837.

MENYANTHACEAE

Menyanthes trifoliata L.   **Bogbean**
                 du **trêfl'ye dg'ieau**
Babington (1839) recorded the Bogbean as 'in
marshes but not very common'. As far as is known, it
has been in only three wet areas: St Peter's Marsh
from where it disappeared when the marsh was
drained; Moulin de Paul mill pond where it was last
seen early this century; the upper part of Bellozanne
Valley from where Guiton saw a flowering specimen
in 1917. In the Société's botanical report for 1928
Attenborough stated that Bogbean was last seen in
1918 but gave no locality.
G last record 1907.

Nymphoides peltata (S. G. Gmelin) O. Kuntze
                 Fringed Water-lily
Well established in a small man-made pool in a
stream running through the wood at Egypt, Trinity in
1981, J. C. Fluck. A non-native, its origin in Jersey is
unknown, but it is often planted in ornamental pools.

APOCYNACEAE

Vinca minor L.   **Lesser Periwinkle**
La Gasca listed the Lesser Periwinkle in 1834 and
Lester-Garland (1903) considered it native in the
upper part of St Saviour's Valley, in St Peter's Valley
and in a valley at Rozel but he thought it was more
frequent as an escape from cultivation. It is now difficult to assess the status of many plants, and all found
growing well away from gardens have been mapped.

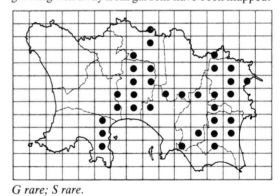

G rare; S rare.

V. major L.   **Greater Periwinkle**
                 d's **êpèrvenches**
A frequent garden escape from at least as early as the
1830s and now thoroughly naturalised on hedgebanks usually close to habitation.
Map overleaf

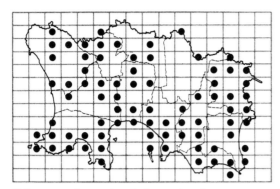

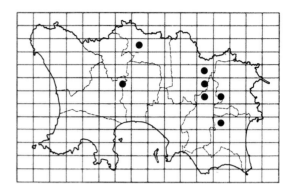

G frequent; A occasional; S occasional.

RUBIACEAE

Sherardia arvensis L.   **Field Madder**
Frequent in dry arable fields and sandy areas.

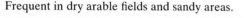

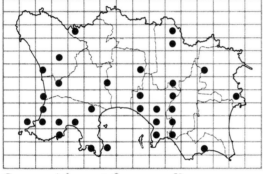

G scarce; A frequent; S common; H common.

Asperula cynanchica L.   **Squinancywort**
Piquet collected specimens from Les Hanières, St
Ouen, in 1884 and 1890. The only known record since
then is one given by Attenborough in the Société's
botanical report for 1946 but this was unconfirmed.
A rare.

A. arvensis L.   **Blue Woodruff**
A casual in St Ouen's Bay, 1884 and 1890, Piquet, and
more recently from bird seed, for example in a
garden at Bel Royal, 1966, H. G. Amy.
G 1900; S 1979.

Galium odoratum (L.) Scop.   **Sweet Woodruff**
(Asperula odorata)   *du ris*
A garden escape which Saunders reported to
Babington (1839) as at Rozel. Piquet later collected a
specimen from near Rosel Manor. By 1926 it
appeared to be increasing slightly and Ariste wrote
that it was in several localities. Some of the records
on the map are of single large plants but at Trinity
there is a patch about ten feet long on one roadside,
Mrs M. L. Long.

G. uliginosum L.   **Fen Bedstraw**
La Gasca's and Saunders' records from the 1830s
were both rejected by Lester-Garland (1903) and
there is still no confirmation. They are thought to be
in error for *G. palustre.*
G no confirmed record.

G. debile Desv.   **Slender Marsh Bedstraw**
No satisfactory record. Druce's specimen from
Beaumont in 1906 was determined as *G. palustre* by
Professor E. F. Warburg. Louis-Arsène's specimens
labelled as from St Brelade, 1924, and mentioned in
the B.E.C. *Report* for 1924 are not necessarily from
Jersey (see *Watsonia* 14: 167–176). The origin of the
post-1930 record in the *Atlas of the British Flora*
(1962) is unknown.
(?)G 1838, 1891 and 1976; S rare.

G. elongatum C. Presl   **Great Marsh Bedstraw**
Inner edge of reed bed, St Ouen's Pond, 1983. The
identification is based on the descriptions in *Flora
Europaea* and the *Excursion Flora of the British Isles.*
No chromosome counts have been made. See the
next species.

G. palustre L.   **Lesser Marsh Bedstraw**
Frequent in inland damp places. In past accounts of
Jersey's flora, this species and the above were not
separated; nor were they in the survey 1960–70.
While the great majority of the records will be of this
species, the map should be treated as a composite
one.

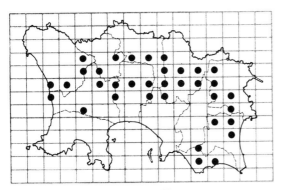

G local; A occasional; S rare; H rare.

G. verum L.   **Lady's Bedstraw**
                                            du **myi d'mielle**

Subsp. *verum*   Common on light sandy soil.

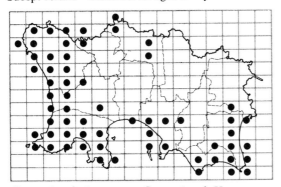

G occasional; A common; S occasional; H common.

G. mollugo L.   **Hedge Bedstraw**
Common in hedges and on rough côtils.

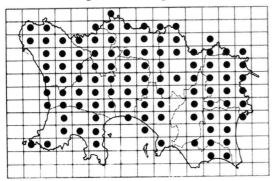

G common; A rare; S common; H occasional.

G. x pomeranicum Retz.   **A hybrid Bedstraw**
G. mollugo x **G. verum** (*G. ochroleucum*)
The hybrid between Hedge and Lady's Bedstraw has been reported from several areas where the parents grow together: West Mount, Les Quennevais and

Portelet Bay, Lester-Garland (1903); Portelet and St Ouen, 1906, Druce; near Pont Marquet Station, 1920, A. J. Binet; St Brelade, 1925, Miss A. B. Cobbe; roadside above L'Étacq, 1958, Mrs J. Russell; La Route de Noirmont, 1983, Mrs M. Case. *G 1883, 1907; H 1979.*

G. album Miller   **Upright Hedge Bedstraw**
Listed by La Gasca in 1834 and by Piquet in 1851 and 1896 but the records are unconfirmed.
G ? A 1932; S error.

G. saxatile L.   **Heath Bedstraw**
Locally frequent on heathland above the cliffs of the coast.

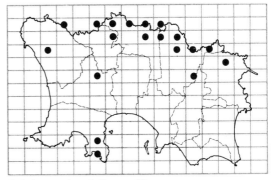

G ? A occasional; S rare; H rare.

G. aparine L.   **Cleavers**
                                   *d'l'***hèrbe à tchilieuvre**

Common, often abundant, in hedges and among rank vegetation. *Eune tchilieuvre* is a grass snake and the Jersey-Norman-French name probably refers to the way the plant snakes up through a hedge. The adhesive fruits are *des p'tits prannants*.

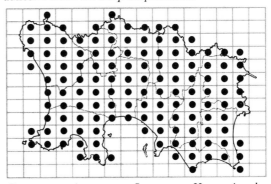

G common; A common; S common; H occasional.

Cruciata laevipes Opiz   **Crosswort**

Miss E. H. de Feu found Crosswort on La Rue de l'Est, Fort Regent, in 1958. It was still there in 1959 but disappeared in the early 1960s.
G error; A 1962.

Rubia peregrina L.   **Wild Madder**

Locally frequent in bushy places on the cliffs.

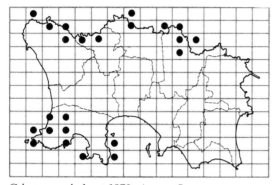

G last record about 1870; A rare; S rare.

CONVOLVULACEAE

Cuscuta europaea L.   **Greater Dodder**

Recorded by La Gasca in 1834 and Piquet in 1851 but it is presumed that the following species, from which Greater Dodder was not separated in early Floras, was intended.

C. epithymum (L.) L.   **Dodder**
                              d'la **touothelle**

Subsp. *epithymum* A locally common parasite particularly on Gorse which it festoons and sometimes almost engulfs with its threadlike stems and small pink spherical flower clusters. Normally it is an annual but D. McClintock found it overwintering on gorse in May 1953. Other host plants include Woodsage, Lady's Bedstraw, Bell Heather, Red Bartsia, Lucerne and Bracken. No special search has been made for its hosts.

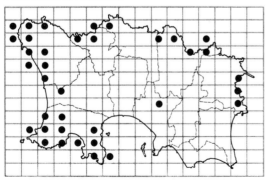

G local; A frequent; S occasional; H occasional.

Calystegia soldanella (L.) R. Br.   **Sea Bindweed**
                        des **veîl'yes dé sablion**

Locally frequent on the sandier parts of the coast.

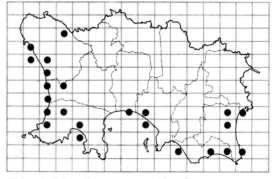

G local; A locally common; H locally common.

C. sepium (L.) R. Br.   **Bindweed**
                              des **veîl'yes**

Subsp. *sepium* Frequent in dampish places. Ereaut in his *Hortus Siccus* of 1847 labelled his specimen *manchettes à la Vièrge* which, roughly translated, means 'elbow length sleeves of the Virgin Mary', a fanciful but highly descriptive name.

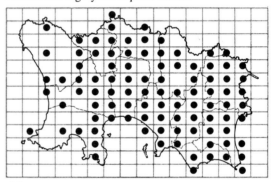

G frequent, with the hybrid with subsp. silvatica *rare; A locally common; S occasional; H occasional.*
Subsp. *roseata* Brummitt One record: Bonne Nuit, 1961, Mrs J. Russell.
G occurs.
Subsp. *silvatica* (Kit.) Maire *(C. silvatica)* This Bindweed from south Europe was not recorded in Jersey until 1956 but it had obviously been here for some time previously. It tends to be a plant of disturbed ground and the edges of rubbish tips. Recently it seems to have decreased, perhaps because of the tighter States' control of dumping.

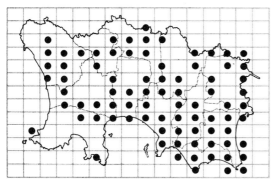

G frequent; A locally common; S occasional.
Subsp. pulchra (Brummitt & Heywood) Tutin (C. pulchra) One record: overgrown garden Mont Arthur, 1960, Miss E. F. P. Thomson.
G 1970, 1971.

Convolvulus arvensis L.   **Field Bindweed**
des **veîl'yes dé r'lié**

Lester-Garland's comment in 1903: 'Ubiquitous. By far too common.' is still true.

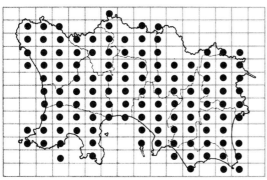

G common; A common; S common; H frequent.

HYDROPHYLLACEAE

Nemophila menziesii Hook. & Arn.   **Baby Blue Eyes**
A specimen of unknown origin is in Ereaut's *Hortus Siccus* of 1847. The species occurs in gardens but is nowhere naturalised.
G 1970.

BORAGINACEAE

Lithospermum officinale L.   **Common Gromwell**
Recorded in error for the next species in the Société's botanical report for 1971.
G last seen 1970.

L. purpurocaerulea L.   **Purple Gromwell**
(Buglossoides purpurocaerulea)
One record: La Route des Mans, St Brelade, 1971, Mrs E. M. Towers.

L. arvense L.   **Field Gromwell**
(B. arvensis)
A rare casual not seen recently. Babington (1839) recorded it simply as 'On cultivated land'. Piquet listed it likewise in both 1851 and 1896 and collected a specimen from St Ouen's Bay in 1900.
G 1885, 1890; A 1900, 1971.

Echium vulgare L.   **Viper's-bugloss**
Viper's-bugloss has always been rare in Jersey and has not been seen for twenty years. La Gasca listed it in 1834 and it was collected at long intervals during last century and in the beginning of this. In 1923 Attenborough recorded it in a quarry near La Corbière where it remained, by the path near the overgrown quarry east of La Rosière desalination plant, until the 1960s. In 1933 he recorded it from 'a new station at St Mary', stating later (pers. comm.) that this was near Le Creux de Vis. J. C. Fluck found one plant on disturbed ground near there in 1961. Several plants were found east of Portelet Inn car park in 1964 by J. C. Fluck. The rarity of Viper's-bugloss in Jersey and Guernsey is unexpected considering its quantity in Alderney and Herm.
G last seen 1958; A locally frequent; S rare; H locally common.

E. plantagineum L.   **Purple Viper's-bugloss**
d'la **grâsse-g'linne**
In 1689 Dr W. Sherard found this 'In the sandy Grounds near St Hilary plentifully' (see the Introduction) and the species, sometimes called Jersey Viper's-bugloss, is still locally plentiful on light soil. The best-known locality is above Beauport where some of the fields have been purple with it for years. Druce's description of the colony and of his finding of it in 1906 (*Journal of Botany* XLV: 424) could equally well have been written in the 1970s and early 1980s: 'On the slope of a hill near Beauport there were some hundreds of a tall fasciated form three to four feet high; in one instance at least the flattened stem was ten inches across and had on it 438 fully expanded flowers. The plants attracted my attention more than a mile away'.

Plants were particularly plentiful after pigs had been kept in the fields. Similarly on a côtil at Les Hâtivieaux, St Ouen, where Purple Viper's-bugloss had been occasionally seen in the past, it was suddenly abundant on one part in 1981, 1982 and 1983 after horses had been allowed to graze the côtil. This particular part had been much used by the horses for their droppings. It is therefore suggested that the species likes disturbed ground with a light soil rich in nitrogen. The fields at Beauport are no longer being farmed so Purple Viper's-bugloss may decrease there. In all colonies fasciated forms occur remarkably freely.

The species was featured on the 9p stamp issued by the Jersey Postal Authority in 1972.

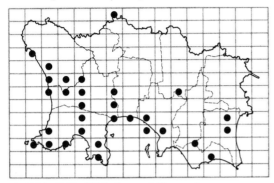

G 1886, 1891, 1894; S error? H error?

E. pininana Webb & Berthelot   **Giant Echium**

Giant Echiums seed themselves freely in several gardens and in 1981 two young plants c. 50 cm high were growing on a heap of soil tipped where a reservoir was being formed near La Rue de la Campagne, St Ouen. These disappeared but in autumn 1982 the remains of two fully grown plants which had flowered and fruited were found on an earth bank of tipped soil about 150 yds away – the same two plants moved in the construction work?
G scarce; A rare; S occasional; H rare.

Symphytum officinale L.   **Comfrey**

Recorded frequently since first noted by Babington (1839) but considerable confusion exists between this and Russian Comfrey. It is now thought to be rare in wet places.
G rare; A rare; S 1905; H 1980.

S. asperum Lepechin   **Rough Comfrey**

Druce recorded this at St Catherine and St Brelade in 1906/7 (*Journal of Botany* XLV: 423). There is no supporting specimen in his herbarium, and as he added '(*asperrimum* Donn), the fodder plant' he presumably intended the following species.

S. x uplandicum Nyman   **Russian Comfrey**
S. asperum x S. officinale   *d'la* **console**

Russian Comfrey, which occurs occasionally in all but the west of the island, is the most likely Comfrey to be seen. A. E. Wade stated that though very popular from about 1870 onwards when it was imported into Britain from Russia, it was probably introduced earlier under the erroneous name *S. asperrimum* (*Watsonia* 4: 117–118). It was under this name that it was introduced into Jersey as the following extract from the first *Report* (1834, p. 7) of the Jersey Agricultural and Horticultural Society shows: 'The *Symphytum asperrimum*, or prickly comfrey, . . . is

under trial by the Honorary Secretary, who will report upon it in due time'. The Honorary Secretary, Col. J. Le Couteur, later Sir John, duly reported (1837, pp. 15–16): 'I consider it to be of sufficient value, to recommend it to the attention of every experimental farmer who will find a small portion of it very acceptable in July and August, when green forage begins to fail.' The present population is presumably from these introductions.
G scarce; A locally frequent; S 1977.

S. orientale L.   **White Comfrey**

Only one early record exists, Piquet's in 1908 from a lane near St Helier. This may have been by the steps down St John's Road where Mrs M. L. Long found it in quantity in 1969. It disappeared in the mid-1970s. There are four other records: sandpits north of St Ouen's Pond, 1958, Mrs G. F. Johnson; Bellozanne Valley, 1958, D. McClintock; still in quantity on the east side of La Route de l'Aleval where it was first found about 1975, Mrs M. L. Long; wall at Mont Mado, 1982 and 1983, Mrs M. Pett.

Anchusa officinalis L.   **Alkanet**

A specimen labelled 'Jersey 1847' but with no specific locality is in 'Mrs Robinson's' herbarium in the British Museum. There is no local knowledge of the plant.
G error.

A. azurea Miller   **Large Blue Alkanet**
(*A. italica*)

One record: L'Étacq, 1900, Lester-Garland.

A. arvensis (L.) Bieb.   **Bugloss**
(*Lycopsis arvensis*)   *d'la* **p'tite g'linne**

Subsp. *arvensis*   Frequent on light soil.

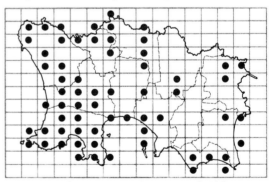

G occasional; A frequent; S occasional; H frequent.

Pentaglottis sempervirens (L.) Tausch ex L. H. Bailey
(Anchusa sempervirens) **Green Alkanet**

Green Alkanet is frequent along hedgebanks of the interior and is occasionally abundant. Lester-Garland (1903) thought it was native in at least one locality but otherwise was an escape from cottage gardens. Druce considered it was native to Jersey. It is not now seen in gardens and if not native, then it is thoroughly naturalised, and has been recorded since 1832 (Gay).

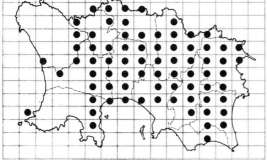

G scarce; S rare.

Borago officinalis L. **Borage**
du **bouôrrage**

Borage, still used as a herb in drinks, is frequent on roadsides and disturbed ground. It was first noted by Gay in 1832 and was recorded by Babington in 1839.

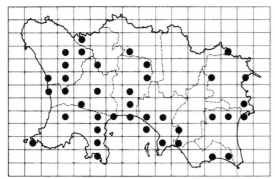

G occasional; A occasional; S locally frequent.

B. pygmaea (DC.) Chater & W. Greuter
Slender Borage

H rare (Jethou).

Myosotis arvensis (L.) Hill **Field Forget-me-not**

Only very occasionally seen. Any plant suspected of being the common English Field Forget-me-not should be looked at closely. Early and Changing Forget-me-not are much more likely to be found. Babington (1839) recorded it as common and Piquet

(1896) as frequent on roadsides. This is no longer true – and perhaps was not at the time, as Lester-Garland (1903) gave only three localities and stated that it was not common.

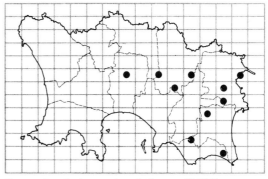

G occasional; A occasional; S rare; H 1889.

M. ramosissima Rochel **Early Forget-me-not**
(M. collina) *dé l'*ouothelle dé souothis

Common on light soil.

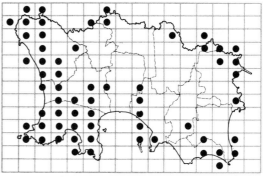

G, A, S and H frequent.

M. discolor Pers. **Changing Forget-me-not**
(M. versicolor) *dé l'*ouothelle dé souothis

Subsp. *discolor* Common on light soil. Var. *pallida* Bréb. with white flowers and yellow-green foliage also occurs.
Subsp. *dubia* (Arrondeau) Blaise Lester-Garland considered this frequent in Jersey (*Journal of Botany* 1920) and it still occurs.

Map overleaf

125

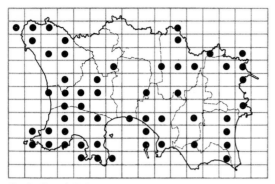

G, A, S and H frequent.

M. sylvatica Hoffm. **Wood Forget-me-not**
des **yeux d'la Vièrge**

A rare garden escape nowhere naturalised, first recorded by Babington (1839) near St Helier.
G 1969; A rare; S rare.

M. secunda A. Murray **Creeping Forget-me-not**

The nomenclature within this section of the *Myosotis* genus has changed over the years. Babington's 1838 specimen of *M. repens* belongs here (det. D. Welch) and so does Lester-Garland's (1903) *M. palustris* var. *repens* which he stated was common. Recent records suggest that this may be only slightly commoner than *M. laxa*. These Water Forget-me-nots are difficult to separate and it may be that they have been under-recorded. The maps must be read with this in mind.

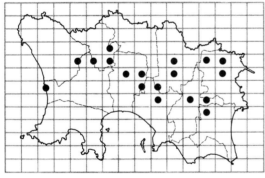

G rare; A frequent; S rare.

M. sicula Guss. **Jersey Forget-me-not**

On 10 June 1922 A. J. Wilmott found this forget-me-not growing in damp places on Ouaisné Common and the following day he found it in a second locality – by the edge of the small pool on the Noirmont headland. It was last seen on Ouaisné Common by Miss M. McC. Webster in 1957 but was still in good quantity by the Noirmont pool until the late 1970s. Gorse then began encroaching on the pool and it became overshadowed by willows. Only a few plants could be found in 1983 so some conservation work was carried

out to restore the former open, sunny habitat which had suited Jersey Forget-me-not. This species occurs nowhere else in the British Isles or the Channel Islands.

M. laxa Lehm. **Tufted Forget-me-not**
Subsp. *caespitosa* (C. F. Schultz) Hyl. ex Nordh. Lester-Garland (1903) considered this rare but during the survey it was recorded almost as frequently as *M. secunda*. See that species. D. Welch determined one of Babington's 1838 specimens as this.

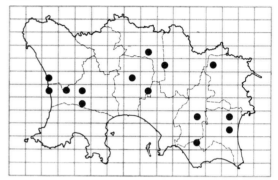

G more frequent than M. secunda.

M. scorpioides L. **Water Forget-me-not**
(M. palustris)

La Gasca recorded this in 1834 and Babington (1839) and Piquet (1851) both stated it was frequent in marshes. No supporting specimens are known. It is thought that most records were probably not of *M. scorpioides* as known today since in the past this name covered most of the forget-me-nots of damp places. Lester-Garland (1903) considered it rare and gave two records, one of his own from St Ouen's Pond and the Rev. W. M. Rogers' from Waterworks Valley. In 1983 R. W. S. Knightbridge found it in two adjacent fields in Vallée des Vaux and similarly in the valley running south from St Mary's Church.
G 1866.

Lappula squarrosa (Retz.) Dumort.
(Echinospermum lappula) **Bur Forget-me-not**
Two records: St Ouen's Bay, probably introduced with foreign seed, 1898, Piquet; rubbish heap near Georgetown, 1899, Lester-Garland.

Cynoglossum officinale L. **Hound's-tongue**
Recorded by Babington (1839) and Piquet (1851 and 1896) from Les Quennevais, and last collected from there in 1876 by Melvill.
G rare; A claimed; H common.

VERBENACEAE

Verbena officinalis L.   **Vervain**
d'l'hèrbe d'grâce

Though Vervain is frequent on roadsides and similar dry places, it always seems an unexpected pleasure to see it. The Jersey-Norman-French name *d'l'hèrbe d'grâce* may come from this or from that it was considered a holy plant in the past, much used medicinally.

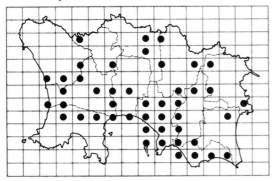

G rare; A rare; S last record 1892.

CALLITRICHACEAE

Callitriche truncata Guss.

Short-leaved Water-starwort

G locally abundant in the past, last seen 1968.

C. stagnalis Scop.   **Common Water-starwort**

Probably the commonest of the Water-starworts. Babington's specimen originally labelled *C. verna* var. *platycarpa* from St Lawrence in 1838 (Hb Cantab.) is this species (det. Dr J. P. Savidge who has helped greatly with this Genus), and so is Lester-Garland's, originally labelled *C. verna* from a stagnant ditch at L'Étacq in 1899 (Hb Kew). There may still be confusion between these species, and *C. obtusangula* is hardly separable when sterile. The following map is therefore a composite one of all species and is included merely to show that Water-starworts are not as rare as Lester-Garland's 1903 Flora and individual records would indicate.

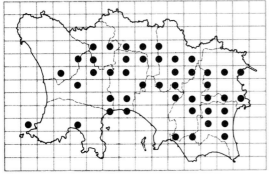

G common; A rare; S common.

C. obtusangula Le Gall

Blunt-fruited Water-starwort

St Peter's Marsh, 1852, Piquet, and 1876, T. B. Blow both det. Savidge (Hb Oxford); Bellozanne Valley 1877 and 1906/7 Druce (*Journal of Botany* XLV: 421); 1899, Lester-Garland *fide* Schotsman (Hb Kew); Georgetown, Lester-Garland (1903); La Becquetterie, 1968, Mrs D. L. Le Quesne; Grouville Marsh, 1970, Dr J. G. Dony. See *C. stagnalis*.
G rare; H 1958.

C. platycarpa Kütz.

Various-leaved Water-starwort

Some records in the past of *C. verna* may belong here. There are recent records from two ditches in St Clement where it was frequent in 1968, Mrs E. M. Towers, confirmed Dr Savidge who thought a specimen from the narrow 'canal' through Samarès Manor grounds was 'possibly *C. platycarpa*'. See *C. stagnalis*.
G only certain record 1894; S 1842, 1896.

C. hamulata Kütz. ex Koch

Intermediate Water-starwort

Recorded from St Peter's Marsh, Gorey and a pond near Noirmont, Babington, (1839); quarry near La Corbière, 1899, A. Bennett and Grand Val, 1900, Lester-Garland, both *fide* Schotsman (Hb Kew); ditch near St Ouen's Pond, 1917, Attenborough; Portelet, 1925, Ariste; Ouaisné Common pond, 1930, I. A. Williams; pool at Grosnez, 1958, confirmed Savidge.
G rare; H 1957.

LABIATAE

Ajuga reptans L.   **Bugle**

Recorded by Saunders (Babington 1839) from St Saviour's Valley and Ereaut collected a specimen in 1847, but how wild the plants were is unknown. Bugle is often planted in dampish gardens and sometimes escapes through the gate or hedge but it is never seen at any distance away from houses.
G frequent.

A. chamaepitys (L.) Schreb.   **Ground-pine**

A specimen collected by C. J. Tempère in August 1876 and labelled only 'Jersey' is in the Birmingham University herbarium. There is no local knowledge of this species in the Channel Islands. Tempère similarly collected *Teucrium chamaedrys*, Wall Germander, and both must be considered extremely doubtful except as fleeting garden escapes.

Teucrium scorodonia L.   **Wood Sage**
d'l'ambrais

Subsp. *scorodonia* Common on the cliffs and dry hillsides, and sometimes locally abundant.
Map overleaf

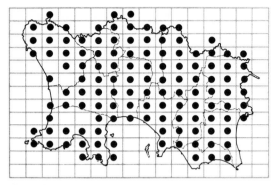

G, A, S and H common.

T. scordium L.   **Water Germander**

La Gasca's record of 1834 was rejected by Lester-Garland and it has never been confirmed.
G last seen 1925.

T. chamaedrys L.   **Wall Germander**

Specimens collected by Tempère in 'Jersey' in the 1870s are in the Belfast and Birmingham herbaria but see Ground-pine. 'In a lane at Trinity, Dr Stanley', Piquet (1851). This is presumably the record given in the *Phytologist* (1853). Later Piquet crossed out the entry in his 1851 list and did not include it in 1896.

Scutellaria galericulata L.   **Skullcap**

Skullcap was recorded last century from the Town Mills Pond, the brook at Millbrook, St Peter's Marsh and, in Piquet's 1896 list, from the mill stream between the second and third mill in St Saviour's Valley. This was probably near the Moulin de Paul millpond, the only locality given by Lester-Garland in 1903. Skullcap still grows near Moulin de Paul but with the changes made in the 1950s it is now by the side of the north end of Grands Vaux reservoir.
G rare.

S. minor Hudson   **Lesser Skullcap**

Lesser Skullcap is still in good quantity in some of the boggy places on or near the cliffs. All the areas on the map were known last century. In addition, it was reported from La Saline in 1919 and from the east of Bouley Bay in 1922. Plants may still be there, overlooked.

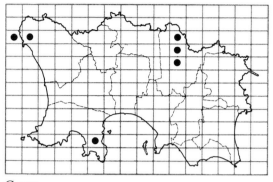

G rare.

Marrubium vulgare L.   **White Horehound**

Last century, when White Horehound was used medicinally, both Babington (1839) and Piquet (1851) described it as common. As its use diminished, so the quantity of plants diminished. By 1896 Piquet could only record it as frequent and by 1903 Lester-Garland thought it rare. During the survey it was occasionally found on disturbed ground, usually on light soil.

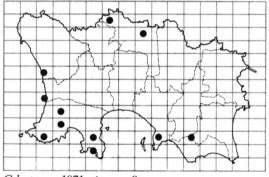

G last seen 1971; A rare; S rare.

Galeopsis angustifolia Ehrh. ex Hoffm.

        Red Hemp-nettle

Druce collected a specimen from Pont Marquet in 1907. It was a solitary plant which he considered a casual and which he originally named *G. ladanum* (*Journal of Botany* XLV: 425).

G. speciosa Miller   **Large-flowered Hemp-nettle**
(*G. versicolor*)

Babington (1839) gave Saunders' record but suggested that it might be only a variety of the following. There has been no confirmation of the record which was rejected by Lester-Garland (1903).

G. tetrahit L.   **Common Hemp-nettle**

Frequent last century according to Piquet in his 1851 and 1896 lists, and Lester-Garland thought it not common in 1903. In recent years it has been recorded, rarely, from a few cultivated fields.

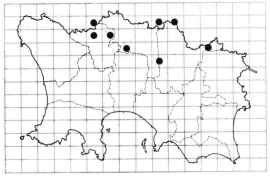

G last seen 1969; A occasional.

Lamium maculatum L.   Spotted Dead-nettle

A garden escape recorded three times: by mill stream, Grève de Lecq, 1956; Le Hocq Marsh, 1961, Mrs J. Brooks but habitat now gone; near Grouville Church, 1969, Mrs E. M. Towers.
G one record.

L. album L.   White Dead-nettle

White Dead-nettle, a common plant of English roadsides, has always been rare in Jersey and is practically unknown in the other Channel Islands. Babington (1839) gave only a record of Saunders' and Piquet described it as rare in 1851 and very rare in 1896. The only place it persisted for any length of time was near the farm at Crabbé. Guiton, reporting it in 1916, stated that it had been there for some years. It was still there in the late 1960s but now seems to have gone. In the 1960s it was recorded from an unexpected number of places. These are shown on the accompanying map but it had gone from most, if not all except that above Grève de Lecq Valley, by 1983. It was sometimes needed as a specimen for drawing or identification in school examinations in the 1960s, and at least part of the increase came from its being deliberately planted out, so that a supply was at hand when required.

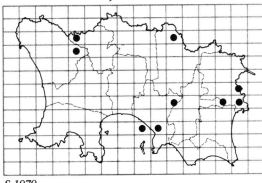

S 1979.

L. purpureum L.   Red Dead-nettle
                                        d'l'enchens

Common on roadsides, on derelict land and as a weed of cultivation.

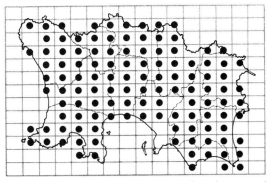

G frequent; A common; S occasional; H last record 1890.

L. hybridum Vill.   Cut-leaved Dead-nettle

Widespread on cultivated land but not as frequent as the last species.

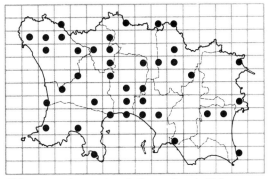

G frequent; A occasional; S occasional; H frequent.

L. amplexicaule L.   Henbit Dead-nettle

Subsp. *amplexicaule*   Frequent on cultivated land.

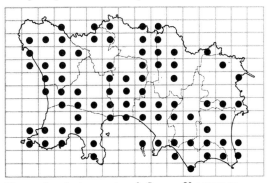

G occasional; A occasional; S rare; H common.

Lamiastrum galeobdolon (L.) Ehrend. & Polatschek
(Lamium Galeobdolon) **Yellow Archangel**
Subsp. *galeobdolon* A rare native species. Yellow
Archangel occurs in damp thickets on the north coast
and has been known in the valley running down to St
Catherine's Bay from Rosel Manor since at least 1853
when a record of Piquet's was given in the *Phyto-
logist*.
G the garden 'Variegatum', one locality.

Leonurus cardiaca L. **Motherwort**
du **picot**

A rare casual with scattered records from 1839
onwards. There have been three since the Occupation (1940–45): Devil's Hole, 1949, Attenborough; rubbish dump, North Canal, St Ouen, the
late 1950s; near Les Creux, St Brelade, 1961, J. C.
Fluck.
G not seen wild this century; S rare.

Ballota nigra L. **Black Horehound**
du **meuthe-en-c'mîn**

Subsp. *foetida* Hayek Locally frequent on roadsides and disturbed ground.

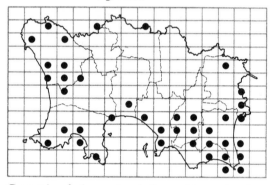

G occasional; A occasional; S rare; H occasional.

Stachys officinalis (L.) Trevisan **Betony**
(Stachys Betonica)
Locally frequent on the cliffs and cliff heaths.

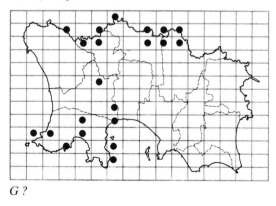

G ?

S. germanica L. **Downy Woundwort**
An undated note by Babington in his own copy of his
Flora states that Dr Bromfield found this in St Peter's
Valley, but Babington queries the record and there
has been no confirmation. This may be the basis for
the otherwise untraceable record for Jersey given in
The Wild Flowers of Guernsey.

S. sylvatica L. **Hedge Woundwort**
d'l'ortchie puante
Frequent on hedgebanks and roadsides.

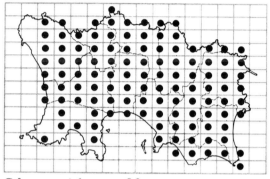

G frequent; A frequent; S frequent.

S. palustris L. **Marsh Woundwort**
d'l'orvale
Locally frequent in damp areas.

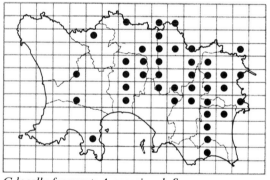

G locally frequent; A occasional; S rare.

S. x ambigua Sm. **A hybrid Woundwort**
S. palustris x **S. sylvatica**
Plants intermediate between Hedge and Marsh
Woundwort occasionally occur and are presumed to
be hybrids. The first record was by the French
botanist, J. Gay, in 1832. The name Woundwort
comes from the use of this and the previous species
for staunching blood.
G occurs.

S. annua (L.) L.   **Annual Woundwort**

Two records: Attenborough had a specimen, which he suspected was a casual, brought to him from Les Quennevais in 1923; rubbish dump, Trinity, 1959, Miss E. H. du Feu.

S. arvensis (L.) L.   **Field Woundwort**

Frequent in cultivated ground.

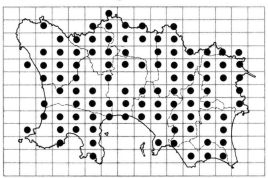

G common; A occasional; S occasional; H occasional.

Nepeta x faassenii Bergmans ex Stearn
                                        Garden Catmint

Occasionally planted out on wild hedgebanks where it may survive for a few years, but does not become naturalised.
G 1958; A 1972.

N. cataria L.   **Catmint**

Recorded last century by La Gasca in 1834 and Babington in 1839, and collected in 1855 by J. Piquet from the road between Le Marais, St Ouen, and L'Étacq (conf. E. F. Warburg) and in 1869 by F. Piquet. It may have been cultivated in the past as a medicinal herb.

Glechoma hederacea L.   **Ground-ivy**
                                        du **tèrrêtre**

Frequent on grassy hedgebanks and in shady places, usually on dampish soil.

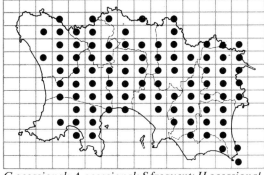

G occasional; A occasional; S frequent; H occasional.

Prunella laciniata (L.) L.   **Cut-leaved Selfheal**

A 1932.

P. vulgaris L.   **Selfheal**

(Brunella vulgaris)
Common in grassy places.

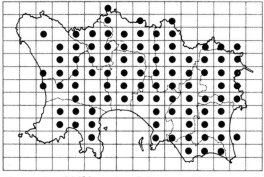

G occasional; A frequent; S frequent; H occasional.

Melissa officinalis L.   **Balm**
                                            du **piment**

Subsp. *officinalis* Still occasionally found by roadsides as an escape from cultivation, as it has been since records began last century.

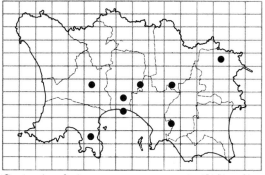

G occasional; A rare.

Acinos arvensis (Lam.) Dandy   **Basil-thyme**

'Melissa acinos' was stated by Babington (1839) to have been found by Saunders 'On hillsides by the road to St Peter's' and was stated by Attenborough to have been found by a visitor on an old wall at Beaumont in 1953. No specimens exist and as *Melissa officinalis* is known in St Peter there may have been a confusion of names.

Calamintha sylvatica Bromf.   **Common Calamint**

Subsp. *ascendens* (Jordan) P. W. Ball Three records: garden escape, Mont à l'Abbé, 1919, A. J. Binet; St Brelade's Bay Hotel, 1961, D. McClintock; above Beaumont, 1969, Mrs E. M. Towers.
G ? H claimed.

C. nepeta (L.) Savi   **Lesser Calamint**

Piquet listed this as 'Very rare near L'Étacq' in his 1896 list but there is no specimen, whereas there is a specimen of *Nepeta cataria* from near L'Étacq in 1855. Some confusion is suspected.
G local; H frequent.

Satureja montana L.   **Winter Savory**

One record: 'Introduced. Spontaneous in gardens', 1911, Piquet (Druce, *Journal of Botany*, 1911).

Clinopodium vulgare L.   **Wild Basil**

Subsp. *vulgare* A specimen collected in August 1898 by Piquet and labelled only 'Roadsides, rare' is in the Société's herbarium.
A rare.

Origanum vulgare L.   **Marjoram**

A rare garden escape last century but not seen since 1900.
G last seen 1890s; A 1966.

Thymus vulgaris L.   **Garden Thyme**

On a wall top, 1961 and 1973, D. McClintock.

T. praecox Opiz   **Wild Thyme**
                                        d'la **sèrpiliéthe**

Subsp. *arcticus* (E. Durand) Jalas (*T. serpyllum*) Large patches of Wild Thyme, smothered with purple flowers in summer, occur commonly on the dunes and heaths. More open, trailing plants grow on banks and over rocks elsewhere near the coast.

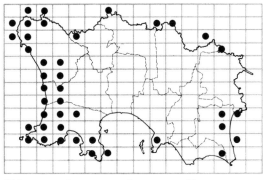

G frequent; A common; S common; H common.

T. pulegioides L.   **Large Thyme**
(*T. Chamaedrys*)

Druce thought some plants he saw between Pont Marquet and St Brelade in 1906/7 might be this but the description of them (*Journal of Botany* XLV: 425) does not seem to make them significantly different from *T. praecox* and no specimens exist.

Lycopus europaeus L.   **Gipsywort**

Locally frequent in wet places.

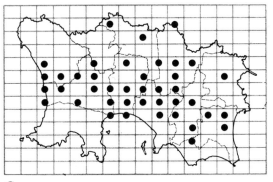

G rare.

Mentha pulegium L.   **Pennyroyal**

In 1981 Pennyroyal was found in good quantity, looking native, in a damp grassy field south of The Grove, Mont Cambrai, and it is still there. Last century it grew in St Peter's Marsh and on Gorey Common but the only other record of it as a native plant this century was by Attenborough in 1916 from near the rifle range at Crabbé. In the past Pennyroyal was occasionally used to try to form aromatic lawns which would require little cutting. In 1958 a few plants were found in a lawn in the grounds of Samarès Manor. Miss E. H. du Feu refound it there in 1959 but it has not been seen recently.
G last seen 1924; S 1902.

M. arvensis L.   **Corn Mint**

Lester-Garland (1903) stated that Corn Mint was rare in his experience but Piquet had assured him that he had seen it frequently. Babington, much earlier, had also recorded it as frequent. It may be that as cornfields disappeared from Jersey, so did Corn Mint. In the survey it was found only five times and only in small quantity each time.

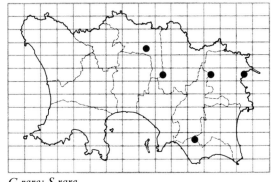

G rare; S rare.

M. x verticillata L.   **Whorled Mint**
M. aquatica x **M. arvensis**

One record: St Peter's Valley, 1930, I. A. Williams (Hb Kew).
G rare; S 1892.

M. x gentilis L.   **Bushy Mint**
M. arvensis x **M. spicata**

One record: Mont Mado quarry dump, 1966, J. C. Fluck, conf. Dr R. M. Harley.
G 1968.

M. aquatica L.   **Water Mint**
           d'la **menthe sauvage**

Common in wet places.

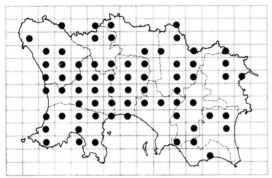

G frequent; A frequent; S occasional; H local.

M. x piperita L.   **Peppermint**
M. aquatica x **M. spicata**

Recorded by La Gasca in 1834 and Ereaut collected a specimen in 1847 for his *Hortus Siccus*. In 1961 J. C. Fluck gathered n. m. *citrata* (Ehrh.) Briq. in Vallée des Vaux where it was probably planted.
G last record 1926; A occasional; S 1957.

M. x maximiliana F. W. Schultz   **A hybrid Mint**
M. aquatica x **M. suaveolens**

One record: Val de la Mare, St Ouen, 1957, Miss M. McC. Webster, det. R. Graham.

M. spicata group   **The Spicata Mints**

As knowledge of this group has increased its nomenclature has changed and it has not always been possible to equate even some relatively recent names with present ones with certainty. The following account should be read with this in mind.

M. suaveolens Ehrh.   **Round-leaved Mint**

Lester-Garland's '*M. rotundifolia* Huds.', which he recorded (1903) as local in damp low-lying meadows in most of the main valleys and in the low-lying parts of the east, is thought to have been Round-leaved Mint. This is still roughly its distribution.

G locally frequent; S 1841; H ?

M. x rotundifolia (L.) Huds.   **A hybrid Mint**
M. longifolia x **M. suaveolens**

A record given as this cross in the Société botanical report for 1961 was probably referable to *M. x villosa*. No specimen is available.

M. x villosa Huds.   **A hybrid Mint**
M. spicata x **M. suaveolens**

Both '*M. x cordifolia*' and '*M. x niliaca*', which were reported occasionally during the survey in the 1960s, probably belong here. The n. m. *alopecurioides*, Apple Mint, has been rarely recorded.
G rare.

M. spicata L.   **Spear Mint**
           d'la **menthe dé gardîn**

Recorded by Lester-Garland (1903) as a garden escape under the name '*M. viridis*'. Garden Mints, referable to *M. spicata*, still occur occasionally as escapes.
G occasional; A last record 1957; S rare; H 1957.

M. longifolia (L.) Huds.   **Horse Mint**

Horse Mint was recorded last century by Gay, Babington and Piquet but recent work by Dr R. M. Harley has shown that all records of this species from north-west Europe belong to *M. spicata*.
G ?

Salvia pratensis L.   **Meadow Clary**

Babington noted, without date, in his own copy of his Flora that H. W. Taylor had found one plant, a non-native, on Witches Rock (St Clement).
A one plant in the 1950s.

S. x sylvestris L.   **A Sage**
S. nemorosa x **S. pratensis**

One record: near 'Maine' Hotel, 1882, Rev. J. Leitch (Hb Carlisle).
G 1898, and three other Sages all of ?garden origin have been reported once each.

S. verbenaca L.   **Wild Clary**
           *d'l'***hèrbe à la danme**

Locally frequent in dry areas near the coast. This is a polymorphic species, one variation of which used to be called *S. Marquandii* Druce or *S. clandestina* L., Guernsey Sage. Many attempts were made in the past to find this in Jersey but all the specimens so labelled seem to be in error.

Map overleaf

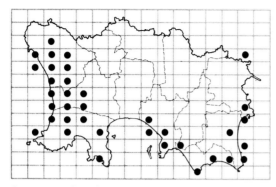

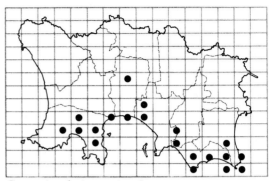

*G occasional, with 'S. marquandii' rare; A frequent;
H rare.*

G occasional; A occasional.

SOLANACEAE

Nicandra physalodes (L.) Gaertn.   **Apple of Peru**

Usually a casual occasionally found on rubbish
dumps or on light soil, but it can become established
as in the field at the junction of La Route de l'Étacq
and La Route des Salines where it has been known
for more than fifty years, sometimes in quantity.
Ereaut collected a specimen in 1847.

L. chinense Miller   **Duke of Argyll's Tea-plant**

One record: near Millbrook, 1965, Mrs E. M.
Towers, det. Dr F. H. Perring.

Atropa bella-donna L.   **Deadly Nightshade**
d'la **chrysanthème au dgiâbl'ye**

Not known wild in the island this century and may
never have been so. Babington (1839) gave a
Saunders record from St Clement. In 1851 Piquet
wrote: 'Formerly found at St Clement but since
destroyed'. In 1894 he wrote in his copy of Babington:
'I have found this plant in fruit in a field at St
Clements Oct 4/94'. In 1896 he listed it as: 'In a field at
St Clement, very rare'. There are two specimens
collected by him in the Société herbarium, one
labelled: 'Lane at St Clements 1898' and the other:
'Waste places, very rare, 1899'. Lester-Garland
(1903) was not convinced that Deadly Nightshade
had ever been wild in Jersey and relegated it to his
'Ambiguities and Errors . . .' stating that: 'Mr Piquet
tells me there used to be one fine plant in a lane near
the house called Maitlands, St Clement's'. One
wonders why Piquet did now show him the specimens
if he considered them genuinely wild. Guiton
collected a specimen from a garden plant in St
Saviour in 1900. This dangerous plant is often, in
error, said to be common in Jersey. This is because of
confusion with Black Nightshade *Solanum nigrum* or
Woody Nightshade *S. dulcamara* which are much less
poisonous.
*G last recorded in the 1840s, probably planted;
S ?error.*

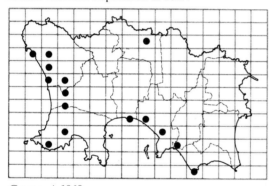

G rare; A 1969.

Lycium barbarum L.   **Duke of Argyll's Tea-plant**

Much planted as a windbreak along the south coast
and occasionally naturalised. There was some difficulty in deciding when to record a plant, i.e. how
naturalised it was. A map is given merely to show that
there is a fair amount of the Duke of Argyll's Tea-
plant in the island outside gardens. Piquet first listed
it from St Aubin's Bay in 1896 'but probably an
escape'.

Hyoscyamus niger L.   **Henbane**
d'la **hannebanne**

Recorded last century from 1834 (La Gasca)
onwards, usually as scarce or rare, but by 1903
Lester-Garland thought it very rare and decreasing.
The last record in the Société's botanical reports is in
1923 from near La Corbière by C. Chapman.
G last record 1933; A rare; H 1889 and 1922.

Physalis alkekengi L.   **Bladder Cherry**

No satisfactory record. Specimens collected from St Helier, 1850, and St Ouen's Bay, 1900 by J. Piquet (Hb Oxford) and 'in old gardens', 1869, by F. Piquet (Hb Société Jersiaise) are *Nicandra physalodes* Apple of Peru. It is therefore presumed that J. Piquet's record from Mont Néron (St Helier) given in the *Phytologist* for 1853 was in error. No specimen is known supporting the 1974 record given in the Société botanical report.

P. angulata L.   **A Bladder Cherry**
G 1975.

Salpichroa organifolia (Lam.) Baillon   **Cocks-eggs**
G locally plentiful.

Solanum nigrum L.   **Black Nightshade**
                                 du **vèrjus au dgiâbl'ye**

Subsp. *nigrum* Common on cultivated and waste land. While it is inadvisable to eat the black berries of this plant, they are not virulently poisonous like the large purple-black berries of Deadly Nightshade which does not grow here and with which this is often confused.

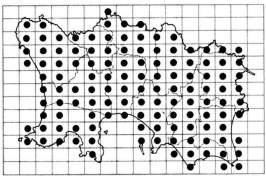

G frequent; A occasional; S frequent; H frequent.

S. chenopodioides Lamarck   **Tall Nightshade**
See *S. sarrachoides* Green Nightshade.
G rare; S 1961.

S. luteum Miller   **Red Nightshade**
Subsp. *luteum* 'S. *villosum* Lam.' which Attenborough found in a sandy field near Bel Royal in 1917, may belong here.
Subsp. *alatum* (Moench) Dostál   Rare and not seen recently. It was listed as *Solanum nigrum* var. *rubrum* by Gay in 1832 from Les Quennevais and later as *S. nigrum fructo rubro* by W. Christy in 1836 from Les Quennevais and Petit Port. Babington (1839) gave Christy's record and called the plants *S. nigrum* var. *miniatum*, as did both Lester-Garland (1903) who said the variety occurred in small quantity at La Pulente, and Attenborough who found it in St Ouen's

Bay in 1915. *S. nigrum* var. *ochroleucum* which Attenborough stated had occurred in Jersey is included here in *Flora Europaea*.

See Attenborough's account of *S. nigrum s.l.* in the Société's botanical report for 1917.
G last century only.

S. sarrachoides Sendtn.   **Green Nightshade**
Though the first record was only in 1930 when I. A. Williams found it at Waverly Farm, St Brelade, and in an arable field near La Moye, St Brelade, Green Nightshade is now sometimes common in arable fields lying fallow in autumn and on consolidated rubbish dumps. Black Nightshade may also be common in the same areas but no hybrid has yet been found in spite of careful search. Previous records of *S. chenopodioides*, Tall Nightshade, belong here.

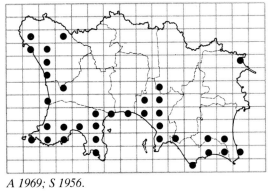

A 1969; S 1956.

S. dulcamara L.   **Bittersweet**
                                 *d'l'*amièrdoux

Frequent in damp overgrown areas and on rocky shores where the plants tend to have somewhat fleshy leaves.

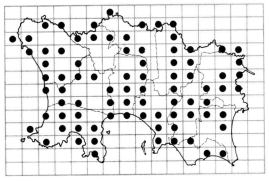

G frequent; A occasional; S frequent; H frequent.

S. tuberosum L.   **Potato**
                                 des **patates**

Potatoes appear regularly on rubbish dumps as throw-outs from cultivation or from the kitchen. They can produce tubers and set seed but do not persist for more than a year or two.
G, A, S and H as in Jersey.

S. laciniatum Aiton   **Kangaroo Apple**

In 1962 one plant of Kangaroo Apple appeared on a compost heap in St Clement and in 1967 another appeared in a hedge of a nearby field, La Houguette, close to the Mont Ubé light, Mrs L. A. Morris. Their origin is unknown. There were no plants in gardens in the area. In 1969 J. R. Palmer reported it as spreading out of the Churchill Memorial Park at St Brelade and growing on the hillside behind the Park. Since then it has occasionally appeared spontaneously in gardens, on rubbish dumps, sometimes in quantity, and by roadsides, usually in the south of the island. Plants normally live for several years and though a hard frost kills them, viable seed is set. The apricot-coloured, elongated, tomato-like fruits are poisonous. The main increase was in the 1970s, so the map includes all records 1962–1983.

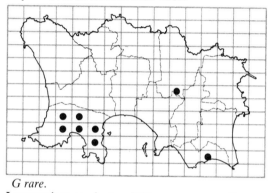

G rare.

Lycopersicon esculentum Miller   **Tomato**
                                                  des **tomates**

Tomatoes have appeared, self-sown, on most of the rubbish dumps and sewage compost heaps since the Occupation (1940–45) and in the 1950s plants bearing ripe fruit were seen in joints between the paving stones of the less-frequented streets of St Helier. In 1972 several plants were growing well on the Île Percée, some with good fruit. These plants were presumably from seeds in gull droppings.
G occasional; A occasional; S occasional; H Longue Pierre 1969.

Datura stramonium L.   **Thorn Apple**
                              du **pommyi du dgiâbl'ye**

Although Piquet stated in both his 1851 and his 1896 lists that he considered Thorn Apple to be naturalised, Lester-Garland (1903) and Attenborough (1919) called it a casual. Information gathered in the last thirty years overwhelmingly supports Piquet. Plants are sometimes so abundant in a field that the crop has been thought to be Thorn Apple. It is particularly persistent and has been in some fields as long as can be remembered. When the old buildings on the site of 4 Hill Street, St Helier were demolished in the 1960s to make way for the new offices of the Midland Bank, the site lay open for over a year and Thorn Apple grew in quantity on the

open ground. Was it from seed lying dormant there from before the previous building was erected? Similarly when the flats of Clarence Court were built in Clarence Road, Thorn Apple grew on disturbed ground round the site and was along the sides of the entrance road for some years after the flats were occupied. A poisonous plant, its somewhat disagreeable odour and the prickles on the 'apple' make it unattractive to children. The flowers are normally white but plants with purple flowers f. *tatula* were seen in a field near La Forge, St Mary, in 1961, and Mrs Rayson reported some in a back-garden in Roseville Street in the mid-1950s and the 1960s. An illustration by Pandora Sellars is opposite page 118.

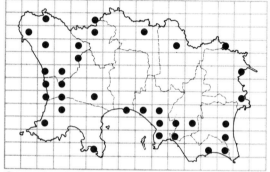

G occasional; A rare; S rare.

D. innoxia Miller   **Great Thorn Apple**

Several plants in 1976 in a small area on the west side of Mont Cochon, near St Andrew's Park. The area had been disturbed for the first time for many years and is now built over.

Nicotiana species   **Tobacco**

Rare escapes, nowhere naturalised. On 10 October 1942, during the German Occupation, L. Sinel wrote in his diary: 'Large quantities of local-grown tobacco are on sale'. The species is unknown but J. C. Fluck reported *N. rustica* at Georgetown in 1967 and Miss J. English found about six plants of *N. sylvestris* in a patch of old rubble on Les Landes in 1969. Sweet Tobacco, *N. alata* was recorded from a wall in Vallée des Vaux in 1927 by Ariste, from a sand dune at Le Bourg in 1960 by J. C. Fluck and it was growing on Mont Mado rubbish dump in 1969.
G rare; A 1976.

BUDDLEJACEAE

Buddleja davidii Franch.   **Buddleia; Butterfly-bush**

Mrs L. A. Morris remembers Buddleia growing wild, as a weed, in a field called La Cannevière along the Coast Road, St Clement, in 1927. The winged seeds of this Chinese plant are blown far and wide by the wind with the result that plants can be found in places as varied as overgrown côtils in the country and chimney stacks in town. Its main spread has been in the last forty years.

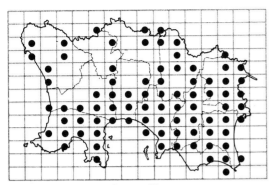

G frequent; A 1967; S rare; H rare.

SCROPHULARIACEAE

Mimulus guttatus DC.   **Monkey Flower**

Monkey Flower, a garden escape, was first noted in the late 1930s by N. Le Brocq. In the 1950s Miss France found it in the stream between Don Bridge and Pont Marquet, and in 1962 Mrs H. M. Cash reported it as abundant in a wet area to the north of Mont du Bu de la Rue, St Lawrence. During the survey 1960–70, new localities continued to be found and the map shows its distribution by 1970. Perhaps because of the warm wet winter of 1982/3, 1983 was an exceptionally good year for it and it was abundant in many areas. R. W. S. Knightbridge in a survey of wet meadows in 1983, confirmed that it is still spreading.

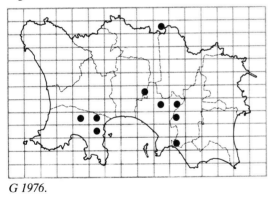

G 1976.

M. moschatus Douglas ex Lindley   **Musk**
G rare garden weed.

Verbascum blattaria L.   **Moth Mullein**

Listed by La Gasca in 1834 without locality, by Piquet in 1851 from St Helier and St Saviour and by him again in 1896 as: 'On cultivated land, very rare. St Saviour'. The only record this century is of one plant in 1959 on a consolidated dump of rubble in the valley west of La Ville des Quennevais. J. E. Lousley who confirmed the 1959 specimen considered that mulleins sent to him in 1962 were garden forms of

hybrid origin with *V. blattaria* as one parent. These were found by J. C. Fluck growing wild over a small area at Grève d'Azette.
G two early records; S 1872.

V. virgatum Stokes   **Twiggy Mullein**
G last record 1982.

V. phlomoides L.   **Orange Mullein**
Reported five times from rubbish dumps during the survey in the 1960s but not seen recently.
G rare; S 1958; H rare.

V. densiflorum Bertol.   **Dense-flowered Mullein**
A plant of the previous species growing on a dump in Waterworks Valley in 1960 was recorded as this in error because of a confusion of *Verbascum* names at the beginning of the survey.

V. thapsus L.   **Great Mullein**
                            d'la **molène**

Subsp. *thapsus* A native species widespread on disturbed ground and sometimes locally plentiful on heathland after fires, as on Portelet headland in the late 1970s.

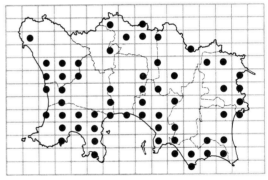

G local; A rare; S rare; H rare.

V. speciosum Schrad.   **Hungarian Mullein**
One record: rubbish dump near Town Mills, 1960, Miss P. Donaldson and Miss D. C. Mauger, det. J. E. Lousley.

V. pulverulentum Vill.   **Hoary Mullein**
One record: St Ouen's Bay, 1885, A. Ley (Hb Birm. Univ.).
G error.

V. nigrum L.   **Dark Mullein**
                            d'la **molène**

Subsp. *nigrum* A native species, occasional on hedgebanks and grassy places in the interior and north of the island.

Map overleaf

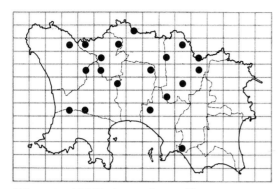

G last record 1947; A rare; S rare; H rare.

V. bombyciferum Boiss.   **Broussa Mullein**
G rare.

V. phoeniceum L.   **Purple Mullein**
The 1960 Jersey record given in *The Wild Flowers of Guernsey* requires confirmation. Its source is unknown.
G one plant 1968.

Scrophularia scorodonia L.   **Balm-leaved Figwort**
                                         d'l'orvale
Dr W. Sherard found Balm-leaved Figwort: 'By the rivulet sides betwixt the port and St Hilary' when he visited Jersey in 1689. See the Introduction. This is the common Figwort of Jersey and not the following species in spite of their English names. Lester-Garland (1903) stated that this rare English plant was in: 'Hedges and thickets. Abundant' and Druce commented that it was: 'Common not only in "hedges and thickets" but on banks and walls' (*Journal of Botany* XLV: 424). This is still true.

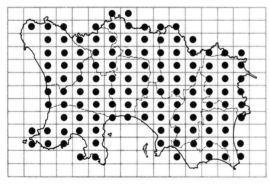

G common; H frequent.

S. nodosa L.   **Common Figwort**
Rare and no locality is at present known. Babington's 1839 record is unlocalised. Piquet crossed out both the original entry in his 1851 list and an additional one in 1856, and at some unknown date replaced it with

'Wet woods, St Peter's Valley'. He repeated this in his 1896 list adding a little more detail: 'Near a mill-stream in St Peter's Valley, rare'. Lester-Garland (1903) stated that it was in a wood near Trinity Manor and N. Le Brocq claimed to have found it in Rosel Manor grounds in the late 1930s. There have been only three records since: three plants in a hedge near Rockmount, Jardin d'Olivet, Trinity, 1957; one plant in St Peter's Valley, 1958 and about ten plants on the sides of a path in a wood south of Quetivel Mill in Waterworks Valley, 1974, Mrs M. L. Long.
G last record 1968; S rare; H rare.

S. auriculata L.   **Water Figwort**
(*S. aquatica*)
Rare in wet places: Gargate Mill, St Peter's Valley, Babington (1839); St Ouen's Pond and St Peter's Marsh, Piquet (1851); Vallée des Vaux, 1882, Rev. J. Leitch (Hb Carlisle); foot of Mont Pinel, St Ouen, 1890, A. J. Binet. Water Figwort still grows at St Ouen's Pond and at the foot of Mont Pinel.
G frequent; A occasional; S occasional; H rare.

Antirrhinum majus L.   **Snapdragon**
                                  d'la **dgeule-dé-lion**
Subsp. *majus* Occasionally naturalised on old walls. No map is given because of the difficulty of deciding when a plant is wild. It also occurs on rubbish dumps and disturbed ground.
G rare; A 1900; S rare; H 1958.

Misopates orontium (L.) Rafin.   **Lesser Snapdragon**
(*Antirrhinum Orontium*)
Locally frequent in cultivated ground.

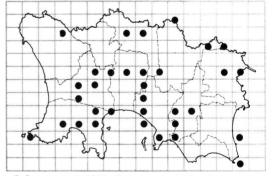

G frequent; A 1970; S common; H local.

Chaenorhinum minus (L.) Lange   **Small Toadflax**
(*Linaria minor*)
Babington (1839) gave a Saunders record but later crossed it out in his own copy of his Flora. Piquet added: 'On the Quenvais, Mr Barker' to his 1851 list at some later, undated time and in 1896 he listed it as rare on Les Quennevais though he told Lester-

Garland (1903) that he had never seen it. Perhaps he meant that he had not seen it growing because a specimen labelled as collected in St Brelade in 1854 by Mr Barker is in the Piquet herbarium bought by Druce (Hb Oxford).

G error.

Linaria purpurea (L.) Miller   **Purple Toadflax**

Introduced. An occasional but persistent garden weed, as in the Howard Davis Park where Burdo knew it before the war. The flowers are sometimes pink.

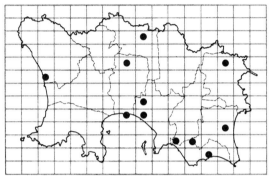

G occasional; S rare.

L. repens (L.) Miller   **Pale Toadflax**

Rare on hedgebanks. Lester-Garland (1903) reported it in the valley by the side of Mont les Vaux, St Aubin, where it was still present until the 1970s. Similarly a patch found in Bellozanne Valley in 1954 remained for many years. It was also found near L'Étoquet, St Ouen, in the survey of the 1960s. Previous records include: near Tabor Chapel, 1871, F. Piquet; 'Past the china-stone quarries', 1880, and Beaumont New Hill, 1888 where it was still present in 1916, A. J. Binet; near St Peter's Barracks, 1900, S. Guiton; near Grève de Lecq, 1916, near Léoville, 1917 and at Le Sauchet, 1918, Attenborough.

G rare; S 1841.

L. pelisseriana (L.) Miller   **Jersey Toadflax**

An extreme rarity not seen recently but the terrain of Mont au Guet, its *locus classicus* overlooking St Ouen's Bay, is unaltered and it may well reappear.

This essentially Mediterranean plant was first found by Babington on 24 July 1837. In his diary he wrote: 'Returning home (with W. Christy and R. M. Lingwood from St Ouen's Pond) by St Peter's after passing a mill, we ascended a hill, and found near to its summit a *Linaria*, much too advanced to be decided, but probably *Pelisseriana*'. The following year he returned and confirmed the identification, finding it in flower on 5 June 1838 and collecting the specimen illustrated on Plate 2832 of the Supplement to *English Botany*. Attenborough, who found it on 19

May 1926, wrote in the Société botanical report for that year: 'The finding of this plant which was thought to be extinct was a source of great satisfaction to the writer who had vainly searched for it during the last twenty years!' The 'new locality' which he mentioned in the Société's botanical report for 1928 was nearby (pers. comm.). Jersey Toadflax was found in roughly the same region at long intervals until the late 1940s when it was last seen there by O. Buckle (pers. comm.).

Its history in St Brelade is more vague. Lester-Garland (1903) stated that Guiton had discovered a second station at St Brelade where the plant was plentiful, but A. J. Wilmott, writing in his diary on 8 June 1922, stated that Guiton told him that: 'his sister brought some dozen stalks in a bunch of wild flowers from Mont Fliquet. Whereupon he told her to take him back immediately but they failed to refind the place (known within a little) and have never found it since'. This story has been handed down from one generation of botanists to another, since Guiton first saw the picked flowers, but for Fliquet read Fiquet and for sister read wife. In the late 1950s history repeated itself. Mrs J. Russell, a visiting botanist from England who has helped to gather much information on the Jersey flora, met a local woman near La Corbière. On learning that Mrs Russell was interested in plants, the woman told her that when she last picked some flowers along the south-west coast, she had found a little flower which she had not seen before. There was only the one and she picked it. The description given of it fitted Jersey Toadflax. The woman added that she had never seen another.

In the 1947 Société botanical report Attenborough stated that a schoolboy had found it near St Aubin and later (pers. comm.) he said it was on the rock face on the east side of Mont les Vaux.

In 1955 Miss J. Pallot, now Mrs J. Machin, found it on an overgrown hedgebank at St Martin among Nettles and Red Campion. The habitat was so different from the one in the west of the island that the plant is thought to have been a casual.

L. maroccana Hooker f.   **Garden Linaria**

A 1973.

L. vulgaris Miller   **Common Toadflax**

Frequent on hedgebanks.

Map overleaf

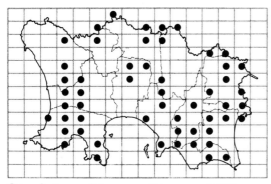

G local; A rare; S frequent; H last record 1962.

L. supina (L.) Chaz.   **Prostrate Toadflax**
G 1858.

Cymbalaria muralis P. Gaertner, B. Meyer & Scherb.
           Ivy-leaved Toadflax
Subsp. *muralis* Piquet did not mention this south
European plant in his 1851 list but by 1853 he had
found it in St Clement's Lane (*Phytologist* 1853).
Lester-Garland stated (1903) that it was thoroughly
naturalised, and it is now common, usually on walls.
By the time the seeds are ripe, the stalk bearing the
seed-capsule has turned away from the light and
buried the capsule in a dark crack in the wall. The
seeds are then ready to continue the colonisation of
the wall.

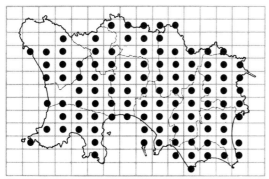

G common; A occasional; S locally frequent; H local.

Kickxia elatine (L.) Dum.   **Sharp-leaved Fluellen**
(*Linaria Elatine*)
Subsp. *elatine* Piquet listed this in 1896 as frequent
in cultivated fields and gardens while Lester-Garland
(1903) described it as a not common colonist of
cultivated ground. Today it is decidedly rare though
recently there has been a slight resurgence and it was
seen in 1979 in gardens at Gorey, Mrs H. Baker, in
Devon Gardens, J. C. Fluck and at Les Hâtivieaux,
St Ouen. In 1980 and 1981 it was abundant on a grave
in St Lawrence Churchyard, Mrs M. L. Long.
G scarce; A 1900; S occasional; H occasional.

K. spuria (L.) Dumort.   **Round-leaved Fluellen**
(*Linaria spuria*)
One record: St Ouen's Bay, 1837, Babington (Hb
Cantab.).
G claimed; S 1892.

Digitalis purpurea L.   **Foxglove**
                 dé l'ouothelle dé brébis
Subsp. *purpurea* Always common but exceptionally abundant in 1978 when huge areas both on the
north coast and in the inland valleys were sheets of
purple.

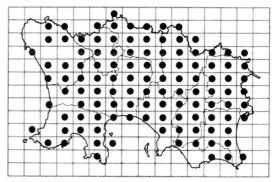

G local; A locally frequent; S common; H common.

Erinus alpinus L.   **Fairy Foxglove**
Fairy Foxglove was growing wild on the top of a wall
at Rosel Manor in the 1960s, Mrs M. L. Long.
G two records.

Veronica serpyllifolia L.   **Thyme-leaved Speedwell**
Subsp. *serpyllifolia* Common in moist grassland,
paths and waste places.

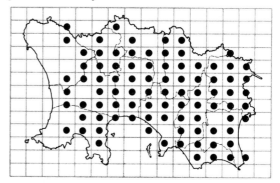

G common; A 1976; S frequent; H frequent.

V. officinalis L.   **Heath Speedwell**
Local. Babington (1839) and Piquet (1851) described
Heath Speedwell as common. It is possible that this
speedwell which is sometimes called Common
Speedwell was just assumed to be common because
of its name. Later Piquet (1896) listed it as rare and

the only locality he gave was Vallée des Vaux where it still grows, Miss E. H. du Feu. A. J. Binet found it in 1889 in Waterworks Valley near the foot of Le Mont du Bu de la Rue, and it still also grows there, Miss D. C. Mauger. Lester-Garland (1903) thought it rather rare and gave four localities: St Aubin, Noirmont Warren, Grands Vaux and Bouley Bay. Ariste found it at Noirmont in 1925 and it was by a path behind Noirmont Manor in 1969, D. J. Clennett, though it has since disappeared from there. New recent localities are: Beaufort Square where it was a garden weed from 1966 to at least 1971, J. C. Fluck; in good quantity on headland east of the Devil's Hole, 1967, Mrs D. L. Le Quesne, and still there; Le Don Gaudin, St Peter's Valley, 1983, Mrs M. L. Long; north-facing slope on Les Quennevais near La Carrière Quarry, 1983, Mrs P. Anderson.
G last record 1901; A rare; S rare; H common.

V. chamaedrys L.   Germander Speedwell
du **tèrrêtre**

Subsp. *chamaedrys*   Common on hedgebanks and heaths.

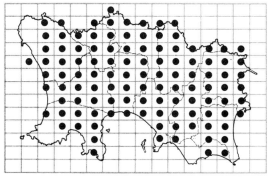

G frequent; A frequent; S common; H frequent.

V. scutellata L.   Marsh Speedwell
Rare. Marsh Speedwell has had a continuous history in or near Grouville Marsh since at least 1873 when it was found there by Dr M. M. Bull (Hb Oxford). In 1915 Attenborough stated that it was fairly plentiful in the marsh. The latest record, R. W. S. Knightbridge 1983, is from a wet meadow just south of the marsh. A specimen was collected by the Rev. J. Leitch at St Ouen's Pond in 1882 (Hb Carlisle).
G 1790.

V. beccabunga L.   Brooklime
d'la **bêle**

Common in wet places but strangely missing from most of the coast.

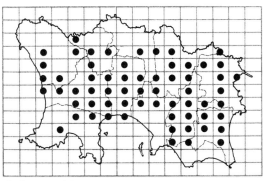

G decreased from common to scarce; A occasional; S rare.

V. anagallis-aquatica L.   Blue Water-speedwell
This and the following species were not separated until comparatively recently. Few specimens exist so it has not been possible to assign all the old records to their correct species. Neither is known in Jersey in 1983 but much suitable habitat still exists. Past records of Blue Water-speedwell are: Grève d'Azette, 1838, Babington, conf. P. D. Sell (Hb Cantab.); La Moye, 1906, Druce (Hb Oxford); Quennevais, 1933, A. J. Wilmott (note in his diary). It remained near Don Bridge, Les Quennevais, from where it was recorded for the *Atlas of the British Flora* in the late 1950s, until the habitat was destroyed in the 1960s.
A rare.

V. catenata Pennell   Pink Water-speedwell
See the above species. Two specimens were collected from Samarès Miles last century: 1851, J. Piquet (Hb Oxford), and 1869, F. Piquet (Hb Société Jersiaise).
G rare.

V. arvensis L.   Wall Speedwell
Common on walls and banks and it often studs short turf on the cliffs and dunes with specks of sapphire-blue in early spring.

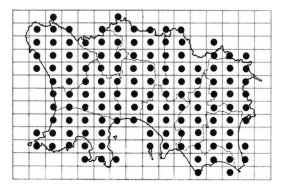

G common; A frequent; S common; H frequent.

V. peregrina L.   **American Speedwell**

A rare garden weed originally from America. Until recently all the records were from St Saviour: St Saviour, 1859, Mr Wolsey (*Phytologist* 1859); St Saviour, 1876, Dr M. M. Bull; plentiful in the yard of Alphington House, St Saviour, Miss D. Higginson, and in the near-by nursery gardens, Lester-Garland (1903). The only records since then have been from Samarès Manor grounds in 1958 and Deputy M. Bonn's garden at Oaklands, St Peter, in 1981.
G error for Jersey.

V. agrestis L.   **Green Field-speedwell**

Only occasionally seen during the survey of the 1960s, usually on disturbed or cultivated ground. This species, like the following, was described as common last century though Lester-Garland (1903) thought it was far less common than the next. It may be that Common Field-speedwell (Buxbaum's Speedwell) which arrived towards the end of last century, has taken their place.

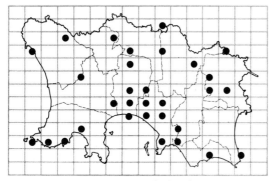

G scarce; A rare; S last record 1896; H rare.

V. polita Fries   **Grey Field-speedwell**

Now only occasionally seen, but described as common last century and by Lester-Garland (1903). See *V. agrestis* above.

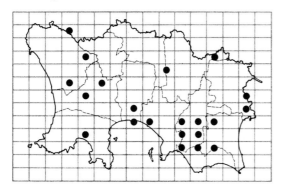

G scarce; A rare; S 1958; H last record 1894.

V. persica Poiret   **Common Field-speedwell**
(*V. Buxbaumii*)

When Piquet compiled his 1851 list, he did not mention Common Field-speedwell (Buxbaum's Speedwell). At some unknown, later date he added it with the comment: 'On a hedge near the avenue to Mr Nicolle's Farm, St Saviour'. Between then and 1896, when he compiled his next list, it became common and it still is. The first known Jersey specimen is F. Piquet's, dated 1871.

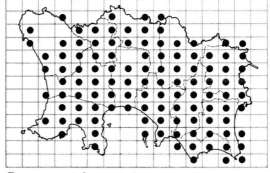

G common; A frequent; S common; H frequent.

V. filiformis Sm.   **Slender Speedwell**

First recorded in 1929 by Ariste from near 'la route de la Trinité'. This Persian species would have come to Jersey as a desirable rock garden plant and then escaped into the lawn, hedge and roadside. The eastern bias of its distribution is interesting as most garden escapes have a southern or haphazard distribution.

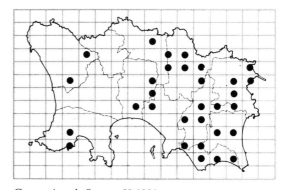

G occasional; S rare; H 1932.

V. hederifolia L.   **Ivy-leaved Speedwell**
                                         du **tèrrêtre**

Common since records began. Two subspecies are present, see confirmation below, but their relative frequencies are unknown. The map includes both.
Subsp. *hederifolia* St Clement, 1838, Babington; Jersey, 1957, W. B. Gourlay. Both det. M. Fischer (Hb Cantab.).

Subsp. *lucorum* (Klett & Richter) Hartl   Roadside bank near Beaumont, 1957, Miss V. M. Leather, det. M. Fischer (Hb Cantab.).

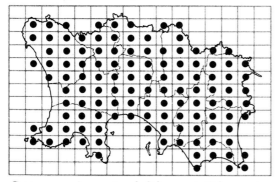

G common; A occasional; S frequent; H frequent.

Hebe x franciscana (Eastwood) Souster
H. elliptica x **H. speciosa**   **Hedge Veronica**
Hedge Veronica, mistakenly called *Hebe* x *lewisii* in the past, is planted as a hedge along parts of Victoria Avenue and occasionally elsewhere. Seedlings are sometimes seen. It is not normally used as hedging in the countryside so there is no Hedge Veronica 'presence' in Jersey as there is in the Isles of Scilly.
G frequent; A occasional; S occasional; H occasional.

H. salicifolia (Forster f.) Pennell
                    Narrow-leaved Veronica
G garden wall.

Sibthorpia europaea L.   **Cornish Moneywort**
In 1689 Dr W. Sherard found Cornish Moneywort on a moist wall in Grouville. See the Introduction. Babington (1839) and Piquet (1851 and 1896) recorded it as common and Lester-Garland (1903) thought it frequent. It was still frequent on moist shady hedgebanks until the drought of 1976 which affected it badly but it is now recovering.

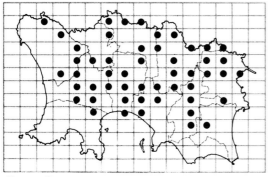

G rare; S rare.

Euphrasia arctica Lange ex Rostrup   **An Eyebright**
Subsp. *borealis* (Townsend) Yeo   Claimed by Druce to have been collected at St Ouen and St Aubin in 1906 but the specimens are *E. nemoralis*.

E. tetraquetra (Bréb.) Arrondeau
                    Western Eyebright
                    *d'l'*aphrasie
Locally frequent and the overwhelming majority of Jersey's Eyebrights are this species. No other has been recorded recently but no serious study has been made of them. Babington (1839), Piquet (1851 and 1896) and Lester-Garland (1903) recorded only '*E. officinalis*', a name no longer in use because of its ambiguity. That this is the species they intended is confirmed by P. D. Sell and P. F. Yeo determining Babington's specimen labelled *E. officinalis* from St Ouen's Bay in 1837 as *E. tetraquetra*.

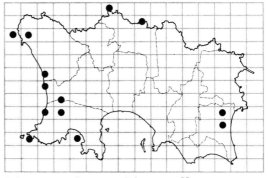

G frequent; A frequent; S frequent; H common.

E. nemorosa x **E. tetraquetra**   **A hybrid Eyebright**
G 1958.

E. nemorosa (Pers.) Wallr.   **An Eyebright**
Specimens labelled by Druce as '*E. borealis* Wettst' from St Ouen and St Aubin in 1906 belong here and I. A. Williams collected a specimen from sandy ground near the Racecourse, Les Quennevais in 1930, det. H. W. Pugsley.
G, A and S occasional.

E. confusa Pugsley   **An Eyebright**
G 1866 and 1968; A rare; S 1928.

E. stricta D. Wolff ex J. F. Lehm.   **An Eyebright**
G rare.

E. micrantha Reichenb.   **An Eyebright**
G one record.

Odontites verna (Bell.) Dum.   **Red Bartsia**
(*O. rubra*)

Subsp. *serotina* (Dumort.) Corb.   Until recently Red Bartsia was an extremely rare plant in Jersey.

143

Babington (1839) recorded it without giving a locality and Piquet in 1851 could only write: 'In a field. Rare. Mr Ereaut'. Later he crossed this out and put: 'Field at St Clement', from where he collected a specimen in 1866. By 1896 this was still the only place in which he knew it. Meanwhile, A. J. Binet had found it in the north of St Ouen's Bay in 1892. It was still rare in the early 1940s but in 1946 Attenborough found it in plenty on Don Bridge Racecourse. By the 1950s it could be found fairly easily in the Les Hanières region, St Ouen, and by 1980 it had become locally abundant in St Ouen's Bay. It also occurs, rarely, elsewhere.

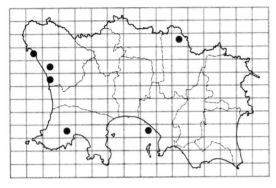

Parentucellia viscosa (L.) Caruel   **Yellow Bartsia**
First found by Dr W. Sherard in 1689 in moist places by 'the port', see the Introduction, and a specimen 'Gathered by ye Revd Mr Clark' in Jersey between 1730 and 1740 is in the Dillenian herbarium, Oxford. Other past records suggest that, as now, it has always been locally plentiful. In 1983 it was abundant at St Ouen's Pond after the wet winter 1982/83. Lester-Garland (1903) also recorded it from Samarès and R. W. S. Knightbridge listed it as rare in a field there in 1983.

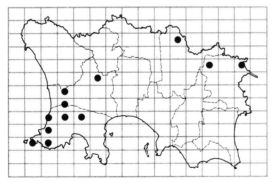

G scarce; A occasional; S frequent; H 1889 Jethou rare.

Pedicularis palustris L.   **Marsh Lousewort**
Babington (1839) recorded this from St Lawrence Valley but Lester-Garland (1903) rejected it and there is still no confirmation.
G as Jersey.

P. sylvatica L.   **Lousewort**
Subsp. *sylvatica* Locally common in wet places but so abundant in some areas in 1978 as to form carpets of pink.

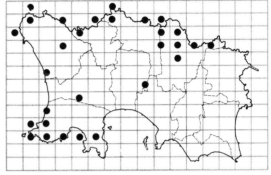

G local; A occasional; S common.

Rhinanthus minor L.   **Yellow Rattle**
(*R. Crista-galli*)   *des* **sonnettes**
Local. In the past Yellow Rattle was recorded from Samarès Miles, near St Ouen's Pond, Bouley Bay, Rozel Bay and Le Sauchet. More recent records are from Les Quennevais, 1950s; La Corbière, 1960s, Mrs E. M. Towers; Mourier Valley, 1970, Dr J. G. Dony. It still grows in all three places sometimes in abundance.
G rare.

ACANTHACEAE

Acanthus mollis L.   **Bear's-breech**
Garden escape or relic. This huge plant is capable of flourishing long after the garden of which it was originally part has disappeared, and if it thrown out with garden rubbish, it can become established and survive among native vegetation, including thick bramble scrub. Viable seed is set and the seedlings grow to maturity. A flourishing clump at Archirondel has been there since at least the 1930s; a large old-established patch on waste ground at Five Oaks brick works was removed when the site was developed in the 1960s; it was well naturalised among dense vegetation round a pool on the Jardin d'Olivet in 1962 and it has been growing for many years on the uncultivated part of West Mount.
G occasional.

OROBANCHACEAE

Orobanche species   Broomrape

Three species, *O. purpurea*, Yarrow Broomrape, *O. minor*, Common Broomrape and *O. rapumgenistae*, Greater Broomrape, have been well-known in Jersey since records began, and also a fourth, *O. maritima*, Carrot Broomrape, if this is considered a species distinct from *O. minor*. Five other species have been recorded at various times but with some of these there are identification difficulties. A paper entitled 'Notes on Jersey Orobanches' by Attenborough appeared in the 1938 botanical report of the Société. Attenborough was the premier field botanist in Jersey for many years but he collected no *Orobanche* specimens, so there is no check on his notes – though it must be said that some *Orobanche* species are difficult to name even with a specimen. The authors of the account of the *Orobanche* genus in *Flora Europaea* comment on its 'intrinsic taxonomic difficulties'. All the known information about these five species is included in the accounts of them.

O. ramosa L.   Hemp Broomrape

La Moye, 1913, A. Webster, det. H. W. Pugsley. The specimen was originally labelled *O. purpurea* and was in C. E. Salmon's herbarium (*Journal of Botany*, 1940). Salmon's herbarium is now in the British Museum's herbarium but the specimen could not be found when D. McClintock looked for it recently. The error has usually been in the other direction, branching *O. purpurea* being taken for *O. ramosa*. The source of an earlier record given in W. J. Hooker's *British Flora* (1842) cannot be traced. The main host plant, Hemp, used to be grown as a crop.
S ?1833.

O. purpurea Jacq.   Yarrow Broomrape
(*O. caerulea*)

Local on Yarrow. Some years it is more plentiful than others. J. T. B. Syme found it near St Aubin in June 1853 and wrote in the third edition of Sowerby's *English Botany* (1863–92) '. . . I have collected it only in Jersey, where it is abundant, apparently preferring the tops of walls which have a turf coping'. It is as well that it was abundant, because in the British Museum herbarium there are three sheets of flowering spikes which he collected near St Aubin and altogether they contain fifty-six specimens.

The distribution map (1960–70) indicates that it is more frequent round the east, south and west coasts than either inland or along the north. Records from the past, going back to 1836, come from the same regions, though in a good year plants may well be found elsewhere. The summer of 1978 was an excellent one for Broomrapes, including the Yarrow Broomrape, and that year it was reported as plentiful in St Lawrence Churchyard which is deep in the

interior. Regrettably, the more recent years, 1981, 1982 and 1983 have been exceptionally poor.

Piquet's specimen from a wall top in 1871 was determined as var. *tapeina* Beck by Beck (C. E. Salmon, *Journal of Botany* 1927).

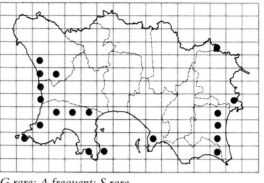

G rare; A frequent; S rare.

O. alba Stephan ex Willd.   Thyme Broomrape

In Attenborough's paper (see above) he stated of the Thyme Broomrape, '. . . one of our rarer species as it occurs in St Ouen's Bay only' and in the next year he repeated this in a paper on the calcareous flora of Jersey. In the Société's botanical report for 1954 he stated that 'Specimens were found' but there are no specimens in the Société's herbarium. There is plenty of Thyme in St Ouen's Bay and on Les Quennevais so Thyme Broomrape may well exist in Jersey.
S ?1892.

O. loricata Reichenb.   Oxtongue Broomrape
(*O. Picridis*)

In his paper on Broomrapes (see above) Attenborough stated of *O. picridis* F. W. Schultz, 'This species is more widely distributed [than *O. elatior*]. It occurs at Gorey, the Quennevais and St Ouen's Bay . . . In Jersey this plant does not grow on *Picris hieracoides* but on certain of the *Umbelliferae*, e.g. *Smyrnium olusatrum*'. In the Société's botanical report for 1946 he claimed that it was unusually abundant in St Ouen's Bay, and in 1955 he claimed to have seen it again. There are no specimens in the Société's herbarium to support the records. The only other claim, from sandhills in St Ouen's Bay by H. F. Parsons, was relegated by Lester-Garland (1903) to his ambiguities and errors list.
G 1892.

O. minor Sm.   Common Broomrape

This is still the commonest species in Jersey, as it has been since Babington recorded it in 1839, and it may well be under-recorded on the map. It can usually be found every year in good quantity on light soil. Host plants have been given as Red Clover, Soft Clover,

Lucerne, Sea Holly, Wild Carrot, Buck's-horn Plantain, Cat's-ear and Mouse-ear Hawkweed. It has also been seen parasitising garden plants. Attenborough mentioned var. *flavescens* Regal where he said the whole plant was lemon yellow and that it was generally found on Buck's-horn Plantain. H. F. Parsons collected var. *concolor* from St Ouen in 1883 (C. E. Salmon, *Journal of Botany* 1927).

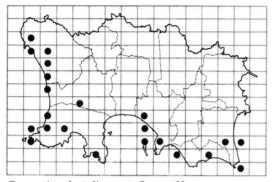

G occasional; A frequent; S rare; H rare.

O. maritima Pugsley   Carrot Broomrape
(O. amethystea)

The authors of the *Orobanche* account in *Flora Europaea* consider that this may be only a variety of *O. minor*. Whether a full species or not, it has been recorded in Jersey in considerably varying quantity since the middle of last century. Henslow (1858) found it parasitical on Sea-holly and abundant in St Ouen's Bay. Sea-holly seems to have been its chief host last century but Lester-Garland stated (1903) that it was 'Parasitic upon *Daucus* as a rule, more rarely upon *Eryngium*', and Attenborough (1939) agreed. In the 1950s and 1960s it was an extremely rare plant, the only place where it could regularly be found being on the side of Le Mont du Vallet, above L'Étacq, St Ouen, and then only two or three spikes per year. There were single records from La Corbière and La Grosse Tête. This rarity continued until 1978. Wild Carrot is always common in the west of Jersey but in 1978 it grew in almost unbelievable abundance. This may well have been connected with the long drought and summer heat of 1976 and the mild wet winters of 1976/7 and 1977/8. Wherever Wild Carrot grew in the south-west, west and north-west in 1978, then Carrot Broomrape also grew in abundance. In many places, as near Grosnez Castle, there was such a forest of Carrot Broomrape spikes that it was impossible to walk without knocking some of them over. The numbers decreased almost as rapidly as they had increased and by 1981 it was difficult to find Carrot Broomrape without a search. Identification was based on the description of *O. maritima* given in

the *Flora of the British Isles* 2nd ed. (1962).
G rare; A occasional; S rare; H last record 1925.

O. hederae Duby   Ivy Broomrape

Rare and recorded only six times: Mont Orgueil, E. D. Marquand, and St Helier Harbour, Lester-Garland (1903); near Gorey, 1923, J. E. Woodhead; Bellozanne Valley, 1929, Mrs T. W. Attenborough; garden, Mont Gras d'Eau, St Brelade (probably from seed accidentally brought from Herm), 1958; Mont Orgueil, 1960, P. J. O. Trist. Its rarity is extraordinary considering its quantity in the northern Bailiwick and the amount of its host plant, Ivy, in Jersey. A thorough search of the Gorey district might produce more records.
G common; A rare; S frequent; H rare.

O. elatior Sutton   Knapweed Broomrape

In the *Journal of Botany* (XLV: 425) Druce wrote, '*O. ritro* Gren. & Godr. forma *hypochaeroides* Beck in lit. On the sands of St Ouen's Bay Mr Lester-Garland showed me (in 1907) a very beautiful species growing on *Hypochaeris radicata*. It was of a bright citron-yellow colour, not only in the flowers, but also the bracts and stem. The older bracts were marked at the midrib with bright yellowish-brown. The curiously conical head of the partially open-flowered spikes was also remarkable. The plant was very glandular. The type has only been found in a few localities near Marseilles. The existence of another undoubtedly native Mediterranean species in the island is very interesting.'

There were several records in the next few years: '– on *Hypochaeris radicata* on the sandhills of St Ouen's Bay. It was growing in one place', 1913, A. Webster (B.E.C. *Report* 1913); in fair quantity in St Ouen's Bay, 1917, Attenborough; St Ouen's Bay, 1923, W. C. Barton (Hb Birm. Univ.) with the comment in the *Journal of Botany* for 1923 '. . . in good quantity this year. I counted over thirty plants in one square yard of ground'.

In his 1939 paper (see above) Attenborough wrote 'This is our rarest species and is only found in one spot in St Ouen's Bay . . . The stem is from 4 to 6 inches high and of a lemon yellow colour. The whole plant is densely glandular and pubescent. The corolla is also very glandular and hairy and is about three quarters of an inch long. The plant has a rather ghostly appearance, being very visible in the dark. It grows on *Hypochaeris radicata* only'.

In the Société's botanical report for 1945, just after the German Occupation (1940–45), he commented 'The series of bunkers in St Ouen's Bay have endangered . . . *Orobanche ritro* though here the destruction of the unsightly bungalows may do good.' There have been no post-Occupation records.

O. rapum-genistae Thuill.   **Greater Broomrape**
(*O. major*)

Subsp. *rapum-genistae* Since the 1930s Greater Broomrape has been seen only on the coastal cliffs of the south-west between La Moye and La Corbière. The records from the past were more widespread: Bouley Bay, Babington (1839); the hill behind First Tower, Babington (1839) and Piquet (1851); Water-works Valley, Lester-Garland (1903) and Druce (1923). A. J. Binet was the first to record it, in 1891, from the south-west coast. It parasitises Broom, particularly the prostrate subspecies, and more rarely Gorse.
A locally abundant.

LENTIBULARIACEAE

Pinguicula lusitanica L.   **Pale Butterwort**

Saunders' record, given by Babington (1839), was rejected by Lester-Garland (1903) and it has not been confirmed.

Utricularia minor L.   **Lesser Bladderwort**
G 1790.

U. vulgaris L.   **Greater Bladderwort**

Saunders' record, given by Babington (1839), was rejected by Lester-Garland (1903) and it has not been confirmed.

PLANTAGINACEAE

Plantago major L.   **Greater Plantain**
      du **pliantain**

Subsp. *major* Common on roadsides and similar dryish areas.
Subsp. *intermedia* (DC.) Arcangeli Two records: Les Quennevais, 1837, Babington (Hb Cantab.); sandpits north of St Ouen's Pond, 1982.

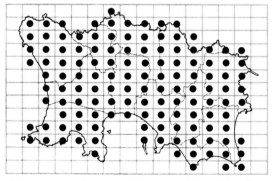

G frequent; A frequent; S frequent; H occasional.

P. coronopus L.   **Buck's-horn Plantain**
      d'la **cône dé chèr**

Subsp. *coronopus* Common in low or open turf, particularly round the coast, and often abundant

where trampling or motor traffic has eroded the turf.

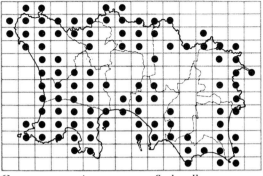

G common; A common; S locally common; H common.

P. maritima L.   **Sea Plantain**
      *d'l'*ancelée d'falaise

Frequent on rocky coasts within reach of the sea spray. It may be under-recorded as it probably grows on most of the inaccessible parts of the north coast.

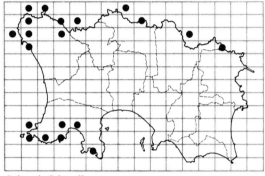

G local; S locally common.

P. media L.   **Hoary Plantain**

A casual specimen was collected by Piquet in St Ouen's Bay in 1854, and a letter in the *Evening Post* (1911) from W. P. J. Le Brocq reported it in a lawn at Pontac. Otherwise this common English plant was unknown in the Channel Islands until 1960 when Miss E. H. du Feu found upwards of forty plants in St Saviour's Churchyard where they had every appearance of having been established for many years. The species still grows there. Babington (1839) recorded it as common but, realising his error, he crossed it out in his own copy of his Flora.
G error?

P. lanceolata L.   **Ribwort Plantain**
      *d'l'*ancelée

Common, often abundant. In 1981 it was luxuriant and dominant over some entire fields grazed by cattle at St Ouen. Lester-Garland described plants with peculiar heads of flowers var. *sphaerostachya* Martens & Koch and these still occur.

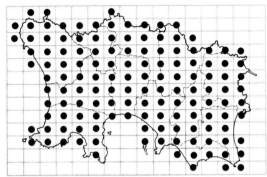

G, A, S and H common.

P. arenaria Waldst. & Kit.   **Branched Plantain**

A rare casual: 'Only a few specimens', 1878, C. J. Tempère (Hb Birm. Univ.); waste ground La Fontaine, St Peter, 1911, W. P. J. Le Brocq (Hb Brit. Mus.); St Ouen's Bay, 1912, Piquet (Hb Société Jersiaise). One plant, originally reported as *P. psyllium* byMrs F. Evans from sandhills in St Aubin's Bay in August 1848 (*Gardeners Chronicle* 31.12.1848 p. 86), was later thought to be the following species. This was probably the source of the record given in Hooker's *Student's Flora* for many years, a record quoted by Lester-Garland.

P. sempervirens Crantz   **Shrubby Plantain**
(*P. cynops*)

F. Naylor saw several specimens which he identified as *P. cynops* in St Aubin's Bay in 1859 in the same area as Mrs Evans' plantain (see above). He therefore considered that Mrs Evans' plant was also *P. cynops* (*Trans. Bot. Soc. Edin.* 1860, 7: 466).

Littorella uniflora (L.) Ascherson   **Shoreweed**
(*L. lacustris*)

Shoreweed has been known in three localities. Babington (1839) stated that it grew in St Peter's Marsh but there were no other records from there even before the marsh was drained. Piquet (1851 and 1896) stated that it was abundant near St Ouen's Pond. A. J. Wilmott and Ariste collected specimens from there in the 1920s and it was still present in the late 1950s. The Rev. W. W. Newbould found it at St Brelade, presumably on Ouaisné Common, and it continued to be known there – abundantly in 1899 according to Piquet on a herbarium sheet – until 1956. It has not been seen recently but it may well still be in both the latter localities, except that the margins of St Ouen's Pond are somewhat overgrown and Ouaisné Common suffered badly in the drought of 1976.

CAPRIFOLIACEAE

Sambucus ebulus L.   **Dwarf Elder**

Claimed by La Gasca (1834) and Saunders (Babington, 1839) but rejected by Lester-Garland (1903) and there has been no confirmation.
G very rare.

S. nigra L.   **Elder**
                         du **seu**

Common on the cliffs and in hedges inland. In 1941 during the German Occupation (1940–45) Elderberries were on sale in the market in St Helier for 1/– per lb. In the last few years, entire hedges of Elder have been planted to replace elms.

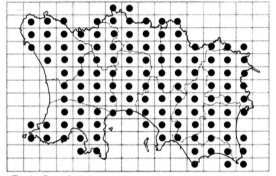

G, A, S and H frequent.

Viburnum opulus L.   **Guelder Rose**

La Gasca's record (1834) was rejected by Lester-Garland (1903). In 1958 Mrs M. L. Long found it growing on Mont Ubé but it is no longer there.

V. lantana L.   **Wayfaring-tree**

La Gasca's record (1834) was rejected by Lester-Garland (1903) and there are no other records.

V. tinus L.   **Laurustinus**
                         du **laurientîn**

Garden escape or relic. Ereaut collected a specimen in 1847 for his *Hortus Siccus* but how 'wild' it was is unknown. Ariste wrote 'Acclimaté à Jersey' against a specimen he collected in St Martin in 1925 and J. C. Fluck collected a specimen in 1964 near the German Underground Hospital, St Lawrence. It was naturalised in the woods of Noirmont Manor in the 1950s and 1960s but they have since been cleared.

Symphoricarpos albus (L.) S. F. Blake   **Snowberry**

Introduced, but its history in the island is unknown. It was recorded occasionally in woods and hedges in the interior during the survey.

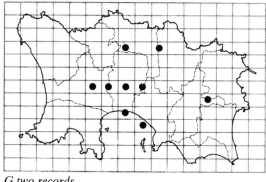

G two records.

Leycesteria formosa Wall.   **Himalayan Honeysuckle**

Ariste found Himalayan Honeysuckle as a garden escape in Vallée des Vaux in 1926. More recently it appeared in the middle of a field at Le Squez, 1965, J. C. Fluck, and since then a large patch has become established in Waterworks Valley, Mrs M. L. Long. It also appears spontaneously in gardens.
G 1958.

Lonicera japonica Thunb.   **Japanese Honeysuckle**

A garden throw-out which during the early 1960s was found flourishing in several parts of the island, usually near where garden rubbish had been deposited. In some areas, it was feared that it might be taking the place of the native Honeysuckle but it then decreased rapidly, perhaps because of the severe winter of 1962/3 though there may have been other contributory causes. It has not been seen recently except on Ouaisné Common.
G rare.

L. periclymenum L.   **Honeysuckle**
    du **chuchet**

Common in woods and hedges.

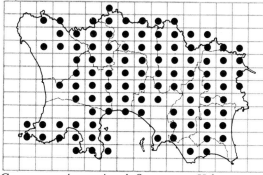

G common; A occasional; S common; H frequent.

L. nitida E. H. Wilson   **Chinese Honeysuckle**

A Chinese plant occasionally used for hedging round gardens or fields. It may well persist where planted. *G occasional.*

ADOXACEAE

Adoxa moschatellina L.   **Moschatel**

A specimen of Moschatel in the Société's herbarium is labelled 'July 1898. Shady woods, rare' by J. Piquet. There is no other mention of this species in Jersey, or indeed in the Channel Islands, and as the locality is not given, the specimen should not be used as a basis for a Jersey record.

VALERIANACEAE

Valerianella locusta (L.) Laterrade
(*V. olitoria*)   **Common Cornsalad**
    d'la **bourse**

Walls and banks. Locally frequent but much less common than the following species. Lester-Garland (1903) stated that the two species were sold in spring in the Jersey market under the name of 'boursette' and were an excellent salad. This practice continued until just before the German Occupation (1940–45).

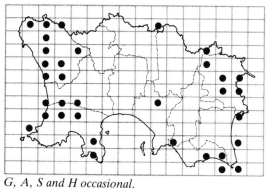

G, A, S and H occasional.

V. carinata Lois.   **Keeled Cornsalad**
    d'la **bourse**

Common on walls and banks.

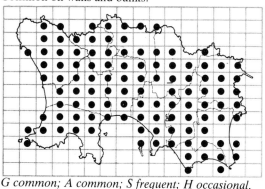

G common; A common; S frequent; H occasional.

149

V. dentata (L.) Poll.   **Narrow-fruited Cornsalad**

La Gasca listed this in 1834 and Babington (1839) claimed to have found it in St Lawrence Valley. Lester-Garland rejected both records but two specimens gathered later exist: Samarès, 1847, H. W. Taylor det. P. D. Sell (Hb Cantab); Trinity, 1908, Piquet (Hb Oxford). See the following species.
G 1888; A 1900.

V. eriocarpa Desv.   **Hairy-fruited Cornsalad**

Babington's '*Fedia auricula β. tridentata*' gathered on 21 July 1837 in St Lawrence Valley was determined as this species by P. D. Sell (Hb Cantab.). Between 1837 and 1907 there were single records from Samarès, St Aubin, Les Quennevais, St Clement and Mont à la Brune. Neither this species nor the above has been refound. Perhaps they were also grown as a salad and died out when eating-fashions changed, or a different species was used.
A rare.

Valeriana officinalis L.   **Common Valerian**

La Gasca's and Saunders' records which were given by Babington (1839) were rejected by Lester-Garland, but Piquet collected a specimen from 'Side of river, Grouville' in 1875 (Hb Oxford).

Centranthus ruber (L.) DC.   **Red Valerian**
                                du **lilas d'Espangne**

Introduced and still abundant locally, forming enormous masses of colour in June, as Lester-Garland stated in 1903. The colour can be dark red, pink (normal) or white.

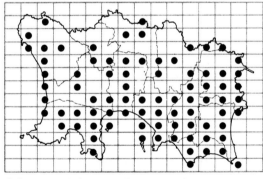

G frequent; A frequent; S occasional; H occasional.

C. macrosiphon Boiss.   **Spanish Red Valerian**

Two records: Dancaster's Farm, St Ouen's Bay, 1901, Piquet, but originally labelled *Valeriana pyrenaica* (Hb Oxford); La Corbière, August 1912, Piquet, but originally labelled *C. calcitrapa* (Hb Société Jersiaise).

DIPSACACEAE

Dipsacus sativus (L.) Honckeny   **Fullers Teasel**

Introduced, probably in bird food, and found rarely on or near rubbish dumps in the 1950s and 1960s. In this, the cultivated species, the stiffer bracts spread horizontally and the heads are used for raising the nap of cloth.
G 1978; A 1958.

D. fullonum L.   **Teasel**
(*D. silvestris*)   *du* **tcheurdron à chorchi**

Local in wet areas.

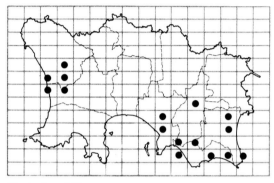

G, A, S and H rare.

Succisa pratensis Moench   **Devil's-bit Scabious**

Locally common most years on the cliffs between Grosnez and La Cotte à la Chèvre, and in more varying quantity in the south-west where it has been reported from the north-facing slopes at La Corbière, from the côtils east of Ouaisné Common and from the cliffs near Bel Croute. Instead of the root of Devil's-bit Scabious gradually becoming thinner as it delves deeper, or separating into several smaller roots, it ends abruptly, as though it had been bitten off. To account for this, stories were told in olden days of the devil biting off its root because be objected to its reputed healing powers. Hence comes its English name. Contrariwise, a different story is that the devil did such harm with the plant that the Virgin Mary cut off the root to lessen the evil. (See Sheep's-bit *Jasione montana* for the local name *flieur du dgiâbl'ye*.)
G error?

Knautia arvensis (L.) Coult.   **Field Scabious**

Saunders' record from St Ouen, given by Babington (1839), was not accepted by Lester-Garland. The only confirmed record is from Sorel in 1898 when Piquet collected a specimen – and wrote 'Very rare' beside it.
G rare; A occasional; S rare.

Scabiosa atropurpurea L. **Sweet Scabious**
(S. maritima)

Collected in the 1870s from Les Hanières, St Ouen, and described as well-established there by Lester-Garland (1903). Later Druce stated: 'I believe Mr Piquet sowed the seeds of *S. maritima (S. atropurpurea)* and some other French plants at St Ouens. He showed it me there. It had whitish flowers and has now disappeared' (*B.E.C. Report* 1926). In Melvill's herbarium there is a specimen collected by Piquet from 'hillsides near St Aubin' in 1874. In Ariste's and Louis-Arsène's herbaria there are specimens collected at L'Étacq on 25 July 1924 and T. J. Foggitt collected it from there on 8 July 1926. It has since disappeared, a German bunker being on the exact place.
G 1925 and 1971.

S. columbaria L. **Small Scabious**

Babington's (1839) record of Small Scabious as 'frequent' has always been considered an error. The only other record is in Piquet's 1896 list where he claimed it was rare at St Clement. Lester-Garland (1903) queried this also.
G only Babington's ? record.

CAMPANULACEAE

Campanula portenschlagiana Schultes
Adria Bellflower

A garden escape originally from the eastern Mediterranean occasionally found on the sides of walls where its masses of flowers in early summer produce cushions of blue.
G occasional.

C. pyramidalis L. **Chimney Bellflower**
G occasional.

C. fragilis Cyr. **A Campanula**
G garden escape on one wall.

Trachelium caeruleum L. **Throatwort**

In 1967 Mrs E. M. Towers found Throatwort, a Mediterranean plant, in good quantity on an old wall behind the flats at La Folie at the foot of Mont Félard. It was well established and looked as though it had been there for many, many years. Similarly, in 1977, Mrs M. T. Yandell found it very well established on walls in Grosvenor Street. Both colonies survive in spite of some plants in Grosvenor Street being sprayed with weedkiller later in the 1970s.
G four localities.

Wahlenbergia hederacea (L.) Reichenb.
Ivy-leaved Bellflower

There are five past records of this species which is at present unknown in the island. W. C. Trevelyan found it in 1833 in a bog in the upper part of St Peter's Valley (Babington 1839). Someone unknown collected it from 'St Peter' on 7 September 1835 (Hb Cantab. ex Hb Casborne). J. Lloyd, writing in the *Phytologist* (1859), claimed to have '. . . found upon some marshy ground *Ranunculus ophioglossifolius, lingua, flammula, Wahlenbergia hederacea* and *Bartsia viscosa*'. The marshy ground must, from the other species named, have been the St Peter/St Lawrence Marsh. In 1903 the Société Jersiaise was given an album of paintings titled *Jersey Wild Flowers* by B. H. Gosselin Lefeuvre of Guernsey. In it there is an exquisite painting of this beautiful little plant. The other paintings are all flowers known to grow in Jersey, including some Jersey rarities not found in the other Channel Islands. Babington noted, without a date, that H. C. Watson had found it at Bouley Bay. Lester-Garland (1903) rejected Trevelyan's record but he may not have known of the others. Ivy-leaved Bellflower probably disappeared from the Beaumont area when the marsh was drained but does it still grow in some damp meadow elsewhere?
G one record, St Andrew, 1858.

Jasione montana L. **Sheep's-bit**
des flieurs au dgiâbl'ye

Common in dry places, particularly near the coast. The local name for this plant, *flieur au dgiâbl'ye* which I am assured by Dr Le Maistre is correct, probably comes through a confusion of Devil's-bit Scabious with Sheep's-bit. Though superficially they look alike, botanically they are very different. Sheep's-bit, which is not a scabious, is closer to a Harebell than to Devil's-bit Scabious, and the usual reasons for associating the devil with the latter species cannot apply as the root of Sheep's-bit is not 'bitten off' short. See Devil's-bit Scabious.

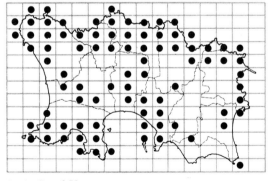

G, A, S and H common.

Lobelia erinus L. **Lobelia**

Single plants are sometimes seen near gardens or rubbish dumps but the species is nowhere established.
G occasional.

COMPOSITAE

Eupatorium cannabinum L.   **Hemp Agrimony**
d'la **jalousie sauvage**

Subsp. *cannabinum* Frequent in overgrown wet areas.

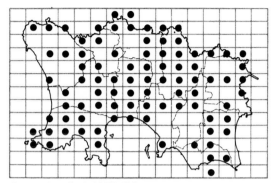

G occasional; A 1977; S frequent.

Solidago virgaurea L.   **Goldenrod**
d'la **vèrge d'or**

Frequent on rough hillsides and in open woodland. This is a native species as opposed to the following garden escapes.

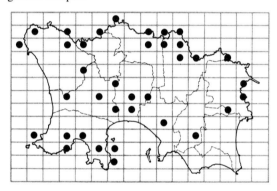

Solidago species   **Garden Goldenrod**

Garden Goldenrods were occasionally seen in the past where garden refuse had been tipped and they would persist for years. With the virtual disappearance of such dumps, and perhaps with Goldenrod declining in favour as a garden plant, none has been seen recently.
G occasional; A occasional; S 1961.

Bellis perennis L.   **Daisy**
des **mèrgots**

Common in short turf. E. B. Syme recorded Hen and Chickens, a form in which several smaller flowers appear on short stalks above the normal flower, in 1853 at St Ouen.

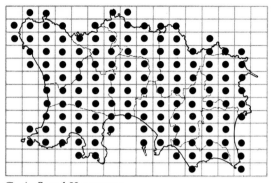

G, A, S and H common.

Aster novi-belgii L. agg.   **Michaelmas Daisy**

Michaelmas Daisy used to be frequent on dumps where garden refuse was thrown, and it would persist, but with the virtual disappearance of such areas it is becoming rare.
G rare.

A. tripolium L.   **Sea Aster**

It is now impossible to tell whether Sea Aster has ever grown in Jersey. Saunders' record in Babington (1839) was rejected by Lester-Garland (1903). Piquet did not mention it in either his 1851 list or his 1896 list and its supplement in 1898. A specimen collected by him in July 1898 is in the Société's herbarium but the specimen sheet carries only the words 'Salt marshes. Rare' i.e. it is not localised, and there is no specimen in his main herbarium now in Hb Oxford. Attenborough claimed in the Société's botanical report for 1947 that he had found Sea Aster in St Catherine's Bay and St Brelade's Bay, and he added that it had been considered to be extinct for many years. There are no specimens to confirm the claim, and while it is difficult to know what he could have confused with Sea Aster, except possibly Michaelmas Daisy, it is perhaps even more difficult to think of it growing in St Brelade's Bay, which is one of Jersey's sandiest bays without a scrap of salt-marsh. At St Catherine's Bay there is one small possible habitat. In the distant past it may well have occurred in the Samarès region of St Clement where there were saltpans.
G rare; A rare.

A. linosyris (L.) Bernh.   **Goldilocks Aster**
(Crinitaria linosyris)

The record in the *Atlas of the British Flora* is based on a specimen labelled as from Jersey in 1840 by Dickson (Hb Cantab.) and should be discounted. See the Introduction.

Erigeron glaucus Ker-Gawler   **Beach Aster**

This blue-green perennial aster from North America is sometimes planted out on banks. It can persist for

many years.
G self-seeds.

E. philadelphicus L.   **Robin's Plantain**
This grew as a weed in a garden near Green Island in
the 1960s and 1970s.

E. acer L.   **Blue Fleabane**
(E. acre)   *d'l'**hèrbe à puches***
Subsp. *acer*   Most years Blue Fleabane is locally fre-
quent on the dunes of Les Quennevais and St Ouen's
Bay.
G rare; A rare.

E. mucronatus DC.   **Mexican Fleabane**
(E. karvinskianus)   *des **mèrgots à pouochîns***
Introduced and now abundant on many walls. Attenborough used to say that this Mexican species was
rare when he first came to the island at the beginning
of the century, and that it was not recorded because it
was not reckoned part of the wild flora. The first
specimen seems to have been collected by Burdo
from a wall at Millbrook in 1925. Attenborough
stated in the Société's botanical report for 1948 that
its quantity had remained the same for many years
but that it seemed to be increasing. Since then it has
increased to such an extent that in some areas few
walls are without it.

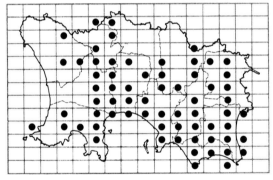

G locally abundant; A 1970; S occasional.

E. canadensis L.   **Canadian Fleabane**
(Conyza canadensis)
Piquet added to his 1851 list at some later undated
time that Canadian Fleabane was in a field at
Millbrook and in his 1896 list that it was on waste and
cultivated ground in St Helier. No localities are given
on the Piquet herbarium sheets dated 1900 and 1910.
Lester-Garland (1903) considered this North
American species to be a casual in St Helier. Since
then it has become frequent on roadsides and dry
areas throughout the island but it may be giving way
to the next species with which its sight records are
inextricably tangled. Canadian Fleabane became
abundant during the Occupation (1940–45) but

diminished greatly in the late 1940s according to
Attenborough.

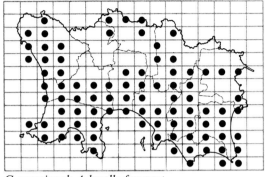

G occasional; A locally frequent.

E. bonariensis Retz.   **Argentinian Fleabane**
This South American alien is sometimes split into two
species *E. bonariensis* Retz. and *E. sumatrensis* Retz.
though A. Cronquist in *Flora Europaea* maintains
that these are the extreme ends of the range of variation of the one species *E. bonariensis*. If the two are
considered to be separate, then *E. bonariensis* was a
common weed in a garden at Millbrook in 1958, Mrs
M. L. Long, and by the early 1960s it was widespread
in the Millbrook–Mont Cochon area. Though still
most often seen in that region it now occasionally
occurs on light soil from St Ouen round the south
coast to Gorey. The rusty brown pappus, the flower-
head bracts with purple tips and the side branches
sometimes overtopping the main stem separate it
from *E. sumatrensis* which D. McClintock called
Guernsey Fleabane in *The Wild Flowers of Guernsey*.
In April 1973 J. B. Marshall identified a specimen
from Mont Matthieu, St Ouen, as *E. sumatrensis*.
Later that year it was found occasionally on roadsides and dry places, inland as well as coastal, and it is
now the commoner of the two. It almost certainly
went undetected for some years prior to 1973 as at a
superficial glance it could be thought a large, greyish,
hairy Canadian Fleabane.
G locally frequent (only E. sumatrensis*).*

Filago vulgaris Lam.   **Common Cudweed**
(F. germanica)
Recorded as frequent by Piquet (1896), and as rare
by Lester-Garland (1903) in dry waste places. It is
still rare, mainly on roadsides.

Map overleaf

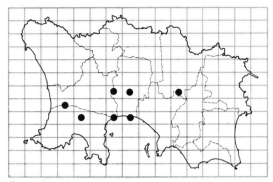

G, A, S and H rare.

F. pyramidata L.   **Broad-leaved Cudweed**

Père Vaniot collected a specimen in St Brelade on 29 August 1881 and Druce collected a young *Filago* at St Aubin in 1910 which, when grown on, proved to be this species (*Journal of Botany* 1911).

F. minima (Sm.) Pers.   **Small Cudweed**
(*Logfia minima*)

Common on dry hillsides and dunes of the west.
G occasional; A locally frequent; S occasional;

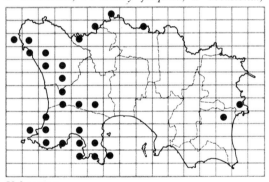

H frequent.

F. gallica L.   **Narrow-leaved Cudweed**
(*Logfia gallica*)

One plant by the roadside, Bouley Bay, 1875, Dr M. M. Bull, who stated that he could not think where it had come from as there was none in the fields round about (*Journal of Botany* 1875; Hb Brit. Mus.).
S 1902 and still there.

Gnaphalium sylvaticum L.   **Heath Cudweed**
(*Omalotheca sylvatica*)

Saunders' record given by Babington (1839) was rejected by Lester-Garland (1903) and there has been no confirmation.

G. uliginosum L.   **Marsh Cudweed**
(*Filaginella uliginosa*)

Common in damp places.

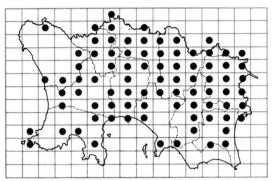

G frequent; A rare; S frequent; H occasional.

G. luteo-album L.   **Jersey Cudweed**

First recorded by Dr W. Sherard when he visited Jersey in 1689. See the Introduction. His statement that it was 'On the Walls and dry Banks very common.' has mystified generations of botanists because Jersey Cudweed is a plant of damp sandy places. The 'walls' are still a mystery but the dry banks can now be explained: Attenborough suggested in the mid-1950s that the area north of St Ouen's Pond be searched as that was the last place he had seen Jersey Cudweed many years ago. Some newly excavated sandpits had filled with water in winter. As the water-level receded in the summer of 1955 Mrs M. L. Long noticed a few seedlings on a soaking wet spit of sand running out into a shallow pool. The plants were Jersey Cudweed and as the summer drew on, and more water evaporated, the whole floor of the sandpit became covered with seedlings. Every year since 1955 if there has been the necessary habitat – wet, open ground which later dries out – then Jersey Cudweed has been present in that area, sometimes in abundance.

In 1689 there was little development round the coast, for example Les Mielles of St Helier, where the hospital now is, were still open and the Parade was a marsh. There would be plenty of 'banks' along the south and west coasts which would be wet in winter but dry out in summer and so provide a habitat for Sherard's 'very common' Jersey Cudweed. An undated, unlocalised specimen is in the collection made by Dr Sherard and may well be from Jersey. A specimen in the Druce collection is labelled that it is ex Hb Dillenius and was collected in Jersey by the Rev. W. Clarke in 1720. Another specimen, still in Hb Dillenius, has 'This specimen was gathered in Jersey by the Rev. Mr Clark' against it. The Rev. Mr Clark(e) was active mainly between 1730 and 1740. See the Introduction. The above collections are in Hb Oxford.

Earlier this century Jersey Cudweed was found only at long intervals but the habitat was not always present. Over the years it has mainly been recorded from St Ouen's Bay, including the land edge of the reeds on the east side of St Ouen's Pond, with occasional records from St Brelade, La Corbière, Grouville, Petit Port and St Helier. Since *G. undulatum*, Cape Cudweed, an alien rare in Britain, arrived in Jersey last century it has frequently been mistaken for this species.

When the name Jersey Cudweed came into use is unknown. Petifer (1712) and Smith (1824) called the species Jersey Live-long. An illustration by Pandora Sellars is opposite page 103.
G scarce; A 1973.

G. undulatum L.   **Cape Cudweed**

First collected in 1888 by J. F. Richards, who told Druce that it seemed to be 'quite naturalised in Jersey' (B.E.C. *Report* 1892). In 1892 A. J. Binet wrote in his diary that '. . . The whole of the W side of the cliff overlooking the Westmt garden is covered with the parallel stems of this plant'. Lester-Garland (1903) described it as locally common. It has now spread over most of the island and is sometimes abundant after fires.

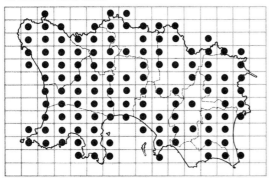

G common; A locally frequent; S common; H occasional.

Anaphalis margaritacea (L.) Benth.

Pearly Everlasting

A specimen collected in 1847 is in Ereaut's *Hortus Siccus* but there is no information as to its status and the plant may have been of garden origin. Marquand (1901) stated that he had seen a specimen from Jersey. Perhaps he did, but a specimen of Cape Cudweed, collected in 1898, was originally labelled as this species. No foundation is known for the statement in Hooker's *Student's Flora* (1870) that Pearly Everlasting was naturalised here at that time. It is not now and probably never has been.
G three claims.

Inula helenium L.   **Elecampane**

A garden escape first reported by Saunders from near Bagatelle (Babington, 1839) and collected by the Rev. W. W. Newbould from St Catherine's Bay in 1841/2. Piquet (1896) listed it from a wood near Swiss

Valley, though in earlier, undated notes he had stated it was in a valley near Bagatelle and then in the upper part of a meadow above Swiss Valley. Lester-Garland (1903) stated that Guiton found it in Queen's Valley but a specimen collected by Guiton in 1900 was from a meadow near Swiss Valley. Many of these confusing localities may have been the same. It has not been recorded since, though no particular search has been made.
G rare.

I. conyza DC.   **Ploughman's-spikenard**

Always rare. Babington (1839) gave W. Christy's record from a lane above Beaumont. Piquet collected specimens from St Clement's Bay in 1851 and from St Lawrence in 1900 (Hb Oxford) and Vaniot collected it near Sion Chapel, St John, in 1881. The only place it seems to have occurred with any regularity is near Pont Marquet where A. J. Binet found it in exactly the same place in 1891, 1915 and 1919, and Miss E. H. du Feu then refound it near Pont Marquet in possibly Binet's locality in 1957. It has not been seen since. There are a few claims from areas like the rocks near La Corbière where the habitat is wrong. Confusion with the following species is suspected in these claims.
G very local; A occasional; S rare; H local.

I. crithmoides L.   **Golden Samphire**

Local within reach of the sea spray.

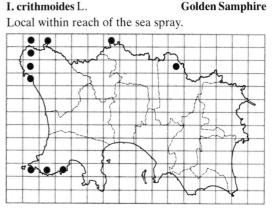

G locally plentiful; A occasional; S locally frequent.

Pulicaria dysenterica (L.) Bernh.　　**Common Fleabane**
Common in damp places.

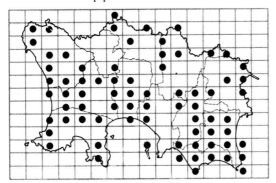

G, A, S and H frequent.

P. vulgaris Gaertn.　　**Small Fleabane**
Not seen since last century. Lester-Garland stated that Piquet collected a specimen in 1862 but the only specimen now in Piquet's herbarium (Hb Oxford) was collected by 'Mr Naylor' from a marsh at Gorey on 9 September 1861. The only other records are Babington's (1839), from a bog near St Clement, and he noted in his own copy of his Flora that the Rev. W. W. Newbould had found it at St Aubin. No supporting specimens are known for these latter.
G last record 1877; S 1872.

Guizotia abyssinica (L. fil.) Cass.　　**Niger**
A bird seed alien first reported from Mont Mado rubbish dump in 1969 by J. R. Palmer and later found on the dumps at the north end of St Ouen's Bay in the 1970s.
G 1975.

Bidens tripartita L.　　**Trifid Bur-marigold**
One small plant was found by Mrs E. M. Towers in the stream near Tesson Mill, St Peter's Valley in 1968. Most other records are about the middle of last century when it appears to have been widespread, being reported from wet areas in Grands Vaux, St Clement, St Peter, St Brelade and St Ouen. J. Piquet collected a specimen from Le Marais, St Ouen, in 1852 (Hb Oxford) and F. Piquet from St Ouen's Pond in 1869 (Hb Société Jersiaise) where Attenborough saw it flowering in 1910.
G two centuries ago only.

B. cernua L.　　**Nodding Bur-marigold**
Not now known in Jersey but there are three old records: St Lawrence Marsh, 1842, Rev. W. W. Newbould (Hb Cantab.) and 1852, Piquet (Hb Oxford); plentiful in St Peter's Valley, 1845, J. Atkins (letter to Babington).

Helianthus annuus L.　　**Sunflower**
　　　　　　　　　　　　　　　un **tournésol**
When there were rubbish dumps in the post-war years, this could normally be found growing on them. The origin would be seed in bird food.
G rare.

H. rigidus (Cass.) Desf.　　**Perennial Sunflower**
Established by the edge of a north coast dump for a few years in the 1960s but now gone.
G occasional.

H. tuberosus L.　　**Jerusalem Artichoke**
Plants survived for a few years on at least three dumps in the 1950s and 1960s but nowhere is it established in the wild as it is in parts of Europe.
G 1970.

Ambrosia artemisiifolia L.　　**Ragweed**
Piquet collected a specimen in St Ouen's Bay in 1906 and A. J. Robinson found it in quantity in 1953 in a field above Trinity Hill on the west side. A few plants were still there in 1958.
G one plant 1963.

Xanthium strumarium L.　　**Rough Cocklebur**
One locality only, a disused quarry opposite Tesson Mill, St Peter's Valley, from where Piquet collected specimens in 1896, 1897 and 1899. There are no later records of this American species and the quarry has now been developed.
G 1890.

X. spinosum L.　　**Spiny Cocklebur**
A South American plant collected in St Ouen's Bay by Piquet in 1899 and 1900.

Spilanthes decumbens (Smith) Moore　　**Spilanthes**
G 1923–26.

Schkuhria pinnata (Lam.) Thell.
　　　　　　　　　A South American Composite
G 1980.

Galinsoga parviflora Cav.　　**Gallant Soldier**
In November 1960 A. J. Robinson found Gallant Soldier, a native of South America, in a field in the south of St Martin. Half the field was broccoli and the other half was tomatoes yet the Gallant Soldier was abundant throughout the field and could not be found in any of the surrounding fields. How it arrived in such quantity is unknown. Similarly near Pontac in 1964 and at Millbrook in 1967 particular areas were full of it yet it could not be found nearby. There were occasional records elsewhere and the map shows its

occurrences between 1960 and 1970. Since then it has continued to be found occasionally but it has not made the impact on the flora that might have been expected considering its quantity locally in the 1960s.

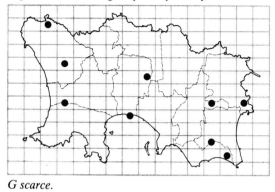

G scarce.

G. ciliata (Rafin.) Blake   **Shaggy Soldier**

Louis-Arsène showed me this Central and South American species growing sparingly in one of the vegetable gardens, and commonly in another, in the grounds of Highlands College in 1958. He said he thought it had come in from France with vegetable seed. In 1965 Mrs E. M. Towers found one plant near a car park in St Brelade's Bay and the map shows where records were made from then until 1970. It was never in the local abundance of Gallant Soldier yet it continues to be seen occasionally.

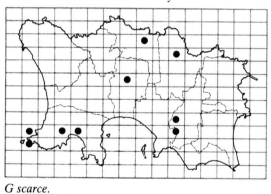

G scarce.

Anthemis arvensis L.   **Corn Chamomile**

Subsp. *arvensis* Babington (1839) and Piquet (1896) stated that Corn Chamomile was common. Lester-Garland (1903) queried this and thought it very rare. The only specimen he saw was Piquet's collected in St Ouen in 1900. Experience in the last thirty years supports Lester-Garland. In 1961 one plant was found in Cap Verd valley, St Lawrence. In 1963 a specimen was collected along La Verte Rue, St Ouen, (confirmed Kew) and plants were found on the site of Brandy's Basket Works, Victoria Avenue,

where a circus had been held.
G 1894; A 1838; A 1897.

A. ruthenica Bieb.   **A Chamomile**

In the *Journal of Botany* (1920) Druce stated that a specimen labelled as collected by Piquet from corn-fields in Jersey in 1900 was *A. ruthenica.* A similarly labelled specimen in the Société herbarium was identified by J. E. Lousley as *A. arvensis.* It may be that Druce meant *A. ruthenica* Bieb. subsp. *requienii* (Schultz Bip.) Nyman which in *Flora Europaea* is stated to be a synonym of *A. arvensis* subsp. *incrassata* (Loisel.) Nyman.

A. cotula L.   **Stinking Chamomile**

Frequent last century according to Babington (1839) and Piquet (1851 and 1896), not common by 1903, Lester-Garland, and now decidedly rare. A. J. Wilmott found it in quantity in a field near Le Sauchet, Rozel, in 1922, and Burdo collected it near there in 1926. A number of plants were found distributed round flat waste ground at Mont Mado quarries in 1963, Mrs D. L. Le Quesne, and also in a field of Gladioli, near Millais, St Ouen in 1968.
G now scarce; A 1899; S occasional.

A. tinctoria L.   **Yellow Chamomile**

One record: on a bank of waste land near La Rue de la Blanche Pierre, St Lawrence, 1964, J. C. Fluck.

Achillea ptarmica L.   **Sneezewort**
                                                   d's **aigrettes**

A garden outcast found on Rozel Hill in the late 1930s by N. Le Brocq, near Causie Lane, St Clement, in 1962 by Mrs L. A. Morris, at Pontac in 1968 by Mrs D. L. Le Quesne and at Les Brulées, Trinity, in 1976 by Mrs M. L. Long.
A rare.

A. millefolium L.   **Yarrow**
                                 d'la **tchèrpentchiéthe**

Subsp. *millefolium* Common in dry grassland, and on roadsides and hedgebanks. The local name means carpenter's herb and Attenborough who was a well-known chemist for many years said that if a carpenter cut himself he would apply this plant to the wound to staunch bleeding. The flowers are occasionally pink instead of the usual white.

Map overleaf

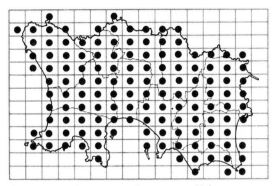

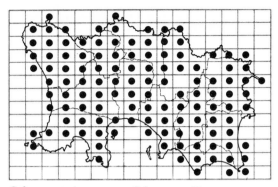

G common; A common; S common; H frequent.

G frequent; A common; S frequent; H scarce.

Chamaemelum nobile (L.) All.   **Chamomile**
(Anthemis nobilis)   *d'la* **canmiéthe**

Still common in damp places. This is the plant from which chamomile tea is made, and in *A Picture of Jersey* (1809) Stead comments that in some areas there are 'great quantities of camomile, which here, in its uncultivated state, is more bitter, though not of so delicate a colour as that raised for sale in England and elsewhere'. G. F. B. de Gruchy in a paper, 'The Court of the Fief and Seigneurie of Noirmont', in the Société *Bulletin Annuel* (1926) states that a tenant of the Seigneur once sued another tenant for picking *amerosque* on his land. De Gruchy translates *amerosque* as Chamomile, rather than as one of the mayweeds, and this seems more likely to be the species involved.

T. inodorum Schultz Bip.   **Scentless Mayweed**
(M. perforata; M. inodora)   *d'la* **m'soûque**

Common on cultivated and disturbed land. In recent years some fields lying fallow in autumn, after tomatoes or another summer crop, have been white with flowers of Scentless Mayweed. Perhaps it or its seeds can survive the various chemicals, now used on farm land, better than other species, and it flourishes in their absence. The map is a composite one of Scentless and Sea Mayweed. See above.
G common; A frequent; S frequent; H scarce.

Matricaria recutita L.   **Scented Mayweed**
(Chamomilla recutita; M. chamomilla)

    d'la **m'soûque**

'Not very common', as Lester-Garland (1903) described it, though widespread.

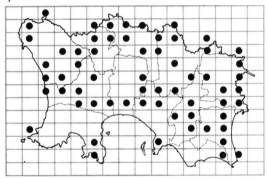

G locally common; A locally frequent; S common; H 1837.

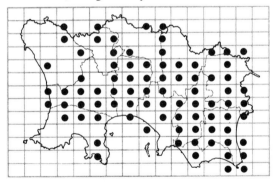

G common; A 1977; S 1872 and 1896; H last record 1893.

Tripleurospermum maritimum (L.) Koch
(Matricaria maritima;   **Sea Mayweed**
M. inodora var. *salina)*   *d'la* **m'soûque**

Common round the coast. This species was previously regarded as either a subspecies or a variety of the following. No separate records were kept during the survey so the map given under the following species is an aggregate one. Druce stated (1907) that he 'looked out rather carefully for transitional forms but did not see them'.

M. matricarioides (Less.) Porter   **Pineappleweed**
(Chamomilla suaveolens)

Not known in the island until a specimen was collected by Lester-Garland from a rubbish heap near Rouge Rue quarries in 1903 (Hb Société Jersiaise) presumably too late for his *Flora of Jersey* (1903). Ariste wrote '*Acclimatée un peu*' against specimens he collected at Beaumont and Fort Regent in 1928. It is now a frequent weed particularly on the

158

compacted soil of areas like field entrances and road-sides.

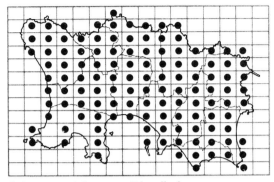

G frequent; A frequent; S locally frequent.

Otanthus maritimus (L.) Hoffmanns. & Link
(Diotis maritima; D. candidissima)   **Cottonweed**

Cottonweed, a native species which was first collected in 1835 and which grew in local abundance in St Ouen's Bay in the 1850s and 1860s, was considered rare by Melvill in 1876.

The building of the sea wall was blamed for its decrease but that particular part of the sea wall, the quarter mile stretch from L'Ouzière Slip northwards, was not built until about 1877 according to a *Report* on the St Ouen's Bay sea walls prepared for the States of Jersey in 1948 by Messrs Coode & Partners. Perhaps preparations for its building began earlier. That the species survived, though in much reduced quantity, is shown by specimens bearing dates in the 1880s in British herbaria and by the entries in A. J. Binet's notebook:

'20/7/90 This though not in bloom is the unmistakeable Diotis – a beautiful plant. Just on the N. side of the end of the outlet to St Ouen's Pond – on the shingle.
. . .

Disappearance of Diotis mar.? In my walk this day 24/4/92 I watched particularly for Diotis maritima which I found last year or the year before. I regret much that during the building of the sea wall, it has either been destroyed or covered over with tons of gravel. This may mean the total disappearance of a very rare plant from our flora. Further on I thought of finding another spec: as I believe Dancaster told me there was one near his house – but did not find it – perhaps because I did not go far enough. –
It has not disappeared. I found it later in the summer – April much too early to look for it.'

The last specimen known of the certainly original population was gathered in June 1897 by Piquet (Hb Birm.). A gap seems to exist between then and 1912 perhaps because an apron was constructed to that part of the sea wall in about 1900 (Coode *et al.* 1948). In that gap Lester-Garland stated: '*Diotis*

candidissima Desf. Only known from one locality, and now destroyed by the building of a sea-wall in St Ouen's Bay.' (*Journal of Botany* 1901, XXXIX: 65) and in his Flora of 1903 he gave it as extinct. Druce visited Jersey in 1906/7 and wrote: 'The locality where I saw this growing in Jersey in 1877 is now covered by the St Ouen's sea-wall. It appears now extinct in the islands.' (*Journal of Botany* 1907, XLV: 422).

A new phase then began, perhaps because Piquet reintroduced it. P. É. F. Perrédès stated of Piquet: 'He procured seeds from Mr Lynch, of Cambridge, started them in pans in his garden, and when they had sufficiently developed, he planted them out in their old locality. Two months before his death (5 September 1912) he was shown a small specimen from the Bay, and his delight was so great that, although unable to walk, he drove out to see it.' (*Journal of Botany* 1912, L: 373).

Records then begin again with Pugsley collecting a specimen in 1914 and A. J. Binet entering in his notebook: 'June 26, 1914 Motored to Pond with Smith and E. Found 3 plants Diotis mar. after (just blossoming) having long ago given up all hope of ever again seeing this plant.' and 'About Aug 13/(19)19. 4 or 5 plants (some small) growing on this date on the same spot. The flower is over and the heads brown with the seeds still hanging on.'

The species survived until the late 1920s. The end is shrouded in mystery particularly as to where in the Bay the plants were growing. W. C. Barton wrote against his specimen: 'Mr Attenborough told me this was from the old station where the plant has reappeared and not from Mr Piquet's place.' Louis-Arsène distributed a large number of specimens, many in seed, in 1925 with a note that '. . . it reappeared some years ago in another place not far from the classical locality, and now seems to be on the increase' and claiming that the plants had been knocked over by children and run over by a vraic cart. In 1958 he took me to the area from where he said he had collected them – by Les Laveurs Slipway at the north end of the Bay. At least three people collected specimens in 1926, though from exactly where is unknown, and in the Société's botanical report for 1927 Attenborough stated: 'It is with great regret that the writer records the destruction of our remaining plants . . . last summer . . .' In later years he used to say that they had been knocked down deliberately with sticks.

The story ends with A. J. Binet's notebook entry: '3 fine plants Aug. 1928'.
G error? A 1838.

Chrysanthemum carinatum Schousboe
Annual Chrysanthemum

Recorded three times as garden escapes but nowhere naturalised.
G 1958.

C. segetum L.   **Corn Marigold**
                     du **mèneleu**

Until recently Corn Marigold was a common plant of arable, acid land but it has decreased considerably since the States of Jersey began giving a lime subsidy to farmers and herbicides began to be used in fields to kill emerging weeds.

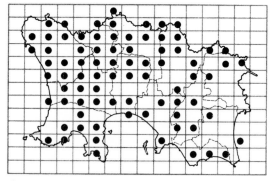

G as Jersey; A occasional; S locally frequent; H rare.

Tanacetum vulgare L.   **Tansy**
(Chrysanthemum vulgare)   *d'la* **t'naisie**

Garden escape occasionally naturalised near houses.

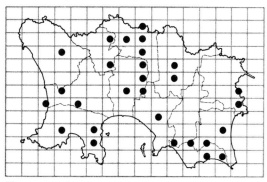

G occasional; A occasional; S rare.

T. parthenium (L.) Schultz Bip.   **Feverfew**
(Chrysanthemum Parthenium)   *du* **maître**

Garden escape, widespread but thinly distributed. It usually occurs near old habitations, particularly at the foot of walls or in uncultivated corners, and is probably a relic from the time when it was used medicinally. Recently there has been an upsurge of interest in its possible medicinal powers and it has been in great demand.

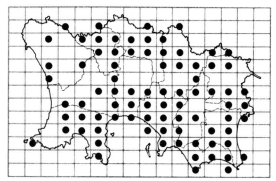

G frequent; A occasional; S frequent; H rare.

T. macrophyllum (Waldst. & Kit.) Schultz Bip.
An east European Composite

Two records: Jersey, 1883, A. Ley (Hb Birm.); Beauport, 1929, Ariste. These were presumably garden escapes as the species is not established in Jersey.

Leucanthemum vulgare Lam.   **Oxeye Daisy**
(Chrysanthemum leucanthemum)   *d's* **ièrs dé boeu**

Common on the cliffs and frequent on hillsides inland. In 1978 it was so extraordinarily abundant on many parts of the coast that, for instance, to observers looking west from Ouaisné Common, Beauport headland seemed to be covered by a thick blanket of snow in June. The long, dry, hot summer of 1976 followed by two mild, wet winters probably affected the species. A relevant paper by Prof. T. W. Böcher, who stated that Jersey's Oxeye Daisy is diploid, is in the *New Phytologist* Vol. 57.

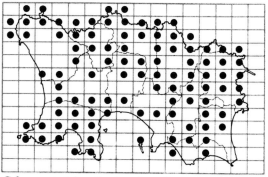

G frequent; A locally abundant; S common; H occasional.

L. maximum (Ramond) DC.   **Shasta Daisy**

A garden escape reported five times in the 1960s. It may persist for a time but is nowhere established.
G two records; A 1967.

Cotula dioica (Hooker f.) Hooker f.
Hairless Leptinella

Well-established in the grounds of Samarès Manor

where it was first noticed in 1958. This New Zealand species may originally have been planted in the 1930s or earlier as a mat-forming perennial instead of grass in a lawn.

C. coronopifolia L.   **Button Plant**
G 1978.

Artemisia vulgaris L.   **Mugwort**
*d'l'***hèrbe d'St Jean**
Common in hedges, cultivated fields and waste places.

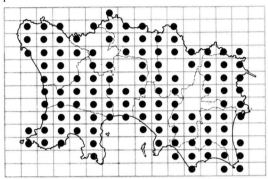

G frequent; A rare; S last record 1892; H rare.

A. absinthium L.   **Wormwood**
*d'l'***absînthe**

Piquet recorded *absînthe* as frequent in waste places and near dwellings last century, and it may well have been, since it was used medicinally. Lester-Garland (1903) considered it very rare and it remains so, being reported from only three localities since his Flora. A specimen in the Société herbarium labelled '*A. maritima,* Anneport, 1912, J. Piquet' is *A. absinthium* and the species was still at Anneport until at least the late 1950s. In 1961 Miss P. Donaldson found one plant on waste land on the site of Brandy's Basket Works on Victoria Avenue, and plants were seen there until 1969. In 1962 Mrs D. L. Le Quesne found one plant on La Mielle, St Clement.
G rare; A occasional; S occasional.

A. maritima L.   **Sea Wormwood**
Lester-Garland (1903) rejected Saunders' record given by Babington (1839). The only other claim for this in Jersey is in the *Journal of Botany* (L: 316) when J. S. Gasking reported it at Anne Port in 1912, stating that he had given the specimen to Piquet. It presumably is the specimen of *A. absinthium* mentioned above.

A. annua L.   **Annual Mugwort**
A bird seed annual reported from the grounds of St

Brelade's Bay Hotel in 1961 by D. McClintock.

Tussilago farfara L.   **Colt's-foot**
Now rare but there seems little agreement on the quantity in the past. Babington (1839) recorded it as 'not rare'. Piquet wrote 'Fields. Too frequent' beside a specimen gathered in April 1896, and stated in his 1896 list that it was common. Only seven years later, Lester-Garland (1903) stated it was rare. It is a plant of heavy clay soil, which is not common in Jersey, so it is of interest that it was recorded from the site of Copp's brickyard at Mont à l'Abbé by N. Le Brocq in the late 1930s and by Mrs E. M. Towers in 1964. It is possible that Guiton's record from Mont à l'Abbé, given by Lester-Garland (1903), was from the brick-works also. In the 1950s A. J. Robinson found it in Huelin's old brickworks at Five Oaks. During the survey Colt's-foot was found in some unusual places where it had not been seen previously, for example by the side of the road at the quarry at La Crête and by the edge of the culvert running across the mudpond at Handois where it still grows. Some of these may well have been deliberately planted by someone who inquired where Colt's-foot grew, because he wanted to pick it and eat it when he was out walking, and who was disappointed to hear how rare it was. The only field since the war with any quantity of Colt's-foot in it, was in the Mont au Prêtre region. There is no local name for this plant, which is perhaps an indication that it has always been at least uncommon. In English, the name Colt's-foot means this species; in Jersey-English Colt's-foot means *Petasites fragrans*.

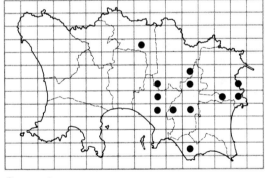

G rare; A rare.

Petasites hybridus (L.) P. Gaertner, B. Meyer & Scherb.   **Butterbur**
(P. officinalis)
Subsp. *hybridus* Rare: bog at St Clement, Babington (1839); in the grounds of Longueville Manor, Piquet, and still by the stream below Longueville Manor, J. C. Fluck; Trinity, 1860, Duprey and 1900, Guiton; Mont au Prêtre, Guiton; near Rozel, Guiton, and still in the valley running down from Rosel Manor to St Catherine's Bay, J. C.

161

Fluck. In 1898 Piquet wrote 'Frequent chiefly near dwellings and certainly introduced', against a specimen.

P. fragrans (Vill.) C. Presl
(Colt's-foot) Winter Heliotrope
du **pas d'âne**

Common on hedge banks and waste places. Originally it would have been a garden plant but it is now completely naturalised. Considerable confusion exists in Jersey over the identification of this plant because its Jersey-English name is Colt's-foot, whereas in English, Colt's-foot is *Tussilago farfara*. Similarly, its Jersey-Norman-French name is *pas d'âne*, whereas in French, *pas d'âne* is *Tussilago farfara*. An illustration by Pandora Sellars is opposite page 134.

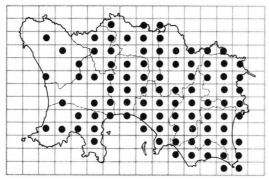

G common; A locally frequent; S occasional; H locally frequent.

Senecio mikanioides Otto ex Walpers   **German Ivy**

N. D. Simpson sent a specimen collected by Miss E. Vachell from a wall at St Catherine in 1923 to Druce and in November 1924, Ariste, Burdo and Louis-Arsène collected specimens from Archirondel. It was soon frequent on hedges in the area and has now spread to other parts of the island. Louis-Arsène stated that it seeded freely but this is not so, at least in the west. Most of the spread would appear to be by human agency, people taking cuttings for their gardens or hedges and then discarding pieces when the plants grow too rampant. The leaves are vaguely ivy-shaped and it is a climber, but it is related to Ragwort and Groundsel not Ivy. This becomes apparent in November when the plant, a South African, produces heads of small, fragrant, yellow flowers. The name German Ivy comes from its superficial resemblance to Ivy and its use as a house plant, often on trellis, in Germany.

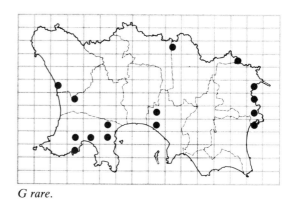

G rare.

S. cineraria DC.   **Silver Ragwort**
(S. bicolor ssp. *cineraria)*

A specimen collected by Ereaut in 1847 is in his *Hortus Siccus* but it may be of garden origin. Druce saw it in 1906/7: 'On a steep bank near St Aubin where it has escaped from a garden but will soon be naturalised' (*Journal of Botany* XLV: 422) and Attenborough stated against a specimen gathered at St Aubin in 1913 that the species was fully naturalised. It was there until at least 1927 (Ariste) but has not been seen since.
G two single plants; A 1977.

S. x albescens Burbidge & Colgan   **A hybrid Ragwort**
S. cineraria x **S. jacobaea**

One record: 1923, Williamson, Tullie House Herbarium, Carlisle, conf. D. McClintock.
G 1980.

S. jacobaea L.   **Common Ragwort**
d's **entaillies**

Common on uncultivated land and in neglected fields.

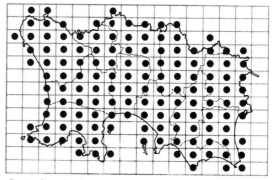

G, A, S and H common.

S. aquaticus Hill   **Marsh Ragwort**
La Gasca (1834) listed both this and '*S. erraticus*'.

162

Lester-Garland rejected both and there has been no confirmation.
G last record 1891.

S. squalidus L.   **Oxford Ragwort**

In 1963 Mrs E. M. Towers found four plants in the Bellozanne Road–St Andrew's Road region. There have been a few plants, never more than four, in the district almost every year since. It seems remarkable that this plant which colonised waste places so quickly in England should not have increased and spread to other parts of the island.
G rare.

S. sylvaticus L.   **Heath Groundsel**
                                    du **s'nichon**
Common on dry hilly places particularly after fires.

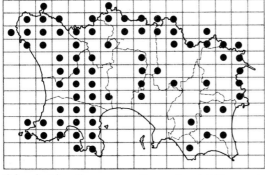

G local; A locally common; S occasional; H frequent.

S. vulgaris L.   **Groundsel**
                                    du **s'nichon**
Common. The radiate form, sometimes called subsp. *denticulatus* (O. F. Mueller) P. D. Sell, is common on Les Quennevais and on the dunes of St Ouen's Bay. Babington (1839) first noted it and Trimen, who saw it in April 1871, wrote in the *Journal of Botany* (IX: 200) that it '. . . made so great a show (on Les Quennevais) that it was hard to believe it merely groundsel'.

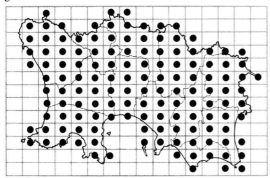

G common; A common; S frequent; H frequent.

S. elegans L.   **Elegant Ragwort**
One wild record: the land end of the causeway to La Corbière lighthouse, 1964, Mrs P. Rixon. This South African annual or biennial has seeded itself freely, unaided, for about fifteen years in gardens at St Brelade and St Ouen, including on gravel paths, yet it seems strangely unable to support itself outside gardens.

S. grandiflorus Berg.   **A garden Senecio**
G rare garden escape.

Calendula officinalis L.   **Pot Marigold**
                               d'la **soucique**
At some time or another, almost every place where garden refuse has been thrown, has had Pot Marigolds growing on it, and single plants are likely to occur along road edges. Rarely, it becomes established as on the hill side at L'Étacq, where it has been known for about sixty years. Jerseymen consider the flowers and leaves indispensable for conger soup, but even the petals alone, sprinkled on top, provide a beautiful garnish.
G frequent; A occasional; S occasional; H 1957.

C. arvensis L.   **Field Marigold**
G locally frequent.

Gazania taxon   **Gazania**
Gazania is occasionally planted on roadside banks of gardens, but one plant, of unknown origin, was found at Le Pinacle by Mrs M. L. Long in 1962. It had disappeared by 1963, probably because of the hard frost of the intervening winter which killed most gazanias in gardens.
G 1947–56, 1982.

Carlina vulgaris L.   **Carline Thistle**
Subsp. *vulgaris*   Locally frequent on hillsides of the coast.

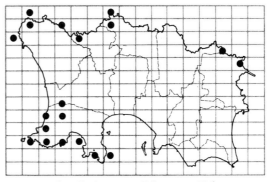

G rare; A locally frequent; S frequent; H frequent.

Echinops sphaerocephalus L.　　**Pale Globe Thistle**

Piquet gathered a specimen on Fort Regent in 1903 and one large plant of an *Echinops* species grew in the sandpits north of St Ouen's Pond from about 1960 to 1975.

Arctium lappa L.　　**Greater Burdock**

In the past '*A. lappa*' was used as an aggregate name. All specimens seen belong to *A. minus*.
G, A, S and H as above.

A. pubens Bab.　　**Babington's Burdock**
G 1951 and 1958; H 1958.

A. minus Bernh.　　**Lesser Burdock**
　　　　　　　　　　　dé l'ouothelle d'âne

Widespread but thinly distributed on waste places, roadsides and overgrown côtils. The fruits are called *des prènants* or *des bouôlîns* in Jersey-Norman-French.

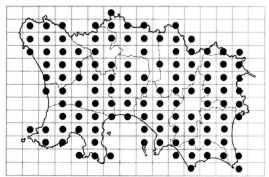

G uncommon; A frequent; S frequent; H occasional.

A. nemorosum Lej.　　**Common Burdock**
G occasional? A last record 1932; S 1892.

Carduus thoermeri Weinm.　　**A Musk Thistle**
G 1982.

C. nutans L.　　**Musk Thistle**

Subsp. *nutans* Musk Thistle seems to have decreased over the years: common, Babington (1839); frequent near the coast on waste ground and stony places, Piquet (1851 and 1896); rather rare, fields and waste places, St Aubin's Bay, Portelet Bay, St Peter's Barracks, L'Étacq, Lester-Garland (1903). It is still to be seen above L'Étacq some years, for example 1983, in good quantity but it seems to have gone from Les Hanières, St Ouen, the only other place from which it has been recorded since the Occupation (1940–45).
G local; A frequent; S 1872; H 1889.

C. acanthoides L.　　**Welted Thistle**

Babington (1839) gave a Trevelyan record in the *Addenda* in his Flora but Lester-Garland (1903) rejected it and it has never been confirmed.
G error.

C. tenuiflorus Curt.　　**Slender Thistle**
(C. pycnocephalus var. *tenuiflorus)*

Still common, often abundant, round the coast.

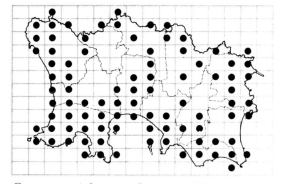

G common; A frequent; S common; H common.

Cirsium vulgare (Savi) Ten.　　**Spear Thistle**
(C. lanceolatum)　　　　　　　　　　*des* **soudards**

Common and sometimes locally abundant but a biennial, so not a persistent weed like Creeping Thistle.

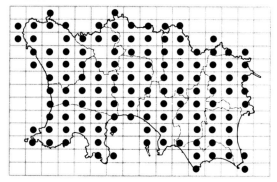

G, A, S and H common.

C. dissectum (L.) Hill　　**Meadow Thistle**
(C. anglicum)

Last century Meadow Thistle grew in two wet areas, Samarès Miles, St Clement, 1854, 'Mr Malcolm', Piquet (Hb Oxford) and by St Ouen's Pond, 1898, Lester-Garland. It was last seen in the St Clement's area in the mid-1920s and was claimed from St Ouen in the late 1930s. It has been reported only at long intervals so may yet reappear though R. W. S. Knightbridge in a detailed survey of wet meadows in 1983 did not record it.

C. oleraceum (L.) Scop.   **Cabbage Thistle**

One record: 'One single plant in the meadows near the second watermill in St Peter's Valley', 1861, Piquet (Hb Oxford).

C. acaule Scop.   **Dwarf Thistle**

Subsp. *acaule*   First reported from Les Quennevais by J. Gay in 1832 and stated to be common there by W. Christy in 1836. It continued to be seen, near where the Wild Privet grows, until 1931 when Burdo collected a specimen but in spite of much searching, and several false hopes where the species reported as Dwarf Thistle turned out to be Carline Thistle, it has not been refound. The area would appear to be relatively unchanged.
G error; A locally common.

C. palustre (L.) Scop.   **Marsh Thistle**
                                              du **tcheurdron**

Common in wet places.

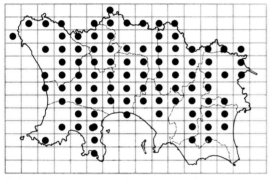

G frequent; A occasional; S occasional; H local.

C. arvense (L.) Scop.   **Creeping Thistle**
                                             du **tcheurdron**

Common. Druce recorded var. *horridum* from St Catherine's Bay and var. *mite* Koch from Pont Marquet in 1906/7 (*Journal of Botany* XLV: 422). This latter may be the same as var. *setosum* Mey listed by Piquet (1896) from Goosegreen Marsh (conf. A. Bennett).

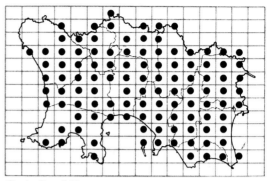

G, A, S and H common.

Onopordum acanthium L.   **Cotton Thistle**

A few unconnected casual records: 1833, 1896, 1920, and finally 1961 when several plants were unaccountably among gorse at La Moye, Mrs M. L. Long, and also on waste ground on the site of Brandy's Basket Works, Victoria Avenue, Miss P. Donaldson.
G only record two centuries ago; S 1881.

Cynara scolymus L.   **Globe Artichoke**

A vegetable-garden reject which can persist for a time on dumps.
A 1974.

Silybum marianum (L.) Gaertn.   **Milk Thistle**

Local on roadsides in the 1950s but decreasing and now rare. Babington (1839) recorded it from St Aubin's Bay, near St Helier, and Piquet (1851) added St Ouen's Bay. It still grows in St Ouen's Bay almost exactly where A. J. Binet saw a 'Splendid specimen in 1st road N of Pond ½ way between shore and hill', and it was still at Mont Orgueil Castle, though just one plant, in the 1970s where Lester-Garland (1903) reported it as abundant. This thistle, with huge blue-green leaves splashed with white, is sometimes called Mary's Thistle, a name which, like the specific epithet *marianum*, comes from its supposed association with the Virgin Mary. In the past the plant was thought to help nursing mothers and the white patches are supposed to be splashes of the Virgin Mary's milk as she fed the infant Jesus. An illustration by Pandora Sellars is opposite page 150.

Map overleaf

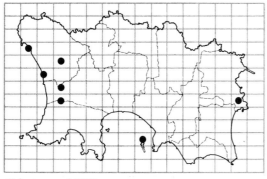

G last record 1977.

Serratula tinctoria L.   Saw-wort
Frequent along the north coast cliffs.

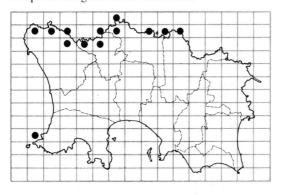

Mantisalca salmantica (L.) Briq. & Cav.
A Knapweed
Considerable confusion has arisen as to which plants Piquet sent to J. G. Baker in 1855. In the *Phytologist* (1858) Baker claimed that *Centaurea clusii* (now named as above) 'has occurred in Jersey only in small quantity and has not been seen since 1855'. Babington made an undated note in his copy of his Flora: '? *Cent. salmantica* St Ouen's Bay. Mr Piquet. Much rarer than *C. paniculata*, both in a lucerne field.' There is no local knowledge of this species in the island and Piquet does not mention it. See *Centaurea paniculata* and *C. leucophaea*.

Centaurea scabiosa L.   Greater Knapweed
Records of this are confused. Lester-Garland (1903) saw a specimen collected by Piquet in 1868 on Les Quennevais. This specimen has not been traced but one collected by Piquet in 1851 in St Ouen's Bay is in Hb Oxford. Lester-Garland also claimed to have seen it himself at the north end of St Ouen's Bay, but Attenborough, in the 1927 Société botanical report, claimed to have found '*C. pratensis* Thuill.' there, and

stated that 'The Centaurea growing in the north of St Ouen's Bay has been named *C. scabiosa*. It has now been determined as this species . . .' i.e. *C. pratensis*. The latest claim is by K. E. Bull by the railway track to La Corbière in 1971.
G ? A occasional.

C. paniculata L.   Jersey Star Thistle
Subsp. *paniculata* This was another of the plants named by J. G. Baker in 1858 from specimens sent to him by Piquet. See *Mantisalca* above. In the same year G. Henslow wrote in the *Phytologist* that '*C. paniculata* (?)' grew in the west of Jersey though sparingly. In 1872 Piquet added it to his 1851 list and stated that it was abundant on a hillside north of St Ouen's Pond. It was still present in small quantity in 1981 but could not be found in 1983.

C. leucophaea Jord.   A Knapweed
Another of the plants said by Baker to have been sent to him from Jersey by Piquet. See *Mantisalca* above. This is presumably why it was entered in Hooker's *Student's Flora* last century. There is no local knowledge of the species.

C. calcitrapa L.   Star Thistle
Babington (1839) saw Star Thistle along St Aubin's Bay near St Peter's Marsh. This would be near the second Martello Tower or the windmill from where Piquet reported it in 1851. The last specimen from that region seems to be in 1874 when Piquet gave one to Melvill. A note by Piquet on a 1902 French specimen in the Société's herbarium states that it was 'formerly abundant near the second Tower, St Aubin's Bay but now extinct'. In 1889 P. Vénet collected a specimen from St Ouen's Bay (Louis-Arsène's herbarium).
G 1890s only.

C. aspera L.   Rough Star Thistle
Subsp. *aspera* Abundant over much of St Ouen's Bay. In 1839 Babington wrote 'Not a native of Jersey though said by Mr Dickson to have been sent to him from that island'. A specimen gathered in Jersey in 1854 and now in the Kew herbarium has 'There is just one plant of it in the island.' written on the sheet beside it. Whether this was true or not, by the 1890s it was abundant in the north of St Ouen's Bay. Plants have occasionally been found on light soil elsewhere over the years, but only in St Ouen's Bay is it established.

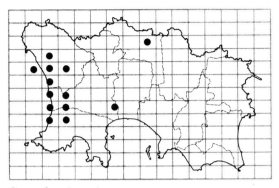

G rare ? extinct; A rare.

C. solstitialis L.   Yellow Star Thistle

Subsp. *solstitialis* A rare casual recorded at long intervals from Babington's time (1839) onwards, always on light soil near the coast. It was last seen in a dry field between Bel Royal and Beaumont by N. Le Brocq in the late 1930s.
G last record 1973; S 1959.

C. diluta Aiton   Lesser Star Thistle

A bird-food casual first found in 1957 above the sea wall between Le Hocq and Green Island and rarely in the 1960s on rubbish dumps.
G casual.

C. jacea L.   Brown Knapweed

Collected at Don Bridge last century by Piquet; in Vallée des Vaux in the 1880s by Dr M. M. Bull, confirmed W. B. Turrill, and near Don Bridge in 1929 and Noirmont in 1949 by E. M. Marsden-Jones and W. B. Turrill.
G 1927.

C. x drucei C. E. Britten   A hybrid Knapweed
C. jacea x C. nigra

At least a dozen records from widely separated places: north end of St Ouen's Bay, Don Bridge, Noirmont, Plémont and Almorah Cemetery, from 1842 to 1960, most confirmed by Marsden-Jones and Turrill who did considerable research work on knapweeds in Jersey. Their Ray Society book *British Knapweeds* (1954) should be consulted. In the Don Bridge area in 1929, they found a population of *C. nigra, C. jacea* and their hybrid but when they revisited Don Bridge in July 1949 'not a single *Centaurea* plant could be found in the neighbourhood. The railway had been replaced by a path and the station had disappeared. With these changes the knapweed population had been exterminated'. Perhaps 1949 was a 'bad year' for knapweeds because the 1960 record of the hybrid (confirmed Turrill) was found near Don Bridge. A few knapweeds still sur-

vive in the fields nearby in spite of housing estates and shopping centres.
G two ? records.

C. debeauxii Gren. & Godron   Slender Knapweed

Subsp. *thuillieri* Dostál (*C. pratensis* Thuill.) Attenborough claimed to have seen this in the north end of St Ouen's Bay in 1927. See *C. scabiosa*.
Subsp. *nemoralis* (Jord) Dostál   If the plants called *C. nemoralis* Jord. in the past are separable from *C. nigra* L. then presumably they belong here. The only claim for this in Jersey is by Druce (1920) who stated that Piquet had collected it at St Saviour.
G ?; A 1958; S 1958; and G, A and S hybrids with C. jacea det. Turrill.

C. nigra L.   Common Knapweed
d'la **bourdonniéthe**

Local. Most knapweeds in Jersey belong here. Lester-Garland (1903) gave only this species and said of the knapweeds 'The forms seem inextricable at present . . . and I . . . call them all *C. nigra* for safety'. Members of the Société's Botanical Section did the same and the following map must be read with this in mind.

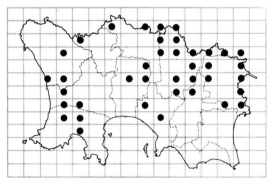

G frequent; A frequent; S common.

C. cyanus L.   Cornflower
des **bliuettes**

Cornflowers were frequent in cornfields last century but corn is seldom grown now, and impurities in seed corn are much reduced, with the result that Cornflowers are decidedly rare. In 1962 they appeared in a field and on a bank where grass had been sown, and similarly in 1968. One plant grew on disturbed ground near Les Quennevais playing fields in 1983.
G rare; A rare escape.

Cichorium intybus L.   Chicory
d'la **chicorée sauvage**

Only occasionally found, but persistent and in quantity when established. Piquet recorded it in 1851 on Gorey Common and it is still in the region. A. J. Binet recorded it from north-east of St Ouen's Pond in 1880, N. Le Brocq from the same place in the late 1930s and it is still on hedgebanks at the foot of Mont Matthieu. Whether or not it was in Jersey before 1834 is unknown. The first *Report* (1834) of the Jersey Agricultural & Horticultural Society stated of Chicory: 'Its culture has been introduced by Colonel Le Couteur who has a *vergée* of it on trial'. By the second *Report* (1835) it had been '. . . found upon trial to be of great value in the present dry season'. Alas, the fourth *Report* (1837) stated: 'The Chicory "Cichorium intybus" which the visiting Committee also noticed was found to be highly productive, but of so laxative a nature, that Cattle lost all flesh if given to them in too large quantities, besides another inconvenience, that of imparting a bitter flavour to milk, these disadvantages led to the abandonment of its culture.'

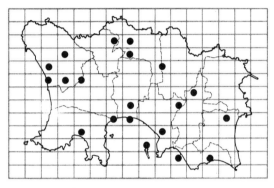

G occasional; A rare; S rare; H 1947.

Arnoseris minima (L.) Schweigg. & Koerte
(*A. pusilla*)   **Lamb's Succory**
Piquet included this in his 1851 list, stating that a Mr Prentice had found it at Grouville. In 1896 he wrote, 'Gravelly places, Grouville, rare'. Lester-Garland (1903) rejected the record and it is still unconfirmed.

Hypochaeris maculata L.   **Spotted Cat's-ear**
Spotted Cat's-ear, a rare plant in England, grows in good quantity between Grosnez and Plémont. Dr J. Frazer collected a specimen in 1876 and it seems to have gone unnoticed until then, though this is not surprising, for it was only noted in England about fifty years earlier. T. C. E. Wells, whose paper on *Hypochaeris maculata* in the *Journal of Ecology* (1976) should be consulted, estimated that in 1972 there were 3,000–5,000 plants at Grosnez (*in litt.*). The species occurs only here and there in western Europe. Wells points out that this discontinuous distribution was interpreted by workers in the 1950s, as that of a relict species which survived during late Glacial times in open areas, such as cliffs, screes and moraines where competition would have been low.

Anyone at Grosnez, even today, in the teeth of a north-west, winter gale will agree that competition was likely to be low. In 1978 almost every plant flowered, which is unusual, but few set seed, snails and rabbits taking a heavy toll. The species is perennial with tap roots which go deep down between cracks in the rocks. Wells suggests (pers. comm.) that from their size, some of the plants might be centuries old.

H. glabra L.   **Smooth Cat's-ear**
Common on the dunes and cliffs of the south-west but easily overlooked. The flower opens only slightly and only does that on sunny (or warm?) days.

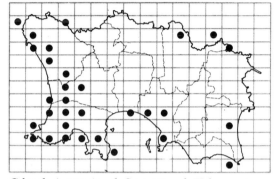

G local; A occasional; S occasional; H frequent.

H. radicata L.   **Cat's-ear**
Common, often abundant, on hedgebanks, road-sides, fields and on the dunes.

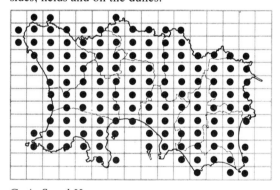

G, A, S and H common.

Leontodon autumnalis L.   **Autumn Hawkbit**
Subsp. *autumnalis* Frequent in fields, on hedge-banks and roadsides. It may be under-recorded because of some members' hesitation in identifying these small dandelion-like species.

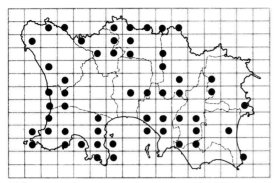

G frequent; A common; S common; H 1890.

L. hispidus L.   **Rough Hawkbit**

Babington (1839), Piquet (1896) and other later botanists claimed to have found *L. hispidus* but as yet not a single specimen has been produced to support any Jersey or Guernsey record. Lester-Garland (1903) stated: 'I have searched for it in vain and suspect some confusion with *L. hirtus*', by which he meant the following species. Druce echoed his words in 1907 and the species has not yet been found.
G errors; A last ?record 1900; S rare; H errors.

L. taraxacoides (Vill.) Mérat   **Lesser Hawkbit**

Subsp. *taraxacoides (L. hirtus)* Frequent in dry grassland and on the dunes but it may be under-recorded on the map. See *L. autumnalis.*

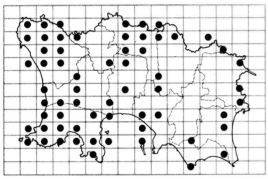

G frequent; A frequent; S common; H frequent.

Picris echioides L.   **Bristly Oxtongue**

Local. All records until after the Occupation (1940–45) were from the south-east. Most still are, but the rubbish dumps of the 1950s and 1960s provided a new habitat on which plants sometimes appeared in abundance. Almost every 'dot' on the distribution map, except those in the south-east, was the site of a dump. In 1982 these dumps are consolidated and covered over, but Bristly Oxtongue remains in the areas.

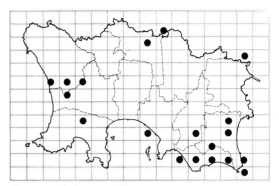

G scarce; A frequent; S rare.

P. hieracioides L.   **Hawkweed Oxtongue**

Subsp. *hieracioides* Local on dry banks and waysides.

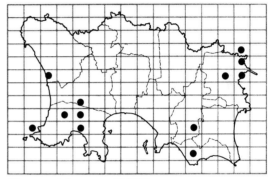

G error; A frequent; H 1899.

Tragopogon porrifolius L.   **Salsify**

Subsp. *porrifolius* Most records are fleeting, but it was reported on the ramparts of Fort Regent in 1851 by Piquet and it was still there up to at least 1926, besides being in other places round about, including La Collette where it still grows. It would originally be an escape from cultivation.

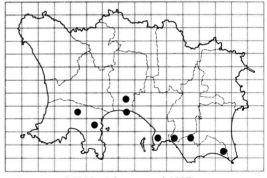

G last record 1958; A last record 1907.

T. pratensis L.   **Goat's-beard**

Babington (1839) gave Saunders' record from fields near St Saviour's Church but Lester-Garland (1903) rejected it and there has been no confirmation.
A rare; S ?

Sonchus asper (L.) Hill   **Prickly Sow-thistle**
                                    du **laiteron**

Common. The subspp. have not been investigated.

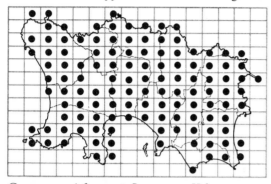

G common; A frequent; S common; H frequent.

S. asper x **S. oleraceus**   **A hybrid Sow-thistle**

Druce identified a plant he found at Rozel in 1923 as this hybrid in error. Stace (1975) determined it as *S. oleraceus.*

S. oleraceus L.   **Smooth Sow-thistle**
                                      du **laiteron**

Common.

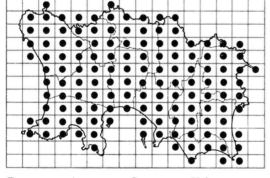

G common; A common; S common; H frequent.

S. arvensis L.   **Perennial Sow-thistle**
                                      du **laiteron**

Subsp. *arvensis* Widespread in fields but it seems to have decreased recently, perhaps through the use of herbicides. It also occurs locally on the cliffs.

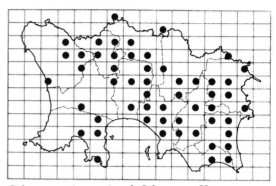

G frequent; A occasional; S frequent; H rare.

Lactuca tatarica (L.) C. A. Meyer
                    Russian Blue Sow-thistle
G 1981/2.

L. serriola L.   **Prickly Lettuce**
G rare.

L. virosa L.   **Great Lettuce**

Lester-Garland (1903) rejected Saunders' record given by Babington (1839) and there has been no confirmation.
G ?

Taraxacum species   **Dandelion**
                                    des **pîssenliets**

Common. Most dandelions are apomictic, i.e. usually set seed without fertilisation, as do brambles, and as with brambles *q.v.* vast numbers of microspecies exist.

The following specimens were collected by members of the Botany Section of the Société Jersiaise and were determined by Dr A. J. Richards unless otherwise stated. Increasing knowledge of dandelions has caused some of the earlier determinations given in the Société's botanical reports to be revised and others omitted. The latest information up to 1983 is given below. Dr A. J. Richards and C. C. Haworth have given considerable help with this difficult Genus.

Section **Spectabilia** Dahlst.   **Red-veined Dandelions**

T. adamii Claire   One of the commoner dandelions, being recorded from fourteen widely distributed places, none of them coastal, 1969–81.

T. britannicum Dahlst.   St Ouen's Pond, 1910, J. W. White and C. E. Salmon, and 1958; Quetivel Mill, 1981.

T. maculosum A. J. Richards   Foot of road wall, St Peter's House, St Peter, 1969 (originally recorded as *T. maculigerum*).

T. naevosum Dahlst. St Martin, 1851, Piquet, det. Dahlst. (B.E.C. *Report* 1931) but the identification is queried by Richards. This dandelion of northern Scotland and Scandinavia is highly unlikely to occur in Jersey.

T. nordstedtii Dahlst. East side of St Ouen's Pond, 1958, 1968.

T. spectabile Dahlst. Jersey (Hb Oxford).

Section **Palustria** Dahlst.   **Marsh Dandelions**
T. sarniense A. J. Richards St Ouen's Pond, 1926, Burdo (originally recorded as *T. austrinum*), and Richards considers '*T. palustre*' St Ouen's Pond, 1949, C. E. Raven, probably belongs here. An earlier specimen labelled *T. palustre* from St Ouen's Pond, 10 April 1914, leg. 'C.N.S.' Nicholson (Hb Brit. Mus.) is also probably this.

Section **Obliqua** Dahlst.   **Dune Dandelions**
T. platyglossum Raunk. Les Quennevais, 1890, leg. J. W. White (Hb Bristol).

Section **Erythrosperma** Dahlst.   **Lesser Dandelions**
T. brachyglossum (Dahlst.) Dahlst. Grosnez Castle, 1925, Burdo; field north-west of St Ouen's Pond and old sandpits north of St Ouen's Pond, 1969; St Andrew's Park at First Tower and dry place Mont Millais Nurseries, 1970.

T. commixtum G. Hagl. Crabière Cottage, La Route des Mielles, 1970.

T. fulvum Raunk. Gravel path at Crabière Cottage, La Route des Mielles, 1958, det. J. L. Van Soest.

T. glauciniforme Dahlst. Crabière Cottage, La Route des Mielles, 1958, det. J. L. Van Soest, and 1970.

T. lacistophyllum (Dahlst.) Raunk. Les Quennevais, 1871, H. Trimen and sandy ground on Ouaisné Common, 1958, both det. J. L. Van Soest; St Ouen and St Helier, 1922, and Pontac, 1924, all Druce, det. Dahlst.; Rozel Fort, 1964, det. Dr A. Melderis.

T. oxoniense Dahlst. Rozel Fort, 1964, det. Dr A. Melderis; field north-west of St Ouen's Pond, 1969; Les Quennevais, 1969 and 1970; sand pit, St Ouen, 1971; Le Chemin du Moulin, St Ouen, 1981.

T. retzii Van Soest Meadow behind Rock View, Pontac, 1970; foot of wall on Le Chemin du Moulin, St Ouen, 1981.

T. rubicundum (Dahlst.) Dahlst. Les Quennevais, '7.4.35' (Hb Brit. Mus.) det. G. Hagland; St Ouen, 1885, A. Ley; Crabbé Rifle Range, 1969.

Section **Vulgaria** Dahlst.   **Common Dandelions**
T. alatum Lindb. f. Roadside at foot of Mont Fallu, 1970.

T. angustisquameum Dahlst. ex Lindb. f. Pontac, 1981.

T. ancistrolobum Dahlst. Les Tours Chapel, 1969.

T. aurosulum Lindb. f. Foot of road wall, Le Rât Cottage, St Lawrence, 1969.

T. bracteatum Dahlst. Field above German reservoir at St Catherine, 1970.

T. cophocentrum Dahlst. Mont Matthieu, St Ouen, and La Hougue Bie, 1970.

T. copidophyllum Dahlst. Waterworks Valley, 1925, Burdo.

T. croceiflorum Dahlst. Crabière Cottage, La Route des Mielles, 1970.

T. dalstedtii Lindb. f. St Peter La Rocque Lane, 1969; Mont du Vallet, L'Étacq, 1970.

T. ekmanii Dahlst. St John, valley south-west of Les Potirons in St Mary and La Route de Manoir in St Ouen, 1970.

T. expallidiforme Dahlst. Les Routeurs, St Peter, 1970.

T. fasciatum Dahlst. Wet field on east side of La Grande Route de Rozel, 1970.

T. fulgidum Hagl. Fauvic, 1969, det. C. C. Haworth.

T. hamatiforme Dahlst. Roadside at foot of Waterworks Valley and Les Vagues, Pontac, 1970; path to Devil's Hole, St Mary, 1971.

T. hamatum Raunk. Roadside near Les Augerez, St Peter, and south of Bel Air, St Mary, 1969; St John, La Grande Route de St Ouen and Waterworks Valley, 1970.

T. oblongatum Dahlst. La Grande Route de St Clement, Ville à l'Évêque at Trinity, foot of road wall in St Peter's Valley and garden at Ozarda, St John, 1970; near La Saline Slip and near the old windmill, St Ouen, 1981 (originally recorded as *T. per-hamatum*).

T. ostenfeldii Raunk. Maison St Louis (Hotel de France), 1881, Père Vaniot (originally recorded as *T. duplidens*).

T. pallescens Dahlst. St Ouen, 1920, Druce.

T. pannucium Dahlst. Field south of Les Augrès Manor, 1970.

T. pseudohamatum Dahlst. Mont Gras d'Eau, St Brelade, 1958.

T. quadrans H. Øllg. Wet field opposite Le Rât Cottage, St Lawrence, 1969; the National Trust for Jersey's property La Grand Côtil de Bouley Bay and near La Saline Slip, St Ouen, 1981 (originally recorded as *T. latisectum*).

T. raunkiaeri Wiinst. Fauvic and field at St Peter, 1969; La Bachauderie, 1970 (originally recorded as *T. duplidentifrons*).

T. scotiniforme Dahlst. ex G. Hagl. Crabière

Cottage, La Route des Mielles, 1970 (originally recorded as *T. melanthoides*).

T. tenebricans (Dahlst.) Dahlst.   Nr Trinity Church, valley south of Les Augrès Manor and by side of La Grande Route de St Ouen near the Manor, 1970.

T. xanthostigma Lindb. f.   St Brelade, 1958.
G Taraxacum species c. 40; A, S and H occurs but species not yet studied in detail.

Chondrilla juncea L.   **Chondrilla**
Piquet wrote in his copy of Babington's Flora that he had seen a few plants near the Square Tower, St Ouen's Bay, near the Pond, and a specimen he collected in St Ouen's Bay in 1905 is in Hb Oxford.

Lapsana communis L.   **Nipplewort**
Subsp. *communis*   Common on roadsides and waste places.

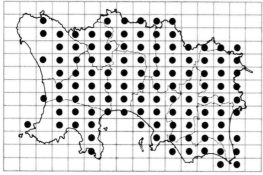

G frequent; A rare; S occasional; H rare.

Crepis biennis L.   **Rough Hawk's-beard**
Babington (1839) recorded this from Fort Regent and other places but later he crossed out the species name and substituted that of Beaked Hawk's-beard. Likewise Piquet had doubts about his 1851 record and the species is not in his 1896 list. Lester-Garland (1903) gives 'Fort Regent, Gorey and Anne Port. Mr J. W. White. St Brelade's Bay'. Unless a specimen can be found to confirm these records, the species should be deleted from the Jersey list. All Guernsey specimens purporting to be this were in error, (McClintock, 1975).

C. foetida L.   **Stinking Hawk's-beard**
One record: waste ground, St Helier, 1910, Piquet (Hb Société Jersiaise).

C. capillaris (L.) Wallr.   **Smooth Hawk's-beard**
(*C. virens*)
Very common. Both var. *capillaris* and var. *agrestis* (Waldst. & Kit.) Dalla Torre & Sarnth. occur, the former usually near the coast and the latter more inland but A. J. Wilmott noted them in 1933 growing

three inches apart near Le Câtel, Rozel.

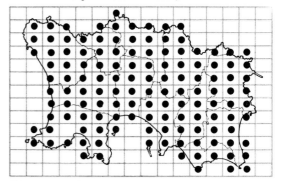

G common; A common; S common; H frequent.

C. vesicaria L.   **Beaked Hawk's-beard**
Subsp. *haenseleri* (Boiss. ex DC.) P. D. Sell (*C. taraxacifolia*)   Common in the past, but now no more than locally frequent.

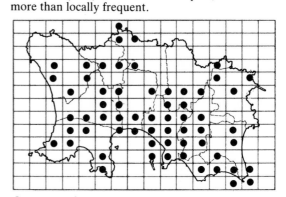

G occasional; A frequent; S occasional.

C. setosa Haller fil.   **Bristly Hawk's-beard**
Two records: St Saviour, Jersey, 1858, det. E. Drabble (Hb Brit. Mus.); 'In a crop, St Helier, T. B. Blow', (1876), Babington's notes in his own copy of his Flora.

Hieracium sublepistoides (Zahn) Druce
                                        A Hawkweed
G three localities.

H. vulgatum Fr.   **A Hawkweed**
Mrs E. M. Towers found a group of plants on the wall of Mont à l'Abbé Cemetery, near the Tower Road gate in 1962 (det. C. P. Andrews) and the plants are still there.

H. strumosum (W. R. Linton) A. Ley   **A Hawkweed**
Miss E. H. du Feu found a hawkweed growing on the wall of St John's Cemetery in 1958. A piece was taken and cultivated, and a specimen from the cultivated plant was determined as this species by P. D. Sell and

Dr C. West. The plant had gone from the wall by 1959.

H. umbellatum L. Umbellate Hawkweed

Umbellate Hawkweeds are locally common on the cliffs and have been recorded from Queen's Valley. Broad-leaved plants, sometimes separated as subsp. *bichlorophyllum* (Druce & Zahn) Sell & West, are the more usual. The narrow-leaved plants are seldom more than 30cm high, as in Guernsey.

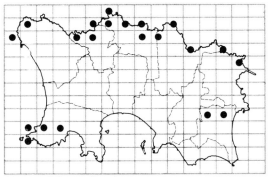

G, A and S occasional.

H. rigidum Hartm. A Hawkweed

Recorded by Lester-Garland (1903) from Water-works Valley.

H. laevigatum Willd. Koch A Hawkweed

Recorded by Babington (1839) but the specimen belongs to the *H. umbellatum* group, Dr C. West *in litt.*

Pilosella officinarum C. H. & F. W. Schultz
(Hieracium pilosella) Mouse-ear Hawkweed

Widespread but much less common than the next species. The subspecies have not been separated. The nomenclature of Sell and West in Stace (1975) has been followed and *Pilosella* placed in a separate genus from *Hieracium*.

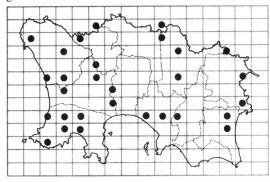

G occasional; A frequent; S occasional; H 1958.

P. officinarum x P. peleterana
A hybrid Mouse-ear Hawkweed
(H. pilosella x H. peleteranum)

P. D. Sell & Dr C. West in Stace (1975) give three records: near Jubilee Hill, 1944, A. J. Wilmott, det. H. W. Pugsley; Plémont and Les Quennevais, 1958, Dr C. West. They also state that the *P. peleterana* parent is subsp. *tenuiscapa* and the *P. officinarum* parent is probably subsp. *concinnata* (F. J. Hanbury) Sell & West in the Wilmott specimen, but subsp. *officinarum* in those of West.
G two records.

P. peleterana (Mérat) C.H. & F. W. Schultz
Shaggy Mouse-ear Hawkweed
(Hieracium peleteranum)

This is the common Mouse-ear Hawkweed of Jersey and much more likely to be seen than the previous species. The subspecies have not been separated but a plant from St John was determined as subsp. *tenuiscapa* (Pugsl.) Sell & West by Dr C. West (Hb Société Jersiaise) and see the above hybrid.

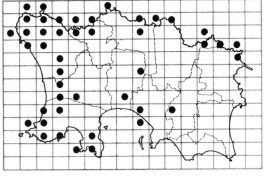

G locally common; A occasional; S occasional; H scarce.

P. aurantiaca (L.) C. H. & F. W. Schultz
(Hieracium aurantiacum) Fox and Cubs

Subsp. *carpathicola* (Naegeli & Peter) Sell & West The Rev. J. W. J. Scott, in his diary, tells of the finding of a colony of Fox and Cubs at the foot of the wall of Les Lauriers, St Peter in 1943. He writes that Attenborough, who identified it for him, said it was a rare alien he had not seen since 1906. It was found, as a garden escape or relic, in several places during the 1960s but it has decreased in the last few years.

Map overleaf

173

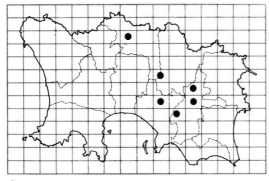

G rare.

ANGIOSPERMAE – MONOCOTYLEDONES
ALISMATACEAE

Sagittaria latifolia Willd. **American Duck-potato**

An introduced American water plant found in abundance in 1961 by J. C. Fluck in an overgrown pool south of Villa Villetri in Vallée des Vaux. Some years later the pool was cleared but the Duck-potato survived and was still present in 1983, R. W. S. Knightbridge.

Baldellia ranunculoides (L.) Parl.
(Alisma ranunculoides) **Lesser Water-plantain**

Rare last century and not seen recently. At various times Lesser Water-plantain has been recorded from St Peter's Marsh, St Ouen's Pond, La Moye Common, 'pond near Noirmont' and the pond on Ouaisné Common. The only records since Lester-Garland's *Flora of Jersey* (1903) are from St Ouen's Pond where specimens were gathered in the mid-1920s and where N. Le Brocq saw it in the late 1930s.
G rare; S 1909.

Alisma plantago-aquatica L. **Water-plantain**
(A. plantago)
Frequent in wet places.

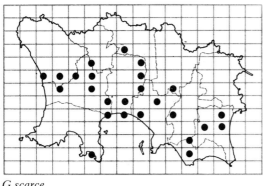

G scarce.

HYDROCHARITACEAE

Hydrocharis morsus-ranae L. **Frogbit**

On 23 September 1911 W. P. J. Le Brocq wrote to the Evening Post giving a list of plants which he had seen in Jersey during the summer and added: 'Though never recorded before, the first plant of this list, viz., Hydrocharis Morsus-ranae, was found in Jersey by Mrs Allen Powles, of Cambridge, who informed me of her discovery, but could not remember its station – which was probably mine of this year, namely St Brelade's. This plant usually floats and cruises from one side of a pond to the other, according to the direction of the wind, but this exceptionally dry summer has caused it to forsake its habits and it is now anchored by rootlets in the peaty bottom of the pond and obtainable dry-footed'. Piquet and Attenborough found it in July 1911 in the same pool, the one on Ouaisné Common, where it was not seen again until the mid-1920s when Louis-Arsène and Burdo collected specimens. Burdo said it was in quantity when he saw it in 1925. Its origin in Jersey is unknown.
G two centuries ago.

Elodea canadensis Michx **Canadian Waterweed**

Collected by Piquet from Town Mills Pond in 1872 but no longer there and not entered in his 1896 list. Piquet also collected a specimen from the small quarry pond on Noirmont in July 1898, and it was from there that Lester-Garland (1903) recorded it, adding 'where Mr Piquet planted it many years ago.' It is not now known wild in Jersey, but it grows in several ornamental private pools so may have the opportunity to colonise wild ones again in the future.
G 1958.

E. nuttallii (Planchon) St John **Nuttall's Waterweed**

Abundant in a pool at Oaklands, St Peter, where Deputy M. Bonn says it was first noticed in 1980. The pool is at the head of one of the streams feeding Val de la Mare Reservoir and though a natural pool originally, it has recently been increased in size, and some water-garden plants were introduced in 1978. The *Elodea* presumably came in with them. A serious attempt was made to clear the pool in 1981 but the *Elodea* was back in quantity in 1982 and 1983.

Lagarosiphon major (Ridley) Moss
  Curly Water-thyme

Abundant in the pools in Mont Mado quarries from at least 1956, and probably from much earlier, to when they were filled with rubbish in the 1960s. Curly Water-thyme, a South African species, is used by aquarists as an oxygenator of water and when thrown away, or deliberately planted, in wild pools it may survive. It was in a pond at Portelet and in the North Canal, St Ouen's Pond in 1956, in a pool on the cliffs

near La Corbière in 1966 (Miss R. Kilby) and abundant in a small pool in the sandpits north of St Ouen's Pond in 1982. It has since disappeared from all except the last locality where it remains in spite of attempts to eradicate it but may well appear for a time in other pools again depending on the vagaries of fashion in water-gardens and fishponds.
G rare; A 1956–63.

JUNCAGINACEAE
Triglochin maritima L.   **Sea Arrowgrass**
Rare where salt and fresh water meet. It was recorded last century from Samarès but Lester-Garland (1903) thought it had become extinct. Attenborough stated in the Société botanical report for 1917 that it was in good quantity in a salt swamp at the base of the cliffs at Le Sauchet and very sparingly at La Saline and in St Catherine's Bay. It is still at Le Sauchet and along the foot of the cliffs in St John. In 1960 Mrs M. L. Long found it by the side of the stream through Beaumont Marsh near the sea sluice, and it is still there in quantity.
G rare.

T. palustris L.   **Marsh Arrowgrass**
Rare and not seen recently. Piquet recorded it from Samarès Miles and St Ouen's Pond in 1851. It remained at Samarès until at least 1958, and after an absence of many years, it reappeared at St Ouen's Pond in abundance on the sides of the North Canal dug by the Germans during the Occupation (1940–45). Attenborough recorded it from there in 1947 and it remained until about the late 1950s. He also recorded it from Le Marais, St Ouen, in 1915.
G rare; A rare.

POTAMOGETONACEAE
Potamogeton natans L.   **Broad-leaved Pondweed**
Known in the deep quarry pool at La Rosière, near La Corbière, from well before the war (Attenborough, pers. comm.) until the quarry was used as part of the desalination plant. A specimen collected from the quarry by J. C. Fluck in 1962 is in the Société's herbarium. Previously it had been recorded from a number of places but see J. E. Dandy's comments under *P. polygonifolius*.
G rare; A locally abundant.

P. polygonifolius Pourret   **Bog Pondweed**
                                               du **vrai d'vivi**
Probably the commonest pondweed in Jersey. J. E. Dandy helped considerably with the naming of pondweeds. In 1962 he stated (*in litt.*): 'I have seen specimens of *P. polygonifolius* dated 1871, 1876, 1877, 1881, 1897, 1898, 1900, 1906, 1907, 1926, 1960 and 1961. Some of these were named *P. polygonifolius* but others were variously named *P. coloratus*,

P. plantagineus, P. natans, P. fluitans, P. alpinus and *P. alpinus* x *polygonifolius* (*P. spathulatus*)! . . . St Ouen's Pond seems to be one of those unusual localities where *P. polygonifolius* (calcifuge) and *P. coloratus* (calcicole) have occurred together'. Potamogetons are extremely difficult to name with certainty. J. E. Dandy specialised in them so, in view of his comments, no old record is given unless confirmed by him. Since Dandy's death A. C. Jermy has identified a pondweed new to Jersey.
G not seen since 1901.

P. coloratus Hornem.   **Fen Pondweed**
In 1962 Dandy stated (*in litt.*): 'Of all the specimens I have seen (from St Ouen's Pond) the only ones which I have been able to accept as *P. coloratus* were collected in 1858 and 1875 (also one from St Peter's Valley dated 1851)'. See *P. polygonifolius*.
G six records to the 1890s.

P. alpinus Balbis   **Red Pondweed**
One record. In 1962 Dandy stated (*in litt.*): 'The only specimen of *P. alpinus* seen from Jersey was collected by Druce in 1907, labelled as from St Ouen's Pond'. See *P. polygonifolius*.

P. x spathulatus Schrad. ex Koch & Ziz
                                     A hybrid Pondweed
Recorded by Druce in error from St Ouen's Pond in 1907. Dandy identified the specimen as *P. polygonifolius*.

P. lucens L.   **Shining Pondweed**
G one locality.

P. pusillus L.   **Lesser Pondweed**
Lesser Pondweed, which had not previously been recorded in Jersey, was so abundant in most of St Ouen's Pond in 1982 that it was difficult to row a boat through it. A. C. Jermy named specimens. No flowering plants had been seen since at least 1949 in or on the open water of the Pond.

It appeared again in great quantity in April/May 1983, though not in quite such abundance as in 1982. By June 1983 a good deal of the surface of the Pond was covered with a layer of yellow-green blanket weed growing on the Lesser Pondweed, so that the Pond presented a most unusual sight. During July the blanket weed began to disappear and an inspection of the Pond on 6 August revealed no living Lesser Pondweed. It may be that the great heat of summer 1983 killed it.

A small quantity was recorded in one of the flooded sandpits to the north of the Pond in 1982 and 1983 by Mrs M. L. Long.

P. berchtoldii Fieber   **Small Pondweed**
G one locality; A 1972.

P. trichoides Cham. & Schlecht.   **Hairlike Pondweed**
G rare.

P. compressus L.   **Grass-wrack Pondweed**
Specimens gathered in Samarès 'Manor grounds in 1958, and thought to be this, were determined as *P. crispus*, in a young and sterile state, by Dandy 1962.

P. crispus L.   **Curled Pondweed**
Many specimens have been confirmed by Dandy and, after *P. polygonifolius*, Curled Pondweed is the commonest pondweed. Records have come at various times from the Grève d'Azette and Samarès region, Grouville Marsh and pools at St Catherine, Avranche Manor and Noirmont and in St Peter's Valley and the Howard David Park. Surprisingly there are no records from St Ouen's Pond.
G occasional.

P. pectinatus L.   **Fennel Pondweed**
Three specimens, all from St Ouen's Pond: 1838, Babington; 1851, Piquet; 1907, Druce, and all determined by Dandy.
G rare.

RUPPIACEAE

Ruppia maritima L.   **Beaked Tasselweed**
Saunders' record given by Babington (1839) was rejected by Lester-Garland and has not been confirmed.
G 1894.

R. cirrhosa (Pet.) Grande   **Spiral Tasselweed**
G rare.

ZOSTERACEAE

Zostera marina L.   **Eelgrass**
d'la plîse

Eelgrass was common until about 1930 when a disease which killed most of the eelgrass in western Europe reached Jersey and almost wiped out the eelgrass beds. Its recovery has been slow but now, some fifty years later, it is growing at extreme low tide, and below, in many of the island's bays. To see it, follow the tide down to low water off, say, Les Laveurs Slip in St Ouen's Bay. Though an ormering tide is preferable, it is not essential: a colony of poorly developed plants which never seem to flower, can be found down 'the boot' at L'Étacq on almost any low tide. The long, grass-green, flat ribbons, usually growing on a very fine gravelly substrata or on good sand, are not parts of a seaweed but are flowering plants of salt water. This and the two following eelgrasses are the only flowering plants which live in the sea off Jersey.
G recovering; A rare; S rare; H local.

Z. angustifolia (Hornem.) Reichenb.
      Narrow-leaved Eelgrass
Two records: St Catherine's Bay, 1887, Richards (Hb Piquet in Hb Oxford); St Clement's Bay, 1902, Piquet (Hb Société Jersiaise). Searches in both areas in 1983 failed to find it.
G rare; H rare.

Z. noltii Hornem.   **Dwarf Eelgrass**
Common on the beaches of St Aubin's Bay and Grouville Bay from about half-tide downwards where the sand is slightly muddy.
H rare.

ZANNICHELLIACEAE
Zannichellia palustris L.   **Horned Pondweed**
This grew in brooks in the Samarès region from at least 1851 to 1900 but it has not been seen there since 1900 when Piquet collected a specimen. In 1982 and 1983 it appeared in abundance at St Ouen in two flooded sandpits to the north of St Ouen's Pond and in a pool in the National Trust for Jersey's property opposite Kempt Tower.
G rare.

LILIACEAE
Asphodelus albus Miller   **White Asphodel**
A small group of plants, presumably garden escapes, were growing on a wild grassy bank at the foot of Mont Rossignol in the early 1970s, Mrs M. L. Long, and they were still there until at least 1980.

Hemerocallis fulva (L.) L.   **Day Lily**
A garden plant often thrown out with garden refuse but nowhere naturalised. Large clumps were established in the past, particularly in the 1960s, on various rubbish dumps, but when the dumps disappeared, so did the Day Lilies.
G three localities.

Kniphofia praecox Baker   **Red-hot Poker**
A spring-flowering Red-hot Poker was established for several years in the 1950s near the foot of Mont Matthieu, St Ouen.
H rare.

K. uvaria (L.) Hooker   **Red-hot Poker**
G two records.

Colchicum autumnale L.   **Meadow Saffron**

Reported in quantity along the old railway line east of Don Bridge by J. C. Fluck in 1963. It was probably planted but is of interest because F. Piquet collected a *Colchicum* at St Brelade in 1869.

Tulipa species   **Tulip**

Ereaut collected a tulip for his *Hortus Siccus* in 1847 but how wild it was is unknown. A few persisted into the 1970s on the dunes behind the site of one of the sea-side bungalows at St Ouen. It is assumed that they came from the garden of the bungalow which was destroyed during the German Occupation (1940–45). Tulip flowers were also seen on most rubbish dumps until dumping was controlled.
G 1969.

Lilium candidum L.   **Madonna Lily**

One spike was flowering in 1977 in the National Trust for Jersey's property opposite Kempt Tower, St Ouen. The plant had obviously been there for many years and it presumably came in with garden refuse before the Trust owned the property. It was last seen flowering in 1980.
G 1958.

L. pyrenaicum Gouan   **Pyrenean Lily**

In the Société's botanical report for 1916 Attenborough stated that this was: 'In a hedge at St Peter's not near any garden, where it has been known for many years'. In 1957 Mrs J. Russell found it under willow bushes in an old sandpit north of St Ouen's Pond. The bulbs were removed in the 1970s when the sandpits were about to be filled. The third record was in 1977 when Mrs K. Le Sueur found at least a dozen flowering spikes by the side of a track near Crabbé. The plants were spread over an area of rough grass about 200cm by 100cm and must have been there some considerable time.

Ornithogalum umbellatum L.   **Star-of-Bethlehem**
                                          d's **étailes dé Bethléem**

Star-of-Bethlehem was first recorded by La Gasca (1834), and Piquet and Attenborough both told of finding single plants. Attenborough further stated in the Société's botanical report for 1917 that the species had the habit of appearing in a sporadic fashion. It was recorded occasionally during the survey but never in quantity.

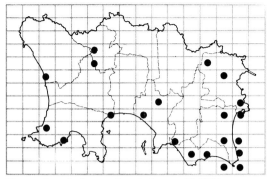

G occasional; A occasional; S rare; H 1937.

O. nutans L.   **Drooping Star-of-Bethlehem**

Three records: 'An spontaneum', 1834, La Gasca; hedgebank, Rozel, 1923, T. J. Foggitt, and Jersey, 1930, R. Meinertzhagen (Hb Brit. Mus.); St Catherine's Point on the grass verge under the cliff, 1964, Miss M. E. Barnsdale.

Scilla verna Hudson   **Spring Squill**

No proven records of this species in the Channel Islands exist. Confusion arises between it and *Romulea* or *Scilla autumnalis*.

S. peruviana L.   **Cuban Lily**

Cuban Lily, a south European species, has survived, untended, where planted along the railway bank near Pontac for at least sixty years.
A 1958.

S. autumnalis L.   **Autumn Squill**

Locally common, sometimes abundant, in short turf usually near the coast. Though called Autumn Squill, the first flowers often appear in high summer. The flowers, usually a pale pinkish blue, are rarely white.

Jersey's race is the same genetically as that in Alderney; Guernsey's and Sark's are the same but different from Jersey's.

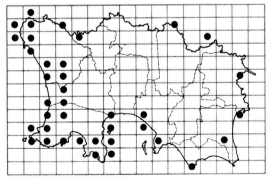

G locally common; A locally common; S common; H frequent.

Hyacinthoides non-scripta (L.) Chouard ex Rothm.
(Scilla festalis) **Bluebell**
des **clioches dé Carême**

Locally common, particularly on the cliffs. Bracken provides the necessary shade in summer.

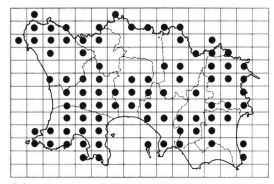

G frequent; A locally frequent; S abundant; H locally common.

H. hispanica (Miller) Rothm. **Spanish Bluebell**

A widespread garden escape though nowhere plentiful. Over a large part of Alderney this bluebell from Spain is now commoner than the native Bluebell so a map of its known distribution here is given. Unfortunately it has probably been under-recorded, many people considering it too recent an escape in many cases to warrant recording. The map may also contain records of hybrids which have gone unrecognised.

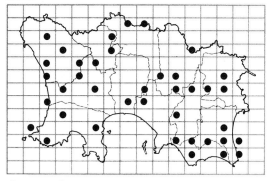

G rare; A frequent; S rare; H ?

Muscari comosum (L.) Miller **Tasselled Hyacinth**

Rare in sandy soil. It was first collected by Ereaut from near the first Martello Tower in St Aubin's Bay in 1847. The habitat there has now gone but plants still occur at the north end of St Ouen's Bay, where Lester-Garland saw it in 1901, and it is still on La Moye golf course where Guiton found it in 1907.

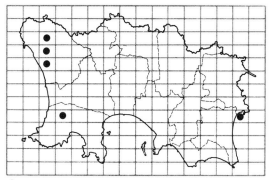

G rare; A rare.

Muscari species **Grape Hyacinth**

Grape Hyacinths of garden origin are widespread but rare, and seldom persist, yet they are frequent garden plants often discarded because they spread too easily through self-sowing. The species are difficult to separate and more than one may be involved.
G ?

Agapanthus praecox Willd. **Agapanthus**

Subsp. *orientalis* (F. M. Leighton) F. M. Leighton
Agapanthus grew for several years on two rubbish dumps in St Ouen's Bay in the 1960s but disappeared when the dumps were covered. It is nowhere naturalised.
G as Jersey.

Allium roseum L. **Rosy Garlic**

A garden escape in small quantity on Portelet Common near the entrance, 1962, Miss P. Donaldson, and still there until at least the late 1970s. Specimens labelled *Allium roseum* were collected by Ariste and Louis-Arsène in 1926 from the Beaumont region.
G scarce; A rare.

A. neapolitanum Cyr. **Neapolitan Garlic**

Ariste wrote on a specimen sheet that this was naturalised on a bank near St Martin though the specimen itself was collected from Highlands College (from the garden?) where he lived in 1926. In 1956 it was found by a field entrance in Val de la Mare, St Ouen and in 1957 a cartload of earth tipped at Grouville Marsh was covered with its flowers in April. It was still rare in the late 1950s but began to spread in the 1960s so that it was then frequent in some areas of light soil. More recently it has decreased and has gone from several of the areas marked on the map.

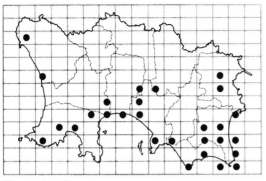

G occasional.

A. subhirsutum L.   A Garlic
A 1962.

A. moly L.   Yellow Garlic
Established in Beaufort Square, Grève d'Azette, for
well over twenty years, J. C. Fluck.

A. triquetrum L.   Three-cornered Leek
                                                d'l'as sauvage
Piquet added Three-cornered Leek to his 1851 list at
some later unknown date, perhaps in June 1858 when
he collected a specimen from St Brelade (Hb
Oxford). He told Attenborough early this century,
that it was rare when he was a young man. By 1903
Lester-Garland thought it 'not uncommon' in the
south, and spreading. Now it occurs over most of the
island except the extreme west and sometimes it lines
roadsides in great profusion. Its flowering stem is
sharply triangular, i.e. three-cornered, not round as
in the majority of bulbous plants.

An illustration by Pandora Sellars is opposite
page 166.

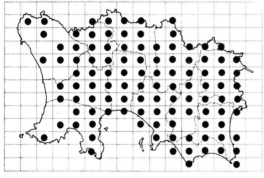

*G common; A locally abundant; S common; H fre-
quent.*

A. ursinum L.   Ramsons
A report by Piquet of Ramsons in a wood at St
Brelade in 1853 was in the *Phytologist* for that year.

He never mentioned it again. Was it perhaps the first
record of *A. triquetrum* which was often called
A. ursinum by visitors during the B.S.B.I. distribution map scheme?
G one record.

A. oleraceum L.   Field Garlic
The only mention of this in Jersey is in a letter from
W. Borrer to Babington in 1851 in which he wrote: 'I
added nothing to the published Flora of the islands
but *Allium oleraceum* which grows with *A. vineale* at
St Brelade's', (Cambridge Botany School library).

A. ampeloprasum L.   Wild Leek
Four records perhaps all from the same site: sands of
St Aubin's Bay, 1878, Piquet and 1883, 1885, A. Ley;
Bel Royal, 1924, F. Robinson. It is strange that this
conspicuous species, which may have been the wild
source of the present cultivated leeks, should have
gone from Jersey when it is still so locally plentiful in
Guernsey and Herm.
G locally common; H locally common.

A. sphaerocephalon L.   Round-headed Leek
                                                  des gênottes
Rare. J. Gay listed it from Les Quennevais in 1832
but no-one else has ever seen it there. The first report
of it from St Aubin's Bay, where it still grows, was by
J. Woods in 1836, and on 25 July 1837 Babington sent
a specimen to Sowerby to be drawn for *English
Botany*. It appeared in a Supplement in 1843, Plate
2813, with the note: 'It appears in great plenty upon
the sandy ground adjoining St Aubin's Bay and varies
from a few inches to nearly three feet in height'. By
the third edition, Vol. IX, 1869, the entry had
changed to, 'Once plentiful, but now becoming
scarce from building being carried on'. In 1889 Binet
wrote in his diary, 'Immediately opposite Bel Royal
on the sandy banks'. Lester-Garland (1903) stated in
his Flora, 'St Aubin's Bay, near Bel Royal, plentiful
but probably doomed'. In 1909 Binet reported it still
there in quantity but in 1919 the diary entry read,
'Have not seen one plant this year'. It was, however,
still present and in the 1927 botanical report of the
Société, Attenborough wrote, 'The existence of
Allium sphaerocephalon is gravely endangered by the
sale of the remaining waste ground at Bel Royal'. He
followed this up in 1933 by writing that it was in
danger of extinction. In spite of these gloomy predic-
tions going back over a hundred years, this Mediterranean species, the Round-headed Leek, which
grows nowhere else in the Channel Islands and only
on St Vincent's Rocks, Bristol, in England, still
survives. It is now dependent on the goodwill of
people living in the area. They are particularly
requested, if they see it coming up on their land, to
give it maximum protection – as it has in England.

The largest colony is on the old railway embankment at the foot of the garden of the house Sea Court at Bel Royal. The previous owner, Mr Belford, was a railway enthusiast and kept the embankment unchanged. His family has done the same. With it, they have incidentally kept one of Jersey's rarest plants.

Four attempts have been made to establish it elsewhere in the island: Druce reported in the *Journal of Botany* for 1913 that Piquet had planted some in St Ouen's Bay; in the following year he stated that E. W. Hunnybun had sown seed on Les Quennevais; Louis-Arsène (pers. comm.) said he had sown seed at Les Hanières, St Ouen; in 1958 when the last building plot at Bel Royal was sold, plants and seed which would have vanished under concrete were taken to a sandy area north of St Ouen's Pond. There has been no trace of the first three plantings or sowings. From the fourth there were a few plants each year until at least 1982 but the outlook is not good, mainly because the dark red spherical flowerheads are attractive and are picked. See *A. vineale*, Crow Garlic, for possible confusion.

A. vineale L.   **Crow Garlic**
d'l'as sauvage

Locally common, sometimes abundant. The normal form is var. *compactum* (Thuill.) Cosson & Germ. but var. *typicum* Aschers. & Graebn. occurs fairly frequently and var. *capsuliferum* Koch has been recorded twice, first by the Rev. W. W. Newbould in 1842 and later by H. C. Watson in 1852. In the 1960s and 1970s, tall plants with large heads of deep red bulbils appeared on land between Bel Royal and Beaumont. From a distance these were often mistaken for Round-headed Leek.

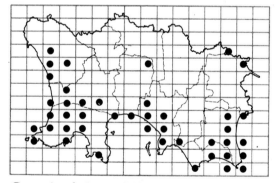

G occasional; A rare; S 1956.

A. cyrilli Ten.   **A Garlic**

Two records of single plants: Mont Mado dump, late 1960s, Mrs M. Pett, and edge of golf course, Grouville, 1982, Mrs M. L. Long, conf. Dr W. T. Stearn. Their origin is unknown.

Nothoscordum inodorum (Aiton) Nicholson
Honey Bells

An alien well-established in the Mont Cambrai and Rue de Haut region from where it was first reported in 1957 by Miss G. Sarre who said she had known it there for some years. It remained more-or-less in the same area in the 1950s and 1960s but since then it has become more widespread. The map gives all records since 1957.

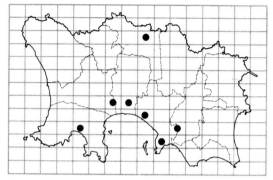

G occasional; S rare; H rare.

Ipheion uniflorum (R. C. Graham) Rafin.
Spring Starflower

Guiton collected a specimen from the golf links, Grouville, in 1921 and Louis-Arsène found it on a sandy area near Pontac in 1926. The first record from the west of the island was in 1956 from the base of a hedge at the foot of Mont Gras d'Eau, St Brelade. It is now widespread round the sandier parts of the south coast but often only as single plants or clumps except in the south-east. A hardy Argentinian and Uruguayan bulbous plant, its attractive blue star-like flowers normally appear early in spring but some years they are so early they appear well before Christmas.

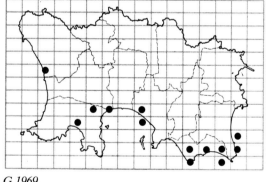

G 1969.

Convallaria majalis L.   **Lily-of-the-valley**

Lester-Garland (1903) rejected La Gasca's 1834 record and though Ariste has a specimen from Noirmont labelled, 'Bois. Cultivée et subspontanée',

180

Lily-of-the-valley is nowhere established in Jersey.
A 1963.

Polygonatum species   **Solomon's-seal**
                                des **plieurs dé Jâcob**

A plant near La Chaire, Rozel, in 1962 was determined as *P. multiflorum* (L.) All. by J. E. Lousley. The hybrid *P. x hybridum* Brügger (*P. multiflorum* x *P. odoratum*) was seen on Mont du Boulevard, St Aubin, in 1963 by J. C. Fluck and it was well established on a rubbish dump at St Ouen in the 1960s. In the mid-1920s there were several records from the woods at Noirmont but expert opinions differed as to whether they were *P. multiflorum* or *P. x hybridum*. *G 1970; S Brecqhou 1957.*

Asparagus officinalis L.   **Asparagus**
                                       *d'l'***aspèrge**

Subsp. *officinalis*   Occasional garden escape on light soil.
Subsp. *prostratus* (Dumort.) Corb.   Rare. J. Woods found it 'On the sea slopes of the hills beyond St Brelade' according to Babington (1839). It is still there and is in good quantity in some years, for example 1979. It is still also in St Ouen's Bay where Attenborough found it in 1912. In the 1917 Société botanical report, Attenborough reported a single plant at Le Saie. The plants are either male or female and unfortunately all the St Ouen plants now seem to be male.
G rare; A only garden escapes.

Ruscus aculeatus L.   **Butcher's-broom**
                                       du **frégon**

Common in many inland woods and local on the coast.

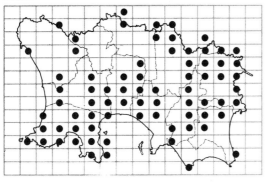

G frequent; A occasional; S rare; H local.

Agave americana L.   **Century Plant**

The Armorican Flora (des Abbayes *et al.* 1971) states that this is frequently planted on the coast of the region and persists, more or less wild. Jersey is given as one locality. While it is true that it has been planted and can survive neglect, nowhere is it established in the wild. The English name comes from the mistaken belief that each plant takes a hundred years to flower. It can flower after ten years according to *Flora Europaea* but usually takes much longer. Though the main rosette dies after flowering, offsets are produced at its base.
G uncommon; S recorded; H rare.

AMARYLLIDACEAE

Amaryllis bella-donna L.

                Jersey Lily or **Belladonna Lily**
                        des **belles-toutes-nues**

Jersey Lilies occur rarely as garden relics, for example on a bank in St Peter near the Airport in the 1960s and 1970s but they have now gone. They are South African flowers which the climate of Jersey suits and they have been grown in quantity in Jersey gardens for many years. In the past, when most country houses in Jersey were built facing south, Jersey Lily bulbs would be planted in a narrow border at the base of the front wall, and in later years, through bulb increase, a thick band of pink flowers on short dark red stems would appear in autumn before the leaves developed. Several properties still possess these borders. The name Jersey Lily which is always used for the species in Jersey when English is spoken, predates the other Jersey Lily, Lillie Langtry. The flower which Lillie Langtry is holding in her celebrated portrait by Sir John Everett Millais is not precisely identifiable. It may be a Guernsey Lily but it is certainly not a Jersey Lily. The name Jersey Lily may have been given to the flower to distinguish it from the Guernsey Lily, another South African species, *Nerine sarniensis*, which is now best as a cold greenhouse plant.
G rare; H planted in the wild on Crevichon by Compton Mackenzie.

Sternbergia lutea (L.) Ker-Gawler ex Sprengel
                                    Sternbergia

Subsp. *lutea*   In the grounds and on the sea slopes outside the walls of Gorey Castle where it had been well-established for many years before 1919 when it was first recorded in the Société's botanical report. It still grows there in good quantity and more recently has appeared spontaneously in gardens in several parts of the island. Its native home is the eastern Mediterranean on stony slopes and in dry scrub. The crocus-like flowers, of a brilliant yellow, are thought by some people to be the 'lilies of the field' which rivalled Solomon in all his glory.
G 1912 and 1965.

Leucojum aestivum L.   **Summer Snowflake**

Subsp. *pulchellum* (Salisb.) Briq. Summer Snow-flake was listed by La Gasca in 1834 as 'colitur'. It is an introduced species which survives competition well in dampish places so that clumps of bulbs can remain and increase long after the garden of which they were once part has gone. For example several huge clumps grow along the old mill leat just below the Val de la Mare reservoir. They were first noted in the early 1950s but had obviously been there for some considerable time. Also many gardeners dislike the masses of dark green leaves and discard the bulbs in the wild, where they survive. Though called Summer Snowflake, flowers can often be found from early January onwards.

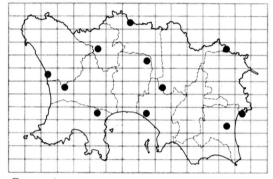

G rare; A rare.

Galanthus nivalis L.   **Snowdrop**
des **bouonnefemmes**

Subsp. *nivalis* La Gasca listed Snowdrops as 'Colitur' in 1834; Ereaut wrote 'Common on hedges' beside a specimen he gathered in 1847; Piquet did not mention them in his 1851 list but in 1896 he included them with the comment 'Hedge banks, very rare; formerly common'. (Did he omit them in 1851 because he still considered them garden plants?) Lester-Garland (1903) gave Piquet's 1896 comment and added 'This seems to be a Jersey tradition. I have never seen it outside a garden or orchard'. Were they really so close to habitation? Today Snowdrops frequently grow on hedgebanks and in woods well away from houses particularly in the east of the island. How some of them arrived it is now impossible to tell. Some are double forms. In the past Snowdrops were much planted in gardens as at St Ouen's Manor and La Hougue Bie. Mrs L. A. Morris's great-grand-father planted out large quantities at Ville ès Philippe about 1880 and her great-aunt and uncle, Mr & Mrs Aubin, planted out Primroses and Snowdrops on the côtils at Belwood, Trinity (pers. comm.).

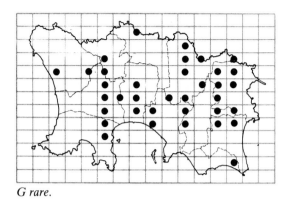

G rare.

Narcissus pseudonarcissus L.   **Wild Daffodil**
des **g'zettes**

Subsp. *pseudonarcissus* A native species locally abundant in woods in some inland valleys and on parts of the cliffs where Bracken provides shade in summer. This is the delicate little daffodil which seeds freely and colonises a whole woodland floor or cliff-side, as opposed to the following species which are often infertile and then spread only by the clump increasing in size. This native species is strangely absent from the other Channel Islands where all daffodils, whether growing in the wild or not, are derived from cultivated plants.

The design on the face (the obverse) of the current £10 note issued by The States of Jersey incorporates a drawing of a Wild Daffodil.

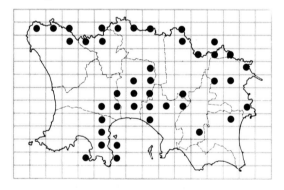

Narcissus cvs   **Cultivated daffodils** or **narcissi**

Cultivated daffodils and narcissi of garden or farm origin, but now growing feral, abound. On two short walks in March 1979, thirty-six different varieties were found, and photographed, in only a small area in the north of St Ouen's Bay. An island-wide systematic search in a good daffodil year, like 1978, might well produce from the wild, flowers of almost every variety grown in the past for ornament or

Opposite, Plate 15 Sand Crocus *Romulea columnae* with Early Sand-grass *Mibora minima* and Mossy
182   Stonecrop *Crassula tillaea*   × 1½

commerce. Fashion is fickle, and varieties grown one year may be a commercial disaster the next, so they are discarded even though the bulbs are sound. Diseased or small badly shaped bulbs are thrown away but many recover. Gardeners want newer varieties, so out go the old ones with the next garden refuse. The result is an extraordinary display in early spring. Many grassy banks between fields are yellow with flowering daffodils. Cauliflowers are sometimes picked in fields where the 'weeds' are daffodils. Areas which were used for the tipping of garden refuse in the past, officially or unofficially, still have daffodils coming up on them year after year. 'Pheasant's Eye', *N. poeticus*, and 'Primrose Peerless', *N. x medioluteus*, were both here when La Gasca compiled his list in 1834, and they can still be found. J. E. Lousley in the *Flora of the Isles of Scilly* (1971 p. 36) surprisingly stated that *N. tazetta*, 'Grand Soleil d'Or', i.e. 'Sols', are almost wiped out in hard winters in the Channel Islands. In direct contrast Deputy H. Vandervliet in an interview (*Jersey Evening Post*, 27 January 1983) advocated their culture, saying that he had grown them commercially for thirty-five years. This would include the winter of 1962/63 one of the worst Jersey has ever known. 'Sols' also survive happily on a few old consolidated rubbish dumps. So do 'Scilly Whites' but 'Paper Whites' suffer badly in a severe winter. There are too many feral daffodils or narcissi to mention each individually and the difficulties in naming some of them seem insuperable. Notes are being kept in the Société's botanical records and will be available to students.

G, A, S and H all have feral Narcissi *locally in quantity.*

DIOSCOREACEAE

Tamus communis L.   **Black Bryony**

A rare native plant of rough places on the north and east cliffs. Babington first recorded it but gave no locality. Piquet added, 'In a lane at Rozel, abundant' to his 1851 list at some unknown later time and collected a specimen from La Saline, St John, in 1895. Meanwhile Vaniot had found it in the '*Vallée allont du clos de l'abbesse de Caen à Ste Catherine*' in 1882. Attenborough who enjoyed walking and climbing on the cliffs stated in the Société's botanical report for 1918 that, 'It really fringes the coast from Mourier Bay to St Catherine's and can no longer be considered a rare plant'. During the survey it was found on only five stretches of coast but Attenborough may well still be right.

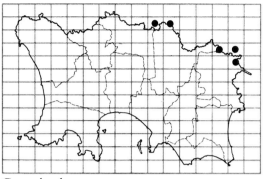

G very local.

IRIDACEAE

Sisyrinchium species   **Sisyrinchium**

Sisyrinchium species are much grown in gardens, and in the post-war years *S. striatum* used to be on most rubbish dumps where it persisted after being thrown out with garden refuse. It has gone, now that rubbish dumping is controlled. *S. iridifolium* subsp. *valdiviense*, sometimes called *S. laxum*, a plant with purple-streaked white flowers, has been an almost ineradicable weed in a garden at St Ouen for more than twenty years but has never 'moved out' of the garden into the wild, though it has had the opportunity. It is now spreading in the gravel paths etc. of St Brelade's Churchyard where it was planted on a grave many years ago.

G rare.

Iris foetidissima L.   **Stinking Iris**

Widespread but sparsely distributed, usually on dry hedgebanks. Though this native species of iris is undistinguished in flower, the 'petals' being thin and greyish-blue, the seed pods contain bright orange seeds and are much used by flower arrangers in autumn. The English name comes from the somewhat disagreeable smell when the leaves are crushed, and it may be this which makes them totally unpalatable to rabbits. See account of the flora of Les Écréhous.

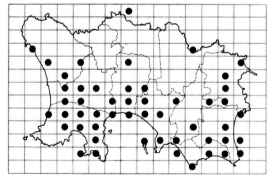

G locally frequent; A frequent; S common; H common.

I. pseudacorus L.   **Yellow Iris**
                                         du **bliajeu**

Common in damp places. The seeds, well roasted,
were used as a substitute for coffee beans during the
German Occupation (1940–45).

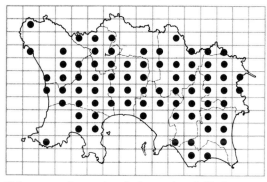

G frequent; A occasional; S occasional; H planted.

I. x hollandica Tubergen   **Dutch Iris**
I. tingitana x **I. xiphium**

Occasionally seen flowering where garden or farm
refuse has been thrown but it does not normally
persist for long.
G occasional.

Iris species   **Bearded Iris**

The large, sterile, early-flowering purple garden iris
I. germanica L. is often thrown out with garden
refuse and it occasionally survives in wild areas for
some years. It has also, rarely, been planted out on
hedgebanks. Hybrid Bearded Irises occur more
rarely as garden throw-outs, for example in the
sandpits north of St Ouen's Pond.
S similar.

Freesia refracta (Jacq.) Ekclon ex Klatt   **Freesia**
G rare escape.

Crocus species   **Crocus**

No *Crocus* species is native or established in Jersey.
Single crocus flowers of garden origin are sometimes
seen in the wild but they do not survive for long. The
source of the *C. nudiflorus* record for Jersey post
1930 in the *Atlas of the British Flora* is unknown.
G two localities.

Romulea columnae Sebastiani & Mauri   **Sand Crocus**
                                          des **genottes**

Subsp. *columnae* Common, sometimes abundant,
in short turf on the cliffs. Its small star-like blue
flowers can be found from the end of March to about
the middle of April or later. Essentially the day
should be warm or the flowers will remain closed.

Rarely the flowers are white.

The first mention of it was in the late eighteenth
century when Captain J. Finlay wróte to Sir Joseph
Banks on 27 February 1787 telling him of it in Jersey,
and describing it, and the Rev. J. Lightfoot wrote
against the species, '. . . *Etiam in Insula Caesarea . . .
prope Grouville in sabulosis . . .* 1787. D. Finlay *qui
example communicavit.*' The specimen was probably
collected between 1779 and 1782 when Finlay was
stationed in Guernsey. See the Introduction.

An illustration by Pandora Sellars is opposite
page 182.

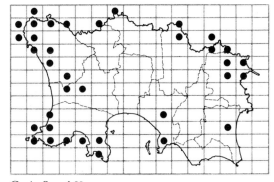

G, A, S and H common.

R. rosea (L.) Ecklon   **Onion-grass**
G locally plentiful (var. australis *f.* alba*)*

Tritonia x crocosmiflora (Lemoine) Nicholson
T. aurea x **T. pottsii**   **Montbretia**
                                          d's **êtchelles dé Jâcob**

A frequent, well-established garden escape. The
cross between these two South African species was
not made until about 1877 in France but plants were
distributed quickly and it has been growing in the
wild in Jersey for many years. The distribution map
well illustrates the random distribution of a plant
which is a hardy garden outcast.

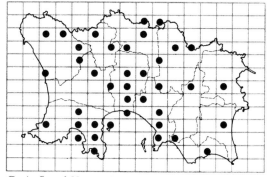

G, A, S and H occasional.

Gladiolus illyricus Koch   **Wild Gladiolus**

One record: Grève d'Azette, 1915, Attenborough (B.E.C. *Report* 1915). This species has not been seen again. A confusion of names is suspected, and that the following species was intended.

G. communis L.   **Jack** or **Wild Gladiolus**
                        d's **êtchelles dé Jâcob**

Subsp. *byzantinus* (Miller) A. P. Hamilton An escape from cultivation which was well-known as such last century though it was not recorded until recently, but see the above species. It is locally frequent in the La Collette area and in the south-east, and single plants are likely to appear almost anywhere on light soil. The map contains only records between 1960 and 1970. Considerably more could have been added in 1980 which was an exceedingly good flowering year for it. Flowering spikes have been seen in habitats as diverse as at the edge of the tarmacadam at the foot of a granite wall in St Ouen; among bracken in the middle of Les Quennevais; near Grosnez and on Green Island. Some of the flower beds by the Harvey Memorial contain it as a weed and it would be a pity if it were ever 'weeded out'.

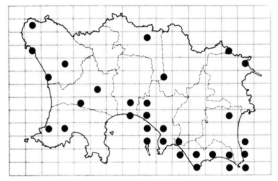

G occasional; A rare; S rare; H rare.

JUNCACEAE

Juncus maritimus Lam.   **Sea Rush**

Local in wet areas on the shore at about high-water mark on a spring tide.

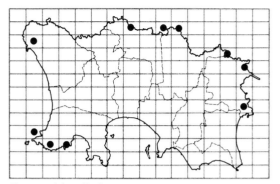

G rare; A locally frequent.

J. acutus L.   **Sharp Rush**

Subsp. *acutus*   Local on sandy areas near the shore. The English and Latin names come from the needle-sharp points of the stiff leaves.

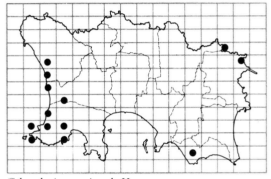

G local; A occasional; H common.

J. inflexus L.   **Hard Rush**
(*J. glaucus*)

Local in wet places. Hard Rush has always been uncommon and remains so, but it is still in all the localities from which it was recorded in the past.

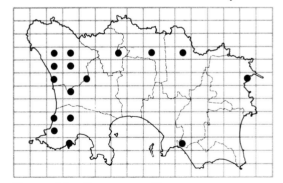

G rare; A locally common; H rare.

J. x diffusus Hoppe   **A hybrid Rush**
J. inflexus x **J. effusus**
Claimed for Jersey by A. Chevalier in 1933.

J. effusus L.   **Soft Rush**
(*J. communis*)   *du* **jonc**
Common in wet places. Clumps of roots were cut in
the past and used as stools. See Purple Moor-grass.
Le Maistre (1966) describes its use in candles and
lights.

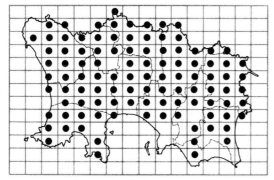

G common; A occasional; S common; H local.

J. conglomeratus L.   **Compact Rush**
Lester-Garland did not recognise this as a separate
species from the last. Babington (1839) recorded it
from St Lawrence but J. Piquet's and F. Piquet's
specimens are, as Lester-Garland said, *J. effusus*.
The first certain record this century seems to be
Ariste's from Bonne Nuit in 1925. During the
1960–70 survey it was found only occasionally and
R. W. S. Knightbridge's survey of wet meadows in
1983 confirms this status.

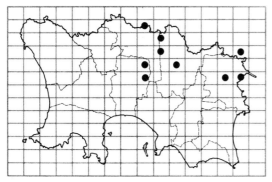

G rare; A rare; S last record 1902.

J. compressus Jacq.   **Round-fruited Rush**
All specimens seen, which claim to be this, are the
following.
G similar error.

J. gerardi Loisel.   **Saltmarsh Rush**
Subsp. *gerardi*   Local where fresh water stands on or
near the shore within reach of high spring tides.

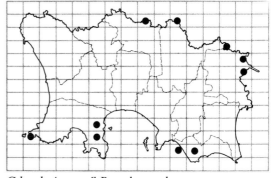

G local; A rare; S Brecqhou only.

J. tenuis Willd.   **Slender Rush**
Ariste collected a specimen from the sides of a path at
Highlands College in 1928 and it may have been there
until 1950 as that date is on one of Louis-Arsène's
specimens but he could not find the plant growing in
the grounds of the College, to show me it, in 1958.
Prof. T. G. Tutin found it on Fort Regent in 1949 and
Dr J. G. Dony in the valley running east from Trinity
School in 1970.
G 1949.

J. foliosus Desf.   **A Rush**
G 1914; S 1953.

J. bufonius L.   **Toad Rush**
Common in damp places.

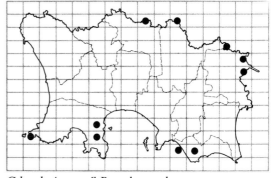

G common; A frequent; S frequent; H common.

J. ambiguus Guss.   **A Rush**
G 1912.

J. capitatus Weigel.   **Dwarf Rush**
Local but occasionally in such abundance that the
short open turf looks reddish-brown when the plants
are in fruit. Some of the earlier inland localities, for

186

example on a hillside near St Lawrence Church and in Vallée des Vaux given by Piquet in his 1896 list, have not been refound.

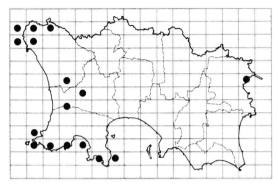

G local; A occasional; S occasional; H rare.

J. subnodulosus Schrank   **Blunt-flowered Rush**
(J. obtusiflorus)
Still at St Ouen's Pond where it was first noted by Babington (1839). F. Piquet collected a specimen from a marsh at Bonne Nuit in 1870 and it was recorded in the Beaumont Marsh region during the 1960–70 survey but it has not been refound recently in either of these places.

J. pygmaeus L. C. M. Richard   **Pygmy Rush**
Recorded from Grosnez by Prof. T. W. Böcher (*New Phytologist*, 1958). Confusion is suspected with the equally small *J. capitatus* which grows at Grosnez and which he does not mention.

J. bulbosus L. (inc. *J. kochii* F. W. Schultz)
(J. supinus)   **Bulbous Rush**
Rare in wet areas. If the records from last century are correct then Bulbous Rush has decreased considerably: common, Piquet (1851); frequent, Piquet (1896); rare, Lester-Garland (1903).

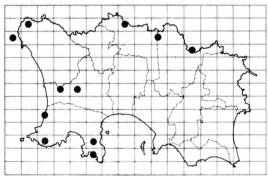

G last record 1891; A last record 1934; S rare; and J. kochii if separable rare in G, A and S.

J. acutiflorus Ehrh. ex Hoffm.   **Sharp-flowered Rush**
Frequent in wet places.

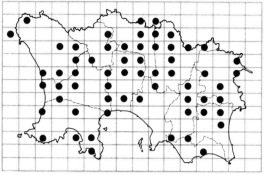

G local; A frequent; S rare; H local.

J. x surrejanus Druce   **A hybrid Rush**
J. acutiflorus x **J. articulatus**
R. W. S. Knightbridge considers that this hybrid may be common where the two parents grow together. Specimens he collected from Le Bourg and Queen's Valley in 1983 were confirmed by C. A. Stace.

J. articulatus L.   **Jointed Rush**
(J. lamprocarpus)
Frequent in wet places.

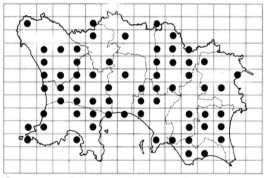

G common; A frequent; S occasional; H 1837 only.

Luzula campestris (L.) DC.   **Field Wood-rush**
Common in grassy places and recorded as such since Babington's time, (1839).

Map overleaf

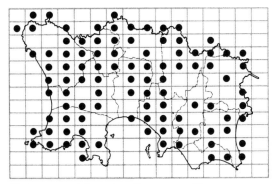

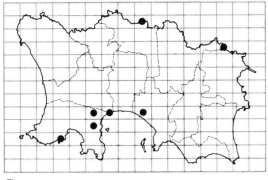

G common; A frequent; S common; H common.

G rare.

L. multiflora (Retz.) Lej.   **Heath Wood-rush**
(L. erecta)
Babington (1839) did not find Heath Wood-rush in Jersey and the only locality which Piquet gives in 1851 and 1896 is St Brelade. Lester-Garland (1903) then described it as frequent and listed several places. Recently it has only been found in Val de la Mare, St Ouen, near La Hague, St Peter, in a valley near Trinity School and at Bonne Nuit. It may well be under-recorded.
G uncommon; A frequent; S rare; H 1957.

L. sylvatica (Hudson) Gaudin   **Great Wood-rush**
Lester-Garland (1903) reported this as plentiful in a gully running down to the sea at Bonne Nuit Bay. In the 1920 report of the Société's Botanical Section, Attenborough stated that it had gone from there but was in a gully in Giffard Bay. In 1958 it was in two gullies in Giffard Bay, in small quantity in one and in great abundance in the other, and it is still present. In 1922 Attenborough recorded it from the cliffs at Noirmont. No systematic search has been made to refind it there and it may well still occur.
G local.

L. forsteri (Sm.) DC.   **Southern Wood-rush**
First listed by La Gasca in 1834 without locality and then recorded by Lester-Garland (1903) from the entrance to the drive by Noirmont Manor and as abundant in a hedge opposite Beau Coin, St Aubin. The species is still in the St Aubin/La Haule region in good quantity and in smaller amounts elsewhere in the island.

COMMELINACEAE
Tradescantia albiflora Kunth   **Wandering Jew**
G 1975 (garden).

BROMELIACEAE
Fascicularia pitcairniifolia (Verlot) Mez
    Rhodostachys
Rhodostachys has been found washed up on the beach in St Clement but is not known to be growing wild in Jersey.
G three localities.

GRAMINEAE
    Bamboo
    du **ros d'gardîn**
Bamboos were much planted in private gardens about a century ago to provide protection from the wind and to supply canes for stakes. Most large properties like the Manors still have ornamental bamboos in their grounds and these are not included in the account. But with the passage of time, smaller gardens have disappeared or changed their positions leaving bamboo clumps or bamboo hedges in the countryside. Occasionally bamboos have been planted in the wild. The 'stands' increase yearly and are likely to remain a permanent part of Jersey's flora unless removed by man. Some bamboos may die after flowering but, contrary to popular belief, this is unusual. D. McClintock an authority on bamboos has named the the following species:

Sasa veitchii (Carrière) Rehder   **Kumazasa**
Valley at Rozel, 1962. This is a broad-leaved grey-green species with white edges to the leaves.

Arundinaria jaunsarensis Gamble   **Anceps Bamboo**
(A. anceps)
The huge clump on the east side of the road at Meadow Bank is Anceps Bamboo. In 1982 and 1983 it was flowering and many canes were dying so that

the once beautiful clump was a sorry sight. It will probably regrow from the rhizomes or from seed.

Pseudosasa japonica (Siebold & Zucc. ex Steudel) Makino   **Metake**
(Arundinaria japonica)

By far the commonest bamboo in Jersey and often found in flower on a close inspection. Two of its distinguishing features are that a quarter of the underside of the leaf is green and the remaining three-quarters are blue-green, and there is but one branch at each node.

Pleioblastus simonii (Carrière) Nakar
       Simon Bamboo

Rozel, 1970. Usually half the underside of the leaf is green and the other half is blue-green, and there are several branches at each node. See the last species.

Phyllostachys viridi-glaucescens (Carrière) A. & C. Rivière   **A Bamboo**

A huge clump and an equally huge clump of *Pseudosasa japonica* have been established for some considerable time in the small valley north of Mont Matthieu, St Ouen.

For an account of bamboos in the Bailiwick of Guernsey see McClintock in *The Wild Flowers of Guernsey* (1975) and in the *European Garden Flora* (1984).

Festuca pratensis Hudson   **Meadow Fescue**
(F. elatior)

Subsp. *pratensis* Records of this and the next species are much confused. Lester-Garland (1903) mentioned it only as at St Ouen's Pond but repeated searches there failed to reveal it, whereas Tall Fescue, *F. arundinacea*, which he did not record from there is frequent. A specimen collected at the foot of Val de la Mare Reservoir in 1961 and recorded as this species was determined as the next by Dr A. Melderis who has given considerable help with the identification of grasses. The only known records are specimens gathered in the Rue des Prés Trading Estate in 1970 by Dr J. G. Dony who also reported it at St Mary and near Highfield, St Saviour.
G scarce.

F. arundinacea Schreber   **Tall Fescue**

Subsp. *arundinacea* Locally fréquent in damp grassland.

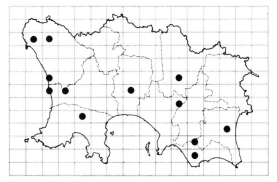

G occasional; A rare.

F. rubra group   **Red Fescue**

The aggregate is common but the quantity and distribution of each species or subspecies in the group need investigation. Subsp. *rubra* and subsp. *arenaria* (Osbeck) Syme are present and a specimen of *F. juncifolia* St Amans is at Kew. Several other species and subspecies almost certainly occur. Dr C. A. Stace of Leicester University and his students are currently working on this group and the following.
G, A, S and H – the group is common.

Festuca ovina group   **Sheep's Fescue**
*d'l'*herbe à moutons

This group, like the above, is common and under active review. Work on it is more advanced so more information is available. The following five species within the group are present and others almost certainly occur:

F. tenuifolia L. was recorded from Grands Vaux by Lester-Garland (1903) and specimens collected by Vaniot in 1881 from Vallée des Vaux and St Helier were confirmed as this by Melderis.

F. ophioliticola Kerguélen subsp. *armoricana* (Kerguélen) Auquier (*F. armoricana*) was stated (*in litt.*) by M. Wilkinson, a post-graduate student at Leicester University, to be covering the dunes at the south end of St Ouen's Bay in 1983, and he determined as this a specimen collected by Vaniot in 1881 also from the dunes of St Ouen's Bay. He further stated (pers. comm.) that it was present on Ouaisné Common in 1983.

F. huonii Auquier was stated (*in litt.*) by Wilkinson to be the common cliff top species of the north coast in 1983.

F. trachyphylla (Hackel) Krajina was collected from the dunes north-east of La Carrière quarry, St Ouen's Bay, by Wilkinson in 1983.

F. longifolia Thuill. was collected from Rozel by Ariste in 1925, det. Wilkinson.
G, A, S and H – the group is common.

x Festulolium loliaceum (Hudson) P. Fourn.
Festuca pratensis x **Lolium perenne**   **A hybrid Fescue**
Babington collected this hybrid naming it *Festuca loliacea* in 1837, Piquet described it as common in meadows in 1851 and it was collected below the Val de la Mare Reservoir dam in 1961, det. Melderis.
G two records.

x Festulpia hubbardii Meld. ex Stace & Cotton
Hubbard's Hybrid Fescue
F. rubra x **Vulpia membranacea**
G rare; A 1933.

Lolium perenne L.   **Perennial Rye-grass**
d'l'hèrbe pèrpétuelle
Common both as a native species and in sown grass-land.

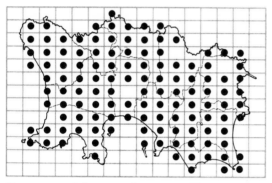

G common; A frequent; S common; H common.

L. multiflorum Lam.   **Italian Rye-grass**
d'l'hèrbe italienne
Italian Rye-grass was only introduced into Britain in 1831 yet by 1836 the Jersey Agricultural and Horticultural Society was recommending it in its third *Annual Report*: 'It is a matter of interest to mark the progress of any new product, in the field of practical husbandry, thus the attention of the Society is called to the culture of the ''Italian Rye Grass'' which has perfectly succeeded in a non-irrigated meadow belonging to your Hon. Treasurer, Mr. Robin. The first crop was fed off between the 14th March and the 22nd of April, it was highly nutritious, and succulent, producing very fine coloured excellent butter'. Italian Rye-grass is now common.

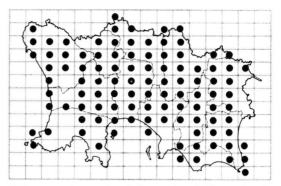

G frequent; A occasional; S occasional; H occasional.

L. x hybridum Haussk.   **Short-rotation Rye-grass**
L. multiflorum x **L. perenne**
Many plants of sown leys and elsewhere seem to be intermediate between these two species and are presumably the hybrid.
G as in Jersey; A 1976.

L. rigidum Gaudin   **Wimmera Rye-grass**
Subsp. *rigidum* One record: bird seed alien, Le Braye Slip, St Ouen's Bay, 1968, Dr J. G. Dony, conf. Hubbard.

L. temulentum L.   **Darnel**
A casual recorded at least nine times since La Gasca first listed it in 1834. The post-war records from a rubbish dump north of St Ouen's Pond in 1956 and the plants found by Miss R. Kilby near Beach Road, St Saviour, in 1970 were probably from bird seed.
G last record 1976; A 1838; S 1874.

Vulpia fasciculata (Forsk.) Samp.   **Dune Fescue**
(Festuca uniglumis)
Dune Fescue is locally common on sandy soil. Stace and Cotton (*Watsonia* 11) have shown that the name *V. membranacea* which was used in Britain in the past for Dune Fescue, covered two species, a diploid and a tetraploid. The name *V. membranacea* has been retained for the diploid, but Jersey's species is the tetraploid and should be called *V. fasciculata*. This species is confined to coastal sandy areas of the Mediterranean and western Europe.

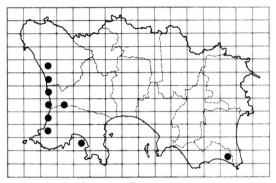

G frequent; A frequent; S error.

V. bromoides (L.) S. F. Gray   **Squirrel-tail Fescue**
(Festuca sciuroides)

Common in dry places, including wall tops.

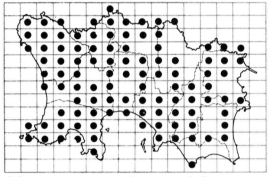

G frequent; A common; S occasional; G common.

V. myuros (L.) C. C. Gmelin   **Rat's-tail Fescue**
(Festuca myurus)

Over the years this seems to have varied in quantity: common, Babington (1839); common, Piquet (1851); rather rare, Piquet (1896); frequent, Lester-Garland (1903). As can be seen from the distribution map it was recorded fairly frequently during the survey.

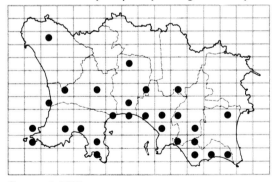

G rare; A 1838.

V. ciliata Dumort.   **Bearded Fescue**
(V. ambigua; Festuca ambigua)

Subsp. *ambigua* (Le Gall) Stace & Auquier   Rare in the south-west. The first record was in 1876 by T. B. Blow, 'from sandy ground close to Grouville Station' (Lester-Garland, 1903), and on the relevant herbarium sheet in the British Museum, Blow wrote: 'One plant snatched from a crack in the platform just as the train was coming in'.

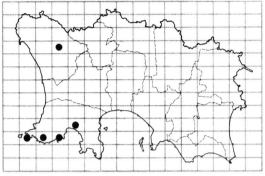

G three records; A 1906.

Desmazeria marina (L.) Druce   **Sea Fern-grass**
(Catapodium loliaceum)

Common round the coast.

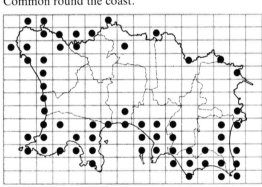

G, A, S and H common.

D. rigida (L.) Tutin   **Fern-grass**
(Scleropoa rigida)

Common in the south and further inland than the last species. Fern-grass was reported as common by all botanists from Babington (1839) onwards as opposed to Guernsey where it appears to have been rare in the past or overlooked.

Map overleaf

191

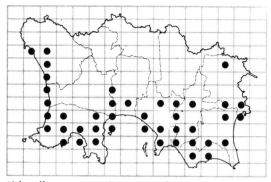

G locally common; A occasional; H occasional.

Poa annua L.   **Annual Meadow-grass**
*d'l'***hèrbe à poules**

Lester-Garland's 1903 comment, 'Ubiquitous. All the year round.' is still true.

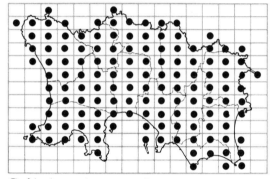

G ubiquitous; A common; S abundant; H common.

P. infirma Kunth   **Early Meadow-grass**

Common on light soil near the coast and in spite of the amount indicated on the map, it is probably under-recorded. It disappears completely, shortly after flowering and fruiting in spring, so summer-time botanists never see it. The first record seems to be Piquet's of 1877, from sandy places near the sea (Hb Brit. Mus.).

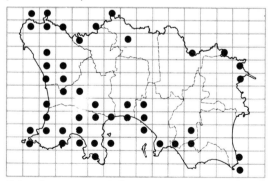

G locally common; A frequent; S occasional; H frequent.

P. annua x **P. infirma**   **A hybrid Meadow-grass**
G plants grown from seed collected in Guernsey were of this hybrid.

P. trivialis L.   **Rough Meadow-grass**
Subsp. *trivialis*   Common.

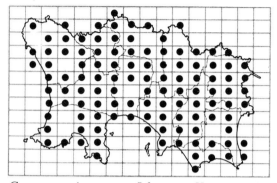

G common; A common; S frequent; H occasional.

P. subcaerulea Sm.   **Spreading Meadow-grass**
Probably more frequent than its few records indicate. Druce reported it in 1907 and it was collected four times in 1968 and 1969. Dr J. G. Dony thought it might be the commonest of the *P. pratensis* group. See the next species.
G frequent; A recorded; S recorded.

P. pratensis L.   **Smooth Meadow-grass**
*d'l'***hèrbe d'pré**

Grasses of the *P. pratensis* group are common, and *P. pratensis* s.s. exists but the quantities of the different species of the group have not been investigated. The map includes all records of *P. pratensis, P. subcaerulea* and *P. angustifolia.*

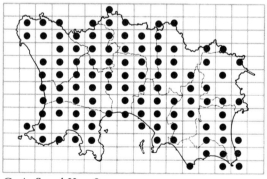

G, A, S and H as Jersey.

P. angustifolia L.   **Narrow-leaved Meadow-grass**
Two records: near Five Oaks, 1968, Dr J. G. Dony, conf. Hubbard, and 1969, Mrs D. L. Le Quesne, det. Melderis, but it may be commoner than these two

records indicate. See the above species.
G as Jersey.

P. chaixii Vill.   **Broad-leaved Meadow-grass**
A 1900.

P. compressa L.   **Flattened Meadow-grass**
Saunders' record given by Babington (1839) was
rejected by Lester-Garland (1903) and has not been
confirmed.
G 1968; S claimed 1872.

P. palustris L.   **Swamp Meadow-grass**
Two records both in 1966: New St John's Manor, J. C.
Fluck; on a newly-made bank outside the electricity
sub-station at the foot of La Haule Hill, Mrs E. M.
Towers; both conf. Melderis.

P. nemoralis L.   **Wood Meadow-grass**
Lester-Garland (1903) rejected all previous records
of this species, except one from Highlands College,
but it was recorded on six occasions during the survey
and most specimens were confirmed by either
Melderis or Hubbard.

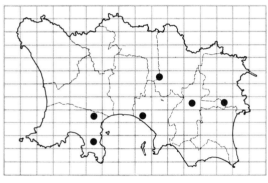

G rare.

P. bulbosa L.   **Bulbous Meadow-grass**
Abundant over small areas. The first records were by
Lady Davy in 1922 from near Fort Henry on
Grouville Common, where both the normal and the
viviparous form were present – and still are – and
from Pontac. N. D. Simpson found it on Les Quennevais near the old racecourse in 1948 and it is still on
Les Quennevais in several places. Thousands of its
small 'bulbs' were lying, looking like chaff, in some of
the blow-outs on Ouaisné Common in the 1960s and
it still grows there in quantity. It flowers early and
vanishes quickly without trace, except for the minute
'bulbs', so that botanists in summer time, or even in
late spring some years, do not see it.

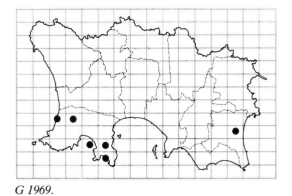

G 1969.

Puccinellia distans (L.) Parl.
(Atropis distans)   **Reflexed Saltmarsh-grass**
Subsp. *distans*   Three records: Georgetown, 1897,
W. M. Rogers; St Luke, 1906, Druce (Hb Oxford); in
quantity in St Aubin's Bay where the St Lawrence
Perquage meets the old railway walk, 1966, Mrs
E. M. Towers (Hb Société Jersiaise).
G rare.

P. fasciculata (Torrey) E. P. Bicknell
(Sclerochloa Borreri)   **Borrer's Saltmarsh-grass**
Subsp. *fasciculata*   Piquet listed this in 1851 and 1896
as rare in St Clement. Lester-Garland (1903) rejected
the records. An unlocalised specimen labelled, 'Salt
marshes, rare, June 1900' by Piquet is in the Société
herbarium.

P. maritima (Hudson) Parl.
(Atropis maritima)   **Common Saltmarsh-grass**
On a detached rock at La Collette from 1870, when
Piquet collected a specimen, until at least 1958 when
it was again collected. Whether it survived the recent
harbour works is unknown. The area, 'the low
cement', was difficult to search by most members of
the Botanical Section of the Société, but Lester-
Garland (1903), who would not have had the same
constraints, failed to find it, which is surprising in
view of its quantity in 1958. It was also found on Les
Écréhous and Les Minquiers in 1958 but it has gone
from Les Minquiers.
G rare; S error.

P. rupestris (With.) Fernald & Weatherby
(Sclerochloa procumbens)   **Stiff Saltmarsh-grass**
One record: Le̦ Marais à la Coque, 1876, Piquet
(Hb Oxford).
G 1968.

Dactylis glomerata L.   **Cock's-foot**
                                   du **pid-d'co**
Still abundant as Lester-Garland (1903) described it.

Map overleaf

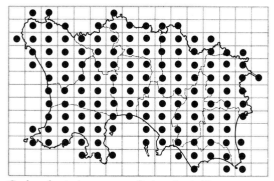

G abundant; A common; S abundant; H common.

Cynosurus cristatus L.   **Crested Dog's-tail**
Common in grassy areas.

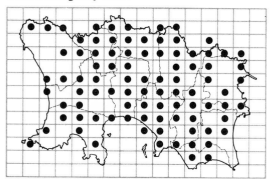

G frequent; A frequent; S frequent; H common.

C. echinatus L.   **Rough Dog's-tail**
In 1689 Dr W. Sherard described a grass thought to be this, as growing commonly on sandy ground. See the Introduction. Last century it seems to have been rare and confined to West Mount and South Hill, St Helier, and to L'Étacq, St Ouen. Druce stated that he was unable to find it in 1877 and thought it varied considerably in quantity from year to year. In 1906 he found it in great abundance and very luxuriant on West Mount (*Journal of Botany* XLV: 427). In the same journal, in 1923, W. C. Barton tells of finding it, in June of that year, growing up to four feet high in the abandoned trenches of the First World War prisoner-of-war camp on Les Quennevais. Attenborough, immediately after the German Occupation (1940–45), wrote, 'One remarkable feature [of the Occupation] has been the abundance of a rare grass, Cynosurus echinatus, which has either enormously increased its known range here or has been introduced during the occupation'. It is now locally common in the south and west.

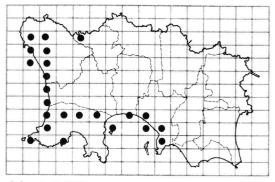

G local; H 1977.

Catabrosa aquatica (L.) Beauv.   **Whorl-grass**
First listed by La Gasca in 1834. Piquet described it as abundant in ditches in Samarès Miles in his 1851 list, but by 1896 it was very rare. Two specimens of Piquet's dated 1856 and 1860 confirm the records. Lester-Garland thought it might be extinct in 1903 and it has not been seen since.
G not seen this century; A rare.

Apera spica-venti (L.) Beauv.   **Loose Silky-bent**
'Bouley Bay; very rare.' according to Piquet in the *Phytologist* for 1853. He never mentioned it again and there is no specimen.
G last record 1958; A 1966.

Mibora minima (L.) Desv.   **Early Sand-grass**
(M. verna)
Common in open turf on light soil, particularly in the west. This is the same distribution as given by Lester-Garland (1903) and Babington (1839). The first record was in 1787 when Lightfoot noted that Finlay had seen it *'in Insula Caesarea'*. Captain Finlay was in the Channel Islands from 1779 to 1782. See the Introduction.

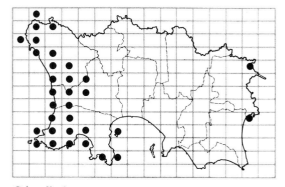

G locally frequent; S 1903; H frequent.

Briza media L.   **Quaking-grass**

Subsp. *media* A patch of a few yards square on Les Quennevais, north-west of Don Bridge, but well away from any house and on land looking undisturbed by man, 1971, K. E. Bull, conf. Melderis. The habitat has since been destroyed. A Saunders' record given by Babington (1839) was rejected by Lester-Garland (1903).
G rare; A occasional.

B. maxima L.   **Great Quaking-grass**
                                   des **lèrmes d'Jâcob**

Locally frequent on light soil most years but of all the south European species in Jersey, this seemed to suffer most in the extreme cold of the winter 1962/63. In the summer of 1962 it was plentiful. In 1963 hardly a plant could be found and it was several years before the numbers were back to normal. The first specimen was collected at St Aubin in 1859 by the Rev. A. M. Norman. Dr M. M. Bull reported to Druce that it was spreading in the 1870s and Druce suggested that it might soon over-run the island (*Journal of Botany* 1879).

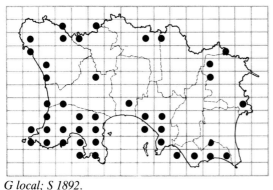

G local; S 1892.

B. minor L.   **Lesser Quaking-grass**

Rare. Ray, in the second edition (1696) of his *Synopsis*, stated that Dr W. Sherard had found Lesser Quaking-grass in Jersey. See the Introduction. A specimen gathered in the eighteenth century and labelled 'In the Isle of Jersey, Hudson', is in the Lightfoot herbarium at Kew. The grass continued to be reported and seems to have been much commoner last century and early this, than it is now. It has occasionally been reported as a casual but the only place where it has occurred regularly during the last thirty years is as a weed in the gardens of Beaufort Square, Grève d'Azette.
G fairly frequent; S locally frequent.

Glyceria maxima (Hartman) Holmberg
(*G. aquatica*)   **Reed Sweet-grass**

La Gasca's record (1834) was rejected by Lester-

Garland and has not been confirmed.
G 1978.

G. declinata Bréb.   **Small Sweet-grass**

Rare: St Ouen, 1906, Druce, det. Hubbard; damp valley between St Brelade and La Moye Station, 1929, I. A. Williams; south side of Val de la Mare Reservoir, 1968, conf. Melderis; meadows north-west of Victoria Village, Trinity, 1970, conf. Hubbard.
G 1891; A 1969; S 1928 and 1978.

G. fluitans (L.) R. Br.   **Floating Sweet-grass**

Common in wet places.

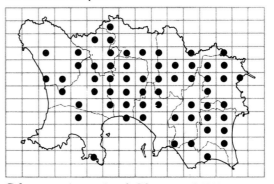

G frequent; A occasional; S last record 1892; H rare.

G. plicata (Fries) Fries   **Plicate Sweet-grass**

H. C. Watson claimed to have found Plicate Sweet-grass by a stream in St Aubin's Bay in 1852, and Druce stated that he had seen a herbarium specimen collected by Piquet from Samarès (*Journal of Botany* 1920).
G last recorded 1901; A occasional.

G. x pedicellata Townsend   **A hybrid Sweet-grass**
G. fluitans x **G. plicata**

Rare: Waterworks Valley, 1897, W. M. Rogers; a specimen from Ouaisné Common marsh was determined as 'probably' this in 1956 by T. G Tutin and it was plentiful in a wet area behind St Clement's Parish Hall in 1981.
A 1953.

Bromus diandrus Roth   **Great Brome**
(*B. maximus*)   *d'la* **droe**

It is not possible to separate early records of this species from those of the next because of difficulties in nomenclature, but the aggregate was common in sandy fields last century. This species is still in good quantity. Plate 2820 in Sowerby's *English Botany* was drawn from a plant collected by Babington at Grève d'Azette on 23 July 1837.

Map overleaf

195

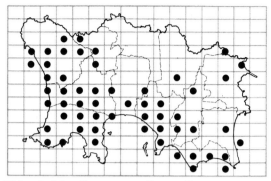

G local; A locally common; S rare; H rare.

B. rigidus Roth   **Ripgut Brome**
(B. maximus ?)

Much less common than the preceding species this century and confined to very sandy soil with somewhat open turf. It is locally abundant over several small areas in St Ouen's Bay and it was found at La Rocque in 1962. Hubbard and Melderis have confirmed specimens.
S rare.

B. sterilis L.   **Barren Brome**
       d'la **droe**

Common on roadsides and on hedgebanks.

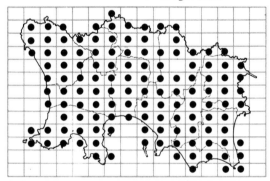

G frequent; A common; S rare; H occasional.

B. tectorum L.   **Drooping Brome**

Specimens were collected in St Aubin's Bay and in St Ouen's Bay in 1900 by Piquet and Guiton.
G 1979.

B. madritensis L.   **Compact Brome**

A grass which Dr W. Sherard found 'on the sandy grounds in Jersey plentifully' in the 1690s has been (? mistakenly) identified as this species. See the Introduction. Early records are confused because of difficulties in nomenclature involving *B. diandrus* and *B. rigidus* but this species, *B. madritensis*, does not seem to have been seen other than near Gorey or

on L'Île au Guerdain this century or last. It is still on L'Île au Guerdain in good quantity but the invading mesems should be kept in check.
G occasional; A rare; S rare.

B. erectus Hudson   **Upright Brome**

Listed by Piquet in 1851 and 1896 from Grouville but the specimen which he labelled *B. erectus* from Grouville in 1856 is the next species, *B. arvensis*.
G 1953.

B. arvensis L.   **Field Brome**

Piquet collected a specimen from Grouville in 1856 (Hb Oxford) and he claimed to have seen it in a meadow near St Ouen's Pond (*Phytologist* 1853).
G 1892 and 1925.

B. secalinus L.   **Rye Brome**

A casual not seen since 1900. Piquet listed it from Les Quennevais and St Aubin's Bay in 1851 and 1896, and Lester-Garland saw a specimen gathered by Piquet in 1872. Specimens from St Clement, 1870, and one labelled only 'Cornfields, rare', 1900, J. Piquet, were confirmed by Melderis.
G rare.

B. commutatus Schrader   **Meadow Brome**

A casual first recorded by Babington (1839) and at long intervals since. The last records seem to be from St Brelade in 1935 and 1936 by J. F. G. Chapple and Lady Davy, det. Hubbard.
G rare; A 1906; S 1907.

B. racemosus L.   **Smooth Brome**

Some confusion of names is suspected in the past. Babington (1839) and Piquet (1851 and 1896) stated that this was common yet Lester-Garland (1903) did not see it and it has not been found since. The only specimen known is one of F. Piquet's, det. Melderis, from St Peter's Marsh in 1870 but it was originally labelled *B. arvensis*.
G scarce; S 1872.

B. hordeaceus L.   **Soft-brome**
(B. mollis s.l.)   *d'la* **droe**

The species is common and has been since records began, but the four subspecies into which it is now split were not separated in the survey because of identification difficulties. Records are only given of the last three subspecies and hybrid when they have been expertly confirmed, but, as Lester-Garland (1903) stated, multitudes of dwarf plants may be found. These occur mainly round the coast on light soil.

Subsp. *hordeaceus* Common both on the coast and inland.

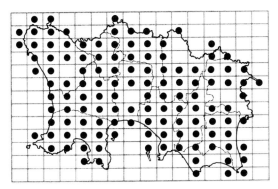

G, A, S and H common.

Subsp. *molliformis* (Lloyd) Maire & Weiller
Melderis thought a specimen gathered in 1968 might
be this, so a search should be made for it.
Subsp. *ferronii* (Mabille) P. M. Sm. Le Mourier
Valley, 1958, confirmed Melderis.
G, A, S and H occurs.
Subsp. *thominii* (Hard.) Maire & Weiller St Helier,
1838, Babington, det. P. J. O. Trist (Hb Cantab.);
grounds of the Imperial Hotel and the dunes of St
Ouen's Bay, 1881, Vaniot, det. Melderis; La Pulente,
La Moye and St Ouen, 1937, J. F. G. Chapple, det.
Hubbard.
G and A occurs.

B. x pseudothominii P. M. Smith

A hybrid Soft-brome

B. hordeaceus subsp. *hordeaceus* x **B. lepidus**

Jersey, 1960, P. J. O. Trist, det. Melderis.
G, A and S occurs.

B. lepidus Holmberg   **Slender Soft-brome**

'A solitary belated plant by the main road from St
Aubin to St Brelade', 1929, I. A. Williams (*Journal of
Botany* 1932 p. 113) and there have been three post-
Occupation (1940–45) claims but none has yet been
verified expertly.
G 1953; H rare.

B. willdenowii Kunth   **Rescue Brome**
(*B. unioloides*)

An introduced South American grass locally
frequent on roadsides. Sir John Le Couteur of Belle
Vue, La Haule, made the following entries about
'*Bromus Schraederi*' (now *B. willdenowii*) in his
record book: 'Sown April 24 – 1867 in drills nine
inches wide. Kept clean by hoeings: in the valley
below the Azalea clump, mown twice. Let it grow on
afterwards for seed – Brown cut it for seed in August.
Saved a cabot of seed or more. Cows and horses eat it
ravenously.
1868 April   Sowed a second piece with this seed in
drills.
1869 Jan 11. This grass is six inches high, fresh and

green.'
No more was heard of the experiment, but it is not
surprising that J. W. White found the grass looking
well-established on a hillside above St Aubin in 1897
since this must have been close to Belle Vue. Meanwhile one of Vaniot's helpers found it on La Grande
Route de St Clement in 1891. The main increase has
been post-war and it occurs so often along roadsides,
particularly at field entrances, that it may be spread
on the wheels of vehicles.

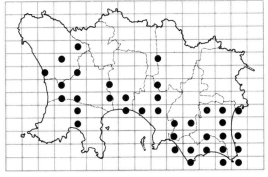

G and A rare.

Brachypodium sylvaticum (Hudson) Beauv.

False Brome

Locally common in shady places.

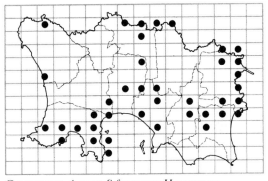

G common; A rare; S frequent; H common.

B. pinnatum (L.) Beauv.   **Tor-grass**
A rare.

Leymus arenarius (L.) Hochst.   **Lyme-grass**
(*Elymus arenarius*)

Not known in Jersey now. There have been four
claims for it in the past. J. Gay claimed to have found
it on Les Quennevais in August 1832 but there would
seem no possible habitat on Les Quennevais then,
nor is there now. W. Christy listed it from St Aubin's
Bay in 1836. His list (*Mag. Nat. Hist.*, New Series 1:
25–28) was of rare British plants which he had seen in
Jersey. The rest of the list is faultless and there seems

197

no reason for rejecting this record. Also a specimen gathered in St Aubin's Bay in 1840 is in Ereaut's *Hortus Siccus*. Piquet collected a specimen in 1911 but there is some difficulty over this. The specimen sheet says near the second tower in St Aubin's Bay but Piquet's son says he found it in Grouville Bay (Perrédès, 1912). Druce in *Plant Notes* in the *Journal of Botany* 1920 stated that it was 'probably planted' but gave no reason for saying this.
G claimed.

Elymus repens (L.) Gould   **Common Couch**
(*Agropyrum repens*)   *du* **bas**
Still common as stated by Babington (1839). The nomenclature and order used by Melderis and McClintock (*Watsonia* 14: 391–395) have been followed for couch grasses. Lester-Garland called the Genus *Agropyrum*.

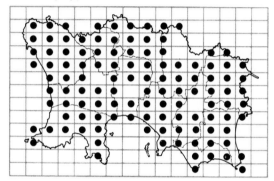

G common; A common; S occasional; H rare.

E. pycnanthus (Godron) Melderis   **Sea Couch**
(*Agropyrum pungens*)
In spite of Lester-Garland's (1903) comments that he had not seen it many specimens from Rozel round the south coast to St Ouen have been determined as Sea Couch by Melderis. It is therefore thought to be frequent in suitable habitats. The var. *setigerus* (Dumort.) Melderis is the commonest, if not the only, variety.
G locally common; A occasional; H rare.

E. farctus (Viv.) Runemark ex Melderis   **Sand Couch**
     du **bas d'sablion**
Subsp. *boreoatlanticus* (Simon. & Guin.) Melderis ('*Agropyrum junceum*') Not as common as last century but still to be found in loose sand round the coast.
G local; A locally frequent; H local.

E. x laxus (Fries) Melderis & D. McClintock
     A hybrid Couch
E. farctus subsp. *boreoatlanticus* x **E. repens**
Four specimens from widely separated areas have

been confirmed by Melderis, so this hybrid, which is difficult for a non-expert to identify, may be locally frequent: St Clement's Bay, 1851, J. Piquet; St Peter's Marsh, 1870, F. Piquet; West Mount, 1961, Miss P. Donaldson; Bonne Nuit, 1963, Mrs D. L. Le Quesne.
G 1958; A 1958.

E. x obtusiusculus (Lange) Melderis &
D. McClintock
     A hybrid Couch
E. farctus subsp. *boreoatlanticus* x **E. pycnanthus**
(*Agropyrum acutum*)
Six specimens from Anneport round the south coast to La Haule and Les Quennevais, ranging in date from 1871 to 1970, have been determined by Melderis. The hybrid is difficult to identify and may be locally frequent.
G occurs; A rare.

Aegilops cylindrica Host   **Goat's-eye Grass**
A specimen was collected at Dancaster's Farm in the north end of St Ouen's Bay in 1901 by Piquet.

Triticum spelta L.   **Large Spelt**
G 1899.

T. aestivum L.   **Bread Wheat**
Occasionally found as a casual from birdseed.
G casual.

Secale cereale L.   **Rye**
G 1968 and 1972.

Hordeum distichon L.   **Two-rowed Barley**
A casual occasionally seen on rubbish dumps.
G occasional; A Burhou 1956.

H. vulgare L.   **Six-rowed Barley**
Recorded from a rubbish dump in the 1960s.

H. murinum L.   **Wall Barley**
     du **blié sauvage**
Subsp. *murinum* Common on dry waste places. The specimen collected by Babington from 'Sands near St Helier' on 18 June 1838 (Hb Cantab.) is the holotype of *H. murinum* L. subsp. *murinum*.

Opposite, Plate 16   Lords-and-ladies, a presumed hybrid (see text) between *Arum maculatum* and
198   *A. italicum* subsp. *italicum*

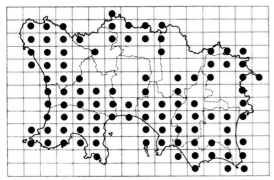

G common; A occasional; S rare; H occasional.

H. marinum Hudson   **Sea Barley**

La Gasca's record of 1834 was rejected by Lester-Garland (1903) and it has not been confirmed.
G ? H 1837.

H. hystrix Roth   **Mediterranean Barley**
G 1838 to 1906.

H. secalinum Schreber   **Meadow Barley**

One record: Le Hocq Common, 1958, Mrs J. Russell.
G last record 1971.

Avena barbata Pott ex Link   **Slender Oat**
G 1970.

A. strigosa Schreber   **Bristle Oat**

La Gasca listed Bristle Oat in 1834 but the next record was not until 1905 when Piquet collected a specimen at Trinity. There were then records in 1906, 1923, 1929, 1930 and lastly in 1958 by R. W. David from near St Ouen's Mill.
G four records; A 1900.

A. fatua L.   **Wild-oat**

Piquet thought this common in 1851 and rare by 1896. Lester-Garland (1903) considered it an occasional casual. Now it is a rare casual.
G occasional; A occasional; S ?1960.

A. sativa L.   **Cultivated Oat**

A rare casual now usually from bird seed.
G casual; A occasional; S 1902; H 1958.

A. sterilis L.

Subsp. *ludoviciana* (Durieu) Nyman   **Winter Oat**
Mont Cochon, 1961, Mrs E. M. Towers and St Ouen, 1981.
G rare and subsp. sterilis; A 1963.

Avenula pubescens (Hudson) Dumort.
(Avena pubescens)   **Downy Oat-grass**

Subsp. *pubescens* Very locally in abundance on Les Quennevais and Druce found it on the slopes of Beauport in 1907. Piquet originally recorded it in 1851 as the following species.

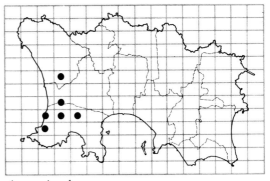

A occasional.

A. pratensis (L.) Dumort.   **Meadow Oat-grass**
(Avena pratensis)
Listed in error for the above by Piquet.

Arrhenatherum elatius (L.) Beauv. ex J. & C. Presl
(A. avenaceum)   **False Oat-grass**

Frequent. Most stems have the 'onion' or 'bulb' at the base and are subsp. *bulbosum* (Willd.) Schlüb. & Mart. to which the alternative English name, Onion Couch, is sometimes given. Subsp. *elatius* also occurs.

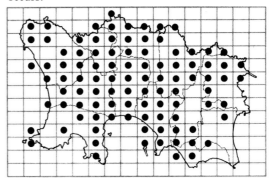

G, A, S and H common.

Gaudinia fragilis (L.) Beauv.   **French Oat**

Two records both by D. McClintock: Pont Marquet, 1954, det. Melderis; rubbish dump at St Ouen, 1958.
G local; A rare.

Koeleria macrantha (Ledeb.) Schultes
(K. cristata)   **Crested Hair-grass**

Locally common on Les Quennevais and further north in St Ouen's Bay.

Map overleaf

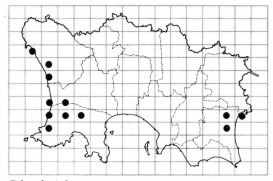

G local; A frequent.

Trisetum flavescens (L.) Beauv.   **Yellow Oat-grass**
(*T. pratense*)

Not seen recently. 'Golden Oat' was one of the constituents in a mixture of 'artificial Grasses' recommended to farmers in 1837 in the fourth *Annual Report* of the Jersey Agricultural and Horticultural Society. Sir John Le Couteur, their secretary, had already been experimenting with it and perhaps that is the source of La Gasca's 1834 record. Later records are: one by Saunders (Babington 1839); Maison St Louis, 1881, Vaniot; Victoria College, 1897, Piquet; St Brelade, 1926, Ariste.
G 1953 and 1980; A occasional; H rare.

Lagurus ovatus L.   **Hare's-tail**
                              des **babinnes-dé-lièvre**

Common, often abundant, in St Ouen's Bay, and in lesser quantity elsewhere round the coast on sandy soil. In the *Journal of Botany* for 1907 (XLV: 426) Druce wrote: 'In 1877 Mr Piquet showed me a small patch, which could have been covered with a hand-kerchief, resulting from some seeds which he had sowed there one or two years before. Now [1906/7] the plant has spread over the whole of St Ouen's Bay, and even some little distance inland on the sand-dunes'. At least five specimens, dated before the 1870s, exist in English herbaria, but they are labelled only 'Jersey' with no specific locality. It is presumed that they are the result of the common mistake of confusing Jersey with Guernsey where the species has grown since at least the eighteenth century. This may have happened when specimens were moved from one herbarium to another which often happened in the past, for example E. Blezard stated (*in litt.*) of the specimens in Hb Carlisle, 'Two specimens of *Lagurus ovatus* with 'Jersey 1838, W. H. White' written underneath have been added by Stevens to his sheet of Babington's Guernsey specimens carrying a Botanical Society of Edinburgh label.' As far as is known, no written record exists and no herbarium contains an adequately labelled specimen before the 1870s. Vaniot's excellent collection, made mainly in 1881, does not contain one. This suggests that Hare's-tail was still rare.

After the severe winter of 1962/63, there were fewer plants than usual in summer 1963, but by 1964 the numbers were almost back to normal, which was somewhat unexpected. This beautiful Mediterranean species, which used to occur no nearer than the Gironde, has gradually been spreading northwards and now occurs plentifully in Normandy. Its fluffy flowerheads have been much used in the Battle of Flowers exhibits since the 1940s, which may explain its spread in recent years to other parts of Jersey.

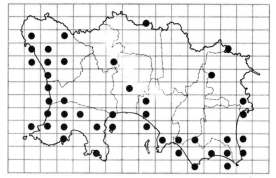

G locally plentiful; A ?1951; S 1892 and 1979; H 1902.

Deschampsia cespitosa (L.) Beauv.

                              Tufted Hair-grass

Subsp. *cespitosa* Two records: Samarès Manor grounds, 1958, D. McClintock; roadside, Ville à l'Évêque, 1959, C. A. Stace.
G 1925; S 1902.

D. flexuosa (L.) Trin.   **Wavy Hair-grass**

Three records: Victoria College grounds, 1897, Lester-Garland; St John's Cemetery, 1958, Mrs J. Russell.
G error; S 1838.

Aira praecox L.   **Early Hair-grass**
                                        du **suthîn**

Common, particularly on light soil. Le Maistre (1966) says it has always been known to farmers as an indicator of acid soil.

200

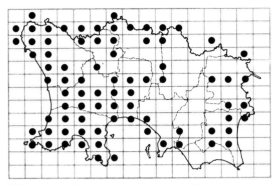

G frequent; A common; S common; H common.

A. caryophyllea L.   Silvery Hair-grass
d'la **finne hèrbe**

Subsp. *caryophyllea*   Common on light soil.
Subsp. *multiculmis* (Dumort.) Bonnier & Layens
St Brelade, 1898, and La Moye, 1899, Lester-
Garland, conf. T. Cope & S. Renvoize (Hb Kew).

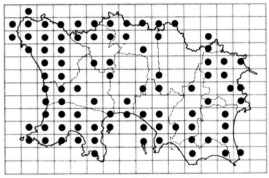

G common; A common; S frequent; H common.

Anthoxanthum odoratum L.   Sweet Vernal-grass
du **tchiândent**

Abundant.

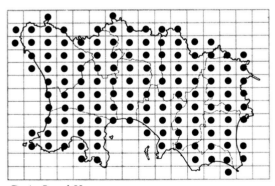

G, A, S and H common.

A. aristatum Boiss.   Annual Vernal-grass
One record: St Brelade, 1879, H. T. Maxwell
(Hb Brit. Mus.).
G ?1897.

Holcus lanatus L.   Yorkshire-fog
d'la **molle hèrbe**

Common, sometimes abundant, as it has been since
records began.

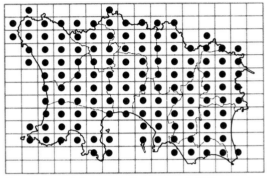

G common; A frequent; S occasional; H frequent.

H. mollis L.   Creeping Soft-grass
d'la **molle hèrbe**

Subsp. *mollis*   As last century, frequently seen but
not as common as the above.

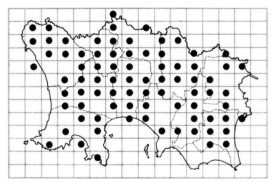

G frequent; A rare; S occasional.

Corynephorus canescens (L.) Beauv.
      Grey Hair-grass

Tufts of this beautiful grey-green and purple grass are
locally common in open turf on sandy areas.

Map overleaf

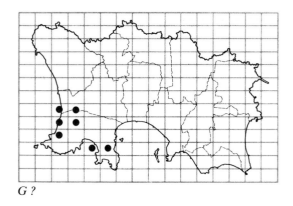

G ?

Agrostis canina L.   **Brown Bent**

Reported from Ouaisné Common in 1954 by D. McClintock, Miss C. M. Rob and W. Sladen; collected there in 1958, Mrs J. Russell (Hb Société Jersiaise) and in 1983 by R. W. S. Knightbridge, who recorded it also in several inland damp areas.
G rare; A rare; S Brecqhou 1902.

A. nebulosa Boiss. & Reuter   **A Bent**

A specimen in the Société herbarium is labelled 'Glyceria distans (Poa) Sea coast rare. J. Piquet'. It is unlocalised and undated, and was determined as *A. nebulosa* by Melderis but should be discounted.

A. capillaris L.   **Common Bent**
(A. vulgaris; A. tenuis)
Common.

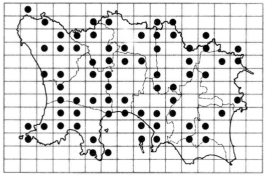

G, A, S and H common.

A. gigantea Roth   **Black Bent**

Many specimens originally thought to be this have later been identified as *A. stolonifera*, including those in the 1960–70 survey, but a specimen gathered at St Aubin by A. Ley in 1885 was confirmed by Melderis and one gathered by Miss E. H. du Feu was confirmed by Prof. T. G. Tutin in 1959.
G occasional; A rare; H (Jethou) 1838.

A. stolonifera L.   **Creeping Bent**
(A. alba)
Common.

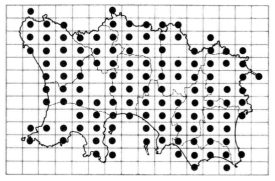

G, A, S and H common.

Gastridium ventricosum (Gouan) Schinz & Thell.
(G. lendigerum)   **Nit-grass**

No satisfactory record. Saunders' record, given by Babington in 1839, was rejected by Lester-Garland (1903) and the specimen purporting to confirm the record given in the 1952–53 report of the Société's Botanical Section, is *Corynephorus canescens.*
G rare; S rare.

Polypogon monspeliensis (L.) Desf.
          Annual Beard-grass
G last records 1889 and 1971.

P. viridis (Gouan) Breistr.   **Water Bent**
(Agrostis semiverticillata)

The first record was by Druce from 'newly-made ground at St Luke's' in 1906. There were no further records until 1962 when Mrs D. M. England found it on a heap of rubble at Bel Royal. Mrs E. M. Towers then added several records in the late 1960s (confirmed Melderis), and the grass has continued to spread. In 1981 it was locally frequent in several areas including by the side of flooded sandpits and by a new private reservoir in St Ouen. Normally it is at the foot of walls which seems the wrong habitat for a species of damp places, but perhaps sufficient water runs down the wall in time of rain for the plants to have damp root runs. The map includes all records up to 1982.

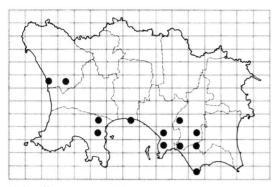

G locally common; A frequent.

x Agropogon littoralis (Sm.) C. E. Hubbard
               A hybrid Beard-grass Bent
Agrostis stolonifera x **Polypogon monspeliensis**
G 1858.

x A. robinsonii Druce   **A hybrid Beard-grass Bent**
Agrostis stolonifera x **Polypogon viridis**
G two records.

Ammophila arenaria (L.) Link   **Marram**
                               du **melgreu**

Subsp. *arenaria (A. arundinacea)* Abundant on the
sands of the coast. Marram has recently been planted
on banks created in Les Mielles, St Ouen, and in
blow-outs on the dunes, in order to stabilise the sand.
The cutting of Marram in Les Mielles is prohibited.
Such conservation measures are not new. On 23
September 1630 the Parish of St Helier prohibited the
cutting of Marram on Les Mielles de la Ville, the sand
dunes near the town. These were to the west of St
Helier and included where the General Hospital and
The Parade now are. Dr Le Maistre (1966) suggests
that the Jersey-Norman-French name may be
derived from the old Norse words *melr* for a sand
dune and *gras* for ?herb.

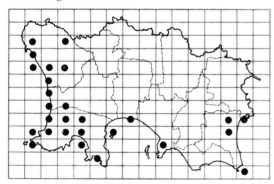

G local; A locally abundant; H common.

Calamagrostis epigejos (L.) Roth   **Wood Small-reed**
This large grass was first listed in 1851 by Piquet from
St Catherine's Bay, where it still grew in 1925
(Ariste), and may still grow. No exhaustive search
has been made – 'cliffs near the sea, Gibraltar at St
Catherine's', according to Piquet's notes in his copy
of Babington's Flora. Piquet then found it at La
Saline, St John, where Attenborough reported it as
abundant just before the war. Unfortunately the
post-war rubbish dumps at La Saline reduced its
quantity considerably but it was found plentifully on
L'Île Agois, St Mary, in 1974.
G rare.

Phleum pratense L.   **Timothy**
                                 d'la **coue**

Subsp. *pratense* This occurs in much of the agricultural grassland. When it first came in is unknown but
it was being recommended as a constituent of an
'artificial Grasses' mixture in 1837 by the Jersey
Agricultural and Horticultural Society in their fourth
Annual Report. Lester-Garland (1903) described the
species as very rare. He may have dismissed this
subspecies because it was sown in leys and considered
only the following, which is indeed rare.
G uncommon; A rare; H 1889.
Subsp. *bertolonii* (DC.) Bornm. Two records both
confirmed Melderis: Maison St Louis, 1881, Vaniot;
grassy field, but not a sown field, near the top of St
Peter's Hill, 1965.

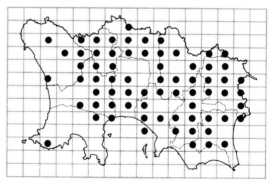

G ?rare; A 1969.

P. phleoides (L.) Karsten   **Purple-stem Cat's-tail**
(P. Boehmeri)
Saunders' record given by Babington (1839) was
rejected by Lester-Garland (1903) and has not been
confirmed.

P. arenarium L.   **Sand Cat's-tail**
Common on sandy ground.

Map overleaf

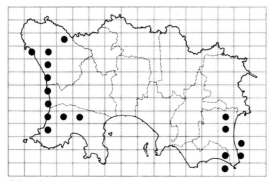

G local; A common; H common.

Alopecurus pratensis L.   **Meadow Foxtail**

Subsp. *pratensis* Common last century according to Babington (1839) and Piquet (1896) but Lester-Garland only gave three localities in 1903, and it was only occasionally found during the survey.

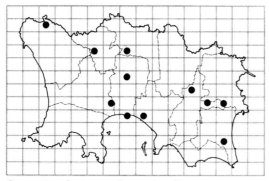

G occasional; A rare; S occasional.

A. geniculatus L.   **Marsh Foxtail**

Still common in wet places, as described last century, but strangely absent from most of the west.

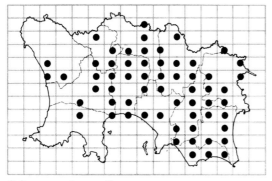

G frequent; A rare; S rare.

A. bulbosus Gouan   **Bulbous Foxtail**
G one locality.

A. myosuroides Hudson   **Black-grass**

A casual recorded at long intervals. La Gasca first listed it in 1834, Babington (1839) gave Saunders' record and Piquet listed it in 1851 and 1896 from Gorey Castle but a specimen he collected from there in 1896 is *A. pratensis*. In 1881 Vaniot collected a specimen on the Longueville Road, perhaps the first correct record. Other records followed: St Helier, 1899, Lester-Garland; Grainville, 1968, J. C. Fluck; near Mont les Vaux, St Aubin, 1970.
G rare.

Parapholis incurva (L.) C. E. Hubbard
               Curved Hard-grass
(*Lepturus filiformis* var. *incurvatus*)
Mr Ereaut found this at La Motte according to Piquet in his 1851 list and Piquet collected a specimen, confirmed Melderis, from La Pointe des Pas in 1852 (Hb Oxford). At some later date, Piquet added to his 1851 list, 'and behind the artillery barracks plentiful. Also in St Ouen's Bay where it grows very large'. It was recorded occasionally during the survey, sometimes in good quantity.

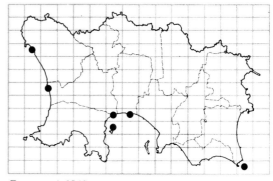

G error; A 1969.

P. strigosa (Dumort.) C. E. Hubbard   **Hard-grass**
Much rarer than the preceding species but still on the St Clement coast where it was first recorded by Babington (1839) and collected by Druce in 1877 and 1906.
G scarce; A 1969.

Phalaris arundinacea L.   **Reed Canary-grass**
               du **riban** (in gardens)
Subsp. *arundinacea* The normal form with unstriped leaves was collected by Piquet from St Peter's Marsh in 1851, and it was still there in 1983 though in very small quantity. It was also growing round a pond south of Ponterrin Mill in 1956.
Var. *picta* L., with striped leaves, the garden form, which was plentiful in Town Mills Pond about the turn of the century, has not been seen there for many

years. It has recently been planted near La Hague Reservoir, St Peter.
G rare; S error.

P. aquatica L.   **A Canary-grass**
A 1979.

P. canariensis L.   **Canary-grass**
                               d'la **canârie**

This was a frequent casual from the middle of last century until a few years ago, but recently it has become rare. Its source was bird seed. The map shows how frequently it was seen between 1960 and 1970. It used to be on most rubbish dumps and on many waste places. Is it that the habitat has gone or have the constituents of bird seed packets changed?

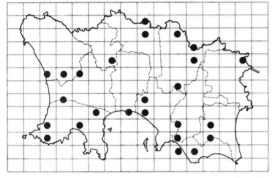

G casual; A rare; S Brecqhou 1902; H 1894 and 1959.

P. minor Retz.   **Lesser Canary-grass**
Dr W. Sherard's Latin description of a grass in Jersey, 'on the seashore over against Normandy' in 1689 (Ray 1690) has been interpreted, questionably, as *Phalaris minor*. See the Introduction. There was no further mention of the grass until it was found by Lester-Garland in 1897 when he gave a specimen to Melvill. By 1900, S. Guiton could write, 'On the south coast in waste and semi-cultivated ground, this fine grass is everywhere to be found' (B.E.C. *Report*). It seemed chiefly to be in the Beach Road/St Luke's Station area and along the railway line east of St Helier, but back in 1898 E. Duprey had written against a specimen that the species had appeared, and then disappeared, from various places. The only records since this flush about the turn of the century, have been in 1925 when Louis-Arsène and Ariste collected it at Samarès and in the 1960s when Mrs E. M. Towers collected it in St Aubin's Bay where it was presumed to be a casual.
G locally frequent; A locally frequent; S 1909.

P. paradoxa L.   **Awned Canary-grass**
G 1900.

Milium effusum L.   **Wood Millet**
Recorded by Piquet from marshes at St Clement in his 1896 list but all known specimens gathered by him, including the one of 1865 mentioned by Lester-Garland (1903), are Agrostises.

M. scabrum L. C. M. Richard   **Early Millet**
G rare.

Piptatherum miliaceum (L.) Cosson
                 Many-flowered Millet
This grows abundantly in a small area of the grounds of Highlands College just above the high retaining wall in Highlands Lane. It was first collected, and labelled as a casual, by Louis-Arsène in 1931 but it may have been grown in the botanic garden which used to be in the area.

Phragmites australis (Cav.) Trin. ex Steudel
(P. communis)   **Common Reed**
                                 du **ros**
Locally abundant in wet places inland and occasionally in small quantity on the edge of the coast where fresh water runs down the cliffs.

In the *Extente* of 1607, five parishes were listed as owing Reed to King James I: St Ouen, St Peter and St Helier 500 quarters, and St Lawrence and St Saviour 300 quarters. These 2,100 quarters were to be delivered between May-day and Michelmas. This due was not mentioned in any other *Extente* and it has not been possible to trace the use to which the Reeds were put, but the following extract for 9 October 1619 from Sir John Peyton's *Booke of Disbursements upon the Castells of Jersey*, may be relevant: 'Paid for 1800 of Reeds at 25s p 100 to cover the Cohu, the Stoore howse at the old Castle and other howses in the said Castle . . . 7l 30s.' Straw, mentioned later in the 1607 Extente, was the normal thatching material but there are records of Norfolk Reed being imported, so home-grown Reed may also have been used. These five parishes would have had extensive Reed beds in 1607. In the past Reeds were also cut for bedding for cattle, a practice which continued up to about 1950.

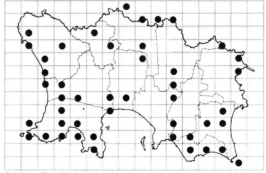

G locally frequent; A locally abundant; S rare; H local.

Cortaderia selloana (Schultes & Schultes f.)
Ascherson & Graebner

Pampas-grass

A garden outcast which sometimes survives. The huge clump near the rock at St Catherine was well-established in 1925 (Ariste). Another clump which was in garden rubbish thrown into an old sandpit north of St Ouen's Pond shortly after the war, survived for more than twenty years but has now gone. Elsewhere it has occasionally been planted out deliberately. Most plants are either male or female, not both, and only the female has the desirable silky plumes. It is therefore grown for preference but male florets must have been somewhere in St Brelade in 1961, because a seedling was found there on a wall. *G rare.*

Danthonia decumbens (L.) DC.   **Heath-grass**
(Triodia decumbens)

Recorded as common by Piquet in 1851 and 1896 and as frequent by Lester-Garland in 1903. It may be decreasing as it was only occasionally found during the survey.

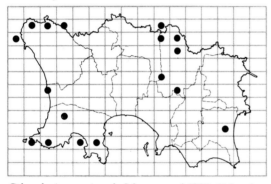

G local; A occasional; S last record 1897; H local.

Molinia caerulea (L.) Moench   **Purple Moor-grass**
(M. varia)   *du* **sectîn**

Subsp. *caerulea*   Locally frequent in rough grassy places. After several years' growth, particularly in a wet area, the hard and compact tussocks of this grass may be more than a foot high and as much across. The best places to see these tussocks are Le Canal du Squez, near Grosnez, and behind the pond on Ouaisné Common. In the past, they were cut and used as milking stools on the farm, and the farmer's wife sat on one in the house. A picture of a Jersey family at home is given in the *Glossaire du Patois Jersiais* (1924), and later by Le Maistre (1966), in the saying: *'lé bouonhomme dans l'bantchet, la bouonne-femme sus l'sectîn et l's êfants sus la jontchiéthe'.* Roughly translated this means that the husband had the place of honour on the sofa by the hearth, his wife sat on a tussock of Purple Moor-grass and the children sat on tussocks of rushes. These latter would

be much smaller than the tussock of Purple Moor-grass and so the family hierarchy was maintained.

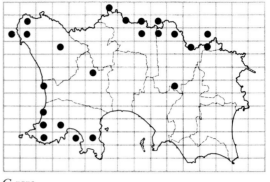

G rare.

Nardus stricta L.   **Mat-grass**

Rare. Piquet found Mat-grass near Bonne Nuit in 1853 and above Bouley Bay in 1864. It remained in the area until at least 1958 when, after intensive searching, a small patch was found above Giffard Bay. In spite of further intensive searching in the late 1970s it was not refound but it may well still exist. *G ?*

Eragrostis pilosa (L.) Beauv.   **A Grass**

Found by Mrs E. M. Towers near Millbrook in 1961, determined Melderis, and still in the area after more than twenty years. In 1981 it was a garden and greenhouse weed near Les Landes, St Ouen.

E. minor Host   **A Grass**

One unlocalised specimen: 'Cultivated ground', 1898, Piquet, determined Melderis (Hb Société Jersiaise).

Eleusine indica (L.) Gaertner   **Wire Grass**
G 1974.

Cynodon dactylon (L.) Pers.   **Bermuda-grass**

Babington noted in his own copy of his Flora that Dr M. M. Bull (d. 1879) had found this in St Aubin's Bay. Two specimens collected by Piquet in 1896 and 1899 are in the Société herbarium, but they are labelled only, 'Seashore, rare' and no locality is given. Lester-Garland did not mention Bermuda-grass in his 1903 Flora. It was therefore with surprise that Attenborough in 1925, when he was judging a children's wild flower competition, noticed a small boy holding a mixed bunch of flowers and grasses, obviously snatched hurriedly from the roadside, and in that bunch was Bermuda-grass. Legend has it that he immediately gave the small boy first prize and set off with him to find it, which they did, on the sandy roadside at the foot of Grève de Lecq Valley, where it still grows. Since the war it has been found in Grouville Bay, St Aubin's Bay and St Ouen's Bay also, sometimes in quantity. Bermuda-grass is a fingered grass and should not be confused with Jersey's other fingered grass, the garden weed *Digitaria sanguinalis*, Hairy Finger-grass.

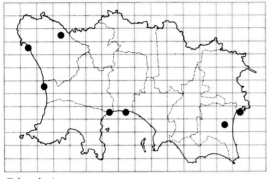

G local; A rare.

Spartina maritima (Curtis) Fernald
(S. stricta)   **Smooth Cord-grass**
Babington (1839) queried the record Saunders gave to him, but still published it. Lester-Garland (1903) rejected it and it has not been confirmed.
G ?1888.

S. x townsendii H. & J. Groves
S. alterniflora x **S. maritima   Townsend's Cord-grass**
Recorded in error in 1958 for the following species.

S. anglica C. E. Hubbard   **Common Cord-grass**
Found in St Aubin's Harbour in 1958 by Mrs M. L. Long. It was first identified as the hybrid *S. x townsendii*, but when more information was available it was realised that it was *S. anglica* and this was confirmed by Melderis. Clumps remained in the harbour for several years but disappeared when the harbour was dredged about 1970.

Panicum miliaceum L.   **Common Millet**
First recorded in 1925 by A. B. Cobbe and seen on most of the rubbish dumps of the island since the war, its source being bird seed.
G frequent; A 1977.

P. capillare L.   **Old-witch Grass**
Two records, both probably from bird seed: garden, St Aubin's Road, 1969, Mrs E. M. Towers; compost heap, Val de la Mare, 1969, J. E. Lousley.

Echinochloa crus-galli (L.) Beauv.   **Cockspur**
(Panicum crus-galli)   d'la **canârie;** *d'l'***hèrbe à pithot**
Frequent in arable fields. Piquet added Cockspur to

his 1851 list in 1857, saying that Ereaut had found it growing wild in a garden at St Helier. Attenborough stated (pers. comm.) that farmers disliked it as they considered it took a lot of goodness out of the land and that there was a legend in the island that it had come in with seed from Lessay Fair. Le Maistre (1966) credits *Phalaris canariensis*, another *canârie*, with this Lessay Fair origin but that is unlikely.

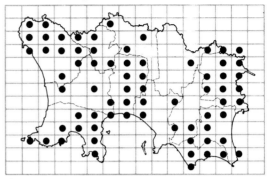

G rare; A rare.

E. muricata (Beauv.) Fern
G 1977.

Digitaria sanguinalis (L.) Scop.
                          Crab Grass or **Hairy Finger-grass**
(Panicum sanguinale)   du **pid-d'alouette**
Widespread on light soil and locally frequent. This persistent annual weed of light soil seems only to have arrived in Jersey in the middle of last century, being first collected at Georgetown by a Mr Purkiss in 1852 (Hb Oxford). Records indicate that though it was still rare in 1866, by 1884 it was very plentiful and by 1896 locally abundant. Normally it is a common garden weed in the south-east but Mrs D. L. Le Quesne and Mrs L. A. Morris reported it almost absent in 1979 and still only in small quantity in the next two years. The reason for this is unknown.

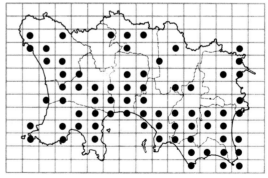

G occasional; S rare.

D. ischaemum (Schreber) Muhl.

Smooth Finger-grass

A specimen was collected in August 1858 from the east end of St Brelade's Bay by H. C. Watson (Hb Cantab.) but specimens collected by Guiton in 1917, and originally determined as this species by E. W. Hunnybun, were later determined as *D. sanguinalis* by Melderis.

Setaria pumila (Poiret) Schultes **Yellow Bristle-grass** *(S. glauca)*

Casual. Three records: among potatoes at La Moye, 1901, Lester-Garland; Victoria Crescent, 1967, and Devon Gardens, Grève d'Azette, 1980, from bird seed, J. C. Fluck.
G casual; S 1961.

S. verticillata (L.) Beauv. **Rough Bristle-grass**

A casual first collected from Le Marais, St Ouen, by Piquet in 1852 and later by Miss E. H. du Feu at L'Étacq in 1959. It was reported frequently in the 1960s, probably from bird seed, but it has not been seen so often recently.

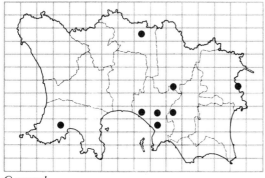

G casual.

S. viridis (L.) Beauv. **Green Bristle-grass**

Introduced. There are two early records: St Ouen's Bay, August 1837, W. Christy (Hb Cantab.); Les Quennevais, 1871, F. Piquet (Hb Société Jersiaise). Lester-Garland (1903) gave three other localities, and Attenborough, in the 1950s, said that he had always known it in a small quarry on Mont Matthieu, St Ouen. A search revealed that it was still there, and it has been seen each autumn since, sometimes abundantly, among White Mustard sown after early potatoes have been lifted. Records increased slightly in the 1960s, the newer ones being of single casuals, presumably from bird seed.

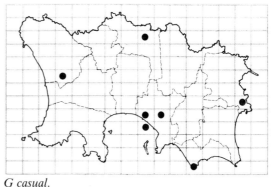

G casual.

S. italica (L.) Beauv. **Fox-tail Millet**

A casual first recorded from a rubbish tip at Gorey in 1957 by Miss M. McC. Webster and the same year it was on a rubbish dump at St Ouen. Like the other *Setarias* this is a common bird seed plant.
G casual.

Sorghum bicolor (L.) Moench **Sorghum**

On a roadside dump, south of St Ouen's Pond in 1964, J. C. Fluck, and later on the roadside on Mont Fallu. It is yet another bird seed plant, like the preceding species.
G casual.

Zea mays L. **Maize**

Several plants were growing on a dump in St Martin in the 1960s. Maize is occasionally grown as an agricultural crop.
G 1967.

ARACEAE

Acorus calamus L. **Sweet-flag**

Piquet planted Sweet Flag in the cliff pool at Noirmont at some unknown date, probably before the 1870s, as F. Piquet has an unlocalised specimen collected in Jersey between 1869 and 1871. W. P. J. Le Brocq told Babington he had seen it in 1888, flourishing. It continued to do so until the 1980s when the pool changed in character and became dank and shaded. Conservation work was begun in 1983 and it is hoped that the pool's previous habitat can be restored.
G Saumarez Park.

Lysichiton americanus Hultén & St John

Skunk Cabbage

Skunk Cabbage was well-established in a wild pool in Vallée des Vaux in 1956 and remained so until removed, presumably for a garden pool, a year or two later.

208

Zantedeschia aethiopica (L.) Sprengel   **Arum Lily**

Arum Lily grows well out-of-doors in Jersey and is a feature of many gardens with brooks or pools, often being planted in the wild part of the garden where it flourishes without attention, for example by the brook which flows down to Rozel. In 1966 Miss R. Kilby reported it as planted in a pool on the cliffs at La Moye.
G rare.

Arum italicum Miller   **Italian Lords-and-Ladies**
du **pitouais**

Common over much of the island. This is the Lords-and-Ladies, the leaves of which first appear between autumn and Christmas, and there are two subspecies in Jersey. The leaves of subsp. *italicum* are white-veined and the lateral lobes diverge; the leaves of subsp. *neglectum* (Townsend) Prime do not have pale veins and the lobes converge, sometimes overlapping. C. T. Prime, an authority on Lords-and-Ladies, stated in 1954 in the *Journal of Ecology* (42: 241) that in Jersey, 'A. *neglectum* [i.e. subsp. *neglectum*] . . . is abundant in the south-east of the island together with the continental *A. italicum* [i.e. subsp. *italicum*], and a continuous intergrading series is to be found. In the north of the island it is much less common; in the central valleys, e.g. Waterworks Valley, Vaux Valley, it is very common, but the plant more closely resembles the British form . . .'. This rough distribution is still true but no attempt was made to map the subspecies separately. The range of variation in the leaves is enormous, and the problems of identification are further compounded by hybrids of both subspecies with the next species. The first record seems to be in 1871 when Trimen and Stratton saw it, and Trimen wrote in the *Journal of Botany* (IX: 200) '. . . this is the only Arum we saw; . . . We noticed leaves with white veins, as in the south of Europe, and also some with dark spots, like those of *A. maculatum* (which probably does not occur in the islands)'. It does occur, see below.

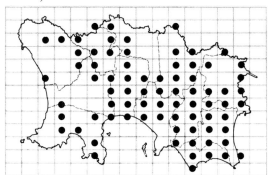

G local; A locally frequent; S rare; H rare.

A. italicum x **A. maculatum**
A hybrid Lords-and-Ladies

Dr C. T. Prime identified an *Arum* sent to him in 1961 from near Crabbé Farm, St Mary, as this hybrid. Other plants not easily assignable to either species were found in subsequent years. When Prime visited Jersey in 1970 he was shown the Crabbé plants *in situ* and also plants near St Mary's Church, at the foot of Jubilee Hill, in Vallée des Vaux and in two places in Trinity. He judged that all of them were hybrids.

In *Hybridisation and the Flora of the British Isles* (Stace 1975) J. D. Lovis and Prime state that hybrids involving both subsp. *italicum* and subsp. *neglectum* of *A. italicum* have been positively identified from Jersey. The illustration by Pandora Sellars opposite page 198 is of one of the Vallée des Vaux plants considered to be a hybrid by Prime though in it the spadix is cream, not pale purple as he and Jovis describe it in Stace. They also state that attempts to cross the species deliberately have failed.

The plants near Crabbé Farm and those at the foot of Jubilee Hill have disappeared through man's disturbance of the areas but new localities continue to be found. The *Arum* complex in Jersey would well repay further investigation.
G one certain record.

A. maculatum L.   **Lords-and-Ladies**
du **pitouais**

Widespread, but not as common as the previous species, and almost absent from the south-east where the previous species is most common. This species is called *A. maculatum* because its leaves are often black-spotted on the Continent. In Jersey the majority are not. Most of the field work on the *Arum* genus in Jersey since c. 1960 has been done by J. C. Fluck.

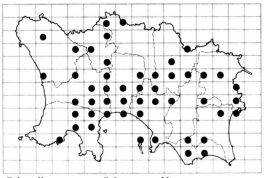

G locally common; S frequent; H error.

Dracunculus vulgaris Schott   **Dragon Arum**

A garden plant occasionally thrown out and surviving until the area where it grows is disturbed again. Over the years it has been seen near Le Hocq, on South Hill, in St Peter's Valley, in Grands Vaux and in the

sandpits north of St Ouen's Pond.
G rare; A 1982.

LEMNACEAE

Lemna polyrhiza L. **Greater Duckweed**
(Spirodela polyrhiza)
One record: stagnant ditches between Georgetown
and Samarès, 1899, Lester-Garland.
G last record 1901.

L. trisulca L. **Ivy-leaved Duckweed**
Rare. Babington (1839) recorded Ivy-leaved Duckweed from marshes near Grève d'Azette but all other
records have come from St Ouen's Pond: stream on
east side, 1900 and 1901, Piquet; south side, Lester-
Garland (1903); north side, 1915, and south side,
1917, Attenborough; in a small man-made pool
north-east of the main pond, 1964, where it appeared
in quantity the year after the pool was dug, and then
disappeared within a year or two.
G two centuries ago only; A locally abundant; S 1872.

L. minor L. **Common Duckweed**
  d'l'hèrbe d'pithot
Common and widely distributed in still water.

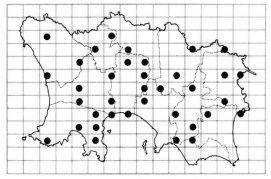

G frequent; A occasional; S occasional; H rare.

L. gibba L. **Fat Duckweed**
Rare. Fat Duckweed was listed by Piquet in 1896
from ditches at St Clement, probably Samarès where
it could still be found in the late 1950s. It was in
Deputy M. Bonn's pool at Oaklands, St Peter in 1982
and 1983.
G ?1900.

L. minuscula Herter **Minuscule Duckweed**
This duckweed from America was growing in the
German Reservoir at St Catherine in 1983, confirmed
A. C. Leslie.

SPARGANIACEAE

Sparganium erectum L. **Branched Bur-reed**
Occasionally found in wet places 1960–70 as the dis-

tribution map shows but R. W. S. Knightbridge
recorded it from several other areas in the east,
south-east and interior in 1983. Cows graze Bur-reed
hard and it may be that the species has increased or
become more obvious now that grazing is reduced.
  Babington (1839) found Bur-reed only at St
Ouen's Pond. Piquet, who listed it in 1851 from 'St
Peter's Marsh and other wet places', thought it
frequent in 1896. Lester-Garland (1903) considered
it 'Not very common', his own records being only
from the middle valleys. Binet's only record is from
Samarès in 1890. Ariste collected a specimen from
Grouville in 1925. In 1980 it was in quantity and
luxuriant by the side of a pool in the valley south of
Mont Misère, St Lawrence.

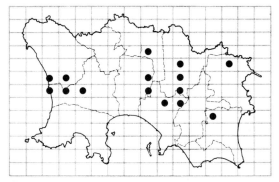

G rare; A rare; H rare.

S. emersum Rehmann **Unbranched Bur-reed**
(S. simplex)
Ereaut's *Hortus Siccus* contains an unlocalised specimen dated 2 August 1847 and Piquet collected one
from Samarès Miles on 31 July 1851 (Hb Oxford,
conf. E. F. Warburg). There was no further record
until the 1920s when Louis-Arsène claimed to have
collected specimens in St Clement on 6 June 1926 and
from Samarès on 1 August 1928. Ariste collected one
from Samarès on 20 August 1928.
G ?

TYPHACEAE

Typha angustifolia L.
  Lesser Reed-mace or **Lesser Bulrush**
Found in two localities by Mrs M. L. Long: wet
sandpits north of St Ouen's Pond, 1960, but the
species is no longer there; Ouaisné Common, 1983,
where it is rare.
G rare.

T. latifolia L. **Reed-mace** or **Bulrush**
It seems extraordinary that this plant was so rare last
century. Piquet listed it only from St Peter's Marsh in
1851, and by 1896 he knew it only from the partially

dried up fish pond at Diélament Manor. Lester-Garland (1903) who did not see it, gave Piquet's records and added that Guiton had told him that it used to be abundant at Les Marais. Which Les Marais is not stated. Guiton found it in the Town Millpond in 1917 and in Samarès Canal in 1918, and Binet found it in Vallée des Vaux in 1919. In all these localities it was reported to be plentiful. Its spread has continued and it is now frequent in wet areas.

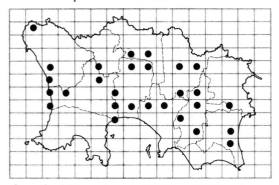

G similar history; A rare; S 1957 and 1958 only.

CYPERACEAE

Scirpus maritimus L.   **Sea Club-rush**
Subsp. *maritimus* Still rare in damp places round the coast, as reported in the past. In 1981 it appeared in a flooded sandpit excavated that year, north of St Ouen's Pond, but the sandpit was filled in with rubble in 1982.

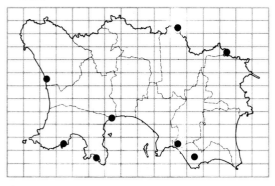

G scarce; A rare.

S. lacustris L.   **Bulrush** or **Club-rush**
Subsp. *lacustris* Often claimed but all specimens seen have been the next subspecies.
Subsp. *tabernaemontani* (C. C. Gmelin) Syme Rare. Recorded by Babington (1839) from St Ouen's Pond and marshes near Grève d'Azette. It was still at Grève d'Azette until at least 1903 (Lester-Garland) but now seems to have disappeared. At St Ouen's Pond it is confined to one clump in the reeds on the east side of the small inner pond, and in 1981 it

appeared by the side of a flooded, newly excavated sandpit north of St Ouen's Pond and it is still there. *G scarce; A last record 1900.*

S. pungens Vahl   **Sharp Club-rush**
Dillenius' edition (1724) of Ray's *Synopsis* contains a record by Dr W. Sherard. See the Introduction. In 1836 J. Woods gathered it on the banks of St Ouen's Pond and the drawing in Sowerby's *English Botany* Plate 2819 was made from a specimen collected there by Babington on 25 July 1837. Lester-Garland (1903) described it as abundant at the Pond and it was still plentiful in the 1940s and 1950s. Gradually it became scarcer probably because it could not stand competition from other vegetation, particularly from a new arrival, the strong-growing *Carex riparia* which was first recorded in the area in 1953, and also from the rank vegetation which grew in shelter provided by a willow hedge planted by a farmer in the 1950s. It has not been seen since the early 1970s but it may reappear.

S. holoschoenus L.   **Round-headed Club-rush**
It is impossible to say whether *Scirpus holoschoenus* has ever grown wild in Jersey, or not. Babington (1839) gave Saunders' record from St Ouen's Bay and Lester-Garland (1903) rejected it. A specimen labelled that it was collected from St Ouen's Pond, Jersey, on 24 July 1923 by J. E. Woodhead is in the Lancaster herbarium. On 19 August 1928, Ariste gathered specimens from the botanic garden at Highlands College and wrote on the herbarium sheet 'Signalé à St Ouen par Saunders'. On 1 September 1928, Louis-Arsène collected 25 specimens from some unlocalised place in Jersey; at a later date, he similarly collected 94; and then in August 1931, he collected 19 specimens labelled as from St Ouen's Pond. This is a total of 138 specimens. Arsène's herbarium was discussed in a paper in *Watsonia* (Le Sueur 1982). Normally the specimens would be dismissed, as having come from the botanic garden, but here there is Woodhead's record to consider. J. E. Lousley, learning of Woodhead's record, searched St Ouen's Pond without finding the species, or any suitable habitat. Woodhead told Lousley and McClintock that he could not remember finding it at the Pond and it was a surprise when it turned up in the collection he made that day, but there was nowhere else from which it could have come. If all the specimens are as labelled, did Woodhead find it only for Louis-Arsène to exterminate it? Or is it still present eluding all search?
G error.

S. setaceus L.   **Bristle Club-rush**
Occasional in damp places.

Map overleaf

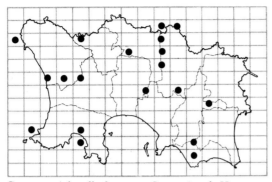

G scarce; A locally frequent; S occasional; H rare.

S. cernuus Vahl   Slender Club-rush
(S. Savii)

Occasional in damp places. Usually, but not invariably, the flowering heads have only one spikelet.

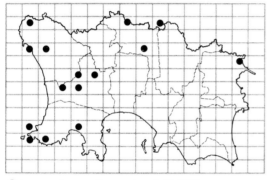

G scarce; A rare; S occasional; H 1837.

S. fluitans L.   Floating Club-rush

Increasingly rare. At various times since 1832 it has been reported from Grosnez and near Le Pinacle, St Ouen's Pond, Ouaisné Common, St Peter's Marsh, St Brelade's Bay and Grouville Marsh. The only post-war records are: La Rosière, 1956, but destroyed in the building of the desalination plant; near Le Pinacle, 1958; above Le Beau Vallet, Les Landes, 1983, R. W. S. Knightbridge.
G one old ?record.

Blysmus compressus (L.) Panzer ex Link   Flat-sedge
G one record, 200 years ago.

Eriophorum angustifolium Honck.
Common Cotton-grass

Rare. Babington (1839) reported Common Cotton-grass from a bog at La Moye, where Piquet later found it in abundance, though it has now gone with the draining of the land. F. Piquet collected a specimen from La Pulente in 1870 but it is not known there now. It is still in the three other places from which it was recorded last century: St Ouen's Pond, the Canal

du Squez on Les Landes and near Egypt, Trinity, in all of which it is decreasing.
G now very rare.

Eleocharis quinqueflora (F. X. Hartmann) O. Schwarz
(Scirpus pauciflorus)   **Few-flowered Spike-rush**

Rare. In the Société botanical report for 1919 Attenborough recorded finding this in a marshy place on Les Quennevais. Burdo found it there in 1929 and with Attenborough's directions, this minute plant was refound in 1958. Babington (1839) and Piquet (1851 and 1896) reported it from St Ouen's Pond but Lester-Garland said he had searched for it there in vain, and so have recent botanists.
G rare; A rare.

E. acicularis (L.) Roem. & Schult.
Needle Spike-rush

La Gasca listed this in 1834 and a specimen collected by Piquet from Bouley Bay in 1851 is in Hb Oxford. The record in the Société's botanical report for 1916 is in error – the specimen is a *Scirpus*.
G error.

E. palustris (L.) R. Br.   Common Spike-rush
(Heleocharis palustris)

Locally frequent in wet areas.

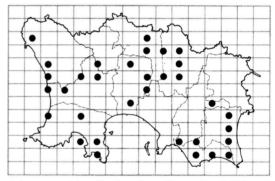

G frequent; A locally abundant; S occasional; H local.

E. uniglumis (Link) Schult   Slender Spike-rush

One record: Samarès Miles, 1851, Piquet (Hb Oxford).

E. multicaulis (Sm.) Desv.   Many-stalked Spike-rush
(Heleocharis multicaulis)

Rare. The only records last century were from near Grosnez (Babington 1839 and Piquet 1896). Lester-Garland (1903) thought it frequent and gave five localities: St Brelade's Bay, St Ouen's Pond, L'Étacq, Bouley Bay and Giffard Bay. Between 1960 and 1970 it was found only in Le Canal du Squez near

Grosnez, above Giffard Bay and in Ouaisné Common Marsh.
G rare; A rare.

Cyperus longus L. Galingale
du **han**

Common in wet places. Galingale, *han*, is so strong when dried that in the past it was an extremely valuable plant, being used in place of hemp for cords and ropes. Matting for floors, tethers for cows, and halters and collars for horses were made of it. Its strength was also used in the old custom *faithe braithe les peîles* (*faire braire des poêles*) on St John's or Midsummer Eve to keep evil spirits away. A *peîle*, i.e. a huge *bachîn* which is a large brass jam pan, was partially filled with water, some metal utensils were placed in it and the rim was tied round with a cord of *han*, Galingale. A number of strings of *han* equalling the number of people participating, were then attached to this cord. To quote Plees (1824): 'When these strings are sufficiently moistened, the persons assembled take hold of them, and drawing them quickly through their hands, a tremulous vibration is excited in the boiler (*la peîle*), and a most barbarous, uncouth, and melancholy sound produced. To render this grating concert still more dissonant, others blow with cows' horns and conchs. This singular species of amusement continues for several hours . . .'.

Les Hannièthes in St Ouen and La Hannièthe in St Martin and Grouville were so named because *han* grew there.

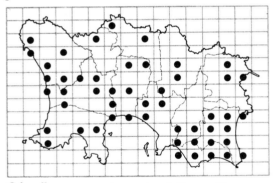

G locally common; A occasional; S rare; H rare.

C. eragrostis Lam. Green Cyperus

J. C. Fluck found this South American species in 1961 growing in a water garden by the stream running through Vallée des Vaux. There was no further record until 1967 when one clump was found, in the wild, at the top of the south arm of Val de la Mare Reservoir and it has since been found in several widely scattered localities. Most cyperuses need a wet habitat, and nurserymen stock Green Cyperus for water-side gardens, but it appears equally at home on roadsides. All records from 1961 are on the map.

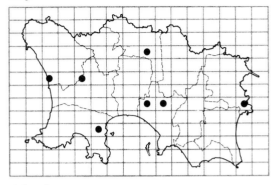

G locally common.

C. fuscus L. Brown Galingale

Listed in 1832 by J. Gay from St Brelade and a specimen collected on 17 September 1842 by the Rev. W. W. Newbould from St Peter's Marsh is in Hb Cantab. It must have disappeared fairly soon after this because St Peter's Marsh and the wet places in St Brelade were well searched last century and this was a species for which Jersey botanists, at least, were looking. Lester-Garland (1903) not knowing of Newbould's specimen rejected Gay's record which had been given by La Gasca.
G one ?record.

Cladium mariscus (L.) Pohl Great Fen-sedge
du **pavis**

In great quantity at St Ouen's Pond where it has been known since the middle of last century (Piquet 1851). Babington and his *aides* (including W. Christy), Saunders, Gay and La Gasca, did not see it in the 1830s. It would seem impossible for any botanist at St Ouen's Pond to miss so huge a plant, even if it were not then in its present quantity, so one must conclude that the species arrived there only about the 1840s. This would appear to be confirmed in Ansted's book *The Channel Islands*. In the first edition (1862), *Cladium* was said to be rare at St Ouen's Pond. In the third edition (1893), Piquet who wrote the section on botany, stated that: 'A very curious sedge-like plant is now common on the east margin of St Ouen's Pond, the seeds of which were probably brought over by some water-bird, bittern or coot. It is the *Cladium mariscus*'. Piquet, who was a highly observant chemist, interested in all plants, implies in this statement that he knew of *Cladium* nowhere else in Jersey, in the wild or in a garden. Nevertheless Le Maistre (1966) stated that it was grown in small ponds in the past because of its use in making halters, chairs etc. and it was mixed with clay to form hard floors. This was almost certainly Galingale, *han*, and not *Cladium*. If *Cladium* was the species involved. one can only marvel at the fortitude of the men and women who worked with the leaves which have barbs on the edges and on the keel, and can cut the flesh of the unwary like a razor. In Norfolk, where *Cladium* is abundant over huge areas, it is sometimes used for thatching.

Schoenus nigricans L.　　　　**Black Bog-rush**

A rare native plant of marshy areas or wet cliffs. Three localities: St Ouen's Pond (Babington 1839) and still there until at least 1926 when Burdo collected it, but it has not been found post-war; near St Brelade (Babington 1839) and this locality is probably the same as Attenborough's Mont Fiquet in 1918 and J. C. Fluck's Beauport in 1961 where it still grows; Les Quennevais, 1871, Trimen, and still there in 1958.
G rare; A locally common.

Carex paniculata L.　　　　**Greater Tussock-sedge**

Subsp. *paniculata* Piquet noted in his copy of Babington's Flora that Greater Tussock-sedge was abundant at La Saline and also in Les Mouriers Bay, St John, on 24 June 1896. Huge tussocks of this magnificent sedge were still growing half way down the cliffs between La Route du Nord and the sea in the late 1960s but have not been seen since the area nearby was used as a rubbish dump.
G scarce; A occasional.

C. vulpina L.　　　　**True Fox-sedge**

Earlier records of *C. vulpina* belong to the next species because of changes in nomenclature.

C. otrubae Podp.　　　　**False Fox-sedge**

One of the more frequent, though still only local, sedges of wet meadows. Except for a record by Lester-Garland (1903) from Grands Vaux, all past and present records are near the coast.

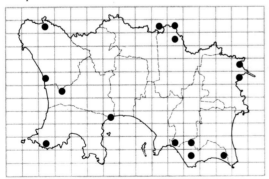

G frequent; S rare; H occasional.

C. x pseudoaxillaris K. Richter　　　　**A hybrid Sedge**
C. otrubae x **C. remota**

In Druce's *Comital Flora of the British Isles* (1932 p. 122) 'C. x axillaris' is given for Jersey. The source of the record is unknown.
G 1890.

C. spicata Hudson　　　　**Spiked Sedge**
G one locality.

C. muricata L.　　　　**Prickly Sedge**

Subsp. *lamprocarpa* Čelak　Frequent on dry banks. Most recent records come from the south and west but Lester-Garland (1903) also recorded the species from St Catherine and Gorey Castle.

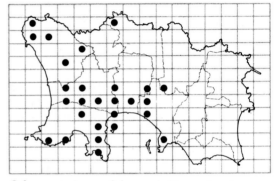

G frequent; A rare; S frequent; H occasional.

C. divulsa Stokes　　　　**Grey Sedge**

Subsp. *divulsa*　Rare in three localities: La Moye, Babington (1839), and Piquet collected a specimen from there in 1900; Gorey Castle, 1923, Druce, 1925, Ariste, and near there, 1965, J. C. Fluck; La Becquetterie, St Clement, 1961, Mrs J. Brooks, and confirmed from there in 1966, A. C. Jermy.
G 1852 and 1891; A rare; S occasional (including subsp. leersii *in A and S).*

C. arenaria L.　　　　**Sand Sedge**

Common in sandy areas round the coast and surprisingly on a grassy slope on the cliffs west of Grève de Lecq.

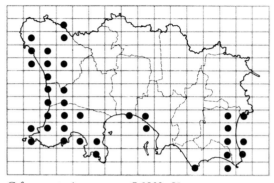

G frequent; A common; S 1902; H common.

C. disticha Hudson   **Brown Sedge**
G one locality.

C. divisa Hudson   **Divided Sedge**
Lester-Garland stated that the Rev. P. N. Playfair found Divided Sedge in 1901 in 'St Ouen's Bay on a bank at the edge of a ditch a little south of the Pond . . .' It was still there in the 1960s.

C. remota L.   **Remote Sedge**
Rare. Reported from about ten places from 1839 onwards. The three most recent localities are Gorey Castle, the valley from Rozel to St Catherine's Bay and near Millbrook.
G occasional.

C. ovalis Good.   **Oval Sedge**
Only occasionally seen but still one of the more likely sedges to be found in a wet meadow inland.

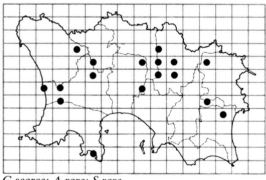

G scarce; A rare; S rare.

C. echinata Murray   **Star Sedge**
Rare in 1899 according to Piquet who at various times recorded it from St Brelade, Bouley Bay and Bonne Nuit. Lester-Garland described it as frequent and added Waterworks Valley and Grands Vaux. During the 1960–70 survey it was found in small quantity in four places: Bouley Bay, La Ville à l'Évêque, marsh

below Trinity School and Val de la Mare Reservoir valley.
G rare; A rare.

C. hirta L.   **Hairy Sedge**
Piquet (1851) described Hairy Sedge as common and it is still one of the sedges most likely to be seen, especially inland.

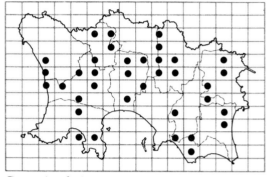

G occasional; A common.

C. riparia Curtis   **Greater Pond-sedge**
In good quantity on the north side of St Ouen's Pond. It was well established when found in 1953.
G scarce.

C. pseudocyperus L.   **Cyperus Sedge**
Still among the reeds of St Ouen's Pond where it was found by Lester-Garland in the dry summer of 1900.

C. vesicaria L.   **Bladder-sedge**
G two ?records.

C. pendula Hudson   **Pendulous Sedge**
In 1891, one of Vaniot's helpers found Pendulous Sedge at the base of the cliffs at La Saline, St John. Members of the Société's Botanical Section found it further along the coast in 1921. Post-war it was growing well in the valley which now contains Val de la Mare Reservoir, the building of which it survived, and by the side of the stream in St Peter's Valley. The species is certainly native on the cliffs and may be in the two inland localities mentioned. More recently, because of its beauty, it is being increasingly planted in gardens and has been seen as a garden escape or garden throw-out in several places. The map contains all records of Pendulous Sedge seen outside gardens since 1960.

Map overleaf

215

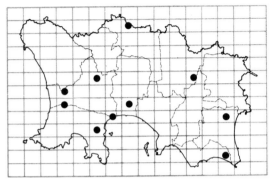

G local; A local; S 1976.

C. sylvatica Hudson   **Wood-sedge**

Subsp. *sylvatica* In 1981 Mrs E. M. Towers found Wood-sedge growing at the entrance to the drive of a house in Rue de Haut, St Lawrence. Its origin is unknown – it was not planted.
G rare; S 1978.

C. flacca Schreber   **Glaucous Sedge**

Subsp. *flacca (C. glauca)* Still to be found in nearly all the areas from which Lester-Garland reported it in the past: St Brelade's Bay, Les Quennevais, St Ouen's Pond, L'Étacq, Bouley Bay, Samarès Meadows, St Helier – as can be seen from the distribution map given below.

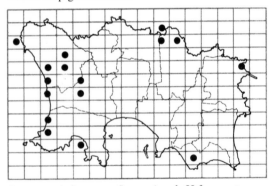

G scarce; A frequent; S occasional; H frequent.

C. panicea L.   **Carnation Sedge**

Carnation Sedge may be decreasing. Lester-Garland listed seven places where it had been seen up to 1903. Since 1960 it has been seen only in the marsh on Ouaisné Common, at St Ouen's Pond and in Le Canal du Squez, St Ouen.

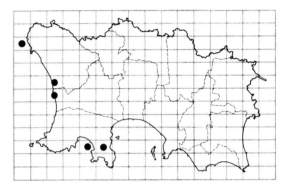

G rare; A occasional.

C. laevigata Sm.   **Smooth-stalked Sedge**

Local in damp fields of rough grassland, but sometimes abundant, even dominant, as in the valley between Ville à l'Evêque and Les Vaux, Trinity, in 1970. Nearly all the records from the past are also in the Trinity region.

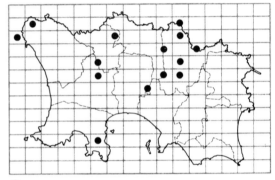

G rare.

C. binervis Sm.   **Green-ribbed Sedge**

Rare. In 1851 Piquet reported it as plentiful on the hills between Bouley Bay and Rozel. Lester-Garland (1903) gave a record by W. M. Rogers from Bouley Bay and added that it was abundant in Bonne Nuit Bay and Giffard Bay and that he had also seen it in Grands Vaux. The only post-war records are from Bouley Bay Hill, Les Landes and Ouaisné Common.
H rare.

C. distans L.   **Distant Sedge**

Rare. Piquet called Distant Sedge common in 1851 and frequent in 1896, but one of his specimens labelled *C. distans* in the Société herbarium is *C. laevigata* so some confusion is suspected. Lester-Garland thought it rare and gave only two localities – a stream on the cliffs at Grosnez from where it seems to have disappeared, and Samarès Meadows where it was still growing in 1958.
G occasional; A rare; S rare.

C. punctata Gaudin   **Dotted Sedge**

Dotted Sedge occurs in only a few places, but sometimes in local abundance, where fresh water runs off the cliffs on to the beach. It was first recognised in 1901 in Giffard Bay by Lester-Garland.

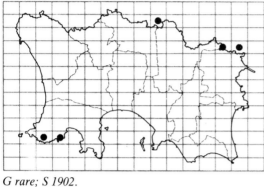

G rare; S 1902.

C. extensa Good.   **Long-bracted Sedge**

First reported by Piquet in his 1851 list from the 'Waterfall near the Pinnacle Rock, St Ouen'. Between then and 1960 it was noted in several places at the foot of cliffs round the coast, and it was refound in all of them, except the initial Pinnacle locality, during the 1960–70 survey.

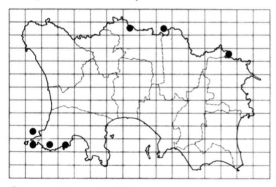

G scarce; A rare; S 1976.

C. flava group   **Yellow-sedge**

The aggregate is still frequent in damp places on the cliffs, as Lester-Garland stated in 1903, and most recorders during the survey echoed his 1903 cry, 'I do not understand the segregates'. The following three species within the complex occur and any records ascribed to particular species are given:

C. lepidocarpa Tausch   **Long-stalked Yellow-sedge**

Les Quennevais, 1851, Piquet, det. E. Nelmes; Petit Port, 1925, Ariste.
G error.

C. demissa Hornem.   **Common Yellow-sedge**

Grosnez, 1925, Ariste; St Ouen's Pond, 1956, D. McClintock; Les Platons, 1968; and a Jersey specimen was determined as this by E. Nelmes (B.E.C. 1947).
G occasional; A occasional; S occasional; H rare.

C. serotina Mérat   **Small-fruited Yellow-sedge**

Subsp. *serotina* Collected several times from St Ouen's Pond last century, and once from La Moye in 1837, all expertly determined R. W. David *et al.*
G rare; S 1902.

C. pallescens L.   **Pale Sedge**

Lester-Garland (1903) rejected a Saunders record given by Babington (1839) but a specimen gathered by Piquet from a marsh at La Motte in 1851 is in Hb Oxford.

C. caryophyllea Latourr.   **Spring-sedge**
(*C. praecox*)

Either this sedge has decreased considerably or it has been much under-recorded recently. Babington (1839), Piquet (1896) and Lester-Garland (1903) all described it as common. During the survey it was found only on Ouaisné Common, in St John's Churchyard, in Mourier Valley and in Bouley Bay.
G rare; A rare; S occasional; H rare.

C. pilulifera L.   **Pill Sedge**

Subsp. *pilulifera* Local and never in quantity.

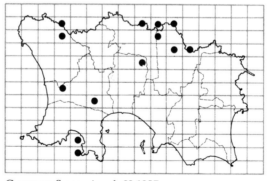

G scarce; S occasional; H 1957.

C. nigra (L.) Reichard   **Common Sedge**
(*C. Goodenovii*)

Plentiful east of St Ouen's Pond; otherwise rare.

Map overleaf

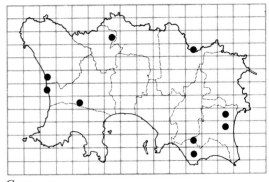

G scarce.

C. acuta L. Slender Tufted-sedge

Two records: weed in crack in edge of ornamental pool, Samarès Manor, 1958, but now gone; disturbed ground, Les Prés Trading Estate, 1970, Dr J. G. Dony, and still there.

C. pulicaris L. Flea Sedge

Local in wet areas. In the past it was recorded from La Saline to Bouley Bay in the north, and La Corbière to La Moye in the south. In the survey it was found only from Giffard Bay to Bouley Bay, and at Noirmont.
G very rare; A rare.

ORCHIDACEAE

Epipactis palustris (L.) Crantz Marsh Helleborine

Rare in wet places. Babington (1839) recorded it from Les Quennevais and St Ouen's Pond. It was last seen on Les Quennevais in 1952–53 by Attenborough, who stated that it had reappeared northeast of the golf clubhouse after an interval of several years. It is now thought to have gone from there because of the area being 'tapped' for water and so becoming drier. The habitat at St Ouen is unchanged and though Marsh Helleborine has not been seen there since 1960 it may well reappear.
G last seen c. 1901.

Listera ovata (L.) R. Br. Common Twayblade

Common Twayblade used to be abundant in a copse in Trinity Manor, according to Ereaut, presumably in 1847 the year in which he gathered a specimen for his *Hortus Siccus*. Since then it has been recorded from a number of places in none of which it seemed to survive, for there is no second record from any of them: Vallée des Vaux (1851); Moulin de Paul, 1896; Mont à l'Abbé, 1902; Samarès Manor, 1922; Bellozanne Valley, 1928; near Le Couperon and woods at Rozel at some unknown date. Innumerable open woods and copses have been searched since the mid-1950s, without success, but the Common Twayblade may still occur in Jersey.
G not seen for 80 years.

Spiranthes spiralis (L.) Chevall.
(Spiranthes autumnalis) **Autumn Lady's Tresses**

Autumn Lady's Tresses, a small orchid with white, almond-scented flowers spiralling round the stem, is frequent on long-established short turf. The easiest places to see it in late August or September are the churchyards of St Brelade, St Clement, St Lawrence, St Martin, St Peter and St Saviour, and the Mont à l'Abbé, Green Street, Almorah and St John's Cemeteries though it occurs frequently on lawns and in short wild turf elsewhere.

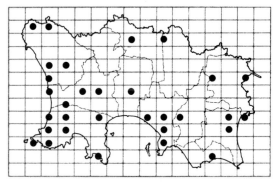

G occasional; A frequent; S occasional; H last record 1930.

S. aestivalis (Poiret) L. C. M. Richard
Summer Lady's Tresses

Extinct? Killed by collectors? Babington first saw Summer Lady's Tresses on 24 July 1837 at St Ouen's Pond and returned the next day to collect a specimen to send to Sowerby for him to draw for a supplement to *English Botany* (Plate 2817). A note in the supplement states that it was discovered in 'Jersey in a wet sandy spot upon the banks of St Ouen's Pond, but it is far from plentiful even there and has not been gathered in any other part of the island'. This resulted in many collectors coming to Jersey to secure one of the rarest of British wild orchids for their herbaria. Many of these collections assembled in the past have now been given to museums, and there is hardly a major museum herbarium in the country which does not contain a specimen of Summer Lady's Tresses from Jersey. Some contain more than a score, most complete with the root tubers. This orchid is decreasing throughout its range in Europe, so it might have gone in any case, but it would seem impossible for any rare species to withstand the depredations of so many collector-botanists.

Its history this century is obscure and the following account is based mainly on conversations with Attenborough (1883–1973) in the late 1950s and 1960s when his memory was becoming dimmed. He settled in Jersey about 1911 but on an earlier visit, perhaps 1906, he found it, picked it – which was the usual thing to do in those days – and took it to show Piquet in his chemist's shop. Piquet looked at it with some surprise, mingled with great pleasure, and exclaimed, 'Ah, my boy, you've got it!' and took a bottle of perfume off a nearby shelf for Attenborough to give to his girl-friend, the daughter of a rival chemist. This shows the attitude of the time towards rare plants. Later Attenborough was most distressed when people brought to him in his chemist's shop in Conway Street, wild orchids which they had picked. It also indicates that the orchid had become extremely rare. Attenborough found it again from about 1910 to 1917, but there were no more from 1917 until about 1925, when he found just one, and no more later. Louis-Arsène arrived in Jersey in the early 1920s. A specimen gathered by him, labelled St Ouen's Pond, 1926, is in the British Museum herbarium. Was it Attenborough's single flowering spike? (Attenborough did not keep a herbarium and by the mid-1920s he would not have picked a rare orchid.) Or was it not from Jersey at all? In Louis-Arsène's herbarium in Jersey, one sheet contains four specimens, complete with tubers, labelled as from St Ouen's Pond in August 1928. These specimens, like many of the other rarities in the collection, almost certainly did not come from Jersey (Le Sueur 1982) but if they did, then he may have been responsible for the final disappearance of one of Jersey's most beautiful wild orchids.

The flowering spike of Summer Lady's Tresses is surrounded by a rosette of leaves at the base of the stem. Autumn Lady's Tresses can easily be distinguished from it because the rosette of leaves is at one side of the flowering spike, not surrounding it, and it may not appear until the flower is over.
G last seen 1914.

Platanthera bifolia (L.) L. C. M. Richard
Lesser Butterfly Orchid
In the Société botanical report for 1922, Attenborough stated: '*Habenaria bifolia*, Br. The Butterfly Orchis was found on the Quenvais by Lady Davy. It was last noted by Mr. R. R. Lemprière at La Coupe many years ago'. It has not been possible to trace Lemprière's note. In 1937 Attenborough erroneously stated that Lady Davy had found this in 1924 instead of 1922. Lady Davy originally recorded the species erroneously as *Habenaria virescens* which is a synonym of *P. chlorantha*, the Greater Butterfly Orchid. The specimen proved it to be this species.

P. chlorantha (Custer) Reichenb.
Greater Butterfly Orchid
Reported in error for the previous species.

Dactylorhiza majalis (Reichenb.) P. F. Hunt & Summerhayes
Subsp. *praetermissa* (Druce) D. M. Moore & Soó
Southern Marsh Orchid
Local in damp meadows. Since the survey it has been noted in Le Marais, St Ouen. There was some confusion over the name of this species in the past. It is the *Orchis latifolia* of Babington and Lester-Garland, and the *O. incarnata* of Piquet.

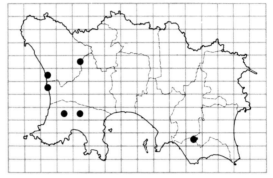

G local; A rare.

D. maculata group   **Spotted Orchid**
(Orchis maculata)   *d'la* **coue dé r'nard**
Both *D. maculata* (L.) Soó, the Heath Spotted Orchid, and *D. fuchsii* (Druce) Soó, the Common Spotted Orchid, occur but the records are inextricably mixed and many were simply of a 'Spotted Orchid'. More work is required to sort out their distributions but they occasionally occur together as at St Ouen's Pond and near La Ville à l'Évêque, Trinity. The aggregate is one of the commoner orchids occurring in damp meadows. A map is given of the aggregate but the orchids are probably under-recorded because of the difficulties some recorders found in separating the species and their unwillingness to record only the aggregate.

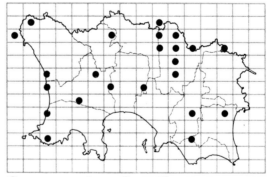

G uncommon; A rare; S rare; H rare.

D. x transiens (Druce) Soó   **A hybrid Spotted Orchid**
D. fuchsii x **D. maculata**

Plants intermediate between *D. fuchsii* and

D. maculata occur at St Ouen's Pond and are presumed to be the hybrid.
G occurs.

D. x grandis (Druce) P. F. Hunt **A hybrid Orchid**
D. fuchsii x **D. praetermissa**
See below.

D. x hallii (Druce) Soó **A hybrid Orchid**
D. maculata x **D. praetermissa**
Plants with the Southern Marsh Orchid as one parent, and either the Common or Heath Spotted Orchid as the other parent, occur at St Ouen's Pond.
G occurs.

Orchis morio L. **Green-winged Orchid**
Subsp. *morio* Locally frequent in meadows and on the dunes though it seems to be decreasing. Babington, who did not record the Green-winged Orchid (1839), was here at the wrong time of year but Saunders might have been expected to tell him of it, had it been a common plant. Ereaut collected a specimen in 1847, and Piquet (1851) considered it rare. By 1871 Trimen could describe it as abundant on Les Quennevais (*Journal of Botany* IX: 200) and Lester-Garland (1903) as abundant at St Ouen's Pond. It was still abundant in both areas until the late 1970s when it suddenly decreased considerably at St Ouen's Pond and in 1983 there were only c. 30 flowering spikes in the north-east fields. This may be partly due to a rise in the water-table in the meadows but it has also gone from the drier areas. It was still common on Les Quennevais in 1983 but it has decreased from its former abundance. This orchid, being an early flowerer and purple, is often erroneously called the Early Purple Orchid in Jersey. It can be distinguished at a glance by its leaves being unspotted and by five of the 'petals' of each flower coming together at the top to give a hooded effect. Its numbers are declining elsewhere in Europe, also for no apparent reason, so it will be interesting to follow its fortunes in Jersey.

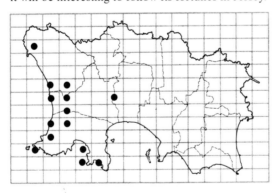

G known only 1890–1924; A locally frequent; H 1922.

O. militaris L. **Military Orchid**
A claim based on a withered specimen found on Les Quennevais in 1923 was later withdrawn (*Journal of Botany* 1923 and 1926).

O. purpurea Hudson **Lady Orchid**
A withered specimen collected on Les Quennevais in 1923 by Miss E. Vachell and originally identified as *O. militaris* was later determined as *O. purpurea* when Louis-Arsène claimed to have found this species in the same area. A specimen in Ariste's herbarium on 2 July 1929 confirms its presence in Jersey. Attenborough, in error in 1937, gave the date of the first specimen as 1926 and stated that it was 'Orchis fusca'.

O. mascula (L.) L. **Early Purple Orchid**
Subsp. *mascula* Rare, widespread, and often seen only as single plants. It may be increasing on Les Quennevais. Strangely, it has been seen in St John's Churchyard, 1901, Lester-Garland; St Saviour's Churchyard, 1958, Miss E. H. du Feu, where it still grows; and in Green Street Cemetery, 1963, Mrs M. L. Long.

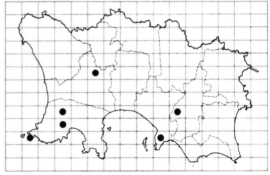

G rare; S 1896; H 1955.

O. laxiflora Lam. **Jersey** or **Loose-flowered Orchid**
  des **pentecôtes**
Subsp. *laxiflora* Locally common, sometimes abundant, in wet meadows. Two consecutive entries in Babington's diary for 1838 run:
'June 5th. Went by La Haule to the Quenvais and St Ouen's Pond, where I gathered *Orchis laxiflora*, then by the water-mill (gathering *Linaria Pelisseriana* on the hill side) to St Peters, and home by the marsh, in which I found *Ranunculus ophioglossifolius*.
June 6th. Went before breakfast to St Peter's Marsh to gather *Ranunculus ophioglossifolius* for Sowerby. Sent it off that day together with *Orchis laxiflora*, *Linaria Pelisseriana*, *Polygala oxycantha*, and *Festuca sabulicola* for him to draw for the "Eng. Bot. Suppl." Walked to St Saviour's Valley.'

In the supplement to *English Botany* Sowerby gave

Babington's note: 'Almost every wet meadow and bog in the islands of Jersey & Guernsey is ornamented by a profusion of this plant. The specimens figured (*E.B.S.* Plate 2828) were gathered by the writer of this at St Ouen's Pond June 9 [should be 5] 1838'.

The number of Jersey Orchids at St Ouen's Pond varies with farming practice. Some years there are enormous numbers in the grassy fields skirting the back of the Pond. Though the Pond is the locality usually given for the orchid, it grows in other areas of St Ouen and in several fields at St Clement. A field at La Becquetterie, St Clement, was purple with them in 1965, and it was almost impossible to set foot in the field without crushing some. Unfortunately many of these were destroyed when the Baudrette Brook was culverted but there are plenty in the fields to the south and east of the Rue des Prés Trading Estate. Piquet listed it in both 1851 and 1896 from St Peter's Marsh and Attenborough gave the Marsh as one locality in 1937. Later he stated in the Société's botanical report for 1940–45 that the site, which had been one of the best, had been destroyed during building operations. Lester-Garland (1903) stated that it grew in Grands Vaux and Attenborough that he had found it near Gorey in 1937. It used to grow in damp areas on Les Quennevais but the habitat now seems to have gone.

Modern farming practice or other development is eventually likely to change many of these old water-meadows, so in 1972 the National Trust for Jersey bought two fields north-east of St Ouen's Pond where the orchid grows in profusion. It is hoped that at least these two fields will contain the orchids permanently.

The English name, Jersey Orchid, has been used for many years in the main Floras of the British Isles. The Jersey-Norman-French name, *des pentecôtes*, indicates roughly the time of year when they flower, Pentecost or Whitsuntide, i.e. after the spring orchids but before those of full summer.

The orchid was depicted on the 7½p stamp issued by the Jersey Postal Authority in 1972 and an illustration by Pandora Sellars is opposite page 214.
G locally common.

O. x alata Fleury   **A hybrid Orchid**
O. laxiflora x **O. morio**

Recorded at St Ouen's Pond in 1914 by Attenborough in the Société's botanical report for that year, and Druce wrote: 'St Ouen with both parents. Our member Mr T. W. Attenborough sent me dried specimens and describes them as seeming to partake of the characters of both species . . .' (B.E.C. *Report* 4:25). This is the record mentioned by P. F. Hunt in Stace (1975) where it is given for Guernsey in error for Jersey.

Attenborough later found it on Les Blanches Banques. Presumed hybrids continue to be seen.
G 1949.

Aceras anthropophorum (L.) Aiton f.   **Man Orchid**
Piquet claimed to have found the Man Orchid at Rozel in 1853, in seed, (*Phytologist* IV) but he did not include it in his 1896 list so presumably he withdrew the record.

Himantoglossum hircinum (L.) Sprengel
                         Lizard Orchid
Three flowering spikes were found on Les Quennevais on 26 June 1918 by Attenborough according to the Société's botanical report for that year (not 1916 as he later stated). Plants continued to be found there up to 1946. In 1961 C. J. Cadbury found 16 flowering spikes between Le Chemin du Moulin and La Grande Route des Mielles, St Ouen. Plants remained in the area until about 1970 when the top soil was suddenly removed to open up a sandpit.

Anacamptis pyramidalis (L.) L. C. M. Richard
                      Pyramidal Orchid
The first record is Guiton's from the north end of St Ouen's Bay in 1900. It was reported on Les Quennevais in 1915, at La Rocque in 1934 and by St Catherine's Breakwater in 1947. It has continued to be found in all these places and is now very locally common in the north of St Ouen's Bay.

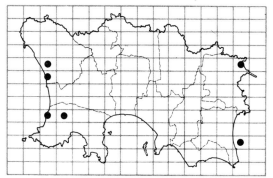

G very rare; A locally common.

Ophrys sphegodes Miller   **Early Spider Orchid**
Subsp. *sphegodes* The Early Spider Orchid was discovered on Les Quennevais by Lester-Garland in 1910, according to Attenborough (1937), and it could still be found there until 1929.

O. apifera Hudson   **Bee Orchid**
Subsp. *apifera* The Bee Orchid was discovered in St Ouen's Bay by Lester-Garland in 1902 and Attenborough and Guiton saw one plant at the south end of the Bay in 1915. The same year they found it near La Tête des Quennevais, very sparingly. The last record was in 1946 when Attenborough saw one plant on Les Quennevais.
G rare; A rare.

A. retroflexus L.   **Common Amaranth**
du **chuchot**

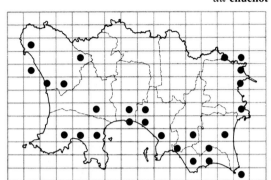

G rare; A rare; S 1898; H 1958.

For text see page 27

Saponaria officinalis L.   **Soapwort**
(S. Vaccaria)   *des* **mains jointes**

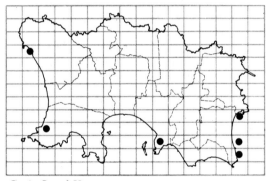

G, A, S and H rare.

For text see page 39

222

LES ÉCRÉHOUS

In 1309 Les Écréhous had no cultivatable land and no house except the 'Chapel' according to the Assize Roll of that year. The next known comment, relating to vegetation, is Père Noury's in the Société's *Bulletin Annuel* for 1892 where he states that each year a labourer could make about ten haycocks of inferior hay.

L. V. Lester-Garland visited Les Écréhous on 18 June 1896 and a list of the 45 species which he recorded is in the Société's *Bulletin Annuel* for 1898. Some information may then be missing because T. W. Attenborough and S. Guiton visited the islets in 1915 and claimed to have brought the total number of species up to 53 by adding five new species though one was already on Lester-Garland's list. Information may be missing again between then and 1928 when a Société expedition studied many aspects of Les Écréhous. After listing a few species including two new ones, Attenborough stated in the expedition report in the *Bulletin Annuel* for 1933 that 'no fewer than 66 species occur in this limited area.' If true then 15 records made between 1896 and 1928 have not been found, though some of the species may have been subsequently re-discovered. Since 1958 several expeditions have been made to Les Écréhous and the known recorded species number 66 again.

The most interesting species is *Anthriscus sylvestris* Cow Parsley which has seldom been seen on the main island of Jersey. Lester-Garland's unspecified orchid in fruit has long been considered a Bluebell which he does not mention. Attenborough commented in the report of the 1928 expedition that 'It is certain that the vegetation would be of even greater luxuriance but for the destruction caused by the rabbits.' The rabbits disappeared but some were introduced again in the early 1970s. By April 1975 Le Maître Île presented an extraordinary sight. The rabbits had eaten every scrap of vegetation except the Stinking Iris and were dying from starvation rather than eat that. As soon as the remaining rabbits were removed, the vegetation returned and the island was green again.

From the end of the Occupation (1945) to the coming of the rabbits, Le Maître Île was a grassy islet, except for the 'marsh' area where Tree-mallow was dominant, and it would have been possible to cut a small amount of inferior hay from it as in Noury's time. Tree-mallow has now spread over the whole of Le Maître Île and the grass is much reduced in quantity.

All species recorded for Les Écréhous are listed below. The dates of the early records are given and an asterisk means that the species has been seen in the last twenty-five years. More species associated with man will probably be added to the list soon because of the increased use of Les Écréhous by visiting yachtsmen.

Asplenium marinum	Sea Spleenwort	1928, *
A. billotii	Lanceolate Spleenwort	1915
Urtica urens	Small Nettle	*
Rumex crispus	Curled Dock	1896, *
Beta vulgaris subsp. *maritima*	Sea Beet	1896, *
Atriplex laciniata	Frosted Orache	1915
A. hastata	Spear-leaved Orache	1896, *
Stellaria media	Common Chickweed	*
Cerastium diffusum	Sea Mouse-ear Chickweed	1896
Sagina apetala subsp. *erecta*	Annual Pearlwort	1896
S. maritima	Sea Pearlwort	*
Spergularia rupicola	Rock Sea-spurrey	1896, *
Silene maritima	Sea Campion	1896, *
Ranunculus ficaria	Lesser Celandine	*
Cochlearia danica	Danish Scurvygrass	1896, *
Capsella bursa-pastoris	Shepherd's-purse	1896, 1928, *
Sinapis arvensis	Charlock	1896

Umbilicus rupestris	Pennywort	1896, *
Sedum anglicum	English Stonecrop	1896, *
Rubus sp.	Bramble	1896, 1928, *
Vicia sativa subsp. *nigra*	Vetch	1896
Medicago lupulina	Black Medick	1915
Trifolium campestre	Hop Trefoil	1896, *
T. arvense	Hare's-foot Clover	1896, *
Lotus subbiflorus	Hairy Bird's-foot Trefoil	1896
Geranium molle	Dove's-foot Crane's-bill	*
Euphorbia helioscopia	Sun Spurge	1896
E. portlandica	Portland Spurge	1896, 1915
Lavatera arborea	Tree-mallow	1896, *
Anthriscus sylvestris	Cow Parsley	1896, 1928, *
Crithmum maritimum	Samphire	1896, 1928, *
Petroselinum crispum	Parsley	1928
Anagallis arvensis	Scarlet Pimpernel	1896, 1928, *
Armeria maritima	Thrift	1896, *
Limonium binervosum	Rock Sea-lavender	*
Centaurium erythraea	Centaury	1896
Myosotis ramosissima	Early Forget-me-not	1896
Solanum nigrum	Black Nightshade	1915
Plantago coronopus	Buck's-horn Plantain	1896, *
P. lanceolata	Ribwort Plantain	1896
Bellis perennis	Daisy	*
Senecio jacobaea	Common Ragwort	*
Carduus tenuiflorus	Slender Thistle	1896, *
Cirsium vulgare	Spear Thistle	1896
Sonchus asper	Prickly Sow-thistle	1896
S. oleraceus	Smooth Sow-thistle	1896, *
S. arvensis	Perennial Sow-thistle	1896
Taraxacum sp.	Dandelion	1896, *
Scilla autumnalis	Autumn Squill	1896
Hyacinthoides non-scripta	Bluebell	1928, *
Iris foetidissima	Stinking Iris	1896, 1928, *
Juncus maritimus	Sea Rush	1896, *
J. gerardii	Saltmarsh Rush	*
Luzula sp.	Wood-rush	1896
Festuca rubra	Red Fescue	1896, *
Lolium perenne	Perennial Rye-grass	1896
Desmazeria marina	Sea Fern-grass	1896, *
Poa annua	Annual Meadow-grass	*
Puccinellia maritima	Common Saltmarsh-grass	*
Dactylis glomerata	Cock's-foot	1896, *
Hordeum murinum	Wall Barley	*
Holcus lanatus	Yorkshire-fog	1896, *
Carex arenaria	Sand Sedge	1896
C. extensa	Long-bracted Sedge	1928
Carex sp.	Sedge	*
Orchis sp.	Orchid	1896

LES MINQUIERS

The first list of plants on Les Minquiers was made by T. W. Attenborough in July 1916 and was given in the Société's *Bulletin Annuel* for 1917. Tree-mallow and Sea Beet were abundant and fine, and Attenborough suggested that the Meadow Brome, which requires confirmation since it is a most unexpected grass for a rocky islet, was introduced. Several visits have been made during the last twenty-five years and the species noted are marked below with an asterisk.

During the autumn or winter of 1972/73 weedkiller was sprayed on about 99% of the vegetation of the island. This extraordinary act is thought to have been connected with an even more extraordinary scheme to plant non-native conifers over all the island in the name of conservation. Les Minquiers is owned by the Crown and an appeal to Her Majesty's Receiver General prevented the trees being planted and so allowed the natural vegetation to return as quickly as possible. This natural vegetation had developed over the centuries and had, until 1973, held together the small amount of soil still present after the erosion associated with the quarrying last century. The vegetation was of a kind adapted to withstand the rigours of winter storms, salt spray and summer drought and the associated insect fauna provided abundant food for migrant birds in spring and autumn. In February 1973 this vegetation cover did not exist and erosion of the bare soil was taking place. By August 1973 the island was green again but looked very different from in the past. Tree-mallows in theory are biennials but in practice many live much longer than two years so that a natural population may contain plants varying from young seedlings to gnarled, weather-beaten specimens several years old. Tree-mallow seeds were unaffected by the weedkiller, so they germinated in abundance and flourished in the absence of competition. In August the plants were growing thickly, young and green, all the same height and looking like a cultivated crop, i.e. the previous age-structure of the population had been destroyed. Gradually it has returned. Sea Beet has recovered but is not back in the cracks in the rocks where it used to give shelter and protection to oystercatcher chicks. Thrift has not been reported recently and nor has Samphire though one plant did survive and was present in 1976. A small area towards the flagpole, which had been the main grassy area had a mass of Smooth Sow-thistle on it in August 1973 and a close search revealed a few grass plants showing some signs of life. The soil-binding grasses are gradually returning but the cover in 1982 was still not as deep or as extensive as it was in 1972.

Rain and storm water collect in small shallow pools on the flattish but uneven rock surface below the 'Terrace'. In 1958 Common Saltmarsh-grass was growing by the edge of the more permanent of these pools. The area has now changed somewhat, perhaps because material was stored in the region when the helicopter pad was constructed, and because the habitat has gone, so have the plants.

Beta vulgaris subsp. *maritima*	Sea Beet	1916, *
Chenopodium album	Fat Hen	*
Sagina maritima	Sea Pearlwort	*
Spergularia rupicola	Rock Sea-spurrey	1916, *
S. marina	Lesser Sea-spurrey	1916
Lavatera arborea	Tree-mallow	1916, *
Crithmum maritimum	Samphire	1916, *
Armeria maritima	Thrift	1916, *
Solanum nigrum	Black Nightshade	*
Sonchus oleraceus	Smooth Sow-thistle	1916, *
'Festuca rigida'	A Fescue	1916
Festuca rubra group	Red Fescue	*
Lolium perenne	Perennial Rye-grass	1916
Desmazeria marina	Sea Fern-grass	1916, *
Puccinellia maritima	Common Saltmarsh-grass	*
Bromus commutatus	Meadow Brome	1916
Elymus farctus subsp. *boreoatlanticus*	Sand Couch	1916
Elymus sp.	Couch	*

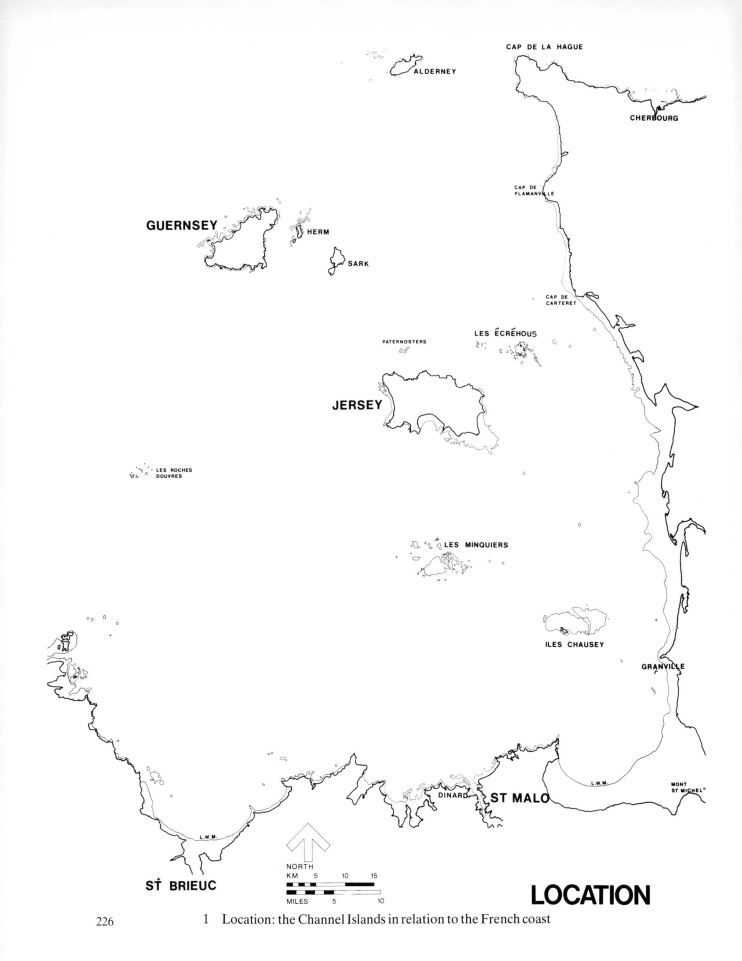

CAP DE LA HAGUE

ALDERNEY

CHERBOURG

GUERNSEY

HERM

SARK

CAP DE
FLAMANVILLE

CAP DE
CARTERET

PATERNOSTERS

LES ÉCRÉHOUS

JERSEY

LES ROCHES
DOUVRES

LES MINQUIERS

ILES CHAUSEY

GRANVILLE

DINARD

ST MALO

L.W.M.

MONT
ST MICHEL

ST BRIEUC

NORTH
KM   5   10   15
MILES   5   10

LOCATION

1   Location: the Channel Islands in relation to the French coast

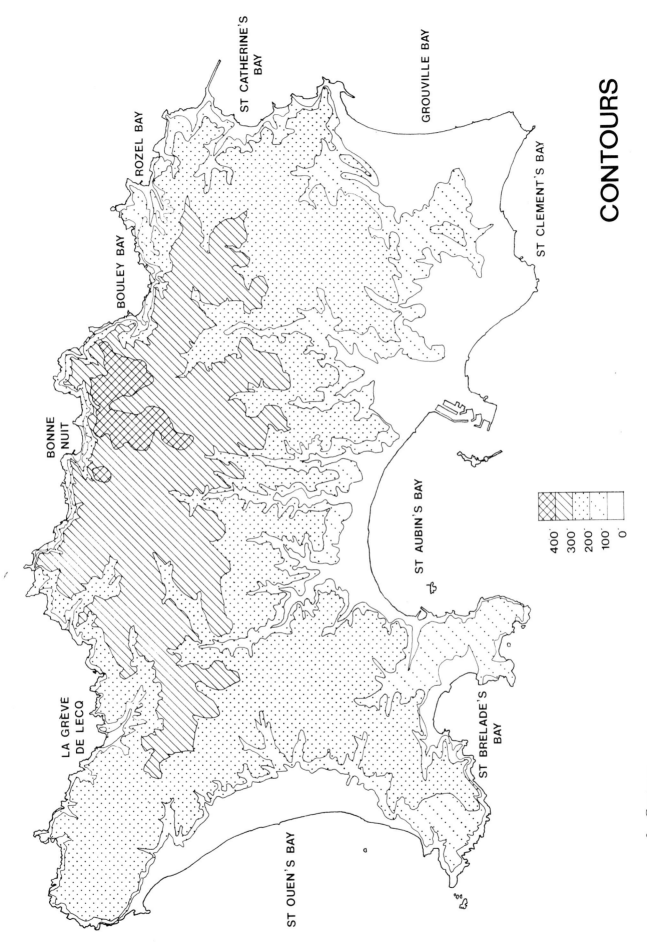

CONTOURS

ST CATHERINE'S BAY

GROUVILLE BAY

ROZEL BAY

ST CLEMENT'S BAY

BOULEY BAY

BONNE NUIT

400'
300'
200'
100'
0

ST AUBIN'S BAY

LA GRÈVE DE LECQ

ST BRELADE'S BAY

ST OUEN'S BAY

2 Contours

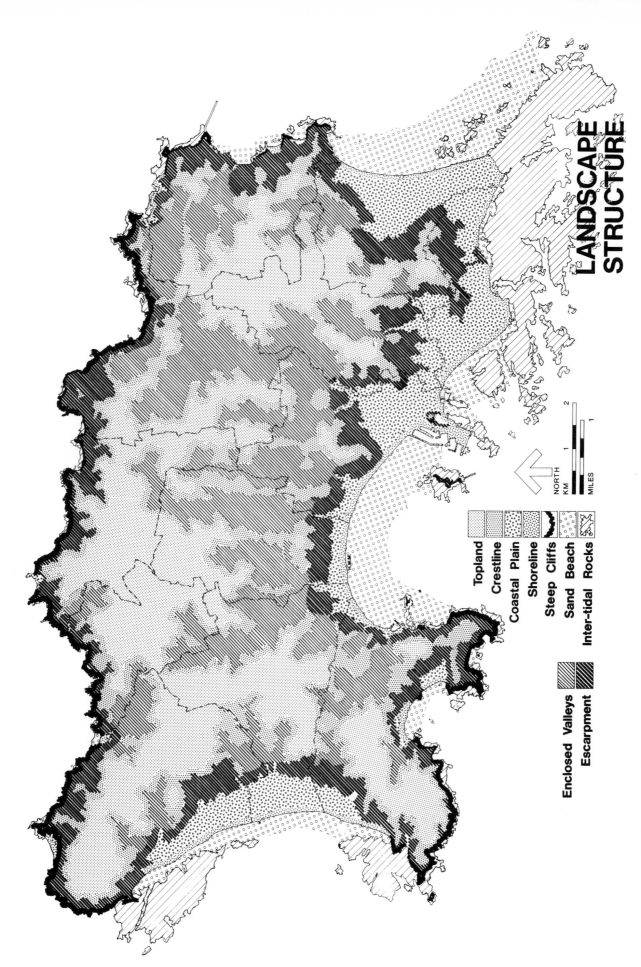

LANDSCAPE STRUCTURE

Topland
Crestline
Coastal Plain
Shoreline
Steep Cliffs
Sand Beach
Inter-tidal Rocks

Enclosed Valleys
Escarpment

NORTH

KM

MILES

3   Landscape structure

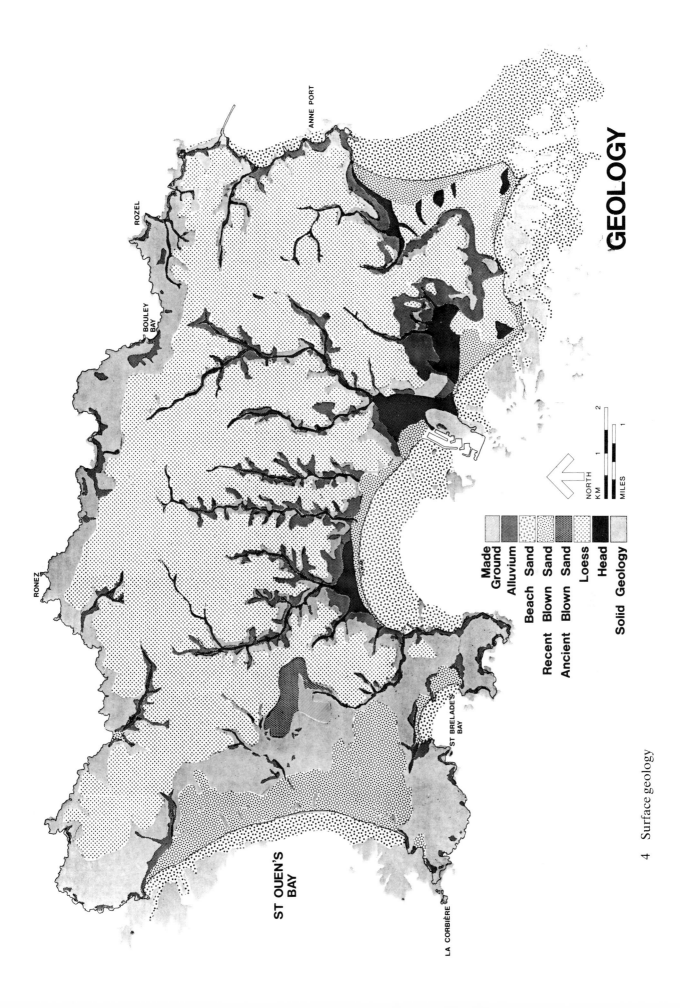

GEOLOGY

ANNE PORT

ROZEL

BOULEY BAY

RONEZ

ST OUEN'S BAY

LA CORBIÈRE

ST BRELADE'S BAY

Made Ground
Alluvium
Beach Sand
Recent Blown Sand
Ancient Blown Sand
Loess
Head
Solid Geology

NORTH
KM
MILES

4 Surface geology

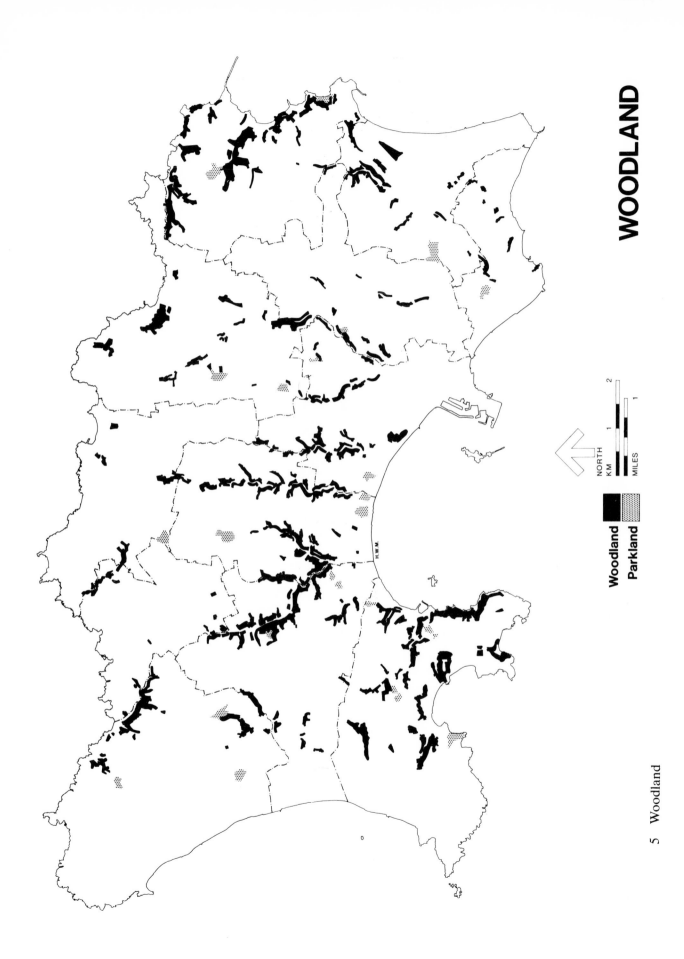

WOODLAND

Woodland
Parkland

NORTH

KM
MILES

5   Woodland

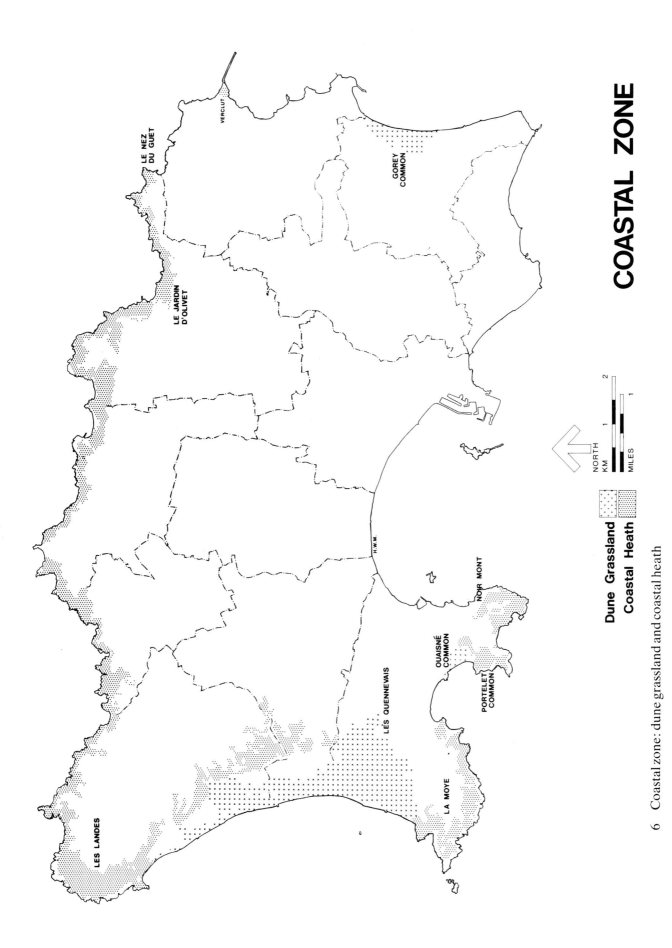

COASTAL ZONE

LE NEZ DU GUET

VERCLUT

LE JARDIN D'OLIVET

GOREY COMMON

LES LANDES

LÉS QUENNEVAIS

H.W.M.

NOIR MONT

OUAISNÉ COMMON

PORTELET COMMON

LA MOYE

NORTH

KM

MILES

Dune Grassland

Coastal Heath

6   Coastal zone: dune grassland and coastal heath

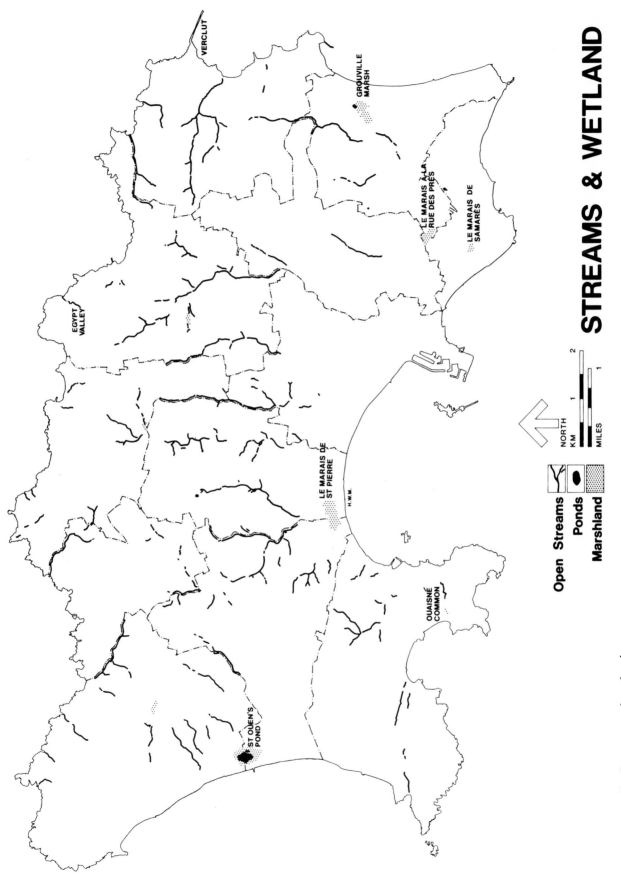

STREAMS & WETLAND

VERCLUT

GROUVILLE MARSH

LE MARAIS À LA RUE DES PRÉS

LE MARAIS DE SAMARÈS

EGYPT VALLEY

LE MARAIS DE ST PIERRE

H.W.M.

OUAISNÉ COMMON

ST OUEN'S POND

NORTH

KM   1   2

MILES   1

Open Streams

Ponds

Marshland

7   Streams and wetland

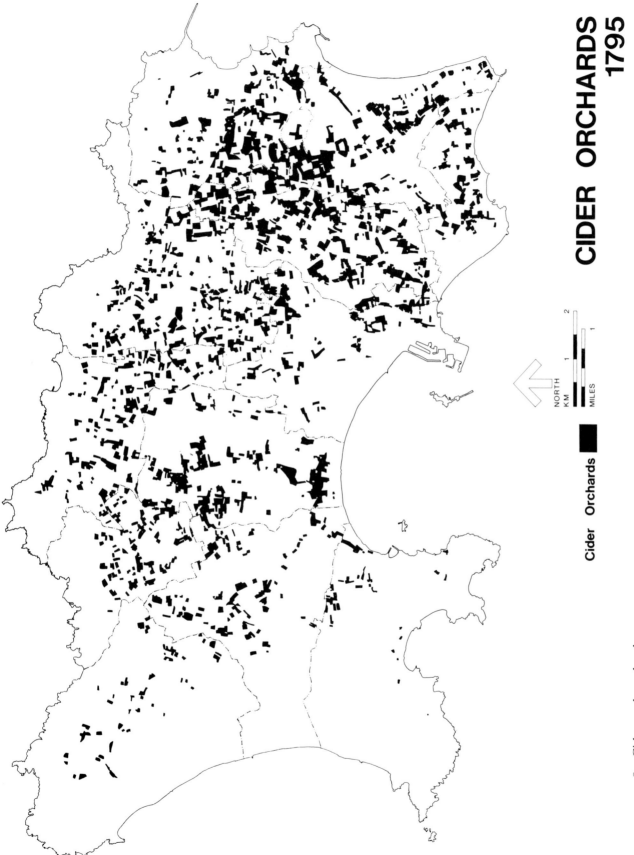

**CIDER ORCHARDS
1795**

NORTH

KM
MILES

Cider Orchards

8   Cider apple orchards

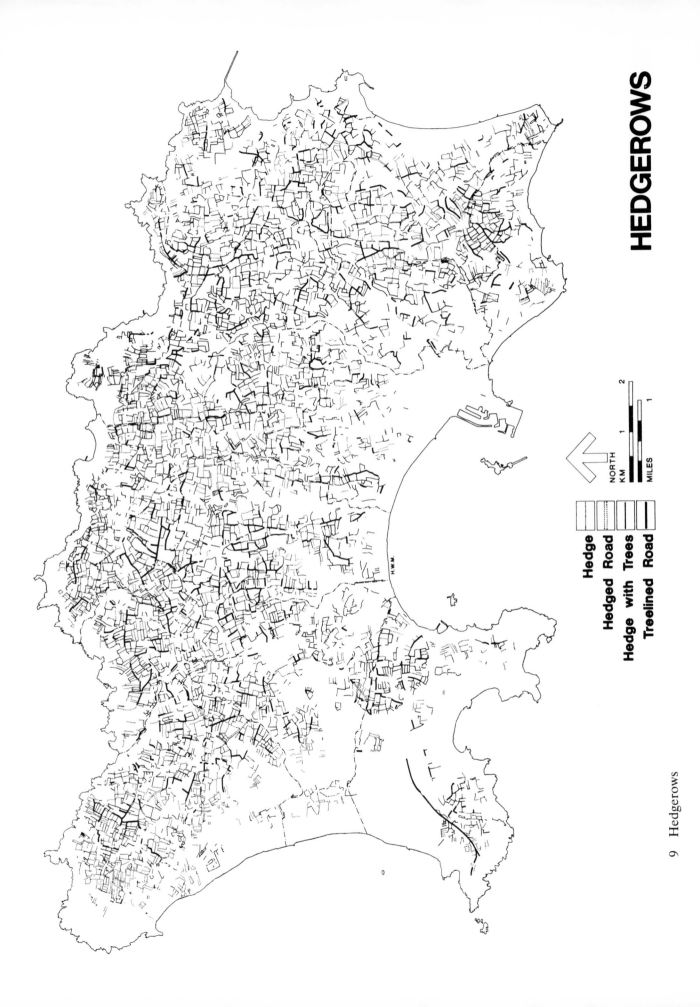

HEDGEROWS

Hedge

Hedged Road

Hedge with Trees

Treelined Road

NORTH

KM

MILES

H.W.M.

9 Hedgerows

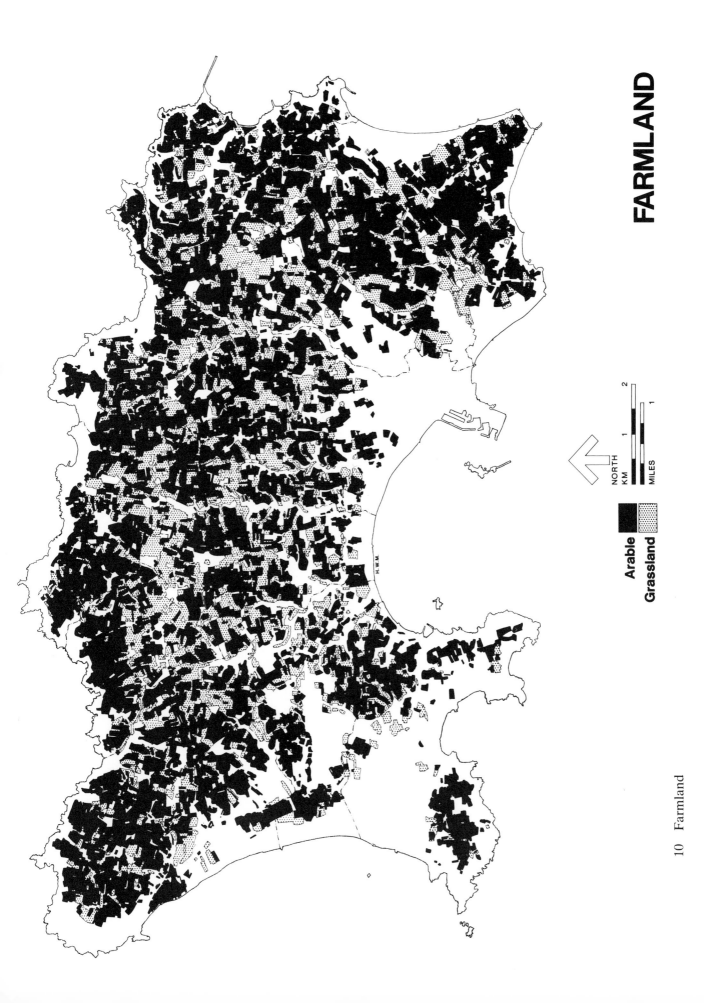

FARMLAND

NORTH

KM

MILES

Arable

Grassland

H.W.M.

10   Farmland

BIBLIOGRAPHY

N. D. Simpson's *Bibliographical Index of the British Flora* (1960, privately printed, Bournemouth) contains on pages 83, 85 and 86 lists of references to the Jersey flora in books, manuscripts, journals and periodicals. Extra sources of information are listed below together with the main Floras used in the preparation of this *Flora of Jersey*. Most references to individual species are cited in the text.

BABINGTON, C. C. (1839). *Primitiae Florae Sarnicae*. London. Author's annotated copy in library, Botany School, Cambridge.

BINET, A. J. (1877–1929). Manuscript diary in library, Société Jersiaise.

CLAPHAM, A. R., TUTIN, T. G. & WARBURG, E. F. (1962). *Flora of the British Isles*, 2nd ed. Cambridge University Press.

CLAPHAM, A. R., TUTIN, T. G. & WARBURG, E. F. (1981). *Excursion Flora of the British Isles*, 3rd ed. Cambridge University Press.

CLOKIE, H. N. (1964). *An account of the Herbaria of the Department of Botany in the University of Oxford*. Oxford University Press.

DE BELLAING, PÈRE (1904). Letter to L. V. Lester-Garland in possession of Mrs M. L. Long.

DES ABBAYES, H. (1971). *Flore et Végétation du Massif Armoricain*, Vol. 1. St Brieuc.

DONY, J. G., ROB, C. M. & PERRING, F. H. (1974). *English Names of Wild Flowers*. Butterworths.

DRUCE, G. C. & VINES, S. H. (1907). *The Dillenian Herbaria*. Clarendon Press, Oxford.

Extentes de l'Île de Jersey 1274, 1331, 1528, 1607, 1668, 1749 (1877–1883). Société Jersiaise.

FALLE, P. (1694). *An account of the Island of Jersey*.

FALLE, P. (1837 ed. Durell, E.). *An account of the Island of Jersey with additional notes by the Editor*.

JERSEY AGRICULTURAL & HORTICULTURAL SOCIETY (1834–1839). *Reports*.

LE MAISTRE, F. (1966). *Dictionnaire Jersiais-Français*. Don Balleine Trust, Jersey.

LE PATOUREL, J. H. (1937). *The Mediaeval Administration of the Channel Islands 1199–1399*. Oxford.

LESTER-GARLAND, L. V. (1903). *A Flora of the Island of Jersey*. London.

LE SUEUR, F. (1976). *A Natural History of Jersey*. Phillimore.

LOUSLEY, J. E. (1971). *Flora of the Isles of Scilly*. David & Charles.

MARQUAND, E. D. (1901). *Flora of Guernsey and the lesser Channel Islands*. London.

McCLINTOCK, D. (1975). *The Wild Flowers of Guernsey*. Collins.

McCLINTOCK, D. (1972). Who was Finlay? *Review of the Guernsey Society* **28**: 73–78.

PIQUET, J. (1851). Manuscript titled 'Catalogue of Plants Indegenous to Jersey one of the Channel Islands' with a few later undated additions and alterations by the author. Library, Société Jersiaise.

PIQUET, J. (1896). The phanerogamous Plants and Ferns of Jersey. *Bulletin Annuel* **3**: 361–382. Société Jersiaise.

PIQUET, J. (1898). Supplement (to the above). *Bulletin Annuel* **4**: 90–91. Société Jersiaise.

PERRING, F. H. & WALTERS, S. M. eds (1962). *Atlas of the British Flora*. Nelson.

POINGDESTRE, J. (1682). *Caesarea*. Manuscript N. 5417 in Harleian Collection, British Museum. (1889) *Caesarea*. Nicolle W. ed. Société Jersiaise.

STACE, C. A. ed. (1975). *Hybridisation and the Flora of the British Isles*. Academic Press.

SOCIÉTÉ GUERNESIAISE (1882–1982). *Report and Transactions*.

SOCIÉTÉ JERSIAISE (1873–1983). *Annual Bulletin*.

WILMOTT, A. J. Manuscript diary at Kew.

Index of Scientific and English Names

Index of Jersey-Norman-French Names